Privatization and Corporate Control
in the Czech Republic

STUDIES IN COMPARATIVE ECONOMIC SYSTEMS

General Editors: Wladimir Andreff, *Professor of Economics at the University Paris 1 Panthéon Sorbonne and Director of ROSES*; Bruno Dallago, *Associate Professor of Economic Policy and Comparative Economic Systems at the University of Trento and President of EACES*; János Kornai, *Allie S. Freed Professor of Economics at Harvard University and Permanent Fellow at Collegium Budapest, Institute for Advanced Studies*; and Hans-Jürgen Wagener, *Professor of Economics and Vice-Rector at the European University Viadrina at Frankfurt/Oder*

Recent developments in different economic systems have presented new challenges to economic theory and policy. Scholars in comparative economic systems have to debate and clarify the nature of the economic system, its place within the economy and the dynamics of its transformation in a comparative perspective.

This series is designed to contribute to the debate and advance knowledge in the field. It provides a forum for original comparative research on the economic system and economic performance including important aspects such as economic institutions and their change, economic actors and policy instruments in the transformation process.

The books published in this series are written by leading international scholars writing in a theoretical or applied way and using either country-specific studies or cross-country comparisons. They show how economic analysis can contribute to understanding and resolving one of the most important questions facing the world at present and in the future.

Titles in the series include:

Struggle and Hope
Essays on Stabilization and Reform in a Post-Socialist Economy
János Kornai

The Transformation of Economic Systems in Central Europe
Herman W. Hoen

The Political Economy of Pension Reform in Central–Eastern Europe
Katharina Müller

Privatization and Corporate Control in the Czech Republic
Clemens Schütte

Privatization and Corporate Control in the Czech Republic

Clemens Schütte
Allianz AG, Munich, Germany

Studies in Comparative Economic Systems

Edward Elgar
Cheltenham, UK • Northampton, MA, USA

Published by
Edward Elgar Publishing Limited
Glensanda House
Montpellier Parade
Cheltenham
Glos GL50 1UA
UK

Edward Elgar Publishing, Inc.
136 West Street
Suite 202
Northampton
Massachusetts 01060
USA

A catalogue record for this book
is available from the British Library

Library of Congress Cataloguing in Publication Data
Schütte, Clemens.
   Privatization and corporate control in the Czech Republic / Clemens Schütte.
      (Studies in comparative economic systems)
   Includes bibliographical references and index.
   1. Corporate governance—Czech Republic. 2. Privatization—Czech Republic.
   I. Series.

HD2741 .S445 2000
338.94371—dc21   00–027264

ISBN 1 84064 411 7

Printed and bound in Great Britain by Biddles Ltd, *www.biddles.co.uk*

To my parents, Helene and Fritz Schütte,
and my wife Dana
in gratitude for their continuing support
and encouragement

Contents

List of Figures

List of Tables

Introduction

As evidenced by the break-down of the Communist bloc, in the long run the viability of a political and economic system substantially depends upon its capacity to provide for an institutional framework producing efficient outcomes of economic activities. The former communist economies failed to solve the problem of scarcity in a satisfactory manner. Improvement of the economic performance in central and eastern Europe should be achieved through institutional change promoting the transformation of formerly centrally planned economies into market economies. The latter are based on individual freedom and the institution of private property which is widely regarded as a necessary prerequisite for efficient production, dynamic competition, structural change and innovatory strength. Yet, privatization alone is not sufficient to improve economic performance in a system characterized by a separation of ownership and control over corporate assets. In the case of single proprietorship merging management and ownership in one person, the problem is not an issue. In modern market economies, however, the problem does exist in the context of large enterprise, especially joint stock companies.

Private property is efficient if management is controlled effectively. Therefore, the emerging property systems of the transitional countries must be provided with mechanisms ensuring that decision-makers always dispose of resources in the interest of the financiers, i.e. equityholders and debtholders. This necessity requires the creation of functioning systems of *corporate control*. Considering established market economies, the transitional countries have a choice between two systemic, mutually not completely excluding alternatives, market-based outsider control or intermediary-based insider control. Meanwhile, they have implemented their privatization programmes and thus have implicitly made a decision in favour of a certain systemic variant.

Why does it pay to examine in particular the Czech model of corporate control? Of course, one answer, addressed to Czech policymakers, goes: to reveal institutional shortcomings and to propose measures to improve the institutional environment. Yet, there are at least three more good reasons why we should analyse the Czech approach to privatization and corporate control. The first reason is the mere pace with which the Czechs have reallocated property rights to the private sector. Apart from Eastern Germany, the Czech Republic has experienced the quickest and perhaps most comprehensive privatization programme in the region. The long-term performance of the Czech economy will depend substantially on the patterns of corporate control that have evolved since October 1991, the starting point of large-scale privatization. Of course, as we know from the experience of mature market economies, the evolution of a full-fledged system of corporate control is a question of decades rather than of a mere couple of years. It takes time for the political decisionmakers to create an institutional environment fitting the economic and cultural peculiarities of a country, and likewise for the guardians of the enterprise sector to learn how to execute effective corporate control. Nevertheless, due to early and rapid privatization, the Czechs have made more headway with corporate control than most other countries of the region. That makes Czech privatization a model case for later privatizers and reformers in other countries. Therefore, it pays to take a closer look at their experience and to make a critical assessment of the fortes and shortcomings of the Czech approach to build up a working system of corporate control.

The second reason why the Czech privatization process is a model case to other reformers is its institutional openness. The Czech approach, using for a large part give-away methods like the famous voucher scheme, only predetermined a temporary primary distribution of ownership titles in many companies. After the termination of voucher privatization, private individuals and institutional investors started to redistribute property rights over the market and to spontaneously design new ownership and control structures of Czech enterprises. Both the voucher scheme in itself and the following redistribution of property rights have been pivotal e.g. for the setting of the capital market and the involvement of banks and other classes of investors in corporate control.

A third argument in favour of analysing the Czech model of corporate control is the controversial economic performance of the Czech economy in the second half of the 1990s. Critics argue that the causes for the current recession might be institutional deficiencies and a merely formal privatization, both acting as a brake to the restructuring of Czech enterprises. If this is true, it pays to inquire into the institutional weaknesses of Czech privatization. On the other hand, according to a recent World Bank report (Pohl et al., 1996), Czech companies have shown a comparatively good restructuring performance in the wake of privatization. The authors use firm-level data of the largest 300-500 industrial firms of Bulgaria, the Czech Republic, Hungary, Poland and Slovakia to measure the restructuring performance of the five countries for the period 1992-1994 and to make projections to 2000. The extent of corporate restructuring is then measured in four ways. First, the export performance of the firms is taken as an indicator of their ability to compete in international markets with high price and quality standards. The result is that exports have grown most in the Czech Republic. Second, the authors measure improvements of production efficiency. Again, variable factor productivity (labour and materials) has increased most in the Czech Republic. Third, firms are divided into five categories according to their degree of profitability or loss. By tracking the movements of each firm within the categories in the mentioned period of time, the authors produce a 'transition matrix' for each country that reflects the percentage of firms in each profit/loss category that moved to another category or maintained its profit level. The result is that Czech loss-makers have improved their financial performance much faster than unprofitable firms in other countries. The Czech matrix compares favourably even to that of the UK which has been added as a Western benchmark. In both countries, most loss-making firms either improve or at least maintain their financial performance, while only a few worsen. The authors extrapolate the past results to the future, thereby assuming the transition matrix of each country to be constant over time (and hence the economic environment encouraging restructuring to be unchanged). They calculate that far fewer Czech firms than other firms will become insolvent by the year 2000 (insolvency means that they can no longer fund their own losses because their net worth has been declined to zero). The fourth restructuring indicator is the level and standard deviation of real rates of return on capital. Interestingly, the Czech Republic has an average rate of return similar to a western economy (UK) and clearly less variation than the other countries under review. The conclusion is that the Czech economic environment both encourages loss-making firms to become quickly profitable and generates a sufficiently high level of competition to prevent excessive profits. The question is, what features of the Czech economic environment have caused the superior restructuring performance? In the eyes of the authors, 'the one important difference is the pace of privatization' (Pohl et al., 1996, p.12). If they are right, the Czech system of corporate control has functioned at least fairly efficiently in the period under review and has produced economic outcomes beating those of other countries in the region. Then the Czech approach to privatization and corporate control could be an appealing option for other reformers.

In the recent literature, several studies have focused upon the institutional development of the private sector and corporate control in the Czech Republic. Brom & Orenstein (1994) point to the continually high control power of the state over the industrial sector after mass privatization. They suppose the Czech government to maintain a large role in many privatized companies due to its direct and indirect shareholdings and tight control of the banking sector. This could enable the state to implement a long-term industrial policy effectively through a group of newly established institutions like the National Property Fund (NPF) and the loan hospital Konsolidacní banka. Furthermore, the authors investigate the activities of the biggest beneficiaries of mass privatization, the so-called investment privatization funds (IPFs) which have evolved spontaneously in the course of voucher privatization. Analysing some main elements of IPF strategy like portfolio concentration and membership on corporate boards, they conclude that the largest funds have taken an active role in corporate governance, at least in terms of gaining board seats and selecting qualified individuals to attend board meetings at privatized enterprises. Like most observers from the Anglo-American world with its firewalls between commercial and investment banking, they are sceptical about the tight ownership links between IPFs and banks with the latter eventually having quite different interests from those of individual investors.

In his survey of the investment policies of the top ten Czech IPFs in the first wave of voucher privatization, Egerer (1994) emphasizes close equity relationships between banks and enterprises. In addition, he reveals that domestic bank-sponsored funds are represented at the boards of more companies than independent funds or those established by foreign banks. Unlike Brom & Orenstein, he argues that banks are using their funds primarily to decrease information asymmetries between banks and enterprises, thus lowering the default risk in connection with bank lending. The monitoring (rather than active restructuring) carried out by the bank-affiliated funds thus largely contributes to the stability of the financial sector.

Coffee (1996) presents a summary of the views of fund managers and company managers on the governance performance of IPFs. He points to a lack of expertise on the part of some directors - in particular those from bank-sponsored funds - about how to increase the performance of a company and how to carry out corporate restructuring. While some restructuring is clearly under way, the role of IPFs in causing it is seemingly ambiguous. In Coffee's eyes, the necessity for the drastic employment reductions reported to him by the management of various firms was obvious to everybody after the loss of the eastern markets in the early 1990s. Inevitable staff reductions were frequently initiated by the management well before mass privatization and, consequently, without IPF instigation. Like Brom & Orenstein, Coffee emphasizes the conflict of interest of bank-sponsored funds which might subordinate the interests of their shareholders to those of their banking parents. However, the only (and fairly weak) evidence presented in favour of the conflict of interest hypothesis is that bank-related IPFs are allegedly seeking excessively diversified portfolios. According to Coffee, the banks prefer their funds to develop relationships with the maximum number of potential corporate clients rather than to execute active governance of only a small number of portfolio firms.

Kenway & Klvacová (1996) assemble data giving evidence of substantial cross-ownership in the privatized financial sector. They suppose cross-ownership to provide incentives for cooperation between IPFs, thus helping to strengthen the governance power of the financial intermediaries as a whole when individually they are weak in relation to firms they own. Moreover, they analyse the replies received to questionnaires sent to the funds industry. Primary goals of the IPFs are reportedly to prevent the firm management from asset stripping, to at least check strategic decisions made by the management and, above all, to appoint qualified managers to the boards of portfolio companies (and to replace the incompetent ones, respectively). From interviews with funds representatives they conclude that the IPFs do not yet have the capacity to execute corporate control in a satisfactory way.

This book pursues both theoretical and empirical ends. After a theoretical analysis of the institutional cornerstones of insider as well as outsider systems of corporate control, it develops institutional recommendations which are subsequently used as a benchmark to assess the performance of the evolving Czech system of corporate control. In its empirical analysis of Czech privatization and corporate control, it presents new evidence on the issues dealt with in the literature above (e.g. on state ownership and control, the concentration of ownership after voucher privatization, the asset structure and governance capacity of funds and financial groups, the board model of the Czech joint-stock company and the governance and restructuring performance of the funds and financial groups). Beyond that, it discusses issues which so far haven't attracted much attention among economists like debt as a control device of Czech enterprises and the role of the capital market in corporate control (including the legal framework of equity control). Some of the major issues discussed are:

- *Role of bank-centred financial groups in the execution of corporate control:* The banks' governance power is based predominantly upon sizeable holdings in their funds and loans to the corporate sector. Their extensive equity involvement in the enterprise sector helps banks to realize economies of scale and scope in the execution of corporate control and brings their governance interest more in line with that of individual shareholders, thereby reducing incentives to enforce a 'satisficing policy' in the board rooms. Bank-sponsored groups have shown a strong interest in active corporate control. Their funds are assumed *inter alia* to provide portfolio firms with better access to finance at comparatively low interest rates. Considering the serious lack of qualified and financially capable direct investors, they have done an important job in spurring restructuring in many companies.

- *Board model of the Czech joint-stock company:* Czech companies enjoy considerable discretion in the design of their company bodies. On the micro level, owners may implement the best board model given the specific ownership and governance situation of the firm. On the macro level, discretion has triggered a trial and error process to select efficient long-term arrangements which may easily produce quite different board arrangements e.g. for different industries. This fact well fits the Czech overall approach to keep the evolving property system open. While most companies made their decision in favour of an Anglo-Saxon unitary board, an increasing number of firms are switching over to the German dual board after the implementation of basic restructuring measures.

- *Institutional environment of debt control:* The institutional environment of debt control is still lagging considerably behind western standards. Apart from delays in the implementation of the necessary legal infrastructure, the main reasons are inexperienced judges and a lack of both will and capacity in the overburdened court system to consequently enforce the bankruptcy law. Therefore, banks have so far been rather passive in triggering bankruptcy and have mostly adhered to loan prolongation and interest collection.

- *Governance structure of banks:* Effective regulation and supervision of the Czech banking industry has been implemented rather late, thus largely diminishing the effects of the balance sheet restructuring carried out by the state and giving way to unlawful and risky actions of banks. Delayed privatization has prevented the big banks from quickly replacing political (and managerial) goals by purely economic ones and giving a higher priority to profit maximizing and sound balance sheets. This has generated inefficiencies in corporate control as well as misallocation of scarce capital.

- *'Openness' of ownership structures:* The voucher scheme paved the way for a vivid market of corporate control which has largely contributed to disciplining the management of widely-held companies. The 'openness' of ownership structures also gave each company a chance to attract a capable owner. It thus mitigated the serious lack of both managerial and guardian competence for many firms. However, the positive effects of open ownership structures have been somewhat reduced by regulation, in particular portfolio restrictions on banks (pushing banks as equityholders increasingly out of the industrial sector) and mandatory bids to protect minority shareholders (but also raising transaction costs of takeovers and thus precluding many eventually capable investors from making an offer).

- *Information efficiency of the capital market:* At present, the information efficiency of the market is low. Scanty information must be put down primarily to liberal disclosure rules and weak enforcement.

- *Minority shareholder protection:* The legal installation of minority shareholder protection took place with considerable delays and only after painful experience with large shareholders exploiting firms at the debit of minority shareholders. Still, there appear to be problems with the actual enforcement and policing of the law.

The book is structured in six chapters. Chapter 1 deals theoretically with corporate control. After an analysis of the control problem in the light of agency theory, it works out some important institutional recommendations for the efficient functioning of both insider and outsider control. It then drafts a theoretical framework to determine which institutional infrastructure of corporate control is fitting which underlying real features of an economy. Finally it discusses the control problem in the specific context of transitional economies and derives institutional preconditions of efficient corporate control.

Chapter 2 presents the Czech approach to privatization including an in-depth description of the voucher scheme. In addition, it discusses the role of the state as company owner after the termination of mass privatization. Chapter 3 identifies the main players in corporate control emerging from an institutionally open privatization process. For this purpose, it comes with the regulation of the big financial groups which spontaneously emerged in the course of privatization. It outlines their role as major players in both the voucher programme and the following process of ownership concentration ('third wave of privatization'), and makes some detailed inquiries into their asset portfolios. The chapter concludes with a measurement of the governance power of various classes of investors in the Czech top 100 companies by turnover.

Chapters 4 to 6 detail the evolution of the Czech system of corporate control after the termination of voucher privatization. Chapter 4 is about equity control and restructuring. It describes and contrasts the structure of the Czech joint-stock corporation as envisioned by law and the Czech board model as observable in reality. Subsequently, focusing upon the powerful bank-sponsored financial groups, it analyses how equity is used as a device of insider control in Czech companies. The chapter tries a detailed assessment of the control performance of the investment privatization funds as main organs of the financial groups to execute equity control over the enterprise sector. To this end, it also presents some evidence about the group's restructuring performance in individual companies.

The performance of debt control is examined in Chapter 5 dealing with the quality of banks' asset portfolios, interenterprise arrears and bankruptcy law as a major institutional tool to exert debt control. In addition, Chapter 5 inquires into the governance structures of the banks which are at the core of the financial groups and hence powerful guardians of the industrial sector.

Chapter 6 deals with market-based control and evaluates the regulation and performance of the emerging Czech capital market. The main part of

Chapter 6 deals with the transparency of the capital market, the protection of minority shareholders and the transaction costs of hostile takeovers. Furthermore, it reviews extensive reform measures lately taken by the Czech authorities to strengthen the capital market and its role in corporate control. The conclusion briefly summarises some of the book's main results.

Most of the empirical research for this book was done while I was a visiting researcher at the Centre for Economic Studies and Graduate Education (CERGE) in Prague. I would like to thank its director, Professor Frantisek Turnovec, and his team for their warm hospitality and support. The conclusions presented in the book are based upon the processing and evaluation of data made available to the author by various local institutions. A partial list includes the economic ministries, the Czech Statistical Office, the Czech National Bank, the Securities Centre, the National Property Fund, the Banking Association, the Association of Investment Funds, the Prague Stock Exchange, the over-the-counter system RM-S and a broad range of newspapers. Empirical data have been complemented by numerous interviews carried out with fund and enterprise managers, bankers, lawyers and state officials. Helpful criticisms and suggestions on earlier drafts of this book by Professors Wladimir Andreff, Bruno Dallago and Jan Winiecki are gratefully acknowledged. I am deeply indebted to Professor Hans-Jürgen Wagener for his steady encouragement and support while I was writing the book. My research work was generously sponsored by the Konrad Adenauer Foundation. The findings, interpretations and conclusions expressed in this book are entirely those of the author and should not be attributed in any manner to Allianz AG.

1 A theoretical foundation of corporate control

1.1 THE CONTROL PROBLEM OF THE MODERN CORPORATION

1.1.1 Asymmetric Information and the Separation of Ownership and Control

The importance of joint-stock companies results from the fact that they permit specialization according to comparative advantages in providing the potentially separable firm inputs financial resources, risk-bearing services, and decision-making (Putterman, 1993, p. 246). In this way great amounts of equity can be accumulated and, by portfolio diversification, risk-return mixes can be realized in correspondence to investors' preferences. The latter, combined with the creation of organized liquid markets for the exchange of risks, leads to a reduction of capital costs in comparison with the classic owner-managed firm, personified by the entrepreneur as both manager and residual risk bearer. Certainly, the separation of ownership and management of resources contains a control problem caused by the special peculiarities in the relationship between the financial risk-bearer (principal) and the charged decision-maker (agent). If this problem is not effectively solved, costs reducing or even cancelling the benefits of risk diversification will arise. In the remainder of this section, the problem of corporate control will be divided into three subproblems, that is into an information problem, an incentive problem of the agent (manager), and an incentive problem of the principal (shareholder).

More than two hundred years ago, Adam Smith (1776, p. 741) stated a control problem dealing with the negligence and profusion of managers in the context of an inquiry into Indian companies: 'The directors ..., being the managers rather of other people's money than of their own, it cannot well be expected, that they should watch over it with the same anxious vigilance with which the partners in a private copartnery frequently watch over their own.' Traditional neoclassical microeconomics, founded in the second half of the 19th century when single proprietorship was still the prevailing form of ownership, treated the firm as an anthropomorphous creation. The

1

assumption of profit maximization as sole corporate objective denied the existence of control problems between owners and managers. As equity ownership became more relevant in the beginning of the 20th century, Berle & Means (1932) documented the tendency towards increasing separation of ownership from management. Inspired by the mere size of the modern corporation and its diffuse ownership, they assumed a high degree of discretion for firm managers, and feared that managers could abuse this discretion pursuing their own ends (p. 121). The Managerial Theory of the Firm, a descriptively oriented branch of the 'Economic Theory of Agency', subsequently called 'Agency Theory', aims at analysing and depicting the agency relationship between shareholders and managers in modern corporations.

The specific feature of an agency relationship is that one party (the agent) independently takes decisions by order of the other party (the principal) (Ross, 1973, p. 134; Jensen & Meckling, 1976, p. 308). An interpretation of the agency as delegation or transfer of property rights illustrates the close entanglement of Agency Theory in Property Rights Theory. Because of different payoff functions of principal and agent, an incentive exists for the agent to increase his own profit at the principal's expense. The possibility of behaving opportunistically is opened to him by an asymmetrical distribution of information between both parties after contract, causing moral hazard. It is costly - possibly prohibitively costly - for the principal to reduce the information asymmetry. Therefore it isn't guaranteed that the agent really pursues the principal's aims. Arrow (1986) identifies two potential reasons for an ex-post information advantage of the agent. Both of them can be applied to the modern corporation:

-   In a 'hidden-action' type principal-agent relation the principal can neither observe all actions undertaken by the agent. Nor, can he infer the effort of the agent. The principal only observes the outcomes of the agent's actions.

-   The agent may also have 'hidden knowledge', i.e. the principal does not know the exact information level of the agent. For that reason he cannot verify whether or not the agent has used his information correctly in the principal's sense. The problem exists independently of the observability of the agent's actions.

Hidden action and hidden knowledge result in an *information problem* offering management a certain degree of discretion to behave opportunistically. Shareholders are uncertain about the quality of the measures taken by management.

1.1.2   Incentive Schemes of Managers and Shareholders

Jensen & Meckling (1976) first systematically applied Agency Theory to the separation of ownership and control in modern corporations. Their model analyses the incentive scheme of a manager who owns a fraction of a firm's stock.[1] The owner-manager will maximize his own payoff function, consisting of different arguments, like his wage, the value of his shares and the value of non-monetary perquisites. The latter cover material profusion, as well as the satisfying of personal needs and ambitions, like the striving for prestige and power. The consumption of 'perks' by the manager, wasting corporate resources, lowers the firm's value. Since the manager does not own the whole equity stock of the firm, the public shareholders have to subsidize the manager's perks. Because of these negative external effects, the manager will consume more perks than a single-proprietor and thus lower the value of the firm at the cost of the public shareholders. *Ceteris paribus*, the fewer shares he possesses the more perks he consumes. Consequently, modern corporations with a strict separation between financial resources and decision-making are in danger of experiencing a most drastic decline of firm value caused by managerial moral hazard.

In practice, managers often link the prestige and power of their position more to the size and growth of their firm than to its profitability. In addition, as Baumol (1959, p. 47) states, 'executive salaries appear to be far more closely correlated with the scale of operations of the firm than with its profitability'. Hence, managers have an intrinsic bias to pursue the growth of a corporation without sufficient regard to profit considerations (cf. Hayek, 1967, p. 308). This can manifest itself in the hiring of too much staff or a non-efficient placing of investment funds. Jensen's (1988, p. 28) 'Free Cash Flow Approach' underlines that managers tend to waste 'cash flow in excess of that required to fund all of a firm's projects that have positive net present value when discounted at the relevant cost of capital'. Managers use the discretion over their cash flow to finance investment projects with lower returns than alternative investments on the capital market, or to preserve inefficient organization structures. Thus, firms will expand beyond their value-maximizing size if the management does not disgorge the cash flow. They can escape from the control of the capital market. The denial of access to future capital is no longer an effective incentive to use resources efficiently (Stiglitz, 1985, p. 139). Owing to management discretion and opportunism, an increase in financial flexibility of the firm causes a decrease of shareholder value.

Diverging risk preferences are an additional component of the conflict between managers and shareholders. By portfolio diversification, shareholders can practically eliminate firm-specific risk. For that reason, they are risk neutral towards the policy of a single corporation and want the management to maximize the expected profit. The value of the manager's human capital depends, to a high degree, on the firm's development as it is highly 'asset specific' or 'job specific', i.e. it is only partly transferable to another job in another firm. For the manager, much of his investment into his own human capital has the character of sunk costs. Besides, he might be liable in the event of insolvency. Since he cannot usually diversify his labour input over many firms, he is rationally risk averse. He can merely try to reduce his risk position, e.g. by diversifying over different fields of business activities or assuring his financial autonomy paying low dividends. Summing up the *incentive problem of the management*, divergent payoff functions, including different arguments and risk attitudes, cause an incentive for managers to increase, with incomplete observability of their actions and knowledge, their own utility at the expense of the shareholders.

Asymmetric information gives rise, together with the manager's opportunism, to *agency costs*, the central instrument of analysis in Agency Theory. They can be defined as the difference between the shareholders' expected benefits in a fictitious, first-best optimum and their real payoff in a second-best world with agency problems (Jensen & Meckling, 1976, S.308). They consist of three components (cf. Jensen, 1988, p. 28; Spremann, 1987, p. 347):

1. Costs of directly monitoring the manager's performance (*monitoring costs*).
2. Costs of restricting the manager's discretion, e.g. a manager's voluntary renunciation of competences, and of implementing proper incentive structures to align his behaviour with shareholders' preferences, e.g. performance-related bonuses and compensating risk allowances if a risk-averse manager's wage is affected with risk (*bonding costs*).
3. Efficiency losses which are incurred in spite of monitoring and bonding expenditures because the conflicts of interest cannot be resolved perfectly (*residual loss*).

While monitoring and bonding expenditures are to a certain extent measurable, the calculation of the residual loss requires the comparison of an actual state with an 'ideal' world, i.e. a general competitive equilibrium with homogenous expectations. Agency costs are therefore an opportunity-costs concept. They are hardly operable as a precise quantitative decision criterium (Spremann, 1987, p. 347 f.). Nevertheless, agency costs are a comprehensive concept to depict the logical solution structure of agency problems. While they are not appropriate for cardinal valuations, they may frequently help to classify institutional arrangements in an ordinal way.

The last component of the agency puzzle in modern corporations is the *incentive problem of the shareholders*. Generally, stockholder meetings, which are an element of the internal governance mechanism of joint-stock companies, are seen as devices to discipline managers. A manager failing to maximize the firm's value can and should be replaced. However, the mechanism can only function on the premises that shareholders expend resources both to obtain information about a management's performance and to evaluate alternative teams or individuals for the job (Stiglitz, 1985, p. 136). But unfortunately, the more dispersed the company stock, the more the costs to gain information exceed the resulting additional individual profit share. Moreover, even for an informed shareholder, it is expensive to persuade other shareholders to replace managers. Therefore, as corporate control has a public-good character, a rational individual, owning only a negligible fraction of the company stock, won't allocate resources to monitor the management (Easterbrook & Fischel, 1981, p. 1171). Nevertheless, individual rationality means, in this case, collective self-harming. Shareholders are representing a 'latent group' (Olson, 1968). They are in a prisoners' dilemma. Effective shareholder control (*equity control*) will only be granted if there is a 'big' shareholder owning a fraction of stock that is sufficiently large to compensate him for his monitoring efforts, even though 'smaller' shareholders will free-ride on the resulting efficiency increase. Ultimately, this boils down to a coordination problem. In widely-held corporations *coordination costs* to organize a joint governance interest in the firm are prohibitive. Indeed, they nip in the bud any incentive to exercise equity control, leaving management with unrestricted discretion. Figure 1.1 illustrates agency and coordination costs arising between various classes of stakeholders.

The three subproblems jointly constitute a multiple principal-(multiple) agent problem (which continues in a chain of agency relations inside the corporation). This threatens to diminish or even to ruin the efficiency advantages of specialization. However, the empirical evidence of developed market economies indicates that there must be governance mechanisms granting the efficiency of the corporate form 'joint-stock company'. Subsequently, there will be identified some agency-costs reducing mechanisms related to equity and debt control which are, above all, focusing the incentive problem of the managers.

1.2 BANK-BASED CORPORATE CONTROL

1.2.1 Control by Equity

The Theory of Complete Agency Contracts (Normative Agency Theory) designs second-best contracts explicitly taking into account diverging

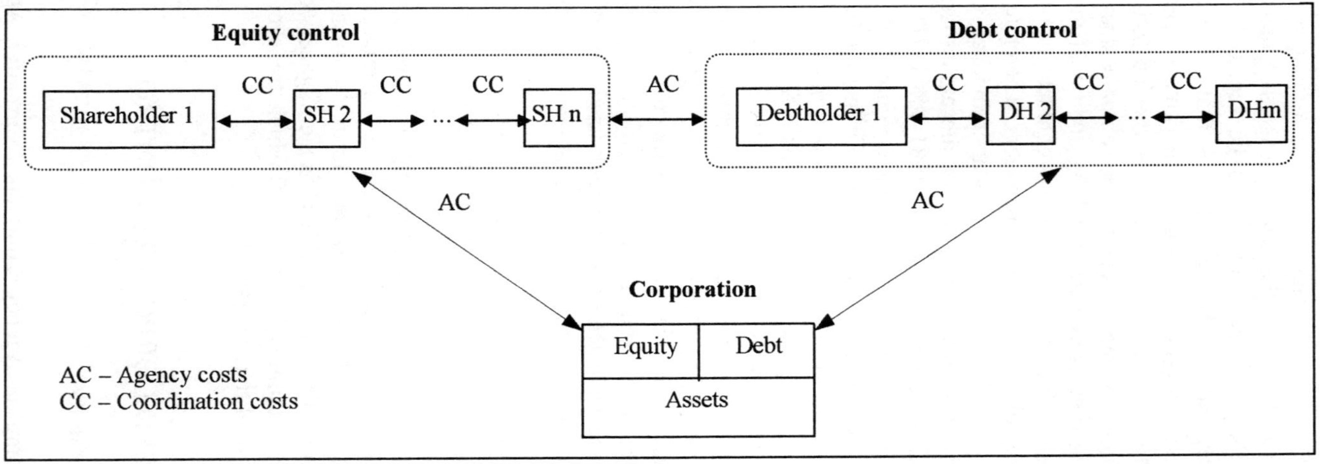

Figure 1.1: Agency costs and coordination costs in the modern corporation

interests, different risk preferences and asymmetric information. *Ex ante* efficient constructions of contracts are deemed possible. Provided that shareholders know exactly the manager's payoff function, his risk preferences and the distribution function of random shocks affecting the production output of a firm, they can design an optimal reward schedule, i.e. a firm-internal governance structure under which the manager willy-nilly maximizes, together with his own payoff, the payoff of the shareholders. As the manager's payoff depends on his performance, his incentives are, by that means, aligned to those of the corporate owners. The latter can cut down monitoring costs. The resulting contract is a formula which determines, dependent on verifiable key variables, the manager's fee. Without denying the relevance of incentive-compatible contracts for a mitigation of the incentive problem of the manager, the complexity of real reward schedules is restricted by bounded rationality of the actors (Simon, 1961, p. xxiv). There are high transaction costs to the contract parties in anticipating the various eventualities that may occur during a long-term agency relationship. The precise and clear formulation of the contract to make it enforceable is also costly. Hence, in a real world of high transaction costs, contracts are less complex than supposed by the Theory of Complete Agency Contracts.

A performance-related fee schedule fixes the distribution of risky production outcomes between manager and shareholders.[2] While risk-neutral shareholders wouldn't mind taking the whole residual risk, risk-averse managers will demand a risk premium compensating them for the utility loss suffered by risk-sharing. The amount of the premium corresponds positively with the variance of random shocks and the manager's degree of risk aversion (Spremann, 1987, p. 344). Compared to a first-best world without asymmetric information, the premium is social waste because shareholders could bear the entire risk without compensation. The fee function is subject to a tradeoff between incentive alignment (lowering monitoring costs) and risk compensation (raising bonding costs): The higher the share of risk borne by the manager, the more effective is the alignment of the manager's incentives to the shareholders' payoff function, but the higher are also the bonding costs borne by the shareholders to compensate the manager for risk-bearing. In this perspective, the optimal incentive contract minimizing agency costs must always be a compromise between 'control of behaviour' and 'risk-sharing' (Schmidt, 1990, p. 24).

An additional institution aligning *ex ante* manager and owner interests are managerial stock-holdings. According to Jensen & Meckling (1976), the divergence of interest between owners and manager can be limited if the manager himself is a shareholder of the firm. In practice, this incentive effect is, at least in certain ranges of managerial shareholdings, diminished by managerial entrenchment. Managers are said to be entrenched if they are virtually uncontestable by shareholder meetings or by takeovers because of the size of their shareholdings and related proxy rights.[3] The portion of managerial shares necessary to become entrenched (either as a single chief executive officer or as colluding collective) depends highly on the equity structure of the firm, i.e. on the resolution of the incentive problem of the shareholders. The more dispersed a firm's 'outside' equity (not held by the management), the greater is the danger of managerial entrenchment. Clearly, entrenchment may motivate managers to pursue their own ends, i.e. perquisites rather than profits, thus raising agency costs.

Agents' opportunism and bounded rationality are turning the attention of Williamson's (1985, p. 29; 1988, p. 570) Transaction-Cost Approach to *ex post* control institutions designed to guard the rights of equityholders. Managers are controlled, among other things, by the company's board of directors.[4] Provided it is adequately designed, the board may be an instrument to preserve the interests of the residual claimants and to secure the asset-specific investment of the community of shareholders (Williamson, 1992, p. 30 f.; 1988, p. 580). Complementary external measures reducing the information problem and protecting equity owners' interests are, for instance, the obligation to disclose information or the scrutiny of the balance by independent chartered accountants.

Thus far, we have implicitly assumed the company to consist of 100 percent equity provided by suppliers who are stepping into a financial relationship with the firm that lasts for the firm's life-time. They possess the right to the firm's residual returns in states when the firm is not bankrupt. As we have seen, there are various *ex ante* incentive-alignment and *ex post* control institutions to protect and enforce their interests, whilst reducing agency costs. We stated that, in a world of incomplete contracts, the distribution of residual claims between pure investors and managers has some effect on the resolution of the agency problem and on the production output. It turns out, therefore, that giving some equity to the management is a part of an efficient governance structure. This view of reinterpreting financial relationships into agency relationships is a clear contradiction of the frequently quoted hypothesis that corporate finance does not matter.[5]

1.2.2 Control by Debt

It remains to be analysed whether the output is also affected by a firm's debt/equity-mix, i.e. the granting of residual claims and control rights to different types of stakeholders in different states of the firm. Which are the links between debt-induced incentives and agency costs? The incentive effects on managers, produced by the firm's capital structure, originate in both the implicit and explicit terms of a contract as well as the control rights attached to the suppliers of finance in each state of the world. The suppliers of debt finance are in a temporary financial relationship with the firm. They control managers through the explicit terms of the loan contract which generally define time and amount of interest and settlement payments. In states of bankruptcy, debtholders become residual claimants and exert control on the firm. They can decide to exchange the firm management. In any case, bankruptcy is expensive for managers because it diminishes their discretion and private consumption ('perks'), their reputation (cutting down the value of their human capital on the market for managers), and increases the probability of discharge. Consequently, an important incentive effect of debt finance stems from the managers' desire to avoid bankruptcy.

Therefore, the design of bankruptcy law is crucial for the efficacy of corporate control. In reality, we can observe quite different approaches to debt control. The principal objective of the US Bankruptcy Code is to maintain the borrower's business as a going concern. In financial distress, the borrower's management can voluntarily file a petition to trigger corporate reorganization under Chapter 11. The filing protects the firm from actions of pre-petition creditors and allows the management to continue to operate and to start restructuring. Control over company assets remains with the borrower (debtor-in-possession). Furthermore, in the US, debt control is seriously weakened by the doctrine of equitable subordination. American law courts often subordinate the claims of senior creditors to those of junior creditors or even to equity if they interfere in the business of borrowers before the filing of Chapter 11 petitions. Each creditor can lose his priority if he has exerted some degree of control over a debtor. Especially secured creditors will regularly refrain from any control action stripping them of their rights to collateral or downgrading their priority. As a consequence of the described institutional barriers for lenders to exert control on borrowers in times of financial distress (both before and after the triggering of Chapter 11), management and shareholders of a borrower gain an enormous bargaining power. Management enjoys remarkable discretion against lenders in virtually all states of the firm, its commitment to loan contracts is rather weak.

On the other hand, the traditional single main goal of German insolvency law is the best possible satisfaction of creditors. It does not aim explicitly at the preservation or maintenance of a debtor's business, but gives priority to the speedy liquidation of assets - even at the expense of the firm's going concern. This puts strong rule-based disciplinary pressure on managers. Lenders can (and do) increase this pressure by use of collaterals and liens on debtors' assets. They give them an additional contractual hedge against managerial opportunism. Effective tools of debt control along with strong institutional incentives to get engaged in equity control[6] were crucial for German banks to become powerful guardians of the enterprise sector.

The antithetical approaches towards debt control in Germany and the US underline the importance of an adequate institutional base of debt control in insider systems where banks and other lenders are to play a most active role in both equity and debt control. With strong and credible bankruptcy laws, banks can make use of debt/equity finance in order to design efficient governance structures at least for bank-dominated corporations. They can thereby induce managers to refrain from opportunistic behaviour and to pursue a corporate policy maximizing the expected value of the firm. Moreover, loose bankruptcy laws are not only weakening the governance power of the banking sector, but also effecting a softening of budget constraints by other stakeholders like trade partners and firm employees.

Beyond bankruptcy law, managers are subject to indirect control exerted by implicit contracts with lenders, including informal conditions of loan renewals or the providing of additional debt finance (Stiglitz, 1985, p. 141). Thus, by committing managers to make payments to lenders, debt finance imposes some serious restrictions on managerial discretion. In particular, managers have to care for the firm's liquidity. The bonding promise to pay out future cash flow limits the possibility of wasting free cash flow.[7] Moreover, it forces managers to restructure the firm in an efficient way and to adopt a corporate policy more closely aligned to the shareholders' interests (Grossman & Hart, 1982, p. 109). In all, debt reduces agency costs by bonding the management through explicit (primarily the threat of bankruptcy) as well as implicit (in particular the terms of loan renewals) contracts.

Nevertheless, debt cannot effect a perfect congruence of managers' and owners' interests because of the antithetical interests of shareholders (profit-maximizing) and lenders (securing liquidity). More probably, it will induce managers to adopt a policy of profit-satisficing, thereby diminishing the risk of insolvency. From the point of view of a risk-neutral shareholder, this is no optimal corporate policy. However, as it is at least closer to the shareholders' interests than eventual managerial opportunism without debt-related incentives, debt is an adequate means to increase the efficiency of a firm.

But debt, affecting the incentive schemes of managers and owners, also evokes agency costs. While the positive efficiency effects depicted above can be realized in a pure form only by a substitution of equity by debt, a negative counter-effect appears for the absorption of additional debt finance to existing firm capital. On the one hand, additional debt imposes a certain discipline on the management by increasing the probability of bankruptcy. On the other hand, it enlarges the management's financial scope, thereby offering him the possibility of wasting or consuming more resources in pursuing private interests.

Furthermore, debt increases bonding costs since debt-induced higher probability of bankruptcy will press a risk-averse manager, who has to invest his human capital into a single firm thereby making it, up to a certain degree, asset specific, to require an additional risk premium for his services (Edwards & Fischer, 1994a, p. 34 f.). The firm may suffer a significant competitive disadvantage, compared to a firm with a lower leverage. In addition, the manager will try to diminish the riskiness of investment projects to lower the probability of insolvency. But that is not efficient from the risk-neutral owners' point of view. The divergence between the degree of risk preferred by the suppliers of equity and the degree aimed at by the management increases.

As bankruptcy is costly for managers, they will in times of financial distress, but before the firm goes broke, more frequently try 'to gamble for resurrection' (Dewatripont & Tirole, 1993, p. 27); that is, to choose excessively risky investment projects instead of safer projects with a higher expected return, but also with a higher probability of bankruptcy. Managers may be tempted to raise additional funds at high interest rates and to place them into high-risk projects whose return distributions have higher variances, even if the statistical means are lower. It grants managers a (small) chance to avoid bankruptcy, thereby defending their discretion against the control of debtholders who could decide to liquidate the firm or sell a share of its assets. Consequently, the threat of debt control evokes perverse incentives for basically risk-averse managers. This can be disastrous if a less risky policy offers a better risk-return mix to the firm and increases its viability, even though leading with a higher probability to bankruptcy. Clearly, we have an efficiency problem.

As long as bankruptcy does not occur, firm control is exercised by equityholders. Unfortunately, even with effective equity control they have no incentive to prevent managers from gambling. On the contrary, in times of financial distress there is an efficiency-reducing incentive congruence between managers and owners. The latter can make money only in solvent states. While owners of companies with limited liability benefit, in states of financial distress, from the upside gains of high risk investments and are therefore prone to take excessive risk, the major part of the costs of downside losses is borne by the lenders (Jensen & Meckling, 1976, p. 334). This obvious conflict of interests between owners and debtholders causes a *debt-induced* agency problem (risk shifting). The distortion of the owners' incentive scheme in indebted firms relates actually to all states of the firm. However, when a firm performs well and has a sound equity base, owners have to bear a bigger part of costs resulting from excessive risks. Thus owners' preference for risk shifting decreases parallel to the firm's debt/equity-ratio. For this reason and because of a remaining discretion for risk-averse managers, who are not prone to gamble in good states, the problem is not as pronounced when the firm is financially sound. But as they will lose their residual rights if the firm fails, the problem may be most drastic in the case of imminent insolvency. Both managers and shareholders are inclined to pursue a risk-seeking corporate policy. The resulting efficiency problem is based *nota bene* not on the separation of ownership and management. It can be resolved efficiently only by uniting all capital claims of a firm, equity as well as debt, in the controlling hand of one institution, representing the management's principal in all states, thereby internalizing all costs and benefits of corporate policy. Otherwise there must always be a debt-induced divergence between efficiency and equityholders' preferences.

1.2.3   Towards an Efficient Capital Structure of the Modern Corporation

But which level of debt is efficient? Or rather, from an agency perspective, which level maximizes the expected value of the firm? In the following, we will identify four types of variables mainly determining the optimal debt level (for a given efficiency of the above listed equity-control mechanisms):[8]

- *Concentration of debtholders*: If the firm's number of debtholders is high, considerable costs of negotiation and coordination bring about a serious incentive problem of the lenders as principals. For this reason, the probability of liquidation in case of bankruptcy increases. As liquidation includes firing the management, it is a 'worst-case' scenario for the managers. Dispersed debt claims therefore increase the probability of managerial gambling in times of financial distress. In addition, they diminish the chance to resolve constructively the solvency problem of an otherwise viable firm that, after insolvency actually occurred, needs restructuring measures rather than liquidation. If there are only a few lenders or even a single debtholder, their motivation to rescue the firm will be greater. Furthermore, as stated above, the relationship between lenders and managers is, despite its rule-governed character, to a certain degree implicit. In a world of imperfect loan contracts, a lender can influence management depending upon his relative power over managers.[9] In such a power relationship the debtholders' position gains its strength not only from the sheer size of a firm's debt/equity ratio, but also from the concentration of debt capital. In times of financial distress, a few strong debtholders probably exert more pressure to pursue an efficient corporate policy on the management than many small ones. Thus, a more concentrated debt structure of the firm significantly lowers coordination costs and renders possible effective control by lenders. In particular, it may help to reduce the problem of perverse managerial incentives (before bankruptcy) and foster efficient solutions for insolvent firms (in the case of bankruptcy). Hence, concentrated debt claims should be linked to a higher debt/equity ratio and vice versa.

-   *Capital base of debtholders*: Even with high debt concentration, efficient debt control presupposes a sound financial position of the lender *vis à vis* his borrower. If the debtholder does not have a sufficiently strong capital base, he might easily suffer financial distress following a debtor's bankruptcy (creditor trap). Thus he will offer further credits to a financially distressed borrower. Then bankruptcy is not a feasible means of disciplining the monitored firm. Consequently, the sounder the capital base of a firm's debtholders, the higher should be its level of debt.

-   *Institutional environment*: The efficiency of debt control is determined by the definition of its institutional environment[10], in particular the design and efficacy of the bankruptcy law. The weaker the control rights of debt-holders and the more expensive the bankruptcy proceedings, the less effectively managers can be bonded to efficiency goals because an attenuation of lenders' control rights automatically enlarges the management's range of discretion, i.e. the amount of states in which they need not fear investors' involvement. If the cost of debt control is prohibitive, a high debt/equity-ratio might lead to serious waste of financial resources by the managers.[11]

-   *Life cycle*: With respect to the problem of free cash flow, the incentives of debt finance depend on the stage the firm reached in its life cycle. A firm rapidly growing on a developing market generally has a lot of highly profitable investment opportunities and no free cash flow. Such a company is subject to the control of the capital market because its financial demand exceeds cash flow. Debt control or a high debt/equity ratio respectively are very important for corporations with large cash flows which already reached the stagnation phase or even need to shrink (Jensen, 1988, p. 31). In these firms managerial bias to waste financial resources may easily dominate efficiency goals.

On the whole, debt is a necessary element of an efficient governance structure which minimizes agency costs. Even without formally modelling the optimal capital structure of the firm, we identified some important variables determining the optimal debt/equity-ratio.[12] In real situations, optimization will be difficult and costly. However, the design of a governance structure including debt will very likely improve the incentive situation of the management from the shareholders' perspective. At this stage, the decisive question runs as follows: Who is ready to design an efficient governance structure at all? As we know, the separation of management and control gives rise to an incentive problem of the principals, i.e. the shareholders. Now this problem is aggravated because we need costly coordination of the interests of owners *and* debtholders as principals of the firm. Therefore, we have to prove whether there exists a suitable institutional solution minimizing the costs of designing an efficient governance structure and eliminating the incentive problem of the principals.

1.2.4   Control by Financial Intermediaries

1.2.4.1   Standard debt contracts and delegated monitoring by financial intermediaries

As the financial need of modern corporations is immense and individual investors prefer portfolio diversification, the incentive problems of dispersed debtholders and owners could justify the existence of institutional investors. Diamond (1984) develops a model which makes monitoring by equityholders completely superfluous and concentrates debt control of firms in the hand of one intermediary. Financial intermediaries can reduce their risk of going bankrupt by diversifying their loan portfolios. Raising the number of stochastically independent loans, the actual aggregate returns converge, according to the Law of Great Number, more and more towards their expected value. Therefore, an intermediary can nearly exclude the incurring of deadweight bankruptcy costs and guarantee payment of fixed interest to the depositors. According to Diamond, a standard-debt contract defines the optimal relationship between intermediary and individual investors as well as between firms and intermediary. Because the intermediary cannot fail, provided that it possesses a sufficiently well-diversified loan portfolio, depositors need not monitor its performance. Diversification together with standard-debt contracts are the key to save agency costs as opposed to non-intermediated relationships between investors and firms or investors' equityholdings in intermediaries. In the presence of private information of the latter, equityholdings require intensive monitoring of the intermediary to maximize its performance. Consequently, it causes a derived agency problem. The efficiency of Diamond's model is conditional on the intermediary's ability to reduce the total agency costs of the system. And indeed, it has a gross advantage in collecting information because, in a non-intermediated system, monitoring (as well as screening) costs are duplicated or, considering the free-rider problem, monitoring is not carried out at all (Diamond, 1984, p. 394). Besides, assuming plausibly fixed costs for the acquisition of corporate information[13], there is strong evidence for economies of scale in monitoring the performance of firms (Diamond, 1984, p. 401). That is why delegated monitoring by intermediaries has a net agency-costs advantage relative to individual borrowing and lending.[14]

While the model's true message is that information for the monitoring of firms is more efficiently gathered by financial intermediaries than by individual investors[15], provided the intermediary's incentives are congruent to the investors' interests, the Diamond model does not deal with the *whole*, and obviously very complex, puzzle of the agency relationship between investors and firms. It is true that it offers a solution for the debtholders' incentive problem by effectively pooling their resources and in this way transforms their agency problem qualitatively, but it does not lead to efficient governance structures of firms. It neglects the incentive effects to managers of powerful equity control. Solely well-diversified and hence risk-neutral shareholders have a strong preference to enforce a corporate policy aiming at profit maximization. Therefore, the standard-debt contract proposed by Diamond is, at least if it is the only way of contracting between investors and intermediaries or intermediaries and firms, not efficient. Besides, it seems to be highly questionable whether solely asset diversification solves the incentive problem of the intermediary thereby making superfluous monitoring of the intermediary by individual investors. Empirical observations lead to serious doubts whether this hypothesis is valid.[16] They rather stress the necessity to implement additional institutions to safeguard depositors' claims.

1.2.4.2 The edge of universal banking

An efficient governance structure of a firm requires an institutional solution that combines both the efficiency advantages of delegated monitoring and control as well as those of uniting a sufficiently large fraction of debt and equity claims in the controlling hand of one institution. Provided it is itself efficiently governed, the resulting intermediary institution will be able to design an efficient governance structure for a firm that complies with the requirements necessary to set up appropriate reward schedules, based upon verifiable and hence contractible signals and managerial residual rights, and to create an optimal financial structure. It 'can then supply external finance to firms in that combination of debt and equity which, by its effect on managerial incentives through debt and equity's return streams and control rights, minimises the agency costs of finance' (Edwards & Fischer, 1994a, p. 43). And whilst eliminating the distortions created by the debt-induced agency problem, it even aligns managerial incentives closer to social efficiency goals.[17]

But which type of financial intermediary is best suited to provide the monitoring and control services? Universal banks might have an edge over other intermediaries with regard to their institutional incentives and efficiency to produce information about their clients. Bank loans typically stand far back in the liquidation claims' line of priority. Thus banks have a special interest in acquiring reliable information about their borrowers. Furthermore, bank debt is 'inside debt' (Fama, 1985, p. 36), that is, banks have access to information about their debtors that is not available to outside debtholders who possess publicly traded bonds and rely on published information about the debtor, e.g. information published by the borrower firm itself or rating agencies.[18] According to Black (1975, p. 326), the ongoing history of a borrower firm, which holds accounts with a bank, conveys useful information. Banks therefore observe the development of a client's balance, i.e. his assets and liabilities, to gain insider information that would be very expensive to acquire for other intermediaries. This theoretic argument is supported in practice by the fact that banks frequently oblige their borrowers to maintain 'compensating balances'. In this context, they can be viewed as devices to generate inside information. Thus, while all types of intermediaries gain by economies of scale, banks derive an information edge from economies of scope in the provision of payment services and the monitoring of firms, making them privileged quasi-insiders. By delegated proxy rights or owning equity in a firm, they can even enhance their insider status and become able to monitor and control firms more efficiently (Saunders, 1994, p. 238). Of course, the latter presupposes the absence of fire walls between the various departments of a bank, especially an unrestricted flow of information between the loan department and the investment arm.

The crucial question is whether banks have a good incentive to execute corporate control. Macey & Miller (1995, pp. 5f.) cast doubt on the efficiency of bank control. They argue that banks have a dominating interest as fixed claimants even if they hold a significant amount of equity, as they are highly leveraged and subject to a mismatch in the term structure of their assets and liabilities that is effected by the high amount of checkable deposits available on demand. We do not deny that such considerations may be of some importance for the governance incentives of banks. But, adverse effects from the term structure of banks' balance sheets can be minimized if banks are allowed to build reserves they can draw from in bad times. This effects an intertemporal smoothing of their balance sheet profits and makes it more attractive to adopt a riskier, yet also more profitable policy in bank-controlled firms. Structural incentives for banks to carry out a corporate policy aiming at profit satisficing rather than profit maximization originate predominantly from other sources. One of them is the asset structure of a bank. A sufficiently large amount of equity shares in firms, directly held by the bank, reduces bonding costs by setting the right incentives for the bank to pursue the interests of shareholders as well. By the same token, considerable debt claims against firms are granting the right incentive to the bank to enforce an efficient risk/return mix for investment and to avoid debt-induced risk-shifting.

On the other hand, the bank's credit exposure to individual firms should not exceed certain critical threshold values. Otherwise, the bank can easily get caught in a creditor trap if its economic survival depends upon the liquidity and financial soundness of one or only a few debtors. If they fail to repay their debt, the bank itself would get into financial distress. In such a situation, banks do not have a good incentive to behave like hard-nosed guardians. They rather tend to soften the budget constraint of the defaulting enterprise and to prolong outstanding loans. Besides, as the debtor firms may anticipate the bank's incentive scheme, the bank cannot then credibly enforce its explicit and implicit terms of the loan contract. The power balance will then be reversed in favour of the debtor. The risk to get caught in a creditor trap is especially high if the asset side of the bank's balance sheet is fraught with doubtful and non-performing loans. This may drastically reduce both the incentive and capability of the bank to execute effective debt control. A sound capital base and a well diversified loan portfolio hence are pivotal for efficient bank-based control.

In sum, a sufficiently diversified intermediary, holding an adequate amount of equity and debt claims, has the right incentive to pursue a corporate policy aiming at profit maximization. Therefore, a universal bank is the type of intermediary most suited to exercise delegated monitoring and control. However, this conclusion is very general in so far as it pins down neither the organizational nor legal structure of the intermediary. In contrast to Diamond (1984), the necessary key features of the intermediary are its wide range of activities to ensure economies of scope[19] as well as the fusion of commercial and investment banking activities enabling the bank to hold equity and giving it the incentive to run a policy efficiently balancing owners' and lenders' interests. In general, these conditions can be fulfilled by a broad scale of structurally different universal banks with the fully integrated universal bank at one end and the financial holding company at the other end.

1.2.4.3 Towards an efficient capital structure of universal banks

The efficacy of intermediary control depends critically on the assumption that the bank has an incentive to fulfil the task of delegated monitoring and control in the intended efficient manner. In principle, the 'efficient-governance-structure' approach of the firm is applicable to banks, too (Dewatripont & Tirole, 1993, p. 13, p. 26 ff.). Bank managers are subject to the same incentive and control mechanisms as managers of non-financial firms. Thus, there must be an optimal capital structure for banks' liabilities, imposing discipline on the management, too. This includes a transfer of control from stockholders to depositors in the event of poor financial performance. Unfortunately, no intermediary-type solution exists since it would perpetuate the problem of delegated monitoring and control. While therefore equity control would be exerted most effectively by big shareholders, debt control is problematical because of the dispersed nature of banks' small depositors. Free-riding and incompetent depositors have to be protected by banking regulation. A monitoring agency can be set up representing debtholders' interests which has two important tasks in banking regulation:[20]

1. To counter *ex ante* the perverse incentive problem of bank managers and bank owners in times of financial distress, it has to adapt their interests by 'net worth adjustments' (Tirole, 1994, p. 477), that is adjustments of the bank's risk-weighted capital ratio (Cooke ratio). A weak financial performance is reflected adequately by a deterioration of the bank's balance sheet. Financial distress (increasing net debt) requires timely recapitalization to counter the incentive to gamble for resurrection. The agency must observe whether a bank meets well-defined capital adequacy requirements, e.g. whether it does not fall below a capital ratio of 8% as proposed by the 1988 international Basle accords. Undercapitalized banks are then obliged to issue new equity.[21]

2. If the financial performance falls below some critical threshold value, the agency will gain complete control of the bank (forced administration). Then, it has to interfere with management in the interest of small and dispersed depositors or, provided there is a deposit insurance, in the interest of tax payers.

The question 'Who guards the guardians?' leads us obviously to the frontiers of theoretic foundations of corporate control. Clearly, compared to the intermediary solution of firm control, the 'efficient-governance-structure' approach to banks, including some considerations of regulation, is not completely satisfactory. While powerful equity control of a bank exerted by large corporate stockholders holds the danger of indirect economic manipulation of the entire industrial sector through the banking sector, dispersed ownership of banks may produce enormous discretion of bank managers and reduce their incentives to maximize the bank's firm value.

1.2.5 Summary: The Institutional Base of Insider Control

Based upon the theoretical analysis above, there can be deduced some critical institutional features of an efficient system of *insider* control, minimizing agency costs and coordination costs.

In the absence of large corporate or individual shareholders, equity control should be conducted by intermediaries to diminish monitoring costs and overcome the incentive problem of the principals (i.e. to reduce coordination costs). For the same reasons, debt control is most effectively exerted by banks.

A controlling intermediary should be both creditor and debtor of a firm. It should exercise both equity and debt control. In this way, it gains from economies of scope and low monitoring costs. Furthermore, only the joint execution of equity and debt control effectively minimizes risk-shifting incentives. Thus a universal bank or bank-centred financial groups with a free flow of information between the investment arm and the department of commercial banking are the types of intermediaries that have the incentive and ability to design an efficient governance structure for a firm.

Efficient debt control requires a working bankruptcy law and a sound capital base of the bank. Furthermore, universal banks have to be controlled effectively for themselves. The dispersed nature of banks' small depositors requires prudential regulation, in particular binding capital adequacy requirements, and a monitoring agency that supervises banks. Besides, banks themselves should be controlled by large shareholders.

1.3 MARKET-BASED CORPORATE CONTROL

1.3.1 The Neoclassical Approach to Corporate Control

Neoclassical microeconomics were founded in the 1870s when single proprietorship was the prevalent form of corporate ownership. Consequently, neoclassical theory for a long time denied the existence of corporate control problems. Rather, the focus was put on the profit-maximizing firm. Berle's & Means' (1932) pessimism concerning managerial discretion and opportunism was responded by Friedman's (1953, p. 22) methodological doctrine that 'firms behave as if they were seeking rationally to maximize their expected returns'. Following Friedman's 'as-if' hypothesis, preferences and motivation of both managers and owners are of no importance for positive economic analysis. Natural selection on the goods markets validates the hypothesis: The determinants of business behaviour do not matter. Managers may even be uninformed and act opportunistically. In the short run, managerial behaviour inconsistent with rational and informed profit-maximization will very likely diminish business resources and the respective firm will not survive for a long time in the market. Clearly, the argumentation reflects a huge confidence in the functioning of the goods markets and the power of competition.

Winter (1964, 1971) disagrees with Friedman, saying that natural selection needs time as competition on goods markets is imperfect. For instance, economic success in any single time period implies nothing about a firm's ability to keep its position in the market in the long run if it is based upon such factors as random or chance. In this case, the firm's behaviour is not consistent over time. Its corporate policy does not comply with a profit-maximizing norm resulting from market data. Thus, no conclusion can be drawn about the firm's future economic success (Winter, 1971, p. 244). Contrary to Friedman, Winter is sceptical about the functioning and selective power of goods markets. Indeed, the neoclassical paradigm of perfect competition on polypolistic and perfect markets is a theoretic construct which cannot be institutionally reproduced in the real world. For that reason, the assumption of profit-maximization as sole corporate objective and Friedman's 'as-if' hypothesis rest on unrealistic premises. According to Demsetz (1969), they rely on a 'Nirvana' approach. Winter (1971, p. 245) asserts that under imperfect competition and a constitutional lack of information firms' decisions are governed by fairly simple decision rules rather than by the outright attempt to maximize profit. Decision rules are changed only in time of crisis. Under normal circumstances, managers tend to apply existing rules and to satisfice profits. As rules can merely outline but not remove managerial discretion, corporate control is back on the agenda.

The final line of defence for the neoclassical dogma results from control market theories, primarily the theoretic constructions of the managerial labour market and the market for corporate control, both of which will be analysed in more detail in the following sections. In accordance with the inherent logic of the control market approach, control inefficiencies on input and output markets are revised by the latent threat of decreasing rental rates of managerial human capital signalled by the managerial labour market or by the privation of managerial control through the market for corporate control. The latter represents the central theoretical approach underlying the mechanisms of market-based outsider systems of corporate control.

1.3.2   The Market for Corporate Control

1.3.2.1   The concept of the market for corporate control

In a neoclassical world, the market for corporate control is the crucial element of a market-based outsider system of corporate control, in which governance is exercised mainly by 'outsiders', i.e. persons 'not presently controlling the affairs of the corporation' (Manne, 1965, p. 113). Marris (1964) first put a difference between the actual depressed market value of a badly run firm as signalled by the capital market and a possible higher value of the same assets if they were managed by a raider, that is a corporation or an individual taking over the firm and using the previously underutilized resources in a (supposedly) more efficient way. The capital gain or opportunity value resulting from this difference provides a strong motivation for raiders to make a takeover attempt. Manne (1965) explicitly introduced the market for corporate control as a permanent institutional device into economic analysis. The asset dealt with in this market is the control of corporations. The right to control a firm is valued on its own as it renders possible speculative gains to a raider.

Conceptionally, the intuition behind the market for corporate control can be sketched in the following way: Bad managerial performance is reflected in comparatively low market prices of corporate stock. A raider hence has an incentive to acquire a strategic stake in the firm, exchange the inefficient incumbent management and install a new one which runs a corporate policy more aligned to the profit interest of the owners. Subsequently, the more efficient policy will cause an increase in the firm's stock price. Thus, the raider can take advantage of arbitrage in time or speculation.[22] The source of the raider's capital gain is a reduction in agency costs, which increases the value of corporate assets under the control of the acquirer as compared to their value when managed by the incumbent management (Easterbrook & Fischel, 1981, p. 1173). There are numerous methods of gaining control of a badly managed firm.[23] In a hostile tender offer, the acquiring entity makes a bid for shares directly to the target firm's stockholders.[24] To encourage them to sell their shares, the bid is made usually at a premium over the company's current market price. The raider specifies the terms of the deal, especially the price and the period for which the bid is valid. The tender is successful if he purchases a strategic stake in the firm, allowing him effectively to control the management. Such a controlling stake may amount to as much as 50% plus one share or only to some 20 to 30%, depending upon the ownership structure of the target. Other possibilities of gaining control are to buy shares gradually on the stock market or to acquire a big stake via block trade from individual or institutional investors. More generally, a non-strategic stakeholder can also acquire control rights without buying additional shares, by initiating a proxy fight. This last possibility is based upon the legal premise that corporate law allows for proxy voting. Then shareholders can empower proxies to exercise the right to vote on a company's general meetings.

The market for corporate control effects an increase in efficiency in the management of corporate resources through two distinct channels. On the one hand, actual changes of corporate control, caused by the described methods, may raise a firm's market price due to restructuring activities and a change of corporate policy. Jensen and Ruback (1983, p. 6) interpret the market for corporate control 'as a market in which alternative managerial teams compete for the rights to manage corporate resources'. From this point of view, the market for corporate control is an integral component of the outside managerial labour market. Management teams are the active players in the market, while stockholders occupy a rather passive role.

Arbitrageurs and takeover specialists are constantly rating firms and competing team offers, including that of the incumbent management team. If the latter fails to maximize a firm's profit, the right to control corporate resources moves, by means of competition between many different management teams, to the team using the firm's assets most efficiently. Comparative superiority of a team is signalled by the amount of the premium which is offered to gain control. Stockholders just choose the highest premium offered to them on the market and thereby contribute passively to the working of the market forces. Their function is that of referees in the competition between the management teams, they reward the highest bidder the right to control the target firm's resources.

On the other hand, the latent threat of a control change provoked by bad management and decreasing share prices, leading possibly to a replacement of incumbent management or at least to a limitation of its discretion, may already help to discipline managers effectively and align their incentives to the objectives of the dispersed owners. To draw out a parallel to Competition Theory, management should be perfectly contestable. If there are no barriers to entrance to the market for corporate control, which are hampering superior management teams from gaining control over a firm with an unsatisfactory performance, potential competition induces incumbent management to make efficient use of firm assets.[25] Both channels will, if they are working according to the neoclassical paradigm, not only align managerial incentives, but probably also lead to efficient governance structures of corporations, including adequate reward schedules, managerial participation and an efficient capital structure.

In a dynamic perspective, the selection process on the market for corporate control implies, *ceteris paribus*, that the probability of the management losing the control rights over firm assets is higher, the larger a company's agency costs. Moreover, contrary to bank-based insider systems of corporate control, market-based outsider systems are offering strong incentives to managers themselves, i.e. to the agents rather than to the principals of a firm, not only to pursue a profit-oriented corporate policy, but even actively to design a governance structure signalling the management's intention to act in the owners' interest. In this way they can enhance not only corporate performance, but also signal their goals clearly and thus reduce the danger of losing control over the firm. For this reason, it is rational for managers to commit themselves effectively to efficiency goals, for instance by boosting the debt and shrinking the equity of the firm. Such a leveraged recapitalization effectively commits managers to reducing free cash flow, while the mere promise to raise dividend payments can be easily broken without incurring a contractual penalty. Added leverage places corporate policy more under the scrutiny of lenders and reduces managerial discretion. The capital market will anticipate this through a higher stock price and, consequently, the likelihood of a control change will decrease.

The efficiency of the market for corporate control and hence the reduction of agency costs are based essentially on three implicit, yet fundamental axioms. Firstly, there must exist a high positive correlation between the performance of management teams and companies' market share price (Manne, 1965, p. 112). While the team perspective underlying the theory of the market for corporate control eliminates the problem of monitoring individual managerial performance (and thus aggravates another problem, namely that of managerial incentives to free-ride on collective performance), it requires that prices on the stock market reflect accurately the relative expected profitability of companies. Capital markets must efficiently process information to offer proper evaluation criteria of managerial performance. Secondly, concerning primarily the motivational structure of raiders, possible perverse incentives evoking inefficiencies in the market for corporate control must be removed. If raiders pursue other goals than to improve managerial efficiency, the positive effects aimed at by the mechanism will not occur. Finally, provided that capital markets are efficient and raiders' motivation is exclusively to boost firm value, the takeover mechanism mustn't be hampered by freeriding shareholders, defence measures by the incumbent management or institutional devices raising the transaction costs of takeovers. As soon as a low share price signals inferior use of corporate resources, control should switch to a management team which is better motivated, more capable of running the firm in the interest of the owners or simply governed more efficiently. In the following sections, we will take a closer look at the three axioms and try to identify some institutional prerequisites for their validity.

1.3.2.2 The informational efficiency of capital markets

The capacity of capital markets to process information has been tested empirically since the late 1960s by countless economists in the context of the so-called efficient market hypothesis. That is the presumption that security prices tend to reflect fully and correctly all available information about the prospects of firms traded on the capital market. Indeed, probably no other working hypothesis of the neoclassical paradigm has been subject to such a vast bulk of empirical examinations. Assessing the results of the literature, Jensen (1988, p. 26) optimistically concludes: 'Although the evidence is not literally 100 percent in support of the efficient market hypothesis, no proposition in any of the sciences is better documented.' Whereas Scherer (1988, p. 73), pointing to exaggerated market fluctuations over time, is rather sceptical about capital markets' ability to estimate the discounted value of future corporate profits appropriately. Subsequently, we are going to elucidate the conceptual basis of the efficient market hypothesis. Then, we will briefly analyse the 'time preferences' of capital markets and identify some problems concerning the empirical corroboration of the efficient market hypothesis.

(i) Theoretical concept

The concept of market efficiency has been theoretically founded by Fama (1970, 1976). Anchored in a neoclassical world without transaction and information costs and with rational behaviour of market participants, the concept presupposes homogeneous rational expectations, 'that is, market participants agree on the implications of available information for both current prices and probability distributions on future prices of individual investment assets' (Fama & Miller, 1972, p. 335). All individuals have identical information sets. The rational use of identical information evokes a unanimous consensus on all market prices. Under those assumptions, security prices must always reflect fully and correctly all available information, markets must be efficient. It follows that prices are freed from their function to coordinate individual plans in market economies. In particular, they are no medium to communicate different preferences, knowledge and assessments among individuals. Strictly speaking, they have no information or signalling function, they are solely a mirror of an inevitable social consensus. The Hayekian problem of decentral knowledge in society is entirely irrelevant. Fama's concept is a static construction without direct empirical relevance (Neumann & Klein, 1982, p. 169).

The hypothesis distinguishes three levels of market efficiency, each dependent on the information set which the market is supposed to process fully and correctly (Malkiel, 1992, p. 739):

- The *strong* form of the efficient market hypothesis assumes that all information known to any market participant is instantaneously and perfectly revealed in security prices. Consequently, given a social consensus on the implications of news, there is no chance of outperforming the market, either on the basis of published news or on the basis of private or insider information. If that was true, information would be of no value for anybody since no investor can take any advantage of it. Yet, high penalties for insider trading, which are observable on many capital markets, give evidence that the exploitation of private information can be very profitable. Moreover, Grossman & Stiglitz (1980) present a theoretical caveat to the idea of strong market efficiency. If no kind of information makes possible profits in excess of the market, who would be willing to spend scarce resources to collect and process information? And, if there was apparently no incentive to do so, how then could the market be efficient (information paradox)? Clearly, the strong version of the efficient market hypothesis must be rejected.

- The relevant information set of *weak* market efficiency comprises all knowledge about past stock prices. Current price changes are independent of price changes in the past. Changes in stock prices are unpredictable and random ('random walk'). Chart analysis isn't helpful because there is no law determining how prices must inevitably move over time.

- Finally, for *semi-strong* market efficiency, the relevant information set consists of all publicly available information, hence the strong form information set less all private information. Fundamental analysis, including the evaluation of balance sheets, the processing of publicized information on corporate policy or R&D and inquiries into the entire economic and political environment of a corporation, is useless.

The weak and semi-strong forms of market efficiency are commonly agreed on hypotheses and seemingly corroborated by an overwhelming majority of empirial tests. But how then can we explain the existence of thousands of highly qualified professionals restlessly collecting information on and assessing the value of firms? The answer is that, in the real world, substantial information costs inevitably generate diverging subjective instead of identical objective information sets. Individual information sets may converge over time because of communication processes in society, but at the same time they permanently diverge due to innovations creating new information. Besides, market participants are not uniform. Their individuality arises from differences in education, intelligence, political and economic intuition or experience. It follows that individuals interpret (even possibly identical) information in different ways. Investors do not draw identical conclusions from identical information. Due to heterogeneous expectations, i.e. diverging subjective probability distributions of future returns instead of social consensus), individual investors can outperform even an efficient market. A superior ability to forecast future returns through subjective probability distributions clearly permits excessive profits. We obviously have to redefine the concept of market efficiency. A tentative definition could be: A market is efficient with respect to news, if the price changes immediately caused by the new information correspond exactly to the price changes that would occur if each market participant knew the news and adapted his subjective probability distribution of returns.

(ii) Empirical evidence

In the past, numerous empirical tests have been undertaken to prove market efficiency.[26] The methodological basis for tests on the semi-strong form of the efficient market hypothesis was founded by a seminal event study of Fama, Fisher, Jensen and Roll (1969), who examined the effect of stock splits on share prices. They suppose managers to be reluctant to decrease dividends. While stock splits themselves do not directly benefit investors (on the contrary, they generate transaction costs), they may be indicators for an increase in a firm's profitability. The announcement of a stock split then reveals the management's faith in future earnings prospects. Efficient markets have to anticipate this information. Fama et al. draw up a sample of firms with stock splits in the past and apply the market model to estimate monthly expected returns for each firm contained in the sample. The difference between actual and expected returns is the monthly excess return (residual) which is attributed to new information not *ex ante* processed by the market. The cumulative average residual over all firms, documented for a period starting 30 months prior to the split and ending 30 months after the same event, ascends significantly before the split. This is ascribed to the market's gradually increasing knowledge of improvements of corporate performance. After the announcement to split which generally occurs shortly before the actual event, excess returns are only random as the market has already fully transformed the news about increased earnings prospects into prices, thereby not permitting systematic excess returns to investors. Hence the cumulative average residual remains broadly constant after the split, too.

According to Fama et al., the adaption path of the cumulative average residual corroborates the semi-strong form of the efficient market hypothesis. The problem is, though, that their study (like hundreds of event studies in the following decades) implicitly is a test not only of the efficient market hypothesis, but also of two other hypotheses:

1. Fama et al. assume that stock splits are strong indicators for increased earnings prospects. In fact, they do not consider alternative causes. For example, stock splits raise the divisibility and saleability of shares, thereby expanding the scope for diversification. Hence, they may attract additional small investors. The management then could use a stock split to detract attention from bad corporate performance. More generally, event studies on market efficiency inherently presuppose a way of interpreting news, i.e. an irrevocable relation between an event and its transformation into a certain probability distribution of future returns. In fact, it then can and must be concluded in which direction prices must adapt in efficient capital markets and whether residuals must be negative or positive with *ex ante* given expected returns. Furthermore, even if the hypothesis as to how news must be transformed into probability distributions turns out to be empirically robust, its implications can always be merely qualitative. It is impossible to state what would be the accurate value of a cumulative average residual and how residuals would evolve over time, provided a market is processing relevant information instantaneously and perfectly. There is no benchmark. Consequently, one can maximally detect *whether* information is transformed by the market, but it is far from clear to which degree it is transformed.

2. As return expectations of individual investors are not directly observable *ex ante* (prior to information disclosure), they are derived by some model of equilibrium, an asset-pricing model like e.g. the market model (used by Fama et al.) or the capital asset pricing model (CAPM). Each model sets up a hypothesis on the shaping of (homogeneous) expectations, which is assumed to be empirically valid.[27]

No doubt, we can only test the validity of three joint hypotheses, i.e. a hypothesis about the adequate relation between news and price changes, another hypothesis about the shaping of individual (homogeneous) expectations and the efficient market hypothesis itself. Therefore, we must look at test results very carefully. For instance, if a study seemingly rejects market efficiency, the reason is that one or more of the three hypotheses are wrong - but which one(s)? Since we know neither all causes and consequences of observable events, nor how exactly people interpret information, it is impossible to measure accurately the degree of market efficiency.

(iii)   The 'time preferences' of capital markets: myopic markets versus myopic managers

A controversial thesis, which can be found in the literature on market efficiency, concerns the link between the market of corporate control and the managerial time horizon. It is suggested that the threat of takeovers might induce managers to shorten their decision-making horizon and to maximize short-term profits.[28] Management thus has strong incentives to neglect the long-term development of the enterprise, to cut down investment projects with long-term benefits and to concentrate heavily on investment with short-term profits. The alleged distortion of managerial time preferences is often attributed to functional deficits of the capital market: The asset-pricing process on the market doesn't allow sufficiently for long-term profits. It systematically undervalues future cash flows in relation to investors' real preferences and expectations. Supposing this criticism to be true, the efficient market hypothesis clearly would have to be refuted since the market obviously doesn't process information fully and accurately.

Yet, it is doubtful whether the assumed distortions really are originating from the market mechanism. There is a difference between shortsighted managers and shortsighted markets (Jensen, 1988, p. 26 f.). Notwithstanding how the capital market values future and near-term cash-flows, managerial incentives are set by a firm's entire governance structure, including reward schedules and managerial participation. Thus, incentives can easily be distorted if a manager holds little stock in his enterprise or the compensation system is based upon accounting values, e.g. accounting earnings, motivating him to pursue myopic 'harvesting strategies' instead of maximizing actual firm value. However, if the capital market accurately reflects investors' expectations and the market for corporate control works efficiently, inferior governance structures should tend to be eliminated.

Of course, markets may produce myopic assessments in the event of insider knowledge or retention of information by the management. Stein (1988, p. 78 ff.) depicts the example of an oil company which might sell its oil reserves for a comparatively low price now or wait until an innovative refinement technique is developed which will make possible sales at a substantially higher price. Stein expects the shortsighted capital market not to recognize the increase in long-term returns which could be realized by selling the refined oil. Under those circumstances, the consequence of a long-term investment and sales strategy is a stock price that is lower than the present value of future profits as expected by the management. Hence the firm is threatened to be taken over by a raider who has obtained the relevant insider information so as to know the firm's true value. Anticipating this, the management has no choice but to implement the inferior policy and sell the reserves immediately in order to eliminate the takeover threat. However, in the real world, a better solution for the management would be to pursue the long-term strategy and to run an adequate information policy, i.e. to inform the market participants on the firm's future prospects. Indeed, the pressure of the market for corporate control induces management not only to pursue a profit-maximizing policy, but also to reveal company information. It thus enlarges the information sets of the market participants.[29]

(iv) Evaluation

As profit expectations are heterogeneous and a superior ability to transform information into probability distributions of future returns may generate excess profits, investors have strong incentives to collect information. Even publicly available infomation may, adequately transformed, evoke results that outperform the market. There may be a number of speculators on the capital market whose record beats the market average in the long term, even though the number is probably small. Furthermore, the rejection of strong market efficiency lets us assume the existence of 'temporarily monopolized information' (Neumann & Klein, 1982, p. 173), that is new private informa-tion which is not instantaneously processed by the market and offers chances to realize abnormal returns. In order to decide whether news is private or public information, whether and to which degree it is already anticipated by the market, and to transform private information into a probability distribution reflecting market chances as exactly as possible, it is necessary to interpret news on the basis of public information. The less public information a market participant has collected, the larger is the likelihood to misinterpret (both private and public) news. It is therefore rational to spend resources on the collection and processing of information.[30]

Investors need information to make adequate assessments of corporate performance. The efficiency of the market for corporate control depends essentially upon both the amount and price of available (public) information. Low information costs can be achieved by strict information disclosure rules for companies. This comprises the periodical revelation of information about corporate performance (balance sheet) and policy (annual report) as well as ad hoc disclosure of news which may directly influence firm value. Furthermore, information must be accurate and easy to interpret. For instance, the processing of balance sheet information based upon replacement-cost accounting is cheaper and more reliable than based upon historical-cost accounting.

Information costs can be reduced, too, through the activities of rating agencies which are specialized in the collection and evaluation of information. They gain from economies of scale and scope in the processing of information. Banks can contribute to efficient equity control in outsider systems, too. Loan renewals signal their judgement on the performance of customers and reveal inside information on companies to the capital market.[31] Banks thus contribute to the informational efficiency of the market. Nevertheless, in order to guarantee a close connection between managerial performance and stock price, the latter must reflect as much information as possible. This can be achieved only if many investors are actively trading their securities on the market, thereby revealing their knowledge and expectations. Such a high degree of market liquidity presupposes, firstly, a high amount of public information to encourage investors to form an opinion on the relative prospects of various corporations. Secondly, liquidity is fostered by low transaction costs of using the capital market, i.e. low trading fees and fragmented share holdings.[32] An institutional environment providing for low information and transaction costs ensures the immediate transformation of relevant news into stock prices and is therefore integral for the efficient functioning of the market for corporate control.

1.3.2.3 Takeover incentives of raiders

Another precondition for an efficiently working market for corporate control is that raiders do not succumb to perverse incentives. A raider launching a bid must aim exclusively at the maximization of the target's shareholder value. In particular, the raider mustn't be motivated to gain control of the target assets in order to excessively diversify his own businesses, to gain a monopolistic market position or to loot the target at the expense of the remaining (minority) shareholders.

In efficient markets, excessive diversification lowers the share price of the raider and raises the probability that he may fall prey to a hostile takeover for himself. This creates a strong disincentive to excessive diversification which possibly could reduce the entrepreneurial risk of the raider company, but at the same time also cuts expected future returns, thereby effecting a suboptimal risk/profit mix.[33] Takeovers which are restraining competition should be blocked by the cartel law.

The problem remains how to protect minority shareholders from oppression by controlling stockholders.[34] In general, there are two alternative solutions. One alternative is to keep controlling shareholders liable for the policy of a corporation. In this case, strong rules and effective enforcement discipline the raider after a takeover. Another solution is to grant minority shareholders an easy and cheap 'exit' from the firm after a takeover, irrespective of the raider's motivation and policy plans. This can be achieved through mandatory takeover bids after one shareholder has purchased a controlling stake in a company. However, the latter may considerably increase the transaction costs of a takeover if the raider has to buy a proportion of the target stock which is higher than the proportion originally planned by him. A raider whose original intention was to buy just a controlling stake in an underperforming firm, say because of limited access to financial resources or risk aversion, then has eventually to take over a much larger stake since each minority shareholder can sell as many shares as he wants after the takeover. Of course, higher transaction costs reduce the rate of takeovers and lower the disciplining threat of the market for corporate control.

Finally, it should be added that effective protection of minority shareholders strengthens the property rights of portfolio investors and increases the trust in the capital market. It cuts the transaction costs of using the market and enhances market liquidity. Thereby, it is conducive to the informational efficiency of the market, too.

1.3.2.4 Transaction costs of takeovers

Transaction costs of takeovers are emerging mainly from three sources, i.e. from managerial defence measures, the concentration of target stock and the bid regulation. Managerial opposition against takeovers comprises a large range of defence tactics like defensive stock repurchase and financial assistance to friendly bidders in order to deter or disable potential or actual hostile bidders from making a bid or accumulating a controlling stake in the target company. The bigger the scope for the incumbent management to build protection devices, the lower will be the success probability of a tender and the higher therefore the transaction costs.

Defence measures can be triggered not only in a takeover battle, but already long before a bid occurs. For example, the incumbent management may entrench itself through cross and circle holdings with subsidiaries and allied companies. If the worst comes to the worst and a sufficiently high proportion of equity is in the hands of friendly firms and companies governed by the potential target itself, the 'target' has effectively left the market for corporate control. At least, a raider has to accumulate a stake higher than that controlled by the incumbent management through the tender offer, whereby the supply of target stock has been shrunk substantially because of the stakes held by friendly investors. If the institutional environment permits such one-sided or mutual entrenchment, the transaction costs of takeovers may be prohibitive.

As already mentioned, concentrated ownership lowers the liquidity and informational efficiency of the capital market. In takeovers, concentrated shareholdings may also raise the acquisition costs of target stock for raiders. The costs of capital 'entrance' into the target rise because of the bargaining power of big 'incumbent' owners as against the raider. The latter then has to pay an additional premium if the incumbent owners know that he cannot purchase the desired amount of shares on the open market or in a bid from the remaining scattered stock.

The transaction costs of takeovers depend also upon the regulation of the bid process. A takeover attempt begins with a tender which can be both conditional on the acquisition of a certain stake in the target or unconditional. In the former case, all tendered shares are given back to the target shareholders if the proportion of shareholders willing to accept the offer is lower than a minimum proportion announced *ex ante* by the raider. Conditional bids may reduce transaction costs as the risk of a failed offer is shifted from the raider to the target shareholders. In addition, the bid may be both partial or full. A partial bid relates only to some fraction of target stock. If the offer is oversubscribed, the excess supply is re-tendered on a pro-rata basis to the shareholders. Partial bids may decrease transaction costs because they reduce the financial risk linked to a successful offer.

Transaction costs may also be prohibitive due to the holdout problem of target shareholders. Grossman & Hart (1980) suggest that small and dispersed stockholders have strong incentives to retain their shares in a bid in order to freeride upon the raider's restructuring efforts after the takeover. The holdout problem is most drastic if, like in the case of Grossman and Hart, shareholders have homogeneous expectations about an increase in the target's stock price after the takeover and if the bid is assumed to succeed with certainty. The fact that, in reality, one can observe successful as well as failed offers, lets us - once again - suppose that expectations both about the eventual performance of the raider and the outcome of the bid are heterogeneous. With this in mind, one can also construct some institutional solutions to mitigate the holdout problem and to considerably reduce transaction costs.[35]

In theory, the holdout problem is overcome most effectively by an offer that is conditional on the tendering of the entire target stock. If the offer is credible, no target shareholder has an incentive to freeride as the mere attempt to do so would thwart the offer. Yet, in practice, such a bid cannot be credible since one single shareholder (e.g. a target shareholder, who expects the company's stock price to increase under the incumbent management for an amount higher than the bid premium offered by the raider, or a manager of the target retaining his own holding in the company) can block it. Raiders therefore make unconditional bids or bids conditional on the purchase of less than 100% of the target stock.

Surprisingly, unconditional bids are more appropriate to overcome holdout incentives than conditional ones. The reason is that it pays for more target shareholders to sell their stock since tendering shareholders realize the bid premium (i.e. the positive difference between bid price and pre-bid market price of a share) irrespective of the outcome of the takeover attempt. All else equal, a rational shareholder will sell if he expects the bid's success probability to be sufficiently low. In a conditional (but otherwise identical) bid, tendering shareholders will receive the bid premium merely if the bid is successful. Yet, in the event of a successful bid, retaining the target stock might have been the superior strategy as it allows shareholders to freeride upon the raider's restructuring efforts.[36] Expecting a sufficiently large increase in the target's share price after a successful bid, it pays to hold out. The incentive to hold out is obviously greater in the conditional than in the unconditional bid. All else equal, more shareholders will sell in the unconditional bid. That's why the unconditional bid has better chances of success and generates lower transaction costs. Lower transaction costs are reflected by a lower minimum bid premium to let the bid succeed.

Besides, as shown by Schütte (1998) in a formal model, partial bids are reducing the holdout incentive more effectively than full bids since even shareholders, who decide to tender all their shares to the raider, will freeride upon the raider's restructuring work if the bid is oversubscribed. This enhances the payoff of the strategy 'sell' relative to 'retain' and likewise decreases the transaction costs of gaining a controlling stake in the target.

In the case of full bids, the holdout incentives of target shareholders can be virtually eliminated by two-tier bids. In such a bid, the raider offers a higher price per share for the first x% of the target stock than for the rest. For example, he may offer a positive bid premium for the first 50% of the target shares tendered to him and a very low price or the pre-bid market price for the remainder. Then, provided the raider has acquired more than

50% of the target stock in the first tier of the bid, he can carry out a so-called takeout merger in the second tier and force reluctant shareholders to sell their stock for the *ex ante* announced lower price. Clearly, two-tier bids are a powerful weapon to overcome shareholder resistance.[37]

1.3.3 Summary: The Institutional Base of Outsider Control

Let us briefly summarize the institutional cornerstones of efficient outsider control: The analysis shows that informational efficiency of the capital market is a crucial precondition for the efficient functioning of the market for corporate control. It follows that, apart from the mere setting up of a capital market, it is of utmost importance to enforce strict information disclosure requirements concerning periodic revelation of balance sheet data and details of corporate policy as well as ad hoc disclosure of relevant news concerning the company. Clearly defined accounting principles lower the costs to process disclosed information. There are accelerator effects of investment in the institutional environment of information disclosure and presentation: An efficient institutional framework will lower information costs and attract the relevant institutional players like rating agencies, investment banks and broker houses which have a professional interest in the gathering and processing of company information. Their activities will further reduce the information costs for all market participants and thus add to the informational efficiency of control markets.

Trust in the capital market can only grow out of an effective protection of minority shareholders. The risk of being oppressed by a controlling shareholder can be lowered most effectively either by offering small investors a fair exit option after a takeover or by keeping controlling shareholders liable for the policy of the corporation.

Transaction costs of takeovers can be cut by an effective institutional restriction of the scope of the incumbent management to implement defence measures against hostile takeovers. Besides, the costs of takeovers can be decreased and market liquidity can be enhanced through an institutional framework that sets incentives for both individual and institutional investors to hold tiny rather than large fractions of company stock.

Finally, the bidding procedure should be regulated in a most liberal way, permitting also conditional and partial bids. Raiders then may design bidding proposals maximizing the success probability of the offer and minimizing transaction costs (given a bidder's goals, financial means and risk aversion). Additional tools like coercive two-tier bids may considerably help to raise the efficiency of the market for corporate control.

1.4 BANK-BASED VERSUS MARKET-BASED CORPORATE CONTROL

1.4.1 Theoretical Approaches to the Comparative Superiority of Control Systems

1.4.1.1 Commitment approach

So far, our analysis has focused on the theoretical development of efficiency criteria for both insider and outsider systems of corporate control. In the real world, control systems have evolved over a long time so as to represent today a fairly efficient institutional response to the social and economic basics of the respective country. One may therefore question whether the highly sophisticated institutional infrastructure of one country would fit the basic setting of another society. Nevertheless, in this section, we are going to draft a theoretical framework to determine which institutional infrastructure is compatible to which underlying real features of an economy.[38] To do this, we will present three different theoretical approaches to evaluate the compatibility of the real economic sphere and the system of corporate control. Let us call them commitment approach, consensus approach and discretion approach.

The starting point of the commitment approach is the tradeoff between liquidity and control for investors. In insider systems with concentrated ownership, large shareholders are strongly and completely committed to stay with the firm even if the stock price deteriorates. This commitment enables owners to engage in long-term relational contracting with other stakeholders, especially with those not involved in corporate finance. The resulting trust relationships are an asset for corporations with production technologies and work organizations requiring high firm-specific (and hence sunk) stakeholder investment.[39] Stable control over the firm by just a few large owners lowers the danger of moral hazard between them and the remaining stakeholders. They support the implicit and legally not enforceable agreement that non-financier stakeholders undertake the specific investment necessary to increase the firm's market value, whereas the investors in control guarantee them a certain value of their specific investment by feeling committed to the durability of the trust relationship. Aoki (1995, p.20) argues that trust relationships are adequate for team-oriented production organization based upon joint task responsibilities and close cooperation of workers. He maintains that they are of less value where the production process is hierarchically organized. This is true if team-oriented production presupposes more individual sunk investment in skills and knowledge which would be drastically depreciated if the worker or manager leaves the firm. Yet, it is far from clear that team-oriented organization generally calls for more firm-specific investment than hierarchic organization.

We can view the problem from the opposite angle, too. Workers and employees of firms can, independent of the amount of relational investment they have undertaken, hedge against unemployment by gathering skills and knowledge which are not specific to one firm or industry. They should be expected, *ceteris paribus*, to prefer jobs that offer them the opportunity to permanently learn and accumulate knowledge and skills useful for other jobs in other firms and industries, too. People with jobs with a very narrow and specific qualification profile are subject to a higher unemployment risk than those with broader skills. They will therefore demand an additional risk premium or an insurance in the form of high investor commitment.

Trust is valuable for the relationship between the firm and external stakeholders, too. This is valid especially for manufacturing companies which produce non-standard goods and enjoy significant market power on factor and product markets. In the automotive industry, for example, both suppliers of intermediate products (e.g. special paints or parts of the engine) as well as dealers of the end product (car) are hit by high substitution costs if they have to change the main contract partner. Suppliers must convert their equipment and reorganize the production process according to the instructions made by another car maker.[40] Dealers trying to switch the car brand face serious substitution costs since carmakers use to geographically segment the market to limit competition among their own distributors. Disloyal dealers thus are in danger not to get access to distribution nets of other carmakers in the region.[41] Without long-term commitment of the firm's investors, external stakeholders will drastically reduce their relational investment or require a high risk premium for it. It pays therefore to create trust and to motivate stakeholders to undertake firm-specific investment.

Long-term commitment is of particular importance for risky start-up enterprises which need, along with venture capital, financial and marketing expertise. The investor's task is frequently not only to provide the firm with capital, but also with entrepreneurial advice (Dittus & Prowse, 1994, p.14). This especially concerns newly founded corporations with low market shares and good growth prospects where the management has a lot of technical expertise in the production sphere, but much less business expertise.

Dispersed owners cannot firmly commit to other stakeholders (Franks & Mayer, 1994, pp.15 f.). If corporate performance and stock price do not satisfy them, they will simply sell their shares and look for alternative investment opportunities promising them higher profits. As their equity stakes are very liquid, the opportunity costs of the investment strategy 'hold' as against 'sell' are too high to make their commitment firm. To put it into Coffee's (1991, p.1330) words: 'While the ten percent stakeholder can be expected to fight, the one percent holder is apt to be a 'sunshine patriot' unwilling to remain on duty during the corporation's winter of discontent.' The upshot is clear: 'Sunshine patriotism' encourages takeover raids. After a successful bid, corporate control shifts to an investor without any trust relationship at stake. The raider can reorganize the corporation without regard of eventual devaluation of the firm-specific investment of other stakeholders. The latter anticipate this danger and refrain from high relational investment in outsider systems.

On the other hand, the impersonal takeover mechanism may also outperform relational investment. In industries suffering from overcapacity of production, uncommitted raiders may make a good job in liquidating and disinvesting corporations with a low market share and poor growth prospects, so-called 'poor dogs'. Raiders committed exclusively to the maximization of equity value can probably cope more easily with downsizing requirements than investors with trust obligations (Dittus & Prowse, 1994, pp.13 f.). Consequently outsider control can achieve a quicker and more efficient reallocation of mobile corporate assets among different industries while insider control enhances the productivity of immobile assets by encouraging relational investment.

No doubt, both systemic variants have their own merits and drawbacks. The commitment approach teaches us that insider systems are relatively superior for industries demanding high relational investment from internal and external stakeholders, for risky start-up enterprises and for firms and industries offering little opportunity to accumulate skills and knowledge with value for alternative jobs. Outsider control can foster the downsizing of industries with overcapacity. During the transition period, both risky start-up enterprises and large, oversized corporations will play an important role. Most start-ups are in urgent need of venture capital and business expertise. Especially as long as business expertise is a scarce production input, they will inevitably rely on banks and other intermediaries attracting and distributing expertise. Moreover, during the transition period, expertise is scarce even in large enterprises with high market shares. They will likewise rely on advice provided by guardians. Corporations with overcapacity belong to the legacy of the past. They are usually privatized former state-owned enterprises or companies still run under the auspices of the government. The size of the overcapacity problem depends not least on the vigour with which the government has privatized and downsized the huge state-owned conglomerates. There is an obvious nexus between the need to downsize and liquidate firms and the privatization programme implemented by the government. Hence, the efficiency of alternative systems of corporate control is linked to privatization, too. Both types of firms, risky start-ups and oversized conglomerates may be of relatively less weight after the development of long-term market structures in the future. Yet, we can only speculate which type of production technology and which type of enterprise will dominate the economy in the long run.

The danger surrounding commitment is that, on the guardian level, trust may easily turn into collusion and entrenchment against control. This is demonstrated by the German model of corporate control and is valid, apart from strong government intervention, for the Japanese model, too. While trust surely fosters specific investment by all stakeholders, entrenchment drastically restricts the incentive to undertake any personal investment at all. Indeed, collusion is imminent in all systems based primarily upon insider control. The question is then: How can we explain the enduring strong performance of the German and Japanese economy in the postwar period? The most conclusive explanation is probably that efficient insider control presupposes high competition on product markets to mitigate adverse incentives. In transitional economies, the entrenchment problem is even more severe than in mature market economies. So-called 'old-boys clubs', i.e. extended personal networks among members of the old nomenclatura, are connecting banking system, enterprise sector and state bureaucracy (Keren, 1995, p.508). Bank-based insider control is likely to strengthen those networks rather than to dissolve them and to introduce market-conforming behaviour of managers. The problem is most serious where vested interests of insiders charged with corporate control prevent urgently needed restructuring of companies. In such cases, arm's-length outsider control may give a better incentive to managers to run a profit-oriented policy and speed up restructuring.

1.4.1.2 Consensus approach

Allen (1993) argues that outsider control by the stock markets may be superior in industries without a consensus about the best corporate policy. He thus diverges from the common assumption of principal-agent theory that the necessity of corporate control comes from asymmetric information and managerial incentives to waste resources. Rather, he supposes managers to be insufficiently informed. In his view, stock market participants who are constantly collecting information and evaluating the performance of publicly listed firms, are playing an important role in checking the strategy run by the incumbent management. Allen supposes stock prices to accurately reflect the weighted opinion of investors on the current policy of a firm, i.e. markets are efficient. Furthermore, he obviously believes that a 'true' evaluation in this sense is identical with an objective and adequate assessment. The price of a firm's stock then corresponds exactly to the judgement made by an investor who knows all relevant information and processes them in a 'right' way: 'The stock price comes to reflect the views of a wide range of different investors and hence is likely to be representative of the true value of the firm' (p.100).

Let us forget for a moment the long history of fads and excesses in speculative stock markets and assume stock price movements to adequately reflect investors' judgement of current corporate policy. Yet, how can stock prices be an objective and 'true' indicator of firm value in a world of incomplete information? Even if they would be, the problem remains that they do not provide much information about which policy is optimal for the firm. Managers cannot conclude the best policy just by analysing the stock price of their corporation and how it is developing over time. So which mechanism selects information on the relative superiority of concrete corporate policies? Unfortunately, in this respect, Allen is rather vague. He seems to suppose that public debate among investors helps managers to gradually improve corporate policy (cf. Allen and Gale, 1995, p.205). Indeed, it seems plausible that public debate and published information enlarge the information set of managers and hence enable them to adapt corporate policy to a changing economic environment. However, discreet intervention in corporate policy caused by hostile takeovers may be a complementary, yet prompter mechanism to reach a consensus on how to run the firm. Management teams getting a long way out of line with the weighted judgement of investors or falling too far beyond the economic performance of their industry rivals fall prey to raider management teams. The takeover mechanism effects an ongoing selection process among alternative policies. Superior policies will survive and trial and error will select the policies that are most compatible to the market environment. In the end, we can observe at least a permanent convergence towards a notional consensus.[42]

Steady selection among policy alternatives and constant checking through public debate are of great importance in monopolistic and oligopolistic industries as well as in sectors of rapid technological change.[43] In both cases the diversity of opinion about the best corporate policy is likely to be large. Selection among different policies will presumably work quicker in competitive industries. All else being equal, the number of policies tested at the same time is higher than in a monopoly, and product market competition substantially spurs the selection process. In competitive industries with well-established technologies the consensus should be higher and the checking role of the stock market is of less relevance. For industries with a high consensus, but where 'traditional' agency problems based upon asymmetric information and opportunistic managerial behaviour are more pervasive, insider control could be superior since it economizes agency costs by avoiding monitoring duplication and by the ability of banks to gain from economies of scale and scope in the execution of corporate control.[44]

In the near future, the transition economies will be dominated rather by traditional industries with well-established technologies and a wide consensus about corporate policy than by young industries without common knowledge on how to manage and to organize their firms. Textile production and engineering will probably outweigh microtechnology and biotechnology. While the consensus problem is of little significance, asymmetric information and managerial opportunism may cause serious problems in absence of managerial reputation based upon past performance in a market economy. According to the consensus approach, this demands primarily insider control. Even monopolists will receive their strategic know-how rather from foreign investors than from selective stock markets. We shouldn't, however, rush to conclusions about long-term comparative advantages and industry structures. Who would have supposed Japan to become a world high-tech leader fifty years ago?

1.4.1.3 Discretion approach

Jensen's (1986) free cash flow theory underlines the managerial incentive to waste cash flow for the funding of investment projects with a negative net present value after discounting at the relevant cost of capital. Debt limits managerial discretion to waste cash flow and thus is a disciplining component of a firm's capital structure. A high debt/equity ratio is an effective device to discipline the management of corporations with large cash flows which already reached the stagnation phase or even need to shrink, i.e. firms with sizeable overcapacities.[45] The management of a young, dynamically growing enterprise faces many profitable investment opportunities. In such companies, expansionary corporate policy driven by managerial reputation considerations causes less damage than in large corporations that frequently grow by diversification without efficiency-enhancing synergies. Especially for industries with large overcapacities, however, cheap access to debt finance could be an asset. From our above analysis we know that debt capital is less expensive in insider systems due to higher risk-shifting incentives in outsider systems. Thus, according to the discretion approach, industries with large overcapacities and poor growth prospects should be subject to an insider control regime.

This conclusion clearly contradicts the lesson from the commitment approach to expose 'poor dogs' to impersonal outsider control. Here we encounter a cardinal problem of all approaches trying to evaluate the relative superiority of certain institutional frameworks for specific economic conditions: They are consistent given the respective underlying assumptions, but focus merely on a small part of a most complex economic reality, i.e. on the benefits and costs of relational investment, the value of a consensus about corporate policy and the necessity to limit managerial discretion in firms with significant free cash flow. It is not least due to the lopsided orientation of all approaches that their results are not always complementary. Therefore, an inevitable precondition for identifying the best system of corporate control is first to clarify which approach is empirically relevant for a concrete economy. Yet, as our theoretical understanding of the complex interdependencies between institutional environment and economic and social basics of a country is very limited, we can assess the performance of a system of corporate control only empirically and necessarily within the broader context of the overall institutional environment it is embedded in. We face a joint-hypothesis problem as we cannot carry out an isolated test on the efficiency of corporate control. A country may boast a strong performance because of its efficient system of corporate control, but possibly also despite weak control mechanisms and because of an excellent educational system, motivated workers or effective cartel laws.

1.4.2 Corporate Control and Systemic Evolution: A Long-term View

Which system of corporate control will best fit the economic and social settings of the transition countries in the long-run? In this respect, we are seemingly suffering from a Hayekian constitutional lack of knowledge - an extremely unfavourable starting point for the attempt to institutionally design a system of corporate control. To make things more difficult, choosing the wrong systemic variant is expensive since, in the long term, the system is path-dependent. The longer one systemic variant has been working, the higher the costs of replacing the institutional infrastructure and implementing another variant. The Japanese postwar experience impressively demonstrates the problems of escaping from an institutional lock-in. Unfortunately, this is valid even for inefficient systemic variants. While the financial systems analysed above have evolved over a long time (most of them in fact over centuries) and could gradually adapt to the demands made by the industrial sector (and vice versa), the transition countries face an institutional vacuum in the financial sphere. They have to implement financial institutions from scratch and hence to create a system of corporate control by design. The danger they are exposed to is to choose a systemic alternative fitting the production sphere badly and thus lowering the overall productivity of the economy.

Considering the constitutional lack of firm knowledge about the working of complex economic systems and about the future economic structure of the transition countries, both the mere transplantation of a Western model of corporate control as well as the constructivistic approach to design an entirely new and untried model are fraught with dangers.[46] The best solution then is apparently to adopt an evolutionary approach and to let the market forces spontaneously select the control system that best fits the economic and social setting. The result of such an approach is a spontaneous mix of insider as well as outsider control structures rather than a plan that precisely predetermines the governance structure of each single industry.

In the beginning of the transition period, banks will dominate capital markets as both corporate guardians and institutions to allocate capital resources. Sophisticated and informationally efficient capital markets are highly complex institutions. It will take some time to build them up. Perhaps more importantly, capital markets need trust to compete successfully with banks. Without a certain reputation that investment is fairly secure and profit-bearing, foreign capital will not find its way to the transition countries on a large scale and scarce domestic capital will be channelled to the banks. In particular, the formerly (or still presently) state-owned banks are drawing on a certain reputation among investors as they have a comparatively big capital base and most of them are implicitly protected by the state not to go broke. The reputation of capital markets depends not merely on the implementation of the institutional infrastructure analysed above, but also on many other factors like the macroeconomic data and political stability of a country. Last but not least, reputation increases over time. Even if the institutional set-up is in place, investors will observe the performance of the market. Stable and continuous long-term growth are important preconditions to create trust and to attract capital. Working capital markets are therefore the results of a successful transition rather than tools to promote the transition itself.

Nevertheless, an evolutionary approach to corporate control requires the institutional development of capital markets from the beginning of the transition period. This is necessary in order to give outsider control a real chance and to initiate a battle of both modes of control as soon as possible. The most important precondition for efficient selection of control structures is effective competition in the product market. Competition may also help to dissolve old-boys clubs. Companies, whose decisions are influenced substantially by personal likes and dislikes, will sustain a handicap in the selection process on the goods markets. The efficacy of the selection process is enhanced by opening the economy to competition from abroad. The same is valid for corporate control: Access to the capital market should be opened to foreign banks, raiders and institutional investors as soon as possible. In the long run, competition will shape an efficient pattern of insider and outsider control mechanisms. Depending on their relative weights, the control systems of the transition countries can be more 'hybridised' than Western models. The advantage of hybrid systems is that they can select the optimal mix of control mechanisms for each industry and even for each corporation.

1.4.3   Corporate Control and Enterprise Restructuring: A Short-term View

Aside from long-term considerations, is there any role for outsider control in the short and medium run? Can the institutional building up of capital markets spur the badly needed restructuring of companies in transition economies? The evolution thus far of corporate control in eastern Europe has been strongly moving towards the bank-based or insider system. Apart from having been endorsed by academics following the developments, it was something of an inevitability. As already touched upon, for a market-based system to have evolved it would have been necessary for liquid (deep) markets to exist. Obviously, this was and still is a problem. Corbett & Mayer (1992) in an early paper on models of corporate governance for eastern Europe take a strong position endorsing a bank-based system. Implicitly calling for an engineering of ownership structures by the state, they write:

> The appropriate ownership structure will place heavy emphasis on control by those who are best placed to exercise it. That will almost certainly mean the enterprise sector itself together with those banks that are closely associated with the funding of industry. (p.70)

The assumption underlying this statement and most of the argument of that paper is that banks are indeed interested in restructuring and would consider loans to firms under their influence simply as a means to an end. But perhaps, and some recent evidence seems to indicate this, banks might use engagements or stakes in companies to hand out loans and thus to increase their business, not seeing the restructuring as the objective, but the volume of loans granted. Concerning the potential role of banks as corporate monitors, Dittus & Prowse (1994) have looked at the viability of the German and Japanese systems as examples of corporate governance in eastern Europe. Their analysis of the banking system leads them to conclude that banks are not likely to live up to the role assigned to them by proponents of these models, at least not in the short- to medium-run. As equity holders, they not only lack the skills necessary for managing large equity portfolios, but are also not particularly interested in developing the capacities to do so. Baer & Gray (1995) examined banks' potential role not as active equity holders, but as active monitors in their capacity as lenders. For the case of Poland they find banks taking an increasingly important role in prompting the restructuring of non-performing borrower enterprises. However, creditors in general 'are still quite passive when it comes to initiating and overseeing the liquidation of non-performing borrowers' and, according to them, delayed privatization has further impeded the process of disciplining poorly performing managers.

Even though there is an initial tendency towards an insider regime, a strong argument can be put forward endorsing the development of institutional elements characteristic of the Anglo-American, market-based system. Both the lack (or scarcity) of know-how and capital are important issues to be dealt with. The basic reason for advocating a parallel development towards a more market-based system of corporate control is the aim to ensure the 'openness' of the system concerning the ownership structure.

What is often disregarded when analysing the functioning and logic of German corporate governance and when speculating about the adequacy of that system for eastern Europe are two structural elements - both of which cannot simply be implemented in transitional economies. First, German bankers and managers have been able for decades and generations to build a professional competence in the field of management that plainly didn't and as yet doesn't exist in eastern Europe, especially referring to the ability to manage complex industrial groups. Managerial capacity has to grow and cannot be transferred *ad hoc* (at least not to a sufficiently high degree).

Second, there is an aspect perhaps best described as 'social norms'. Rock (1995) highlights this element in his critical assessment of 'American Fascination with German Corporate Governance' where he argues that elements of one grown, traditional system cannot simply be transferred into another system of a different history. In Germany, he argues, managers may not be remorselessly adhering to shareholders' interests, but in turn they do not need to have an incentive for every single effort they make. This 'work ethic' lets managers strive to accomplish tasks properly and not be inclined to only do as much as the contract explicitly says and hence compensation is agreed on. Both systems work in their own way - German bankers tend to focus on the long term culturally, even if short-termistic, but controversial action was objectively more profitable.

It can be assumed that the second aspect - 'social norms' - is not yet as well developed among management in eastern Europe as in Germany and may well not develop in the same way. Therefore one important piece of a bank-based system would be missing. How could incentives be imposed on managers if monitors affiliated with banks are given little incentive to engage in monitoring? Clear financial incentives may be an adequate substitute. But incentives of that kind are more a property of the Anglo-American market-based system. Constant changes in ownership structures and the threat of managerial changes in the wake of takeovers may considerably contribute to disciplining the management even in firms where the process of ownership consolidation hasn't yet been brought to an end. Hence the first argument in favour of aiming at policy measures promoting a more liquid stock market.

The preceding point put forward concerning the lack of know-how and capital also points to a promotion of the capital market. Assuming that the stability of ownership structures in eastern Europe has not reached a level as e.g. in Germany due to an initially inefficient allocation of assets[47], then it would be necessary to create an institutional environment allowing for changes of ownership and ultimately control to happen. If the 'best' owner (controlling shareholder) - the owner with the most promising business plan for a specific firm - is not actually the current controlling shareholder, then a legal framework enabling a transfer of control at minor transaction costs would undoubtedly be efficiency-increasing. Control transfers are more costly in a bank-based, insider-dominated corporate than in a financial environment with deep and liquid capital markets, thus creating a further argument for attempting to increase capital markets' liquidity.

The last point supporting a more capital-market-oriented policy is the trivial, but most important one of finance itself. If the creation of an insider-dominated system of corporate control takes its toll on the transparency and regulation of the capital market, then international portfolio investors will disregard that country's stock exchange and move to a market with more favourable conditions. Of course, this will slow down the restructuring process.

1.4.4 Control System and Board Model

So far we have identified the main institutional preconditions for efficient insider and outsider control. We then have argued that, from a long- as well as from a short-term perspective, an evolutionary approach to corporate control is adequate for the countries in transition. As for the institutional environment, that requires the promotion of both modes of control. In this section, we will focus upon the merits of different board models. Indeed, company boards are important tools of equity control. Therefore, we will inquire which board model is most appropriate for the emerging market economies.

In reality one can observe two types of board models which are outlined in Figures 1.2 and 1.3. In the German bank-based system of corporate control, dual boards are an important instrument of the execution of equity control by powerful owners. Whereas in the Anglo-Saxon world, corporate affairs are run by unitary boards which are dominated by the management.

The German joint-stock corporation is governed by two boards, the management board and the supervisory board. The management board

Figure 1.2: Board model of the German corporation

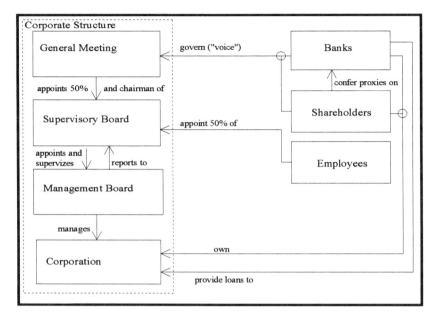

Figure 1.3: Board model of the Anglo-Saxon corporation

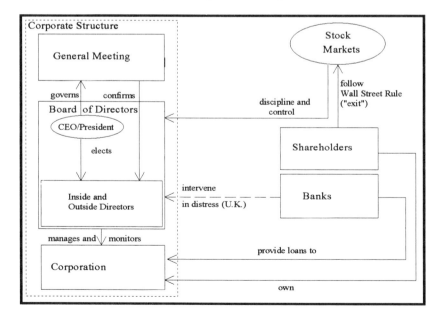

consists of the managing directors who are overseeing rather independently the company's day-to-day business. They are supervised and appointed for up to five years by the supervisory board. German co-determination law stipulates equal representation of owners and employees on the supervisory boards of corporations with more than 2,000 employees. Two thirds of the employee representatives are elected by the firm's workforce, including lower- and mid-level managers, while one third is appointed by the trade unions. The concept of the codetermined supervisory board tries to achieve a structural balance between diverging stakeholder interests like profit maximization, job security and social peace. The broad consent orientation of the German dual board system is emphasized by the strong representation of external long-term stakeholders like creditors, clients, suppliers and public authorities at the supervisory boards. This reflects an effort to consider the corporation as a 'nexus of (implicit and explicit) treaties'. Such a joint participation in corporate governance may help to balance diverging interests in the firm and to encourage stakeholders to undertake more long-term and relation-specific investment based merely upon implicit contracts. In a world which imposes high transaction costs upon the formulation and enforcement of explicit contracts, this leads to efficiency gains.

Nevertheless, large stockholders commanding dominant shares of the voting stock at the general meetings have a decisive influence on firm policy. They elect half of the supervisory board representatives and can choose which stakeholders may co-exercise equity control. Last but not least, they possess a structural voting edge over employees and trade unions as they appoint the supervisory board's chairman whose vote doubles its weight in deadlocks. The dual board system thus enables large shareholders (and the German proxy banks) to exert powerful equity control. In addition, they can, to some degree, restrict managerial discretion and lay down in the charter of the corporation that certain business transactions may be carried out only after prior approval of the supervisory board. The latter is also a major source of non-public information on corporate performance for shareholders as the management board has to report regularly to the supervisory board. It provides owners with valuable insider information which can hardly be inferred from the annual balance sheet. Fundamental decisions such as changes of the corporate charter, the distribution of half of the annual balance sheet profit, new stock issues, mergers and the like, may only be concluded with the consent of the general meeting.

The Anglo-Saxon unitary or one-tier board model does not make an institutional separation between equity control and company management. The board of directors carries out both functions. It comprises the senior management of the corporation and is complemented by a rather small number of outside directors. Widespread equity grants the president (US) or chairman (UK) of the board a powerful position within the company. In practice, he is frequently identical with the chief executive officer (CEO) who heads the senior management. He usually chooses the senior management of the company as well as the other board members, whereas the general meeting merely ratifies his decisions.

In the UK, the Cadbury Committee recently made some recommendations on how to strengthen the accountability of directors. One of its key recommendations is to select at least the outside directors formally by the votes of the entire board (Cadbury, 1995, p.5). From a theoretical point of view, it probably won't cause significant changes in the power structure of boards. The Anglo-American board model (like e.g. the Japanese one) institutionalizes a tension between management and control as the same body and persons are responsible and entitled to run and to control the firm. *De facto*, they have to control themselves. As long as dispersed shareholders behave rationally apathetically, they neither control nor support the outside directors. Both are, however, crucial for strong equity control through boards. Mostly outside directors do not have any strong personal or delegated equity interest in the firm. As their nomination depends upon the vote of the chairman, they have good reason to make a 'good line' to him their first priority. In fact, they are captured and controlled by the chairman. That's why, in reality, boards act as 'rubber stamps' for his actions (Meier & Saba, 1995, p.68). Patronage dominates independence.

Within a system based upon dispersed property, strong equity control through boards is illusionary. Therefore, the two-tier German model would most likely not work in the Anglo-American environment. Consequently, the task of outside directors must be different from that of the German supervisory board. Their contribution to the firm is, first of all, expertise, not corporate governance. The board of directors is a sounding board for the presentation of arguments and comments on corporate policy. The ultimate decision remains, nevertheless, with the inside directors who are dominated by the chairman.[48] The governance performance of the Anglo-American board is, for structural and systemic reasons, apparently poor. Even if a strong owner could probably send delegates into the board and thus exert fairly effective managerial control, the inconsistency of combining management and control in the same body remains. It would be resolved by a German-style institutional separation of both. This, again, is only efficient in a property system characterized by concentrated ownership.

In the end, the efficiency of a board model relies heavily upon the underlying control system and the ownership structures it produces. Strong equity control by large shareholders and proxy banks is institutionally supported by two-tier boards clearly separating company management from equity control. In outsider systems with dispersed shareholdings, freerider problems and portfolio constraints preclude owners from active equity control. Then a one-tier board with outside directors as experts rather than guardians is adequate while equity control is exerted by the market for corporate control.

As argued above, in transitional countries the control systems and ownership structures are only evolving. In the beginning, they depend *inter alia* upon the design of the privatization programme. Yet, provided a country adopts an evolutionary approach to corporate control (as advocated in the previous section), it is far from clear how ownership structures will be in the long run. Therefore, we don't know which board model will be efficient given the ownership structures of a specific branch or even individual companies. On an institutional level, a high degree of discretion in the design of company bodies adequately reflects this uncertainty about future developments. The evolutionary openness of an emerging property and control system calls for an institutional framework that initially shifts the responsibility for the design of company boards largely to individual economic agents. In the long run, the board model of an economy then emerges from a selection process making use of the decentralized knowledge of all market agents. Like other institutions, the efficient board model is generated by the market process rather than by a legal blueprint. In such a setting, the future board model may be hybridized on the macro level while on the micro level it is varying from industry to industry or even from firm to firm due to different governance and ownership structures.

1.5 SUMMARY: SOME LESSONS FOR COUNTRIES IN TRANSITION

Which lessons can be drawn from our theoretical analysis for countries which are only going to create the institutional framework of a market economy? Subsequently we are going to summarize the major results of this chapter in seven institutional recommendations for the transitional countries. They relate to the overall (evolutionary) approach to build up a system of corporate control and to the institutional foundation of both insider and outsider control.

(i) Evolutionary approach
Considering the constitutional lack of knowledge about the future economic structure of the transition countries, both the mere transplantation of a Western model of corporate control as well as a constructivistic approach to design an entirely new and untried model are fraught with dangers.

Moreover, even in the short run, the already existing fundamentals of bank-based insider control in most transition countries are to be complemented by an institutional framework spurring the development of market-based outsider control. This is important in an environment characterized by a political rather than market-induced allocation of property rights, a serious lack of managerial commitment ('work ethic') and restructuring expertise and, last but not least, of finance itself. In a transitional economy, the appropriate approach to corporate control hence is an evolutionary approach laying the institutional foundations of both insider and outsider control. The economic agents then have to design institutional arrangements and governance structures of individual companies while the market forces are constantly selecting. In the long run, the market process is to produce the control mix that best fits the economic reality of a country. The 'battle of both modes of corporate control' will select a control system in which insider or outsider control may dominate or which may be - on the macro level - completely hybridized. In the end, decentral agents and markets decide

- which kinds of control mechanisms will emerge,
- which players will be interested and involved in the execution of corporate control and
- who will be the long-term owners of privatized companies.

One very concrete institutional recommendation deduced from the evolutionary approach to corporate control is the following:

1. *Board model:*
   Companies should be given enough discretion to implement the best board model given the firm's individual ownership and governance situation. Strong equity control by large shareholders is adequately supported by a two-tier board: The two-tier board clearly separates company management from equity control. It thereby avoids the main inconsistency of the one-tier board, namely that the directors have to control themselves. Therefore it is an important tool to foster equity control by banks and other large shareholders. Furthermore, the German-style supervisory board helps to tie stakeholders with diverging interests to the firm. It thus preserves long-term relationships without removing the ultimate control power from the owners. In outsider systems with dispersed equity, freerider problems (and portfolio constraints) preclude owners from active equity control. Then a one-tier board with outside directors as experts rather than guardians is adequate while equity control is exerted by the market for corporate control. As the ownership and governance structures of different companies and industries may vary from each other, reformers should leave owners and managers some scope to draft the board structure that is most compatible to the specific situation of the individual company.

Adopting an evolutionary approach doesn't imply a passive or *laissez-faire* approach of the state. In fact, the state plays an important role. First, *ex ante* it must hedge against inferior economic results wherever possible. This requires the speedy creation of an adequate legal framework. Second, it must constantly monitor the economic process to make *ex post* amendments to the legal framework where it produces inefficient outcomes or sets incentives for opportunistic behaviour. Finally, the state has to screen the activities of the economic agents tightly and to control whether they are sticking to the rules of the game. Effective supervision presupposes both competent supervisory bodies and a strong political commitment to enforce rules.

(ii) Insider control
An evolutionary approach demands the creation of an institutional basis for both insider and outsider control. Efficiency criteria for both systems of corporate control have been deduced in sections 1.2 and 1.3 respectively. As for insider control, the following three institutional recommendations are of major importance for the countries in transition:

2. *Banks groups and equity control:*
    Financial intermediaries play an important, yet different role in corporate control in both systems. In outsider systems, their involvement in corporate control is modest while actively trading pension and investment funds contribute to strong market-based equity control. In insider systems, banks and bank-affiliated intermediaries can be powerful guardians and control companies efficiently through debt/equity finance. Universal banks and bank-centred financial groups have an edge over other investors as they are drawing from economies of scale and scope in the execution of corporate control. In the absence of firewalls, a free information flow between the investment and commercial banking department will minimize agency costs.

    The equity control power of bank groups may come from direct holdings of the bank, from holdings of bank-controlled investment entities like investment funds or unit trusts and from proxy voting. Provided banks have the right incentives to get engaged in equity control, they may also minimize coordination costs. Therefore any regulation limiting the equity investment of banks or bank groups in individual firms should be abolished. Banks should be free to invest in shares. An incentive distortion may result from possible imbalances between banks' shareholdings and the voting power arising from bank-controlled investment vehicles and proxies. While proxy voting has considerable merits in reducing the coordination costs between equityholders, its efficiency can be increased e.g. by making the proxy-voting right conditional on a bank's direct shareholdings in the respective corporation. In a system where banks are controlling firms through debt/equity finance, they should be encouraged to undertake significant equity investments in firms rather than being restricted in the amount they can invest.

3. *Banks and debt control:*

Banks are the main executors of debt control. But, to exert active debt control, they need strong institutional tools including a working bankruptcy law. Effective debt control requires an institutional environment that switches control over assets to creditors immediately when a firm goes bankrupt and does not prevent banks from informal or *ex ante* agreed-on interventions in other states of the firm, especially in financial distress.

In times of transition, an inevitable precondition for effective debt control is the cleaning of the banks' balance sheets. Banks need a sound capital base to become powerful guardians of their debtor firms. Otherwise, they may end up in a creditor trap. Then they cannot credibly put the screws on the enterprise sector to stick to the implicit and explicit terms of a loan contract.

4. *Governance structures of banks:*

Banks themselves must be subject to powerful equity and debt control. Powerful banks exerting active equity and debt control are no threat for countries with insider control mechanisms, but a precondition for efficient corporate control. It is important that banks are effectively self-governed and that their management is contestable. Bank managers have to remain accountable to large shareholders. For that reason, banks should not be allowed to vote at their own general meetings. Furthermore, cross shareholdings among guardian banks must be passive and banks should be restrained from voting at the general meetings of other banks in order to reduce the danger of collusion between the guardians.[49]

The role of the state then is the representation of dispersed and naive depositors, i.e. the execution of debt control over banks by means of standard prudential regulation and supervision. In any case, since the state's dominant interest is that of a fixed claimant, it should refrain from holding equity stakes in banks. This requires the quick and sweeping privatization of the banking system.

(iii) Outsider control

Ownership should be allocated by the market rather than by political decisions. Mass privatization *per se* doesn't produce efficient ownership structures, but can only be the outset of a process of constant ownership changes to find the most efficient ownership structure for a company. In the short run, firms face a serious lack of both managerial and guardian competence, difficult access to finance and an insufficiently developed work ethic. Takeovers at low transaction costs may lower the impact of those adversities by accelerating the finding of efficient ownership structures after privatization.

Spontaneous framing of efficient ownership structures is conditional upon permitting ownership regulation. If the latter is guaranteed, in the long run the market process will select the best owners and equity concentration ratios for individual firms and industries. For instance, banks (along with other large investors) will refrain from relational investment in firms and industries where scattered portfolio investments are producing higher returns on equity. The precondition for efficient ownership evolution is that the institutional environment doesn't generate negative external effects of equity control. This would be the case if banks could misuse their shareholdings to oppress minority shareholders or to talk companies into taking too expensive loans. As already put forward above, the institutional environment must therefore provide for effective minority shareholder protection and a balance between a bank's voting power and equity investment in individual companies. The institutional preconditions for efficient outsider control are spelt out in the final three recommendations.

5. *Protection of minority shareholders:*
Minority shareholders must be protected by law from oppression by large shareholders: without effective protection of minority shareholders, takeovers can become attractive by the mere 'exploitation premium' of raiders. Target stockholders then have to sell their shares just to avoid oppression by the raider after the takeover. The obligation to extend a mandatory and equal bid to all target shareholders after the raider has acquired a certain percentage of the target stock is a simple institutional device to prevent the devaluation of minority shareholder stock. Yet, it increases the transaction costs of bids. Another and more efficient approach would be to make controlling equityholders effectively liable for the policy of the corporation and to punish all actions taken at the debit of minority shareholders. However, such a fiduciary duty requires a most sophisticated legal system in which all kinds of oppression are immediately fined by the courts.

6. *Informational efficiency:*
Capital markets should be transparent so as to ensure information efficiency. The efficiency of the market for corporate control is grounded on market transparency. The latter requires periodial and *ad hoc* disclosure of price-relevant company information. Low information costs enlarge the knowledge of investors and support an adequate judgement of a company's present performance and future prospects. Indeed, there is a self-accelerating effect of information efficiency: The higher the transparency of a market, the more investors are attracted. This leads to permanent checks of managerial performance and, hence, a further increase in the information efficiency of the capital market. A further precondition for informational efficiency is low transaction costs of securities trading which are promoting market liquidity.

7. *Transaction costs of takeovers:*
The regulation of takeover bids should be rather permissive: raiders should be allowed to structure their bids according to their own preferences. In particular, they should be free to make conditional, partial and two-tier bids. In this way, they can minimize the transaction costs and maximize the success probability of bids. All else being equal, permissive bid regulation will lead to a higher number of hostile bids and takeovers and thus enhance the efficiency of the market for

corporate control. On the other hand, the scope of the target management to take defensive measures and to get entrenched must be drastically restricted. Otherwise, the disciplining vigour of the takeover process will be substantially lowered.

NOTES

1. With the firm supposed to be free from debt.
2. In a simple case, the manager's fee function depends only on the production outcome. A risk-averse manager will always choose the combination of a positive fixed fee with a share in the production outcome. Shareholders are constrained by the principals' competition for agents and the individual rationality of the manager who has alternative uses for his human capital. The expected payoff of the manager must not be lower than the utility achievable in other activities.
3. According to Shleifer & Vishny (1990), managers may also entrench themselves by manager-specific investments, i.e. investments in special fields where they have unique knowledge.
4. Williamson refers to the American unitary-board model. In the German dual-board system, supervisory boards control management.
5. See, for instance, the works of Modigliani & Miller (1958) and Stiglitz (1974).
6. The German *Schachtelprivileg*, a cluster of tax provisions to avoid multiple taxation of corporations with interlocking equity stakes, encourages banks to amass equity stakes of at least 10% in industrial enterprises. Besides, banks may enhance their control power by means of proxy voting.
7. Because of missing contractual obligations to pay out an *ex ante* announced dividend, such promises are substantially weaker than debt contracts (Jensen, 1988, p. 30).
8. It is true that the following classification is somewhat arbitrary and there are evident interdependencies between all variables. But, for didactic reasons, it is appropriate to elucidate the complex logic structure underlying the problem of the efficient governance structure.
9. A powerful debtholder who is prone to enter into a long-term relationship with a firm, whilst sharing the firm's risk and influencing corporate policy, thus also changes the quality of a loan contract which becomes a hybrid between a straight debt contract and equity. See also Steinherr & Huveneers (1994, p. 277 f.)
10. The *institutional environment* in the sense of Davis & North (1971, p. 6 f.) 'is the set of fundamental political, social and legal rules that establish the basis for production, exchange and distribution.' Whereas an *institutional arrangement* is an 'arrangement between economic units that governs the ways in which these units can cooperate and/or compete.'
11. In the United States many lenders do not want to get actively involved in a firm's operations because they are afraid of losing the seniority of their claims in the event of liquidation. In certain circumstances, the claims of actively controlling debtholders can even be downgraded to equity.
12. Take notice, again, that we analyse the problem of optimal corporate finance *exclusively* from an agency view and in the context of large enterprise. Different criteria for the construction of an optimal capital structure are analysed by Jensen & Meckling (1976; the benefits of debt, i.e. an increasing level of effort of a risk-neutral owner-manager, have to be traded off against its costs, i.e. an increasing level of riskiness of investment projects), Ross (1977; the benefits of debt, i.e. the signalling of better investment opportunities of a firm without managerial opportunism, ought to be traded off with its costs, i.e. a higher probability of bankruptcy), and Williamson (1988; working out of a microfoundation of the firm, investment projects with low physical asset specification should be financed by debt to cut down transaction costs).
13. Fixed costs are, for instance, caused by investment in information-gathering technology and staff. Hence, the cost for a single intermediary to monitor a set of N firms or projects, with

N>1, is less than the sum of the costs for several intermediaries, with each of them monitoring a subset S of N, with 1≤S<N.

14. Referring to the efficiency of banks' performance, there apparently is a tradeoff between natural economies of scale in the production of information and imminent efficiency-losses caused by a monopolization of the banking sector. Up to a certain degree, dependent on the amount of the bank's private information and sunk costs, potential competition (contestability) can substitute actual competition. However, actual competition still helps to distribute some of the efficiency gains, generated by a bank's monitoring and control services, to naive and incompetent investors (Hester, 1994, p. 139). Clearly, the banks have to withhold a share of the efficiency gains to be compensated for their investment in information technology or additional staff for monitoring and control purposes. Because increasing returns to scale become asymptotically, with growing number of monitored firms, constant returns to scale, competition between several banks is efficient and should be given preference as against the costly (and mostly ineffective) regulation of a monopoly bank.

15. Diamond's (1984) argumentation is inherently static. In a more dynamic perspective, the concept of the learning curve emphasizes the superiority of institutional monitoring, too. Individual investors produce their monitoring services, always and with increasing distance, on a lower part of the learning curve than intermediaries. Thus, they are confronted with higher monitoring costs than the latter.

16. In this context, Dewatripont & Tirole (1993, p. 17) draw attention to the widespread problems of the 1929-33 banking crisis and the recent Savings & Loan Bank's problems in the United States. Of course, one may likewise point to recent problems of the Japanese banking sector.

17. These goals correspond to the owners' interests in absence of debt, i.e. profit-maximization without risk-shifting.

18. Going along with Manne (1965, p. 113, fn.11), the terms 'outside' and 'outsider' subsequently will refer 'to anyone not presently controlling the affairs of the corporation, even though it may include one or more individuals on the corporation's board of directors.' Conversely, the terms 'inside' and 'insider' here relates to all stakeholders governing the affairs of the corporation, like e.g. managers and various types of active investors.

19. To enlarge economies of scope, commercial banking, investment banking, mortgage banking, insurance activities, consulting activities, and other financial services could be integrated within the organization structure of one bank.

20. In general, there are several concrete institutional solutions for a monitoring agency, private as well as public ones. While each of them has some advantages and drawbacks, the design of an optimal institution is hardly feasible. The political independence of a supervisory institution is of great importance. Thus a politically independent central bank might be an appropriate monitoring agency.

21. Tirole (1994, p. 478) proposes, conversely, dividend distributions to reduce the Cooke ratio in the event of strong financial performance. He assumes that owners want to reduce the riskiness of investments when a bank performs well because they do not want to jeopardize their newly gained assets. We do not agree on this point because we presuppose that risk-neutral owners will further try to maximize profits and therefore choose the policy promising the highest expected payoff. On the contrary, there might rather still be an incentive to place funds into too risky projects as, in the absence of an intermediary controlling a considerable share of the bank's equity *and* debt, there remains a distortion of equityholders' interests at the debit of the depositors. But as we supposed before, in the event of a strong performance the effect of this eventual distortion is likely mitigated by the risk-aversion and a remaining discretion of the managers. Besides, it can be countered by further prudential regulation, e.g. liquidity requirements or obligatory maximum shares of large loans in a bank's portfolio.

22. There is a certain distinction between arbitrage and speculation. While arbitrage refers, strictly speaking, to the exploitation of already existing inter-local price differences and sure profits, speculation is characterized by the exploitation of supposed inter-temporal price differences and hence by risky outcomes. As an increase in firm value caused by the raider's reorganization efforts is not sure but can merely be assumed, transactions on the market for corporate control are of a rather speculative nature. Of course, the raider has to contribute not

only capital and the inclination to take risks, but also entrepreneurial competence to raise the target's stock price.

23. See e.g. Röhrich (1994, p. 82 f). and Manne (1965, p. 114 ff).

24. By no means is each tender offer hostile, i.e. in opposition to the incumbent management. Friendly tender offers can speed up the merging procedure of firms. They are agreed on by both sides, raider and incumbent management. Like mergers, they can also be a substitute for a hostile takeover, if the incumbent management sees no way to protect itself successfully from an imminent hostile tender offer and therefore rather tries to improve its position through cooperation and negotiations with the raider. In the latter case, mergers and friendly tender offers have a disciplining effect on the incumbent management and hence must be assigned to the market for corporate control.

25. Contestability and the hidden threat to get the sack in case of inferior performance may well motivate managers to increase their efforts to maximize profits. Of course, they are no remedy against incompetence. A management team incapable of drafting and implementing an efficient corporate policy must ultimately be replaced in an actual takeover.

26. Critical reviews of the relevant literature are presented, for instance, by Elton & Gruber (1991, chapter 15), Malkiel (1992) and Fama (1970, 1991).

27. This problem is widely recognized in literature and referred to as a 'joint-hypothesis problem'. See also Fama (1991, p. 1575 f.) and Malkiel (1992, p. 742).

28. See e.g. Stein (1988) and Scherer (1988, p. 78 ff.)

29. Empirical evidence is rather inconsistent with the assumption of systematically shortsighted markets. For example, price-earnings ratios for stocks of different industries or even only different companies are frequently very diverse. Apparently, investors do not value current earnings and near-term cash flows exclusively, but also growth prospects.

30. It is impossible, though, to specify the optimal amount of costs an investor should spend for the collection of information. Such an optimal degree of information, balancing marginal costs and marginal utility of information gathering, presupposes *ex ante* knowledge of only *ex post* (after resources have been spent) known results. See also Arrow (1962, p. 147). Decisions as to whether and to what extent to stock up on current knowledge are taken by individuals in compliance with hardly generalizable rules. A suitable approach to explain why individuals are motivated to expand their information sets may be the 'satisficing hypothesis', saying that an individual will enlarge his information set as long as the payoff produced by his current conduct (which is chosen by the individual on basis of his present information set) is not exceeding a certain critical threshold value set up by the individual himself.

31. For empirical evidence of banks as vehicles for information generation about corporate clients, see e.g. James (1987), Lummer & McConnell (1989) and Hull & Moellenberndt (1994).

32. The fragmentation of shareholdings makes sure that each investor can sell his complete holding of one stock without provoking a sharp fall in the price of the relevant stock, caused by the mere size of his holding. In other words, the investor's decision to sell depends exclusively upon his expectations about the firm's future performance. An investor holding a significant equity stake in a company may be reluctant to sell his stock because of high transaction costs of 'exit'. Excessive transaction costs hence are preventing him from completely revealing his knowledge and expectations on the market. In this case, the stock price doesn't reflect the maximum amount of information and market efficiency clearly declines.

33. A decrease in profits (per share) may occur, for instance, if the raider has taken over a firm of an industry for which it has no management competence and experience.

34. The implementation of effective minority shareholder protection is also an important institutional challenge for the design of an insider system of corporate control. The problem is at issue in each system where firms can be controlled through equity stakes smaller than 100% of company stock.

35. Grossman & Hart (1980, p.46) argue that the holdout problem can be resolved through the dilution of the property rights of dispersed shareholders. If the corporate charter as part of the firm's governance structure permits a successful raider to exploit minority owners, for example by paying himself large salaries or selling firm assets and outputs below market prices to enterprises owned by the raider, the holdout incentive is drastically reduced. Voluntary dilution of their property rights is even in the best interest of dispersed shareholders since it adds to the

contestability of the management and, hence, sets incentives to pursue an efficient corporate policy.

36.   The condition for superiority of retaining target stock to selling is that the increase in target stock effected by the raider's entrepreneurial and managerial performance is larger than the bid premium.

37.   In addition, the extent of the holdout problem can be limited by the renouncement of mandatory information disclosure for the raider in a takeover bid. Schütte (1998) demonstrates in a game-theoretic framework, that the obligation of the raider to provide detailed information on his identity and business plans to the target shareholders and to meet specified minimum periods of acceptance for the bid considerably reduces the informational asymmetry between both sides. Shareholders can make better assessments on both the restructuring competence of the bidder and the future corporate policy after an eventual takeover. After information disclosure, they will require a higher compensation (bid premium) to sell their shares to the raider. Mandatory information disclosure then leads to higher transaction costs for the acquisition of controlling stakes. Besides, mandatory information disclosure gives rise to freeriding problems among raiders (Easterbrook & Fischel, 1981, pp.1176 ff.). Raiders have to invest substantial information expenditures to identify attractive takeover targets and to design restructuring plans to enhance their performance. These information expenditures are sunk costs once they are made. The revelation of a bidder's private information allows competing raiders to gather relevant information for free. Disclosure thus generates positive external effects to competitors. Other raiders can economize over information costs and thereby improve their position in the bidders' competition. This creates a freeriding incentive for potential raiders and decreases their information expenditures. The transaction costs arising for the raider who must disclose private information are produced by a relative deterioration of his position in the competition with other raiders. Ultimately, it reduces the number of bids and the efficacy of the market for corporate control.

38.   Ideally we would have to integrate political and cultural features into the analysis, too. Yet, as this would go beyond the scope of this chapter, we will concentrate exclusively on economic ones.

39.   Early inquiries into the connections between implicit agreements, long-term relationships and the overall system of corporate finance are provided by Mayer (1988) and Shleifer & Summers (1988).

40.   Substitution costs are much lower for producers of raw materials who are all using the same production technology. For instance, a rancher can replace the butcher to whom he delivers his cattle without switching the production technology as the product is highly standardized. The same is valid for producers of goods which are subject to clearly defined and generally accepted technical norms.

41.   The substitution costs for dealers of highly-standardized mass products on competitive markets are supposedly lower. An insurance agent can switch the insurance company at low cost.

42.   Clearly, in an evolutionary world of permanent economic change, there is by definition no statical equilibrium consensus. Economic change means also a change of the optimal policy response.

43.   See also Grosfeld (1995, p.14).

44.   The consensus approach largely corresponds to the hypothesis of Franks & Mayer (1990, pp.210 ff.) that different forms of corporate control are suitable to correct different types of managerial failure. They argue that insider control is adequate to correct *ex post* failure like inferior managerial performance in comparison with other managers. In fact, if there is a commonly agreed-upon benchmark to evaluate managerial performance, agency costs may be lower under concentrated ownership. Outsider control then is better suited to correct *ex ante* failure like differences in expectations about investment.

45.   In practice, the debt/equity ratio of 'poor dogs' with overcapacities can be boosted through the consequent distribution of all net profits and the use of debt finance as sole source of external funds. Gross investment (i.e. including maintenance investment) then has to be funded exclusively through depreciations and debt finance.

46.   See also Frydman & Rapaczynski (1992, p.266).

47. Many privatization modes like e.g. voucher privatisation produce a political rather than market-induced allocation of ownership.
48. In an econometric study, Morck et al. (1989) assess the efficacy of US boards in disciplining senior management. They found that boards do not generally remove unresponsive managers until the companies significantly underperform their industries. The study hence is evidence of the weak governance performance of US boards.
49. The provisions of German company law, prohibiting firms with equity crossholdings merely from mutual representation at their supervisory boards, are clearly too weak to effectively put a stop to the danger of collusion between financial guardians.

2 Privatization in the Czech Republic

2.1 FEATURES AND INSTITUTIONAL ENVIRONMENT OF CZECH PRIVATIZATION

At the time of the 'velvet revolution' in November 1989, Czechoslovakia not only was the state with the lowest registered share of private ownership among all transition countries. It nearly completely lacked an institutional infrastructure allowing the use of private property for production purposes. The first legislative step towards the foundation of private property as means of production and hence towards privatization was a fundamental amendment of the constitution passed by the Czech parliament in spring 1990. The new constitution guarantees equal legal treatment of all ownership forms, the protection of property of individuals and legal entities by the state and the right of succession (Ufer, 1994, p. 23). It also provides for the transfer of assets from state enterprises into private hands. Furthermore, the constitution places an obligation on the government to protect the property rights of foreign investors in the same way as the rights of domestic firms and to set up the rules necessary for fostering entrepreneurship and competition. The Law on the Formation of Joint-Stock Companies taking effect in July 1990 was a prerequisite for the emergence of large privately-owned firms and the subsequent building-up of a capital market.

Speed, depth and methods of privatization were subjects of a lively political discussion. The *gradualists*, primarily comprising reform communists and social democrats, stressed the high social costs of rapid and comprehensive reform measures. Consequently they argued in favour of gradual privatization to avoid large-scale unemployment and a sharp decline in GDP. In addition, they pointed to the necessity to restructure enterprises and to make markets more functional *before* firms are transferred into private hands (Mejstrík & Burger, 1994, p. 189). The *radicals* led by Václav Klaus preferred a big bang approach with quick liberalization and stabilization. They argued that there is no sense in postponing privatization until enterprises are better prepared and market institutions are built. Firstly, they supposed, the state is not the ideal owner to carry out corporate restructuring. Corporate policy and reorganization is better left to a private owner who should be found as soon as possible. Secondly, and even more important, rapid and deep privatization are inevitable prerequisites to setting up a market environment. Firms have to adapt most quickly to the rules of the market to enhance efficiency. The incentives to do so are substantially weaker under the prevalence of state ownership. This implies the acceptance of institutional gaps and imperfection. Since an efficient institutional framework cannot be created over night, the legal framework of the economy is rather to be developed and improved step by step in response to the revelation of systemic shortcomings.

In the parliamentary elections in June 1990, a broad majority of Czech and Slovak citizens came out in favour of the radical reform approach. The Civic Democratic Party (*Obcanská Demokratická Strana* - ODS) led by Klaus became the strongest force in parliament and Klaus himself was elected Prime Minister. As privatization was the central campaign issue, the election results clearly mirror the far-reaching social consensus to progress quickly to a market economy well half a year after the fall of communism. The major political asset of the radicals was the extreme centralization of power in the Czechoslovak economy. In 1968, the Prague Spring had consequently brought to an end the period of economic and political liberalization enduring from the mid-1960s. The following politics of 'normalization' pursued by the communist regime aimed again at tightly copying the Soviet paradigm and removing most decision-making rights from the level of the individual firm to the centre. In contrast to the development in Hungary and Poland, the rebalancing of powers took place the other way round. In the end, the toppling of managers and workers' councils and the successful *gleichschaltung* of the unions under the past regime enabled the new democratic government to draft a comprehensive privatization plan in a political environment largely free from powerful interest groups trying to abuse their political influence to push through 'social' claims in the course of privatization. The bargaining power of managers and employees was scanty; the unions were discredited as they were considered to have been willing tools of the communist regime rather than the voice of employees' interests. An additional reason for the huge popular support for radical privatization might have been the negative Polish and Hungarian experience of spontaneous privatization casting doubt on both the efficiency and fairness of the gradual approach.

The government's intention to accelerate economic reform and to quickly implement the institutional infrastructure to initiate privatization is documented by the 'Scenario of Economic Reform', a programmatic paper passed by the parliament in summer 1990 which contains the basic strategic decisions concerning how to progress with economic reform. The paper emphasized the priority of strict stabilization, swift liberalization and speedy and equitable privatization. The latter could only be realized by the use of non-standard methods of property transfer. Besides auctions, tender offers and sales widely used in small-scale and large-scale privatization, the Czech privatization concept thus comprised non-standard tools like extensive reprivatization (restitution) and, at its core, mass privatization through vouchers. The implementation of a voucher programme reflects two main objectives of the Czech reformers. Firstly, it should grant the justice of the entire process offering all adult citizens an opportunity to participate in the benefits of privatization instead of distributing them exclusively to a privileged class of managers and employees of better-performing enterprises. Secondly, it should accomplish an acceleration of the transformation and enhance competitive pressure on the enterprise sector. Dispersed ownership was deemed appropriate to support the learning process of citizens and to set incentives to adapt individual behaviour to the market environment ('people's capitalism').

The legal framework of privatization was established by the introduction of several laws between late 1990 and summer 1991. The central rules are contained in:[1]

- the Law on the Alleviation of Some Injustices of Property Disposal (Minor Restitution Act),
- the Law on Out-of-Court Rehabilitation (Major Restitution Act),
- the Law on Land and Agricultural Cooperatives (Law on the Restitution of Agricultural Land),
- the Law on the Transfer of State Property of Certain Assets to Other Legal or Physical Persons (Law on the Privatization of Small-Scale Enterprises) and
- the Law on the Conditions of Transfer of State Property to Other Persons (Law on Privatization of Large-Scale Enterprises).

The organizational and administrative responsibility for the entire divestment process has been accepted by a network of public bodies. The central institutions were the Ministries of National Property Administration and Privatization ('Ministries of Privatization') which were established in both republics in August 1990. They were entrusted with the task of realizing privatization and had the biggest influence on the selection of SOEs to be privatized and the methods applied. Their decision power covered all enterprises founded by ministries of the respective republic. On a local level, the Ministries of Privatization were assisted by a web of district privatization committees whose assignment was actively to identify businesses appropriate to be auctioned off in small-scale privatization. In general, the ministries' role was limited to approving or rejecting the proposals of the committees. In large-scale privatization, they had to review numerous privatization projects of different stakeholders in the enterprises and to compose the most suitable mix of privatization methods for each SOE. They were supported by the founders of the SOEs, that is the branch ministries of the republics. Under the communist regime, these ministries had controlled all enterprises of their respective branches, like manufacturing, construction, foreign trade and so forth. Since the early 1990s, most of them have been melted (for the major part into the Ministry of Industry and Trade) or closed down. Their tasks were to call on enterprise management to draw up a basic privatization project or to prepare a proposal for themselves, to assess all privatization projects submitted in the course of large-scale privatization and ultimately to recommend one project for each enterprise to the ministries of privatization. The founders thus operated essentially as advisory institutions to the privatization ministries.

While the ministries' decisions on the privatization of small and medium-size businesses were definitive and legally effective, privatization proposals concerning firms with more than 3,000 employees and proposals including direct sales of assets or sales to foreign investors were merely of recommendary nature (Klvacová, 1993, p. 22). The recommendations had to be reviewed by an economic council of experts appointed by the responsible government, either republican or federal, and finally approved by the government itself. Surely, most projects submitted by the ministries passed the expert screening without dramatic modifications and were signed by the authorities. Nevertheless, the organization of the decision-making process reflects the government's will to take direct political responsibility for the privatization of large enterprises. This is a striking difference e.g. to the German approach to uncouple privatization from political intervention by setting up an autonomous institution with the sole responsibility to speedily divest state assets. Considering the influential role of the ministries of privatization, the Czechoslovak approach hides the danger of exposing the privatization process to the growing political influence of interest groups and to changes in the political environment. This is precisely what happened in Slovakia under the Meciar regime after the split-off in January 1993. Special treatment of direct sales was intended to reduce the corruption risks inherent to a method that minimizes competition by determining buyers in advance.

The Federal Ministry of Finance had established a privatization department to decide on the privatization methods used for enterprises founded by federal ministries. Compared to the privatization ministries, its significance for the divestment process was rather secondary due to the great preponderance of company assets in the hands of the republics.[2] However, through the ministry's Centre for Voucher Privatization, set up in June 1991, the Federal Ministry of Finance played a key role in the technical organization and supervision of voucher privatization. The centre distributed the voucher books to all participating citizens and oversaw the bidding process, including the setting of initial share prices and the adjustment of prices to demand in subsequent rounds.

In 1991, three Funds of National Property were established with the assignment to administer those state assets still not privatized and to carry out the projects of large-scale privatization in harmony with the decisions made by the Ministries of Privatization or the governments respectively. For those purposes, all SOEs had been converted into joint-stock companies and their shares subsequently transferred to the funds. One property fund had to administer assets of federal enterprises, two funds held shares in republican firms. The proceeds of large-scale privatization collected by the funds were to be used for the compensation of citizens disadvantaged under the old regime, to remedy environmental damages or for purposes of restructuring and recapitalization. It was prohibited by law for the funds to be fed into the state budget. The funds are legal entities put down in the Commercial Register. The executive board of the republican funds are governed by a presidium ('main board') chaired by the responsible Privatization Minister. The other members of the presidium as well as the members of the supervisory board are elected by the republican parliaments. This places the funds under tight political supervision. The funds' responsibilities were strictly divided from those of the ministries. In particular, they had no authority to interfere with the actual decision-making over privatization projects. After the split-off, the federal fund was liquidated and its assets were allotted to the republican funds. Going by the blueprint of privatization, the transfer of state assets will be finished no later than five years after the end of voucher privatization, i.e. in the year 2000. The same date is envisaged for the liquidation of the Czech property fund.

The Czechoslovak concept of privatization can be appropriately described as 'centralized decentralization'. Centralization is achieved by concentrating all decision-making power on a governmental level, i.e. on the level of the ministries of privatization or the republican cabinets themselves. Interest groups, workers and managers had no appreciable influence on the privatization methods applied. Thanks to the quick set-up of an institutional framework that clearly defined responsibilities and procedures of privatization and also drafted a strict timetable for the entire programme, at least the Czech privatization process has so far been largely under stable control by the authorities. The decentralization is effected by the splitting of responsibilities to various bodies. This refers to the basic split between decision-making and implementation, but likewise to the different bodies contributing to decision-making itself. The Ministry of Privatization is effectively prevented from becoming a 'super bureaucracy' with negative impacts on the transparency and supervision of privatization. Decentralization produces a system of checks and balances that increases the mutual accountability of the administrative bodies involved in privatization. The separation of decision-making on one hand and project implementation as well as property administration on the other hand is an important organizational tool to avoid conflicts of interests. A bureaucratic body responsible for all three areas would more likely succumb to the temptation of delaying decision-making and implementation so as not to threaten the legitimacy of its own existence. Clearly, the faster the progress of privatization, the less property remains to administer or transfer and, consequently, the bigger is the pressure to unwind. This bureaucratic disincentive structure could significantly hinder the whole privatization process.

Rapid privatization also demands an immediate toppling of the founding ministries. They are hardly interested in speeding up the privatization of 'their' SOEs since they are losing thereby not only the control of the companies, but possibly even their own *raison d'être*. For that reason, the political discretion of the founders was considerably cut by transferring most of the decision-making power in privatization projects to the newly established Ministries of Privatization. On the other hand, it was sensible to use the founders' inside knowledge on branches and firms and to assign an advisory function to them. The founding ministries were largely involved in the drafting and evaluating of privatization proposals. This certainly eased the burden of the Ministry of Privatization whose staff amounted to no more than 160 persons even in its heyday.

Furthermore, the Polish experience of the late 1980s with the Ministry of Finance as the institution bearing the main responsibility for privatization had raised doubts about the moral willingness of the old-established networks of bureaucrats and enterprise managers not to abuse legal gaps for the 'spontaneous' exploitation of property rights. Eventual participation in the gains of spontaneous privatization adds to the corruption risks of privatization and reduces the incentives of bureaucrats to accelerate the privatization of assets they have been entrusted with. From this perspective, the Czechoslovak approach of setting up completely new institutions (privatization ministries and property funds without any established personnel structures), which are embedded in a system of checks and balances, may be more adequate in allowing the whole process to gain momentum as well as transparency.

The speedy creation and well-balanced nature of the institutional environment certainly helped to make the privatization process more robust against political interest groups and various stakeholders in former SOEs. In the end, both factors together with the strong political will of the government to adhere to the jam-packed timetable of privatization ensured that the whole process has run smoothly over a period of almost seven years.

Today the Ministry of Privatization has already disbanded and, notwithstanding all measuring problems and statistical inaccuracy, the Czech share of the private sector in GDP is topping that of all other transitional economies.

Table 2.1: Private sector share in GDP in transitional economies

Country	1986	1994	1996
Czech Republic	3%	65%	75%
Poland	18%	55%	60%
Hungary	35%	55%	70%

Source: Estimations based upon Milanovic (1991) and EBRD Transition Reports

2.2 LARGE-SCALE PRIVATIZATION

After the decline of the communist regime, the privatization of large enterprises soon became the focus of public attention. Various academic and political interest groups drew up competing proposals including the set-up of a governmental privatization agency similar to the Hungarian approach, the decentralization of the privatization process leaving firm management with considerable discretion on the methods of asset transfer (spontaneous privatization) or several projects emphasizing worker participation and ownership.[3] In the end, the government stuck to the goals of rapid and equitable privatization, pointing to the technical problems and time requirements of standard methods and the lack of fairness and incentive problems of employee ownership. Unlike other transitional countries, the Czechoslovak authorities could design the privatization programme for large enterprises largely free from fiscal constraints since internal and external public debt were negligible. Privatization proceeds hence were no major argument of the government's utility function for the construction of the large-scale privatization programme.

With the government being strongly committed to radical privatization, the discussion increasingly shifted in 1990 to the question of 'how', rather than 'whether', to organize and implement mass privatization. Two alternatives were debated. One proposal was presented by Svejnar (1989) who recommends the transformation of SOEs into joint-stock companies (commercialization) and the distribution of their shares to the citizens through financial intermediaries. Publicly or privately managed mutual funds are to accomplish a sufficient diversification of shares. All individuals hold identical portfolios of shares in the funds. A computerized distribution of shares guarantees a rapid realization of the programme at low cost. The latter results mainly from the easy preparation of share transfers since asset pricing is no longer required. The proposal reveals some striking parallels to the Polish programme designed by Lewandowski & Szomburg (1990). The main advantages of the programme are its equitableness, low costs and perfect risk diversification. However, it reduces the freedom of choice of individual investors. They are not encouraged to collect and process information on companies and cannot arrange portfolios in compliance with individual risk preferences. The lack of active involvement slows down the learning process about the functioning of a market economy. Moreover, if shares are merely allotted to funds and individual investors have neither the opportunity nor any incentive to collect information and to disclose their preferences and expectations in the course of mass privatization, the programme rarely helps to build up the basis for an informationally efficient capital market. In the presence of thin capital markets after privatization, this is a serious drawback. If market prices do not reflect the weighted profit expectations of a large population of active investors, the market's contribution to efficient allocation of scarce capital resources and to corporate control is necessarily rather small.

The second alternative, finally chosen by the Klaus government, was a more evolutionary approach leaving a broad scope for the spontaneous emergence of institutions. The distribution of vouchers which can be invested directly in firms should embolden individual investors to make a comparative evaluation of enterprises. An iterative bidding procedure over several rounds ought to effect a converging of supply and demand for company assets. The result of this more time-consuming process is a tight connection between privatization and the development of the equity market. Asset transfer is preceded by an in-depth evaluation of shares by a multitude of investors. The establishment of privatization intermediaries is left to the market itself. The demand for risk diversification determines the impact of funds upon mass privatization. In contrast to Svejnar's proposal, this programme allows investors to choose an optimal degree of diversification by assigning a part or all of their vouchers to funds and investing the remainder directly in company shares. The role of the state is restricted to finding the balance between supply of and demand for shares over various bidding rounds. No doubt, the organization costs of this procedure exceed the costs of the Svejnar proposal.

As already touched upon, under the communist regime, state enterprises were guided and supervised by a branch ministry ('founder') responsible for matching company performance and plan data scheduled by the central planning bureau and the government. First changes of the governance and ownership structure of large enterprises were launched by the passing of two laws in 1990. The Law on State Enterprises should increase their financial autonomy and control over their disposable profits (Frydman et al., 1993, p.

91). The founders were allowed to split enterprises into smaller independent units. They likewise could convert them into joint-stock companies as defined under the new Law on Joint-Stock Companies. Both laws together built a first legal base for the privatization of large SOEs since they enabled the founders - conditional upon government approval - to enter into joint ventures with private domestic and foreign investors before the passing of an overall concept of large-scale privatization in form of the Law on the Conditions of Transfer of State Property to Other Persons (Law on the Privatization of Large-scale Enterprises) in February 1991. In fact, some spectacular transactions like the joint automotive manufacturing company by Skoda auto and Volkswagen and the purchase of the detergent producer Rakona by Procter & Gamble date back to the period prior to the implementation of large-scale privatization. They reflected a firm commitment of the government to foster large-scale privatization in times of still hot political debates about its actual extent and the methods applied.

The Law on Privatization of Large-scale Enterprises required the federal and republican governments to formulate directives for the implementation of the programme. The founders were charged with the composition of a list of originally 4,129 large SOEs (out of a total of 5,482) to be privatized in two waves until the end of 1996 (UNIDO, 1992, p. 34). Of these, 2,285 SOEs were to be privatized very quickly in the first wave between October 1991 and May 1992, another 1,844 firms were earmarked for a subsequent second wave.[4] For 1,271 SOEs privatization should be postponed to the time after 1996, 82 companies were liquidated in compliance with the bankruptcy law adopted in June 1991. While the decision on how to privatize was made centrally for each SOE, everybody was free to draft a 'project' for a company proposing the application of one or more privatization methods. Large-scale privatization thus amalgamated decentral (drafting of projects) and central (decision making) elements. Privatization projects could cover one or more of the following standard and non-standard methods:

- public auctions or tenders,
- direct sales to predetermined buyers,
- free transfer to municipalities or social securities bodies and
- transformation into joint-stock companies and subsequent distribution of shares (e.g. through the voucher scheme or standard methods).

The transformation of SOEs into joint-stock companies can be followed by various means of distribution to investors, e.g. by direct sales, public offers on the capital markets, transfer as compensation for restitution claims or through voucher privatization. A maximum of 10% of company shares could be sold to employees at a special price.[5] Projects could combine standard and non-standard methods. For instance, a part of the SOE could be sold in a public tender while another part was divested through vouchers. However, due to its political commitment to mass privatization, the government required projects generally to put between 30% and 97% of company shares into the voucher programme. Furthermore, enterprises could be privatized as one piece or split into several business units with their own projects. Indeed, the scope for the design of privatization proposals was immense.

A flow chart of the drafting of privatization projects, the decision-making on them and the implementation of final projects in the process of large-scale privatization is presented in Figure 2.1. The founders were to initiate the drafting of projects. For that purpose, they could either prepare their own draft or place an obligation on firm management to design a project. The latter was the usual procedure. The management then had to come up with a *basic* privatization project and to submit it to the responsible branch ministry before a set deadline. The project had to contain certain mandatory information like the amount of the company's debt, the mode of privatization and the settlement of restitution claims on company assets. The projects also had to inform about the book value of company assets. For this purpose, the Czech Ministry of Finance had emitted rules for the determination of the book value of real property (Kotrba, 1994, p. 164, fn. 27). Nevertheless, the expressiveness of balance sheets remained dubious. Foreign investors with an interest in the acquisition of SOEs were obliged to charge a chartered accountant with the evaluation of company assets. The value estimated after an audit is then the basis for further negotiations with the authorities. This discrimination against foreign buyers constituted an advantage for domestic investors as the asset values guessed by independent accountants mostly exceeded the - in part quite arbitrary - book values which were frequently taken over from the old balance sheets with merely slight corrections.

Apart from the founder and the enterprise management, everybody was allowed to submit a *competing* privatization project. Unlike the basic privatization projects, the competing proposals could also relate merely to parts of the enterprise in question. They did not have to cover all company assets. Provided the competing projects met the valid formal and informational requirements, they were treated on an equal basis by the decision-making authorities. In the beginning, investors drafting competing projects often complained about bad access to company information. The authorities reacted soon and passed a law obliging enterprise management to disclose all relevant information to competing investors. Nevertheless, management normally disposed of an informational monopoly. Along with still existing coalitions with state bureaucrats who were maintaining many board seats in SOEs waiting for privatization, this could have constituted a starting advantage.

Figure 2.1: Flow chart of the process of large-scale privatization

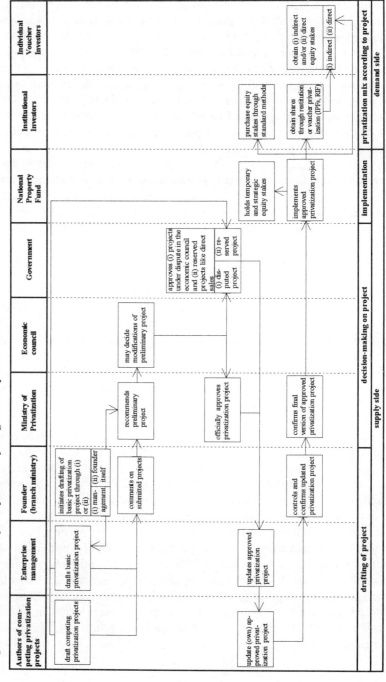

The privatization projects were submitted to the founders who passed them, along with a critical statement, forward to the Ministry of Privatization. The ministry then made a judgement on each project and wrote a recommendation on how to privatize each company based upon the submitted projects. This recommendation was sent to the prime minister and the economic council consisting of the ministers with economic provinces like the Minister of Finance, of Economy, of Industry and Trade and of Agriculture. Provided that they raised no objections, that the recommendation didn't relate to an enterprise with more than 3,000 employees and the project didn't include direct sales or sales to foreign investors, the Ministry of Privatization officially approved the recommendation. After updating by the original author of the successful privatization project, the enterprise management and the founder, the project was handed over to the National Property Fund for implementation. In the event of objections, the economic council drafted a compromise proposal that was then approved by the Ministry of Privatization. The subsequent procedure remained the same. If the economic council couldn't come to an agreement, the disputed project was passed on to the government for a definite decision. The government then sent the approved project to the enterprise management for updating. In the end, the whole decision-making process tried to strike a balance between the interest of the participating protagonists. It aimed at reaching a general consensus. If no consensus could be found, the final decision was made by the government.

Some authors argue that the informational monopoly and rent-sharing between managers and the state bureaucracy (especially the personal networks between managers and branch ministries) indeed enhanced the success of basic privatization projects.[6] This could have resulted chiefly from the fact that the founder is the first 'filter' commenting on all submitted projects. Another reason for a distortion of the decision-making process in favour of managerial projects could be that they compulsorily covered the whole SOE whereas competing projects were allowed to focus just upon certain parts or single plants. They might have left the task of finding solutions for the rest of the enterprise to the Ministry of Privatization. Given the ministry's personnel constraints[7], there were probably incentives to pick out projects covering the entire company.

Empirical evidence seemingly supports the preferential treatment of managerial projects. Until December 1993, company managers along with the founding ministries had been by far the most successful composers of projects. While only 27% of all settled projects were submitted by high-rank company managers, their share in all approved projects amounted to 54% (see Table 2.2). This meant a success ratio of approved to settled projects of 64% for company managers as against an average ratio over all groups submitting projects of 32%. However, apart from the arguments brought forward above, there are two more reasons likewise of importance for the success of managerial projects.

Table 2.2: Approval of privatization projects in large-scale privatization[a]

Project submitted by	Submitted projects			settled projects			
	total	settled	% of all settled projects	approved	rejected	success ratio[b]	% of all settled projects
Company management	5,502 (4,992)	5,116 (3,878)	21% (27%)	2,980 (2,492)	2,136 (1,386)	0.58 (0.64)	40% (54%)
Branch management	710 (711)	689 (562)	3% (4%)	215 (203)	474 (359)	0.31 (0.36)	3% (4%)
Company employees	1,151 (1,141)	961 (88)	4% (1%)	258 (30)	703 (58)	0.27 (0.34)	4% (1%)
Prospective buyer	14,860 (11,478)	12,136 (6,090)	50% (42%)	2,792 (1,254)	9,344 (4,836)	0.19 (0.21)	38% (27%)
Restituted owner	643 (630)	620 (457)	3% (3%)	169 (134)	451 (323)	0.27 (0.29)	2% (3%)
Founding ministry	563 (281)	484 (112)	2% (1%)	392 (78)	92 (34)	0.81 (0.70)	5% (2%)
Consulting firm	541 (527)	497 (331)	2% (2%)	111 (72)	386 (259)	0.22 (0.22)	2% (2%)
District privatization commission	1,143 (1,123)	1,089 (848)	4% (6%)	143 (176)	946 (672)	0.13 (0.21)	2% (4%)
Local authorities	780 (715)	696 (498)	3% (3%)	81 (55)	615 (443)	0.12 (0.11)	1% (1%)
Trade unions	32 (33)	32 (25)	0% (0%)	6 (2)	26 (23)	0.19 (0.08)	0% (0%)
Other	2,003 (1,976)	1,939 (1,485)	8% (10%)	220 (150)	1,719 (1,335)	0.30 (0.10)	3% (3%)
Total	27,901 (23,607)	24,259 (14,374)	100% (100%)	7,367 (4,646)	16,892 (9,728)	0.30 (0.32)	100% (100%)

a Cumulative data as of end-1995, data for end-1993 in brackets.
b Success ratio is defined by the proportion of approved to settled projects of each group.

Source: Ministry for the Administration of National Property and its Privatization of the Czech Republic, own calculations

Firstly, unlike other prospective investors, managers are supposed to have a relative preference for voucher privatization as against other privatization methods. If the voucher method leads to dispersed share ownership, it will ensure managers - in the absence of a working market of corporate control - a high degree of discretion. This explains why basic privatization projects frequently scheduled a considerable amount of company shares for voucher privatization.[8] In many cases, the political commitment of the government to voucher privatization and the anticipation of large participation of citizens in the programme may have aligned the interests of enterprise management and government and laid the political foundations to favour basic privatization projects.[9] This hypothesis is supported by the declining success ratio of company management after 1993. As of end-1995, managers' privatization proposals came to merely 40% of all approved projects which indicates a virtual ending of the managerial success story after integration into the voucher programme had ceased to be an eligible strategy. From January 1994, the distortion incentive in favour of managerial proposals has been at least diminished. Nonetheless, the observable lack of explicit selection criteria among privatization projects (or the fact that they have been kept secret) somewhat reduced the transparency of large-scale privatization and surely was a weak spot of the programme.

A second reason for the comparative success of managerial projects is the uneven distribution of competing projects over enterprises. With an average of 3.125 submitted projects for each enterprise on which a privatization decision was made until end-1993 (3.333 until end-1995), the standard deviation over all SOEs was enormous. A lot of SOEs had twenty or thirty competing projects. The Brno-based milk processing factory Lacrum even attracted as many as 126 competing projects (Frydman et al., 1993, p. 81). But there were many companies on the sideline of investors' interest, too, for which only the obligatory basic projects were drafted.[10] On average, projects drafted by the senior management hence were subject to less competition in the approval procedure than the competing privatization proposals of external stakeholders, lower-rank management and employees. Considering their uneven distribution, it appears fair to say that competing projects have been largely treated on equal footing with managerial ones.

On the firm level, large privatization was a rather lengthy process. The drafting of proposals, their submitting and reviewing by various institutions took at least several months. This is why only 50 projects were settled by the Ministry of Privatization within the first eight months of large-scale privatization until end-1991 (see Table 2.3). The updating of approved projects and their final implementation frequently took many months, too. Thus, merely 20 privatization units were actually passed over to the NPF in the course of 1991 (see Table 2.4). A privatization unit can be defined as *one* tranche of firm equity privatized through the application of *one* privatization method. As each privatization project could propose the splitting of the SOE in question and assign a mix of methods to one firm, the overall number of units approved for privatization is higher than the overall number of approved projects. The latter, in turn, exceeds the number of enterprises whose privatization methods have been decided.[11] As of 31 December 1995, the privatization procedures of 3,552 large enterprises were approved by the ministry. This corresponds to the number of 7,367 approved privatization projects. Hence, on average slightly more than two projects were accepted for each SOE. The property transfer of the companies was to be carried out in 21,605 units/tranches. Consequently, on average, each enterprise has been privatized in roughly six units.

Table 2.3: Progress of large-scale privatization

Cumulative numbers, end of year	1991	1992	1993	1994	1995
Number of privatization projects submitted,	4,656	16,609	23,607	26,614	27,901
of which:					
- decision made	50	10,821	14,374	21,144	24,259
- approved	27	3,029	4,646	6,737	7,367
- rejected	23	7,792	9,728	14,407	16,892
- outstanding	4,606	5,788	9,233	5,470	3,642
Number of enterprises included in submitted projects,	2,277	3,638	4,335	4,638	5,087
of which:					
- decision made	21	2,170	2,694	3,841	4,424
- approved	n.a.	1,871	2,470	3,278	3,552
- rejected	n.a.	299	224	564	872
- outstanding	n.a.	1,468	1,641	796	663

Source: Ministry for the Administration of National Property and its Privatization of the Czech Republic, Czech Statistical Office

The decision-making process itself proceeded mostly very smoothly. Given the long chain of checks and reviews, all involved institutions obviously cooperated well and tried to find a consensus where possible. As a result, during the four and a half years after the start of large-scale privatization in April 1991, 24,259 projects have been settled and the decision on the privatization methods of 4,424 enterprises have been made. The speedy progress permitted the closing-down of the Ministry of Privatization in May 1996. The strict timetable of the voucher programme put considerable pressure on the authorities to speed up decision-making on the bulk of projects submitted already in the beginning of large-scale privatization. Indeed it kickstarted the whole programme. 10,821 decisions were made solely in 1992, i.e. more than 40% of all decisions made until end-1995. Remarkably, the accounting value of the property approved for privatization and passed over to the NPF until end-1992 amounted to some CSK 470,000 million. This is more than 50% of the overall value of property handed over to the NPF until end-1995. Empirical evidence hence confirms that voucher privatization is an appropriate tool in speeding up large-scale divestiture of state assets.

Table 2.4: Methods approved for large-scale privatization by the Ministry of Privatization

Cumulative numbers, book value of property in million crowns, end of year*	units approved and passed over to the National Property Fund					units only approved
	1991	1992	1993	1994	1995	1995
Auction:						
- no. of units	5	336	430	1,700	2,000	2,128
- value of property	n.a.	3,881	5,602	6,777	7,214	9,314
Public tender:						
- no. of units	2	300	500	1,000	1,360	1,394
- value of property	n.a.	10,436	17,962	24,547	29,344	33,001
Direct sale:						
- no. of units	5	986	4,000	8,000	11,000	11,343
- value of property	n.a.	26,613	37,618	54,029	60,160	91,653
Joint stock corp.:						
- no. of units	8	1,218	1,800	1,850	1,870	1,883
- value of property	n.a.	420,171	744,059	748,218	751,418	768,101
free transfer:						
- no. of units	0	1,052	2,500	4,000	4,800	4,857
- value of property	0	9,633	26,942	39,353	47,364	55,749
total:						
- no. of units	20	3,900	9,230	16,550	21,030	21,605
- value of property	n.a.	470,734	832,184	871,965	895,500	957,818

* Columns 2-6 present number and book value of units approved by the Ministry of Privatization and passed over to the NPF. The data of the last column refer to all units approved, irrespective of whether they are passed over to the fund or still in the updating process. The accounting values of units of the last column are calculated by the Privatization Ministry and are different from the book values published by NPF as presented in the preceding columns. The numbers of units contained in the columns 4-6 are estimations made by the author based upon information released by the NPF and the Czech Statistical Office

Source: Ministry of Privatization, National Property Fund and Czech Statistical Office.

Delays of property transfer inevitably emerged in the course of implementation. As of 31 December 1993, for instance, 62% of the assets submitted to the NPF had been privatized in accordance with the approved projects. Substantial time lags between submission and implementation could be observed for auctions (only 54% of assets set aside for auctions were privatized), public tenders (57% of assets privatized) and - rather astonishing - free-of-charge transfers (50% of assets privatized). On the other hand, the transformation into joint-stock companies made fast progress (80% of assets privatized). As of end-1995, 96% of all assets handed over to the NPF were privatized, i.e. transferred to new owners (including public authorities) in harmony with the respective privatization projects. While there was virtually no delay in the transformation into joint-stock companies, some 23% of all other assets were still waiting to be transferred. Conspicuous delays appeared at public tenders (62% of assets privatized) and free-of-charge transfers (67% of assets privatized).

In the case of public competitive tenders, the implementation delay is quite understandable since tenders are very time-consuming. In addition, the budget of the NPF was subject to political debates. As the parliament protracted the approval of the budget, the NPF had to stall the concluding of mandatory contracts with external consulting firms temporarily until a final budget decision was reached. This significantly curbed the implementation of tenders. The regulation of the housing market still is a major impediment to an acceleration of free-of-charge transfers. Many flats and apartment buildings hived off from former conglomerates are to be transferred to municipalities or social securities institutions. However, the prospective beneficiaries' interest in a rapid transference is limited as strict rent control often generates negative income from the rental of real estate. Therefore, public authorities have strong incentives either to protract property transfer until rent control has been relaxed or to make the transfer subject to obtaining financial subsidies from the state.

The major reason for the tremendous overall implementation ratio of 96% (as measured by asset value) is the fact that in cases where a new joint-stock company emerges from a privatization project, its establishment is already considered as the moment of completion of the project. In this view, the project is implemented even if the transfer of shares, e.g. through a public offering or direct sale, has not yet taken place. Moreover, even strategic shareholdings of the NPF are counting statistically as completed privatization projects. Of course, the driving force behind the many establishments of joint-stock companies was voucher privatization. Table 2.5 surveys the transfer methods for stock obtained by the NPF in the course of privatization. By the end of 1995, 97.5% of this stock had been obtained by means of transforming SOEs into joint-stock companies or through takeovers of shares of state-owned joint-stock companies (both of which is filed under the heading 'joint-stock corporation' in Table 2.4). Approximately one half of the shares received in this way has been put into voucher privatization. Concurrently, stock distributed through vouchers constitutes more than 72% of all shares privatized up to end-December 1995. At that point in time, more than two thirds of the entire stock passed to the fund had been privatized and some additional 7% was still waiting to be transferred. Because of the unique nature of the voucher programme for both the overall conception of Czech privatization and the emergence of governance structures, we will have a closer look at it in the following section.

Table 2.5: *Privatization of joint-stock companies by the National Property Fund**

Stages and methods of privatization[a]	Accounting value of stock	% of overall stock taken over by NPF	% of stock privatized so far by NPF
Shares taken over by the NPF	706,444	100.0	-
➢ for implementation of privatization projects[b]	689,055	97.5	-
➢ NPF's investment in securities	11,260	1.6	-
➢ otherwise obtained shares	6,130	0.9	-
Privatized shares	474,630	67.2	100.0
➢ shares sold to the private sector	49,745	7.0	10.5
- public auction	8,274	1.2	1.7
- direct sale to predetermined domestic investors	16,290	2.3	3.4
- direct sale to predetermined foreign investors	13,060	1.9	2.8
- employee shares	2,190	0.3	0.5
- public tender	9,931	1.4	2.1
➢ shares transferred free of charge	424,885	60.1	89.5
- voucher privatization	342,560	48.5	72.2
- to municipalities and social securities	50,146	7.1	10.6
- to RIF (Restitution Investment Fund)	19,674	2.8	4.2
- to EIF (Endowment Investment Fund)	71	0.0	0.0
- for restitution purposes	1,708	0.2	0.4
- to agricultural aid fund	12,162	1.7	2.6
Shares held by NPF as of end-1995	230,124	32.6	-
➢ strategic holdings	176,432	25.0	-
➢ temporary holdings	47,562	6.7	-
Shares not booked as of end-1995	1,690	0.2	-

a Cumulative numbers as of 31 December 1995, accounting value of property in million CSK/CZK.

b Book value of stock taken over from Ministry of Privatization for implementation does not tally with the accounting value established by the NPF. The difference between the book value of input assets (CZK 751,418 million, see Table 2.4) and the accounting value of acquired stock (CZK 689,055 million, see this Table) is due to the requirement to create reserve funds at the establishment of joint-stock companies.

Source: Annual Report of the National Property Fund of the Czech Republic for the Year 1995; own calculations.

2.3 VOUCHER PRIVATIZATION

2.3.1 Supply Side

As for legislation, the voucher programme has been anchored in the Law on Privatization of Large-scale Enterprises since February 1991. The technical realization was defined by two government decrees for the first and second wave of voucher privatization respectively. The decrees mainly define how to purchase investment vouchers and to use them for the bidding for firms. They likewise determine that each adult Czechoslovak (and for the second wave Czech) citizen with a permanent residence on the state territory is allowed to participate in the programme. In addition, they specify some sporadic regulation for investment funds and unit trusts acting as privatization intermediaries.

From a preliminary list of 4,129 SOEs nominated for large-scale privatization in the Czech Republic in 1991, 988 enterprises entered into the first wave of voucher privatization.[12] They supplied shares with a total face value of CSK 212,500 million. 861 Czech firms underwent the second wave, placing shares with a face value of some CZK 155,000 million into the voucher programme. 185 of the second-wave firms offering equity worth CZK 24,000 million had already been included in the first wave. They either supplied property not sold in the first wave or provided the programme with new equity issues. After adaptation by shares worth 8,000 million crowns offered in both waves, the total property supplied in voucher privatization amounts to some 359,500 million crowns.

The companies included in the programme stretched virtually across all branches of the Czech economy with a clear focus on industrial enterprises. By number of companies, 45% of all first-wave firms and 38% of those of the second wave belonged to the industrial sector (see Table 2.6). In terms of face value, their property makes up some 57% of all shares earmarked for voucher privatization. As the resolution of agricultural claims was rather time-consuming, the amount of agricultural property privatized in the first wave was substantially lower than in the second wave. This relates to the face value of agricultural property, but even more to the number of enterprises included in the respective wave.

Compared to the overall economy, the size (by book value as well as number of employees) and profitability of first-wave companies were above average. Relatively high profitability should ensure that participants in the voucher scheme would not end up with worthless shares and eventually lose faith in the entire transformation process. The equity capital of firms offered in the first wave averaged CSK 343 million. The average value for corporations newly established for the second wave reached as much as

Table 2.6: *Supply structure of voucher privatization by branches**

	1st wave				2nd wave				Total	
branch	no. of firms	%	property for vouchers	%	no. of firms	%	property for vouchers	%	property for vouchers	%
Agriculture	176	19	23,002	11	356	41	26,347	17	49,349	14
Industry	434	46	119,084	59	330	38	87,781	57	206,865	57
Other man-ufacturing	122	13	41,698	20	59	7	26,667	17	68,365	19
Non-man-ufacturing	46	5	6,761	3	40	5	6,722	4	13,483	4
Trade & regional	168	17	13,442	7	76	9	7,483	5	20,925	6
Total	946	100	203,987	100	861	100	155,000	100	358,987	100

* Data for first wave exclude federal enterprises; property refers to aggregate face value in million crowns.

Source: Ministry for the Administration of National Property and its Privatization of the Czech Republic; own calculations

Table 2.7: *Supply structure of voucher-privatized enterprises by number of employees**

	1st wave				2nd wave				Total	
no. of employees	no. of firms	%	property for vouchers	%	no. of firms	%	property for vouchers	%	property for vouchers	%
< 50	13	1	2,643	1	27	4	1,500	1	4,143	1
50-100	53	6	4,282	2	69	8	4,688	3	8,970	3
100-500	462	49	35,457	17	456	53	31,722	20	67,179	19
500-3,000	367	39	94,806	47	254	30	52,782	34	147,588	41
> 3,000	51	5	66,799	33	43	5	63,585	42	130,384	36
Total	946	100	203,987	100	849	100	154,277	100	358,264	100

* Data for first wave exclude federal enterprises. Data for second wave exclude 12 unidentified enterprises allotting 723 million CZK to voucher privatization. Property refers to aggregate face value in million crowns.

Source: Ministry for the Administration of National Property and its Privatization of the Czech Republic; own calculations

Table 2.8:   Supply structure by value of stock allotted to voucher privatization*

face value of property for vouchers in million crowns	1st wave				2nd wave				Total	
	no. of firms	%	property for vouchers	%	no. of firms	%	property for vouchers	%	property for vouchers	%
< 50	292	31	8,548	4	335	40	10,741	7	19,289	5
50-100	241	25	17,222	8	244	28	17,539	11	34,761	10
100-500	328	35	71,056	35	235	27	49,182	32	120,238	33
> 500	85	9	107,161	53	47	5	77,538	50	184,699	51
Total	946	100	203,987	100	861	100	155,000	100	358,987	100

* Data for first wave exclude federal enterprises. Property refers to aggregate face value in million crowns.

Source: Ministry for the Administration of National Property and its Privatization of the Czech Republic; own calculations

Table 2.9:   Supply structure by percentage of stock allotted to voucher privatization*

percentage of stock	1st wave				2nd wave				Total	
	no. of firms	%	property for vouchers	%	no. of firms	%	property for vouchers	%	property for vouchers	%
< 34%	40	4	23,629	12	250	29	43,343	28	66,972	19
34% - 50%	71	8	21,074	10	109	13	35,886	23	56,960	16
51% - 96%	440	46	102,618	50	397	46	66,007	43	168,625	47
> 96%	395	42	56,666	28	105	12	9,764	6	66,430	19
Total	946	100	203,987	100	861	100	155,000	100	358,987	100

* Data for first wave exclude federal enterprises. Property refers to aggregate face value in million crowns.

Source: Ministry for the Administration of National Property and its Privatization of the Czech Republic; own calculations about CZK 557 million. The size structure of firms as measured by the number of employees is roughly similar in both waves. The workforce of more than 90% of the companies was 100 to 3,000 employees. 5% of the firms in both waves had a staff of more than 3,000 employees (see Table 2.7). In the second wave, companies over 3,000 employees delivered some 42% of the shares privatized. In the first wave, it had been a mere third of the equity stock supplied.

Supply concentration was very high in both waves. 85 (i.e. 9%) of the first-wave firms and 47 (5%) of the second-wave firms supplied more than half of the shares offered in the respective wave (see Table 2.8). Each of those companies allotted over 500 million crowns of equity to the voucher programme. Adding firms supplying equity with a face value of between 100 and 500 million crowns, 44% of the first-wave enterprises allotted 88% of the shares. For the second wave, supply concentration is even higher. 32% of the companies were responsible for 82% of all shares.

88% of the first-wave firms passed more than half of their stock to the voucher scheme (see Table 2.9). 42% even supplied more than 96%. This is remarkable as each company included in the first wave had to cede 3% of its equity stock to the Restitution Investment Fund (RIF), a subsidiary of the National Property Fund whose assets are determined for the compensation of reprivatization claims under the Major Restitution Act in cases where in-kind restitution cannot be accomplished. Second-wave companies were exempted from this 'collective obligation' but had to transfer equity to the RIF in accordance with the privatization projects. In addition, 1% of their stock was deposited with the Endowment Investment Fund (EIF), another subsidiary of the NPF with the assignment to financially support private charitable foundations.[13] The second-wave companies passed mostly smaller proportions of their stock to the voucher programme. A tentative explanation for this observation is, rather than a declining enthusiasm for voucher privatization, the fact that the majority of strategic enterprises were partially privatized in the second wave. Strategic enterprises are firms from key branches, like utilities, telecommunications and mining, in which the state has a long-term interest or whose ownership structure is politically sensitive. Commonly, just a small proportion of their equity is sold through vouchers while the state holds the majority (possibly together with another strategic investor). A higher share of strategic and politically sensitive enterprises is therefore one factor explaining the smaller proportion of shares allotted by firms to voucher privatization in the second wave.

Apparently companies privatized almost entirely through vouchers are comparatively small in both waves. In the first wave, the 42% of enterprises with the highest proportion of shares for voucher privatization made up merely 28% of the face value of all firms. The top 12% of the second wave contribute no more than 6% of overall face value whereas the 13% of the companies assigning between 34% and 50% of their stock to the voucher programme supply 23%. Roughly speaking, many small companies are privatized predominantly through vouchers while this privatization method tends to be of a rather complementary nature for large companies. Nevertheless, most of the companies placed more than half of their shares into the voucher scheme. Besides, both waves considered, some 65% of all property supplied comes from firms allotting over 50% of their stock to the programme. This means that their ownership structure is essentially determined by the outcomes of voucher privatization.

2.3.2 Demand Side

The organization of the demand side of voucher privatization, i.e. the allocation of shares for investment vouchers, was carried out by the Federal Ministry of Finance (in the second wave the Ministry of Finance of the Czech Republic). For this purpose, it established two Centres for Voucher Privatization (CVP) in Prague and Bratislava which were responsible for setting up an extensive network of 648 registration offices and 5,102 filing counters all over the country.[14] For a fee of CZK 1,050, every entitled citizen could register legitimately for one voucher book per wave. The book constituted a claim to 1,000 voucher points which were to be used for the bidding for companies during the given wave. Voucher holders could consign a part or all of their points to investment privatization funds. This process is referred to as the preliminary or zero round of the privatization wave. For the rest of the wave, the funds then participated in the bidding process like individual voucher holders. Vouchers were not transferable to other persons or entities. Prior to the actual bidding process, the government published a list of companies whose shares could be acquired in the respective wave. The list also disclosed relevant information about the enterprises in question like profit, sales volume, equity as per balance sheet, the proportion of shares supplied in the given wave, indebtedness, net asset value and ownership structure. The list was mailed to all voucher investors at the start of each round. From the second round on, the price list also contained information about the results of the previous bidding round, namely the size and ratio of supply and demand for shares and the number of shares sold to individual investors and IPFs. After all these preparatory activities, the sale of shares for voucher points was performed in several privatization rounds.

The first privatization round was started on the same day as the list of companies was published. From a technical point of view, each round of the bidding process could be chronologically split into four phases. At first the CVP announced the prices of the single joint-stock companies, i.e. the number of shares available for 100 points provided there was no oversubscription. In the first wave, the starting rate was 33.33 voucher points for all shares. Consequently, each voucher book was arithmetically equivalent to 30 shares. Since the face value of one share had been fixed at CSK 1,000 for all enterprises of both waves, 1,000 voucher points tied up with a proportion of 30,000 CSK of the total face value of all first-wave companies.[15] Because of a lower ratio of equity capital to registered citizens, the initial price of the second wave was fixed at 50 points for each share. In the second phase, individual voucher holders and IPFs made their bids. According to individual preferences, each owner of a voucher book could spread his points over a maximum of ten companies.[16] In the following phase, share orders were centrally processed. Thereby, three scenarios had to be differentiated for each company:

(1) If total demand for the shares of one enterprise was lower than or equal to supply, all orders were filled. The remaining stock was offered at a reduced price in the next round.

(2) In the event of oversubscription below 25% ('reducible oversubscription'), the demand of individual voucher keepers was met entirely whilst the demand of IPFs was proportionally cut until excess demand was eliminated. Aside from the hypothetical case of an equilibrium of supply and demand, this was the only way to clear the market for shares of an actual company.

(3) If a firm was oversubscribed by more than 25% ('non-reducible oversub-scription'), all voucher points invested were returned and supplied shares were transferred to the next round.

In the final phase of each round, shares successfully ordered were handed over to the investors. Yet, there was no physical transference. Shares privatized through the voucher scheme are de-materialized and had therefore to be saved onto investors' property accounts at the newly founded Securities Centre.[17] After each round, the Commissions for Fixing Rates of the CVPs could alter share prices of all enterprises for the next round to reduce imbalances between supply and demand. Price adjustments were accomplished according to a complex algorithm whose coefficients varied over the single bidding rounds. By inserting new coefficients into the algorithm, the commissions changed the demand elasticity of prices. Manipulations should accelerate the converging of supply and demand and hence lead to market-clearing outcomes for as many corporations as possible. The algorithm applied has never been made public. It allegedly consisted of some 20 components (Hanousek, 1996, p. 15). Svejnar & Singer (1993) tried to specify the price-setting behaviour of the authorities for the first wave by means of econometric analysis. Their findings are that the price set for the following round is a function mainly of the remaining supply of shares, the ratio of demand and supply from the preceding round and (apart from the first round) the share price of the previous round. The price setting model of Hanousek & Lastovicka (1994) comes to similar conclusions. In practice the key to price setting and hence to manipulation of the coefficients obviously was the assumption of unitary price elasticity of demand for shares of a given enterprise. The shortcomings of such a rough rule of thumb came to light in the third round of the first wave when an immense adjustment of prices caused excess demand for many companies so that only 11.8% of all orders were followed by sales and less than a quarter of the stock supplied was transferred to the voucher investors (see Table 2.10).[18] Similar problems occurred in the second and third round of the second wave in which merely 13.3% and 15.2% of total orders also led to sales of shares.[19] The Ministry of Finance had the discretionary power to terminate a privatization wave at any time. Uncertainty about the number of rounds in both waves should deter investors from strategic behaviour and enforce complete revelation of preferences in each single round. For instance, investors may hope that most of their fellows will use up their voucher points at the beginning of a wave so that the ratio of supply and demand is subsequently becoming more and more favourable. But speculation on undervalued shares in later bidding rounds is dangerous as all points remaining after the last round become invalid. As uncertainty about the final round set incentives to place one's points and thereby to reveal one's preferences from the beginning, it added to the information efficiency of the bidding process.

2.3.3 The Course of Voucher Privatization: Spontaneously Emerging IPFs and the Bidding Behaviour of Investors

The registration for the first wave began rather sluggishly. In November and December 1991, a mere 6.7% of all individual investors registered. Due to aggressive advertisement by IPFs, some 89% of voucher investors entered the programme in January 1992 and ensured a surprisingly high participation rate.[20] 8.57 million citizens of the country (5.95 million Czechs), i.e. about three quarters of all eligible persons, joined the scheme. There are several reasons why the appearance of IPFs enhanced the citizens' willingness to participate:

- *Risk-diversification*: IPFs allow risk-averse individuals to spread their investment over hundreds of enterprises to realize an optimal risk-profit mix.

- *Transaction costs*: IPFs effectively reduce the transaction costs of joining the scheme. It is very expensive for naive individuals to collect information about the

Table 2.10: Supply and demand in voucher privatization according to individual bidding rounds

	first wave (CSFR)					second wave (CZ)				
round	average order price[a]	average sale price[a]	sales in % of total supply	sales in % of round supply	sales in % of round orders	average order price[b]	average sale price[b]	sales in % of total supply	sales in % of round supply	sales in % of round orders
1st round	33.3 (33.3)	33.3 (33.3)	29.9	29.9	37.9	50.0	50.0	13.5	13.5	18.7
2nd round	32.9 (35.2)	43.9 (47.4)	26.0	37.1	52.5	16.9	59.2	23.1	26.7	13.3
3rd round	7.3 (8.7)	31.4 (38.9)	10.9	24.4	11.8	14.3	34.5	19.2	30.2	15.2
4th round	9.3 (11.0)	13.8 (15.5)	12.4	37.2	34.7	25.9	33.7	24.1	54.5	53.8
5th round	11.9 (13.8)	12.6 (14.8)	13.7	65.5	86.5	27.3	27.0	12.2	61.0	77.8
6th round	-	-	-	-	-	23.4	25.1	4.2	53.8	83.0
unsold	-	-	7.2	-	-	-	-	3.7	-	-

a Price in points per share for entire CSFR, price for Czech Republic in brackets
b Price in points per share

Source: Centre for Voucher Privatization, own calculations

83

Table 2.11: Survey of basic data about voucher privatization

	first wave[a]	second wave	total
number of joint-stock companies supplied	988	861	1,664[b]
- of which supplied for the first time	988	676	-
shares supplied (in mil.)	212,5	155,5	359,5[b]
number of citizens registered (in mil.)	5.95	6.16	-
number of IPFs registered	265	349	481[b]
- of which investment funds	265	194	326
- of which open-end unit trusts	-	37	37
- of which closed-end unit trusts	-	118	118
number of individuals placing points (in mil.)	1.76	2.30	-
voucher points consigned to IPFs (in bln.)	4.45	3.91	8.36
- in % of total points	73.3%	63.5%	68.4%
- of which to investment funds (in % of IPF points)	100%	40.0%	71.9%
- of which to open-end unit trusts (in % of IPF points)	-	22.2%	10.4%
- of which to closed-end unit trusts (in % of IPF points)	-	37.8%	17.7%
voucher points placed by individuals (in bln.)	1.62	2.25	3.87
- in % of total points)	26.7%	36.5%	31.6%
voucher points expired (in mil.)	57	38	95
- of which held by individuals (in mil.)	50	33	83
- of which consigned to IPFs (in mil.)	7	5	12
shares supplied per registered citizen	35.1	25.2	-
shares sold (in mil.)	198.0	149.3	347.3
shares left (in mil.)	14.5	5.7	20.2
- in % of total supply	6.8%	3.7%	5.8%
initial rate of shares to points	3/100	2/100	-
number of shares sold (in mil.)	181.8	149.3	331.1
- of which to individuals (in mil.)	63.9	75.1	139.0
- of which to IPFs (in mil.)	117.9	74.2	192.1
average number of shares purchased per voucher book	30.0	24.2	-
- average number for individuals	40.7	33.8	-
- average number for IPFs	26.5	19.0	-
number of companies sold off completely	196	268	464
- in % of all companies supplied	19.8%	31.1%	27.9%

a Czech Republic only
b Data adapted by the part common to both waves

Source: Centre for Voucher Privatization; own calculation

value of the firms supplied. Clearly, funds can draw from economies of scale and scope in information gathering. Besides, because of their frequently excellent contacts to company directors, politicians and ministry officials, they may - legitimately or not - gain from insider information not accessible to individual investors.

- *Competence*: Even if individual voucher holders are well informed, they will not necessarily have the competence to interpret their information in a profitable way. IPFs, however, bundle up scarce branch and investment know-how that is distributed very unevenly among the eligible citizens. On informationally inefficient markets, they can be expected to perform better than naive individual investors.

- *Put options*: The decisive incentive encouraging individuals to buy voucher books were put options offered by many IPFs. *Harvard Capital & Consulting* (HC&C), an investment company managing several IPFs was the first privatization intermediary to launch a sweeping advertising campaign promising each person investing their entire voucher book with a HC&C fund the right to sell their IPF shares for CSK 10,035 to HC&C after one year. The holders of such an option could take advantage of a favourable movement in prices of IPF shares if their value after one year exceeded the promised sum. Passing most of the price risk to HC&C, in the worst case, they still could realize ten times the registration fee. The only risk left to them was the liquidity and seriousness of HC&C to eventually fulfil the promise. While HC&C's cleverness made it one of the biggest investment companies generated by voucher privatization, the successful acquisition strategy was soon copied by dozens of other investment companies. The IPFs of state-owned banks like Sporitelna (CZK 12,000) or Investicni (CZK 11,000) imitated Harvard just like the investment company of the insurance monopolist Ceská Pojistovna (CZK 15,000). In the end, the first wave's leading slogan 'tenfold certainty' made the funds the most prominent phenomenon of the whole programme.

Indeed, investors allocated some 70% of all voucher points to IPFs (73.3% in the Czech Republic, see Table 2.11). It is beyond doubt that the funds bear the main responsibility for the overwhelming popularity of and participation in the voucher scheme. Besides put options, some funds also offered to pay more modest amounts in cash (e.g. 2,000-3,000 crowns) to buy voucher books even prior to the start of the bidding procedure. Various banks granted loans, collateralized by a portion of the shares obtained with the voucher book, to the clients of their funds. However, many of the founders failed to keep their promise or paid off their shareholders after a considerable delay, because of either a lack of liquidity or of disregard for the agreement in absence of effective legal pressure. For instance, HC&C paid off its shareholders only briefly before the preliminary round of the second wave. Delays in the issuing of shares led to further criticism of the funds. Investors learnt from this experience and placed only 63.5% of all points with the IPFs in the second wave.[21] In particular, some large funds shirking their duty to pay off shareholders had to put up with losses of reputation and therefore also reduced demand for their shares.[22] Astoundingly, the funds' adverse behaviour apparently didn't harm the popularity of the whole programme. Attendance at the second wave reached 6.16 million and, hence, even topped the first-wave result of 5.95 million buyers of voucher books.

Fierce competition between 265 Czech first-wave IPFs triggered a strong selection process. Many funds were too small to survive. Their operational costs turned out to be higher than their returns through fees. 47 Czech IPFs of the first wave have merged before issuing their shares. Several small funds with a weak capital base have been liquidated. Nonetheless, the number of IPFs entering the second wave even topped the results of the first wave. The decisive factor for this phenomenon was the introduction of unit trusts with low operational costs. 349 IPFs were registered for the second wave, 155 of which were unit trusts (37 open-end and 118 closed-end trusts). In fact, only 58 out of 194 investment funds had been newly established. 133 of them had already participated in the first wave. The prospects of higher dividend payments due to lower costs of the unit trusts made them a very attractive investment vehicle. While they made up merely about 43% of all IPFs, they obtained 60% of all points consigned to the funds industry. Among the unit trusts, the open-end trusts were relatively more successful than the closed-end ones. The legal obligation to redeem certificates for the net asset value of their proportionate interest in the fund's portfolio (minus a transaction fee) apparently was more attractive for the majority of investors than the put options issued by many investment funds. The 37 open-end trusts, constituting some 10% of all IPFs, collected 22.2% of the points allocated to funds. Though, considering the initial illiquidity of the equity markets and a lack of access to financial means for most funds, the authorities had implemented some protection of open-end trusts by ordering a period of one to three years before the trusts could be opened and redemption could be demanded. After the termination of voucher privatization, roughly 344 investment companies and 481 IPFs operated on the Czech capital market.[23]

The bidding behaviour of funds and individual investors differed from each other in both waves. IPFs tended to place their points in earlier rounds. This was valid particularly for the large funds whose bidding strategy was largely influenced by the objective of not wasting points by the sudden termination of the 'game'. As pointed out by Wijnbergen & Marcincin (1995, p. 6), the put options of the investment companies exerted considerable pressure on the IPFs to avoid the expiry of points since unused points reduce the value of the assets from which funds can draw to pay off their customers. The introduction of uncertainty into the scheme therefore greatly deterred the most powerful players from disguising their preferences. The ministry's decision to terminate the game and the high degree of concentration of voucher points in the hands of just a few big players thus accelerated the incorporation of information into share prices through the bidding process. A certain asymmetry between funds and individual investors was also constituted by the return of IPF points in cases of reducible oversubscriptions. Suppose funds and individual voucher holders displayed, on aggregate, identical bidding behaviour, i.e. allocated identical proportions of their points to all companies. Then they would receive identical amounts of equity per point allotted to a given company as long as there was no reducible oversubscription. Yet, in the latter case, IPF demand is reduced until excess demand is eliminated. Individual investors obtain more stock per voucher point than funds whereas the IPFs get back part of their points. Anticipating this asymmetry, the funds may be under an additional pressure to invest sooner than individual voucher holders. Finally, early placings may reflect the IPFs' endeavour to get hold of strategic shares in certain companies. As average prices decreased in later rounds, IPFs also purchased more 'expensive' shares than individual bidders. In the second wave, differences in the bidding behaviour led to the curious situation that individual voucher holders, while having placed only 36.5% of all points, purchased more shares than the funds.

To clear as many markets for company shares as possible, the authorities made *ex ante* announcements of the last rounds in both waves. Moreover, they recommended all investors to repeat their investment decisions from the previous round in order to largely eliminate existing imbalances. The moral suasion turned out to be successful as both times over 50% of the extant stock was sold. In the Czech Republic, the remnants finally amounted to just 7.2% and 3.7% of the overall supply of the waves. The stock of 196 (19.84%) first-wave and 268 (31.13%) second-wave companies was sold off entirely. In another 293 corporations of the second wave, more than 95% of supplied stock was privatized and in only ten firms was less than half of the supplied equity sold.[24]

2.3.4 A Brief Intermediary Assessment of Voucher Privatization

In spite of various delays and protractions, the voucher programme has been realized most swiftly. After its start in April 1991, it took about four years to draft, examine, decide, improve and finally implement countless privatization projects. Voucher privatization ended on 28 February 1995 when the shares purchased in the second wave were consigned to the property accounts of the Security Centre. The first wave proceeded, from the commencement of the registration of citizens up to the end of the fifth bidding round, in 13 months. The second wave took 14 months. Within a relatively brief period, nearly half of the property of large SOEs has been transferred to the private sector. This is a unique feat, not only compared with the track record of other countries in the region. But since most SOEs have been privatized through a mix of methods, voucher privatization was also the key accelerator for other privatization methods. The tight timetable of the scheme, the adherence of which has been steadily and attentively controlled by an involved and therefore interested public, spurred on the authorities to make quick decisions and to take care of rapid implementations. The involvement of millions of voucher holders in the programme, i.e. the creation of a vast constituency with an irreversible interest in mass privatization, proved to be a powerful control device. The public pressure generated by the participation of large sections of the citizenry effectively bound the government as well as the institutions responsible for the preparation and implementation of privatization projects to the rules of the game and set strong incentives not to protract the whole process. To put it into the words of a political economist: By the arousal of high public demand for the 'good' privatization, the government successfully manipulated its own political incentive scheme so as to make sure that it would *ex post* stick to the privatization goals and timetable set up *ex ante*. From this viewpoint, the voucher scheme is an effective political hands-tying mechanism. It can be concluded that, wherever the speed and scope of ownership transfer matter, voucher privatization is an essential ingredient of the overall package of economic reform measures.

2.4 STATE OWNERSHIP AND CONTROL AFTER VOUCHER PRIVATIZATION

2.4.1 Privatization Halt after Voucher Privatization

What is frequently overlooked in view of the speed and depth of voucher privatization is that the government and the ministerial authorities involved in evaluating and approving privatization projects have hived off a small, but not negligible number of enterprises to remain in public hands and to be controlled by the NPF and the branch ministries until a politically adequate mode of privatization is found in the future. Unfortunately, as turned out soon after the termination of the voucher programme, the privatization of those strategic firms is fraught with many political and institutional uncertainties and risks.[25] By early 1997, the NPF was administering 57 shares in strategic enterprises with a total par value of CZK 170 billion. In addition, the fund was still to complete the approved privatization projects of some 700 firms in which it held equity stakes mostly of under 20%, but in some cases also of up to 100%. The face value of temporary holdings amounted to CZK 35 billion. In sum, the par value of strategic and temporary stakes was roughly equal to the overall value of stock alienated during the first wave of voucher privatization. Most shares are in companies of politically sensitive sectors like energy, banking or metallurgy & mining (see Table 2.12). Therefore, though Czech privatization may have been more vigorous than that of other countries in the region, it cannot yet be considered to be completed.

Table 2.12: Shareholdings of National Property Fund by sectors

All data as of October 1995	No. of firms in NPF portfolio		Overall share in NPF portfolio	
Sector	overall	strategic firms	by face value	by market value
Utilities	33	18	34.0%	39.0%
Transport & telecommunic.	40	3	10.0%	29.0%
Financial intermediation	5	5	5.0%	14.0%
Chemicals & pharmaceutic.	37	5	8.0%	9.0%
Metallurgy & mining	49	9	25.0%	4.0%
Foods, beverages & tobacco	113	3	2.5%	1.4%
Engineering & electronics	157	2	9.0%	1.1%
Services	94	3	1.0%	1.0%
Glass & ceramics	17	-	0.4%	0.5%
Trade	96	3	1.0%	0.4%
Textiles	55	1	2.0%	0.3%
Pulp & paper	31	-	1.0%	0.3%
Construction	84	2	1.0%	0.3%
Agriculture	87	-	0.5%	0.1%
Other branches	15	-	0.3%	0.1%

Source: NPF

After the winding up of the Ministry of Privatization in spring 1996, the drafting and decision-making procedure of privatization proposals on strategic enterprises became largely intransparent. What has been lacking ever since, is an institutional environment that clearly defines responsibilities and competences in this process. In fact, in 1996, privatization projects were approved and implemented only for three strategic firms, the steelmakers Nová hut and Vítkovice and telecommunications monopolist SPT Telecom.[26] All three projects provided merely for a partial denationalization of the companies in question and reserved a majority stake for the state at least for the next years. It seems that political priorities have shifted away from privatization after the successful implementation of the voucher scheme. Neither from the government, nor from the Ministry of Finance has any pressure been exerted on the line ministries to accelerate the completion of large-scale privatization. 31 of the strategic enterprises fall under the responsibility of the Ministry of Industry and Trade alone. Mere reliance upon the branch ministries' intrinsic motivation to give the whole process a new momentum and produce privatization proposals turned out insufficient. Considering the incentive structure of ministerial bureaucrats, this isn't amazing at all. The transfer of strategic stakes into private hands would considerably reduce the power and prestige of the ministries. Moreover, it would release them of one of their major tasks, i.e. participation in corporate control of core industrial and financial companies. The bureaucrats thus would saw off their own branch by spurring privatization. Due both to a lack of enforcement and of a definite timetable, the ministries didn't really feel bound to a swift termination of the entire process of large-scale privatization. From a political economy viewpoint, the parliamentary elections of May 1996 may have added to the reluctance of the authorities to present new privatization projects for sensible enterprises standing in the centre of public interest. Dwindled political support for the mid-right government coalition led to a drastic reduction of its voting share and forced Klaus, ultimately, to govern with a minority in parliament. The situation changed only when some members of the parliamentary opposition left for the government coalition, thus contributing to a stabilization of the political scenery. In January 1997, the government cabinet announced the speeding up of the privatization process again together with the transfer of strategic enterprises. The branch ministries were given two months to submit the overdue privatization proposals directly to the government.[27] Ultimately, the lesson to be drawn from the Czech experience is to define the institutional environment completely at the outset of privatization and to define a binding timetable for the transfer of all enterprises which are to end in private hands. It is much easier to do so in an early phase when a reform-oriented government still enjoys widespread political support than to postpone decisions till later when people are feeling the costs of transformation or have just reached the low of the transformation J-curve.

The privatization of the two mentioned steelmakers indicated a change in the attitude of the government towards the use of MBOs as means of privatization. The senior management teams of both companies bought one percent of the relevant firm along with an option for the purchase of a further 10-15% after five years. Both enhancement and price of the managerial stake are linked to the future performance of the firm, in particular a doubling of the stock price and the meeting of intermediate targets of restructuring which are checked by the government once every six months. The same approach allegedly shall be applied to the privatization of other companies, foremost if there is no foreign investor or political preferences preclude foreign capital from entering the company. Ministerial authorities emphasize, however, that this doesn't mean a new political priority for such leveraged MBOs in general. Outside investors are free to submit better proposals.

After some dubious experiences with foreign investors who didn't stick to their *ex ante* claimed investment targets (like e.g. in the case of the joint venture Skoda auto-Volkswagen), all sales contracts now include detailed investment timetables and high deterring penalties to hedge against *ex post* opportunism and deviations from the scheduled restructuring programme. This is also valid for non-strategic enterprises with long-approved privatization projects. For instance, when one of the leading chemical companies, Silon, was sold to the German direct investor Consil in mid-1996, the sale contract set up by the NPF stipulated that Consil has to invest CZK 900 million with the firm over the next six years. If it doesn't fulfil this contractual obligation, it must pay the part of the money it failed to invest with Silon to the NPF.

Another means used by the NPF to ensure restructuring through new owners and the going-concern of sold enterprises are so-called golden shares (*zlaté akcie*). Rather than classical ownership rights, they are provisions anchored in the corporate charter which grant the NPF certain well-specified veto rights. Normally, they have a time limitation of five years from the transfer of the company to the new owner. Their sense is not to enable the state to actively control company affairs detached from share ownership, but to grant that the owners take regard of several economic and social goals like the maintenance of the integrity of the firm (no asset stripping) and its primary business, the sticking to certain price limits or, quite often, the obligation not to sell company assets to foreign investors or to other buyers at all during a certain period of time. In the end, the function of golden shares is to limit the discretion of private investors. They may, for instance, serve to protect the going concern of so-called family silver, companies with a long tradition and an outstanding reputation which for political reasons are frequently to be transferred only to domestic owners. This is valid for the case of the famous liqueur maker Jan Becher-KV Becherovka, one of the strategic companies. In compliance with a preliminary privatization proposal drafted under the aegis of the relevant line ministry (Ministry of Agriculture) in October 1996, a maximum of 34% out of a total of 94% held by the NPF ought to be offered through public tender exclusively to a domestic investor. Concurrently he would obtain a call option for the purchase of more shares so as to receive a majority stake after two years provided he meets several 'very strict' performance criteria (Hospodárské noviny, no. 204, 17 October 1996, p. 6). Most important, the state would retain a golden share to prevent the private owner from selling the recipe of the liqueur and the trade mark. The same restrictions have been implemented already at the brewery Plzenský Prazdroj along with the obligation of the domestic owners not to sell their equity stakes for several years without prior approval by the NPF.

Yet, the legal basis of the 'golden share' is rather shaky. Neither the Commercial Code, nor any other Czech legislation provides for the implementation of non-equity-related direct intervention of the state in company affairs. So far, no offence against duties resulting from golden shares has come before the courts. Nor did anybody challenge the state of unduly constraining company owners in their business activities. Of course, this doesn't mean that no offences have been committed.

2.4.2   Reactive Control: The State as Company Owner

Notwithstanding the large equity stakes in many temporarily held and especially strategic enterprises (cf. Table 2.13 and Table 2.14) and the resulting high number of board seats[28] taken over by representatives of the fund, the NPF has always taken the line that its job is to divest state property and not actively to intervene in enterprise management.[29]

Table 2.13: Distribution of strategic NPF holdings by size*

Data as of January 1997, size of holding in %	$10 \leq$ s < 20	$20 \leq$ s < 40	$40 \leq$ s < 60	$60 \leq$ s < 80	$80 \leq$ s < 100	s $=100$	total
no. of firms	4	9	31	8	2	3	57

* s=share held by NPF

Source: NPF

While the process of large-scale privatization had been proceeded according to well-defined rules (apart from the depicted delays in the alienation of strategic enterprises), the responsibilities and competences for the execution of corporate control were quite wobbly. A lack of clear institutional arrangements triggered intensive bargaining among various line ministries, the Ministry of Finance and the NPF. In the end, governance competences were allocated on a case-by-case basis to the individual entities. The NPF ceded a good part of the control rights over its portfolio firms without a murmur as it wanted to focus on its original task to implement approved privatization projects. In addition its workforce of some 120 employees (1995) didn't allow a comprehensive execution of corporate control in hundreds of enterprises. As for strategic companies, the majority

Table 2.14: Selected strategic shareholdings of NPF

Sector & firm	total par value in million CZK (by 1-1-1997)	market capitalization in million CZK (by 10-6-1996)	NPF share in % (by 1-1-1997)
Utilities:			
CEZ	59,115	61,819	67.55
16 area energy distributors	486 - 3,869	747 - 4,824	45.93 - 59.13
Telecommunications:			
SPT Telecom	32,209	77,004	51.83
Ceské radiokomunikace [a]	2,260	8,552	70.49
Financial intermediation:			
IPB [a]	5,681	17,731	31.49
Komercní banka [a]	9,502	45,047	48.74
CSOB [a, b]	5,105	-	19.59
Ceská pojistovna (insurer) [a]	2,275	6,781	26.27
Ceská sporitelna [a]	7,600	21,513	45.00
Chemicals:			
Chemopetrol	10,479	13,570	19.57
Kaucuk	4,971	5,906	26.54
Chemické závody Sokolov [a]	1,815	n.a.	73.74
Metallurgy & mining:			
Mostecká uhelná	8,836	2,456	46.29
Nová hut	11,466	3,722	68.25
OKD	24,300	2,280	45.88
Severoceské doly	8,727	4,129	55.00
Vítkovice	13,279	706	68.31
Beverages:			
Plzenský prazdroj	1,939	666	17.07
Jan Becher – KV Becherovka [c]	427	-	94.00
Engineering:			
Aero Vodochody	7,863	716	61.83
Skoda Praha	558	658	54.77

a Market capitalization as of 9 January 1997

b CSOB is not listed at the Prague Stock Exchange. As of January 1997, CSOB's further owners were the Czech National Bank (26.5%), the Slovak National Bank (24.1%) and the Czech Ministry of Finance (19.6%).

c Jan Becher-KV Becherovka is not listed at the PSE.

Source: NPF, PSE, own calculations

of them have been being supervised by the Ministry of Industry and Trade. The informal nature of the agreements on the allocation of governance powers is stressed by the fact that ministerial delegates in the boardrooms have to personally sign a contract on the transfer of proxy rights with the fund. Ultimately, this led to a mix of representatives of various line ministries and the NPF at the boards of strategic as well as temporarily-held companies. The fund is allowed, too, to cede proxy rights to private agents and institutions like investment funds. It did so exclusively in the case of the RIF whose assets are formally owned by the NPF, but managed by a bank-sponsored investment company.

Likewise, there were no firm rules of conduct for the management of equity interests. Rather than the political authorities, the NPF itself had to draw up an internal code concerning how fund representatives have to behave when they are charged with the execution of property rights. The code was finished and approved by the NPF presidium no sooner than in January 1995. It stipulates that no fund representative is allowed to sit on the boards of more than three companies. Except for strategic enterprises, the NPF should attend the general meetings of companies in which its interest reaches at least 20% of the capital stock. In the beginning of 1995, its portfolio comprised 863 interests exceeding this threshold.[30] Furthermore, the fund may send its representatives to firms where it owns more than 25% of the capital stock (but doesn't have to do so). The representatives must have sufficient expertise and self-assertion 'to effectively get through the will of the state'. To make the job attractive for capable and competent managers, fund representatives are permitted to keep all of their board shares (otherwise the fund couldn't pay competitive salaries). The representatives at the general meetings as well as in the boardrooms have to exercise their voting rights in harmony with given guidelines and preceding consultations with the fund's equity interests department. The board delegates (who can be both NPF employees or external consultants) must write biannual reports on their activities. This duty is an important instrument of in-house monitoring and helps at the same time to centrally coordinate the fund's control activities.

The code also defines exactly the discretion of NPF representatives, stipulating in detail which activities have to be okayed *ex ante* by the fund's executive board. The decision scope of representatives in companies in which the fund is holding a stake over 50% is smaller than in firms with minor equity interests. For instance, board representatives may make their own decisions on capital increases or decreases up to 20% of the equity stock in firms where the fund is no majority owner. In other companies, any decision on changes of the capital stock have to be approved *ex ante* by the NPF.

In the judgement of most observers, the NPF's governance activities have been in general quite passive. Rather than to draft its own restructuring plans, the fund's main task is to protect the integrity of corporate assets during the privatization process and to keep a close eye on the behaviour of the incumbent management. This complies with the self-image of the fund. In the view of the NPF, its role as custodian of firm assets was of tremendous importance particularly in the early phase of the privatization:[31]

> The participation of employees of the NPF and competent employees of the line ministries is indispensable in this phase of the privatization process since the majority of managing and supervisory boards initially revealed a too high degree of dilettantism thereby seriously threatening the going concern of the corporations. Disastrous is, for instance, [their] ignorance of the Commercial Code, the Securities Act and so forth. In this context, it must be stated that the representatives appointed to the boards by the NPF are considered important pillars in most company organs (Fond národního majetku Ceské republiky, 1995).

In most companies, the fund has merely reacted to the policy run by the incumbent management and tried to adjust it to its own principles as defined in the code. It didn't try to implement any long-term corporate policy. Instead, its efforts have been directed towards keeping companies in a financial condition that renders possible their privatization in harmony with the relevant privatization project. Therefore, the fund's hands-off approach permitted *inter alia* the restriction of directors' shares to fixed limits and the implementation of a rather cautious dividend policy. In fact, the fund has frequently adjusted the distribution proposals of the management, but also of other minority owners and forced the firms to better retain the capital to finance restructuring. If the performance of the incumbent management was too weak in the view of the fund, it exchanged single managers or entire teams.[32] In companies with foreign direct investors like SPT Telecom (minority stake owned by a Dutch/Swiss consortium) or Skoda auto-Volkswagen (majority in hands of Volkswagen concern), the fund uses its board seats to monitor the restructuring of the majority owner passively and to intervene only in the event of the foreign partner offending against provisions from the sales contract.

So far, the reactive control line has been broken only in some highly indebted companies where the NPF has carried out active financial restructuring in cooperation with the Ministry of Finance and the state-owned loan hospital Konsolidacní banka which is affiliated to the Ministry. In general, financial restructuring is applied as a tool of privatization preparation in corporations where 'it is in the interest of the state for strategic and economic reasons to save the company'.[33] More concretely, capital infusions have been granted to preserve jobs, to blaze the trail for a subsequent direct sale to a pre-determined foreign investor or likewise to maintain key industries with a high importance for the sovereignty and integrity of the country. The last two reasons were decisive, for instance, for the comprehensive financial restructuring of the insolvent manufacturer of aviation products Aero Vodochody. A debt/equity swap carried out in 1996 provided Konsolidacní banka with a 31% stake in the company. Yet, the measure turned out no more than a temporary remedy. The company remained heavily depressed by its current liabilities like wages and social costs and was in urgent need of further capital injections. Not least because of the firm's strategic and political importance for the Czech airforce, the government approved a privatization project drawn up by the Ministry of Industry and Trade to channel another CZK 4.5 billion to the company in preparation for a public tender. The capital was transferred from the resources of the NPF (privatization revenues) and from Konsolidacní banka (ultimately drawing from privatization profits of the NPF, too). The new strategic partner, a Czech-American syndicate built by Boeing, McDonnell Douglas and the Czech Airlines, signed a management contract with the NPF and may acquire company shares gradually according to the fulfilment of the provisions of the contract.[34] Similar solutions have been created or proposed for the financial restructuring of a number of strategic and temporary NPF holdings, e.g. for the integration of the oil processing companies Kaucuk and Chemopetrol into the holding Unipetrol in combination with a strategic equity investment of an international oil consortium.[35]

The most vigorous state intervention in the restructuring process has surely occurred through the banking system. A considerable proportion of privatization revenues were assigned to the recapitalization and financial restructuring of the banks' asset sheets (see section 5.1.2). Moreover, there is some evidence that the state as major owner of the top four banks put the screws on the financial institutes to support some of its policy goals which didn't always comply with sheer profit maximizing. While it is difficult to prove, observers suppose the state to have induced banks to extend loans to troubled firms in 'strategic' (state-dominated) sectors like heavy industry (Pistor & Turkewitz, 1994, p. 44). Besides, as we will argue later, banks were used as means to finance the whole privatization process, sometimes also against their own will and risk preferences. On the other hand, it is an open secret that the state had lost its grip on IPB, the third biggest bank of the country, well before the privatization of the institute. As readily admitted by state officials, control of IPB had shifted to the senior management which was (and still is) supported by a number of allied firms with their own equity stakes in the bank. At the same time, in 1998, IPB was the first bank to be sold off completely to the private sector. And contrary to original plans to privatize all semi-public banks exclusively into the hands of domestic investors, the prospective buyers of the remaining banks will apparently be foreign financial institutions, too.[36]

NOTES

1. See also UNIDO (1992, p. 31)
2. Only a few dozen enterprises had been founded by the federation. Their asset value was equivalent to some 10% of the overall book value of voucher projects in the first wave of large privatization (Frydman et al., 1993, p. 72).
3. Kotrba & Svejnar (1994, pp. 160-163) present a broad overview of several competing groups of privatization proposals discussed in the parliament and the public.
4. Splits, liquidations and a lack of acceptable privatization proposals effected changes in the number of firms inserted into both waves. In the end, the actual numbers of privatized SOEs were 1,788 in the first and 1,459 in the second wave (See Czech Statistical Yearbook 1995, p. 442). At the close of 1993 and 1994, the Czech government approved additional lists containing another 467 enterprises to be privatized. However, as of 31 December 1994, concrete decisions on the privatization modus were made in only 31 cases.
5. In November 1991, the limit was reduced to 5%.
6. See e.g. Flek (1993, p. 5).
7. The ministry's staff contained some 160 persons, spread over six departments. Each department was specialized in the evaluation of projects concerning the privatization of SOEs of certain sectors or branches, i.e. industry, trade, other manufacturing sectors, non-manufacturing sectors and health care (two departments from mid-1993) and agriculture (two departments until mid-1993). The departments' work was internally reviewed by three independent commissions, each of them consisting of four members. Decisions on controversial projects were made by the minister's commission comprising the Minister of Privatization, his deputies and some experts.
8. This is confirmed by Kotrba (1995, pp. 180-194) who presents rich empirical evidence on the strategies of different groups of submitters of privatization projects.
9. Furthermore, the strict timetable of the voucher programme forced the ministry to speed up the decision-making on projects including voucher privatization. Privatization projects for the second wave of the voucher programme had to be reviewed by the end of December 1993 in order not to delay the publishing of the supply list of enterprises inserted into the second wave. Consequently, the projects approved since January 1994 did not include voucher privatization.
10. Kotrba (1995, p. 194 f.) presents a sample of 201 companies, 46 of which attracted only one privatization project submitted by the management. All 46 basic projects without competition could be approved instantaneously.
11. For example, assume an SOE split into altogether five units proposed by two approved privatization projects. This would mean that company equity is divided into five tranches each of which is transferred through another method, e.g. one tranche is inserted into the voucher programme, a second one is sold through an auction, the third one is transferred for free to municipalities and so forth.
12. Originally, 942 Czech, 487 Slovak and 61 federal transformed SOEs had entered the first wave of the voucher programme. Their aggregate face value was CSK 323,100 million for the Czech, CSK 114,400 million for the Slovak and CSK 25,400 million for the federal enterprises. In the run-up to the split of former Czechoslovakia, the federal corporations had been distributed among both republics so that 988 Czech and 503 Slovak enterprises finally underwent voucher privatization. Besides, the value of property earmarked for the voucher scheme had to proportionally correspond with the number of participating citizens in both republics because individuals and IPFs were allowed to allocate points to companies in both their own as well as the other republic. In the end, the face value of the property of Slovak

enterprises joining the first wave of the voucher scheme was cut to CSK 86,900 million. With 5.98 million Czech and 2.58 million Slovak citizens registered for the first wave, the ratio of property per participating citizen amounted to CSK 35,540 for the Czech and CSK 33,682 for the Slovak Republic.

13. A third subsidiary of the NPF, the Equalization Investment Fund, had been established to adjust changes in the balance sheets of enterprises which occurred between the valuation date and the day when balance sheet data of firms contributing to voucher privatization were published. Between the two days, the value of company stock could have changed. This could lead to unjustified discriminations against voucher investors who had to make their investment decisions based on outdated information. The Equalization Investment Fund ought to level out such changes by channelling assets from companies with an increase in stock value to those with a decline. Thereby, it ensured a horizontal wealth adjustment among shareholders.

14. The registration offices were the basic processing site of the voucher programme. They collected the registrations of citizens for both waves. It was at the filing counters that individual voucher holders could submit their orders in the single privatization rounds. 458 of the registration offices and 3,492 of the filing counters of the first wave were located in the Czech Republic.

15. Considering all shares included in the first wave, each voucher book tallied with a face value of some CSK 34,980.

16. This limit was given by the denomination of investment certificates in value classes between 100 and 1,000 voucher points. The investment certificates can be interpreted as 'means of payment' for sales of company shares while the voucher points constitute the currency 'units' of the bidding process.

17. Each participant in voucher privatization, no matter whether individual or IPF, had his own account where shares had to be consigned. After each round, account statements were mailed to the respective owners.

18. The share prices of firms with low demand in the preceding two rounds had been reduced up to as little as 97 shares for 100 points in the case of one company. The CVPs of each republic were empowered to adjust share prices of companies whose headquarters are on the territory of the given republic. Interestingly, the adjustment paths for Czech and Slovak companies took very divergent courses. Demand for Slovak companies turned out to be dramatically minor so that the decrease in prices after the second round was substantially larger in Slovakia. In fact, the third-round prices of Slovak corporations averaged less than one half of the prices in the Czech Republic (17.89 as against 39.22). As the partition of ex-Czechoslovakia was approaching, transfers of share ownership between both republics produced political difficulties and a delay of the completion of the first wave. Due to the relative lack of demand for Slovak companies, Slovak investors were going to acquire significantly more shares of Czech firms than vice versa (22.25 million shares as against 6.00 million shares, IPFs included. Considering the owner structure of IPFs, the difference is even bigger.). This brought about a sizeable increase in foreign capital in the newly established Czech Republic.

19. While the voucher scheme aimed at quick alienation of stock by simulating a market, it should be mentioned that supply prices only converged towards the price level on hypothetical (and perfect) markets. For all shares handed out in the course of the various rounds, prices were - in comparison with this notional benchmark - too high (undersubscription) or too low (reducible oversubscription). In the former case, investors accepting bids basically pay a premium over the equilibrium price on a cleared market. Hanousek (1996, p. 11) turns attention to this point. In the reverse case, the artificial cut of IPF demand allows individual investors to obtain shares of oversubscribed firms at too low prices.

20. The sudden run on voucher books induced the authorities to prolong the registration period for half a month until mid-February.

21. This must also be partially put down to the experience accumulated by investors dealing with market institutions during the 20 months lying between the preliminary rounds of both waves. In the meantime, investors' faith in their own skills of making good investment decisions had grown. On the other hand, this fact indirectly confirms the high relevance of the competence argument put forward above for the initial phase of transition.

22. In the first wave ten IPFs disposed of some 56% of all voucher points passed over to funds. The ten biggest IPFs of the second wave acquired 35% of all points consigned to funds.
23. The estimated number of 344 founders of IPFs is taken from Mejstrík (1994, p. 10).
24. On the other hand, 1.2% of the voucher points in the first wave and 3.3% of those of the second wave remained unused. Only a tiny part of them comes from the IPFs. Probably most funds gave a high priority to using up all points for image and marketing reasons. After the five bidding rounds of the first wave, there were left 498 unlucky individual investors with all 1,000 voucher points unused. The second wave ended disastrously for 277 citizens who failed to make only one successful bid.
25. As Pistor & Turkewitz (1994, p. 29) phrase it: 'The decision to renounce exclusive voucher privatization was not in all cases a decision to retain ownership, but it was a decision to accept a much higher level of uncertainty concerning the rate and extent of the shrinkage of state holdings.'
26. In 1995, no decision on completing the privatization of strategic enterprises had been reached.
27. According to Klaus, it was a mistake not to maintain the original privatization pace and to leave strategic enterprises in a unduly long state of pre-privatization agony: 'I know very well that many productive assets have been lost during this period' (Hospodárské noviny, 26 March 1997, p. 1). As a matter of fact, painful delays in the privatization of strategic companies are also to be put down to more indirect causes. For example, projects on the privatization of the utilities companies which make up some 39% of the NPF's share portfolio by market value so far couldn't be drafted because the government hasn't been able to decide on the mode of price regulation for the highly-monopolized energy sector.
28. According to the former head of the equity interests department of the NPF, Pavel Sanda (1995, p. 31), in early 1995 NPF employees had seats in 177 companies out of a total of about 1,400 firms in the fund's portfolio.
29. This stance has been expressed repeatedly by the former chairman of the fund's executive board Tomás Jezek and maintained by its successor Roman Ceska: ' ... the fund's task is to privatize firms, not to manage them' (Lidové noviny, 11 September 1996, p. 12).
30. Nevertheless, the fund was not prevented from sending its delegates to the meetings of firms in which it owns lower stakes.
31. Quoted from the 'Principles for the participation of NPF employees and employees of other organizations in the organs of joint-stock and other companies', appendix no.1 to the decree no. 1/1994 to the NPF Codex (Fond národního majetku Ceské republiky, 1995).
32. Personnel intervention could be observed e.g. in the case of furniture producer TON Bystrice. The NPF holds a 45% temporary stake in the firm. At the general meeting in March 1996, the NPF rejected the proposals for the personnel composition of the company organs made by the firm's managing board. The fund submitted and got through its own proposal providing for more NPF representatives on both boards. The composition approved by the fund-dominated general meeting is to be maintained until the termination of implementation of the company's privatization project. Afterwards, the new owners ought to convene an extraordinary general meeting to take over control of the firm.
33. Klaus in Hospodárské noviny, 17 October 1996, p. 1.
34. As of summer 1997, the Czech government is discussing the granting of a state guarantee for the purchase of 72 jet fighters to Aero still prior to the testing of the first prototypes which is scheduled for next year (Právo, 9 June 1997, p. 15). Such a guarantee would not only ensure the company full order books for years, but also contribute to financial restructuring more indirectly through a considerable reduction of the interest rate charged on loans to be extended by both domestic and foreign banks to the aircraft manufacturer.
35. The government also played a dominant role in the privatization cum restructuring of the big engineering conglomerate Skoda Plzen. In cooperation with the new (individual) main owner and two banks, it not only rearranged the financial liabilities of the firm, but also reorganized its entire internal structure. The case is depicted in depth in Hayri & McDermott (1995). Other examples for financial restructuring by the state are the recapitalization of tractor manufacturer Zetor Brno and debt reliefs for car maker Tatra Koprivnice and the CKD holding Praha.
36. After the volte-face of the government concerning FDI, the Japanese investment bank Nomura became a strategic partner of the bank.

3 Voucher privatization and the evolution of ownership structures

3.1 RELEVANT PORTFOLIO REGULATION OF FINANCIAL GROUPS

3.1.1 Initial Regulatory Environment of Investment Companies and IPFs

In general, governments implementing a mass privatization scheme can follow two different approaches to voucher intermediaries. Firstly, in pursuance of a top-down approach, they may regulate the occurrence and role of IPFs in detail. This reflects a rather interventionistic stance emphasizing the priority of corporate control, but also revealing some distrust in the ability of the market to provide for spontaneous solutions. The Polish mass privatization programme is the most prominent example for the top-down construction of IPFs. It entails the obvious danger of politicizing enterprise control in the aftermath of privatization (Wagener, 1994, p. 21). The Czechoslovak authorities favoured a more evolutionary or laissez faire approach. Before the start of the voucher programme, it had been anticipated that the vast majority of voucher holders would prefer to invest their points directly into the companies supplied (Skalický, 1994, p. 18). While it was recognized that funds could be a remedy against a lack of corporate control in widely-held companies, their role and importance were not really politically defined. This liberal stance towards privatization intermediaries mirrors confidence in the ability of the market to find a solution for the control problem. Moreover, it leaves the decision on the emerging ownership patterns to the preferences of individual voucher holders and the entrepreneurial initiative of both domestic and foreign founders of IPFs.

It was assumed that the big players on the funds market would be the large domestic commercial banks. With their insider knowledge about supplied enterprises, nation-wide branch networks and reputation, they had a clear edge over eventual competitors. As the banks, with one striking exception, joined the voucher scheme only with a part of their equity stock, control over banks remained for the time being with the state. State control over banks and a clear underestimation of the future role of the IPFs were the main reasons for a virtually complete regulatory vacuum of IPF activities. The Law on Large-scale Privatization of April 1991 only stipulated that voucher points could be used for direct investment into enterprises and for the purchase of shares in 'commercial companies' founded exclusively for the intermediation of points in the voucher scheme, provided those companies obtained a licence from the Ministry of Privatization. Pauly & Tríska (1994, pp. 31 f.) point out that the original version of the law even missed specifying the legal form of the funds. A government decree from September 1991 hastily determined that the 'commercial companies' had to be read as joint-stock companies. The licensing procedure was carried out most smoothly, the requirements to the candidates were rather soft. Mainly, the following criteria had to be fulfilled for the creation of an IPF:

- The founder had to be equipped with one million crowns for each IPF set up.
- The founder had to take responsibility for the fund's management. He himself as well as the mandataries sitting on the boards of the IPF had to possess the necessary managerial and technological know-how to carry on the businesses of the fund. The decree failed, however, to specify the professional qualifications more clearly. The know-how requirement could therefore never be policed and rather treated as recommendation.
- The founding equity of the fund had to be exactly 100,000 CSK and could be increased no sooner than after the completion of the first wave of voucher privatization. The low capital requirement had been deduced from the 1990 Joint-Stock Company Act, the first and still very preliminary codification of legal norms regulating structure and economic activities of Czechoslovak joint-stock corporations. Already on 1 January 1992, the act was replaced by the more sophisticated Commercial Code requiring a minimum capital of one million crowns. This provision was relevant for all IPFs of the second wave if they operated as joint-stock companies.
- The IPF had to inform about its business principles concerning risk diversification, investment specialization on certain industries or regions, liquidity of assets and dividend policy.
- A contract between the IPF and its founder had to specify the management fees to be paid to the founder and the content and frequency of publication of reports.

In addition, the Czechoslovak legal environment provided for a modest number of provisions indirectly concerning IPFs. For instance, the Law on Large-scale Privatization contained a clause prescribing that SOE managers need special government approval for the establishing of subsidiaries. The original objective of this clause was to prevent spontaneous privatization, as observed in Poland and Hungary, by imposing constraints on the disposal of SOE assets (Pauly & Tríska, 1994, p. 34). In the context of voucher privatization, it was assumed that the management of an SOE could establish an IPF in order to invest voucher points in its own company and hence to entrench itself against any control from outside. As a consequence, licences for IPFs founded by SOEs were issued rather seldom. This is why only one of the large financial groups arisen from voucher privatization has been founded by an industrial holding. The investment company Expandia, set up by the chemical giant Chemapol, was the second most successful player of the second wave when it collected more than 300 million voucher points.

Nevertheless, for other founders it was quite easy to obtain a licence. The liberal regulatory approach of the authorities motivated countless financial institutions as well as private entrepreneurs to set up IPFs. After the registration deadline for funds participating in the first wave had expired on 31 December 1991, as many as 429 IPFs entered the programme, 265 of which with the permission of the Czech Ministry of Privatization.[1] The decisive hurdle to be taken was for most founders the short registration deadline only some three months after the publishing of the decree. It made some prospective founders put off their investment activities until the second wave. On the other hand, some founders, predominantly banks, set up even more than one IPF. Agrobanka, the biggest private bank, led the ranking of bank-sponsored investment companies with 17 funds; PIAS, the investment company of Investiční a poštovní banka (IPB), followed with 12 funds. The famous HC&C established 23 funds in the second wave only. Another, yet smaller private sponsor, Cistá reka (Clean River), set up 17 IPFs for the same wave. The overall number of Czech investment companies joining one or both waves of voucher privatization was 186.

This surprising feedback gave rise to a hot political debate on the insufficiency of funds regulation, culminating in an amendment of the mentioned government decree and the passing of a new Law on Investment Companies and Investment Funds on 28 April 1992, some months after the completion of the preliminary round in which points had been consigned to IPFs. The *ex post* legislation concerned both the IPFs' own governance structure and their investment activities (asset structure of portfolio). The most important stipulations concerning the governance structure of IPFs were:[2]

- IPFs can be run exclusively by investment companies which must sign a management contract with the firm. Their founders thus had usually to set up an investment company. Management fees are limited to a maximum of 2% of the average value of the fund portfolio or 20% of its annual profit.
- From the second wave, IPFs have been permitted to be run as unit trusts in addition to joint-stock companies.[3] Unit trusts are no legal entities. They are operated by the founder (investment company) while their property is owned jointly by all investors. Instead of shares, they issue ownership certificates without voting rights. Legislation provides for closed-end as well as open-end

unit trusts. The certificates of open-end unit trusts (*otevrené podílové fondy*) have to be repurchased by the founder at any time while those of closed-end trusts (*uzavrené podílové fondy*) cannot be redeemed but only traded at the capital market. The main advantage of unit trusts as compared to investment funds in the form of joint-stock companies are lower operation costs. For instance, they do not have to incur costs from the organization of annual general meetings.
- Funds have to deposit their liquid means and securities with banks.
- IPFs must not issue bonds.
- Finally, certain groups of persons are precluded from taking seats in the company bodies of IPFs. This related particularly to government officials and civil servants who sat often on IPF boards. It does not lack a certain piquancy that the same bureaucrats sometimes had been deeply involved in the implementation of the voucher programme (Mejstrík, 1994, p. 5). Potential conflicts of interest arising from such constellations should be avoided.[4]

The law also stipulates that IPFs and investment companies may not exert any business other than the administration of asset portfolios. In addition, the law determines disclosure obligations of funds and, in cases of unit trusts, investment companies. They are most liberal, too. The funds or investment companies have to publish information about their economic activities twice a year and the audited annual accounts once a year.[5] Besides, they must publish a prospectus containing information about the investment and dividend policy, the board members and the management fees of an IPF.

The following provisions should grant sufficient diversification of IPF portfolios and thus contribute to the protection of investors. They considerably influenced the funds' investment activities during both waves. The most important regulations affecting the asset structure of the fund portfolios were:

- IPFs are not allowed to hold more than 20% of the equity of one firm. All IPFs managed by one investment company may jointly hold up to 40% of one company.[6] This limit has been later reduced to 20%.
- An equity stake in one firm must, in turn, not exceed 10% of all assets held by one fund and 20% of the assets of all funds managed by the same investment company. The latter provision is, of course, redundant since the 10%-limit for each single IPF already implies that the company's overall stake in one firm cannot legally exceed 10% of its overall assets.
- The maximum value of assets managed by funds or trusts of one investment company or a group of such companies with the same founder-manager may not go beyond 10% of the value of all assets hold by IPFs holding a licence to operate in the country.
- IPFs may not acquire shares or certificates of other IPFs or other investment companies. Nor are they allowed to purchase shares of entities holding a stake of more than 25% in the given fund or its investment company. IPFs and

investment companies founded by banks or insurance companies may not buy shares of any financial institutions.

The last provision ought to prevent excessive concentration of power in the hands of banks. It should also prevent banks from forming competition-reducing alliances through ownership links and from mutual assistance to get entrenched. As we will see, in practice, this legal intention has not been enforced too consequently. The limitation of holdings to 20% of the equity of one firm mirrors political concern that the funds may become too powerful rather than care for sufficient diversification. Obviously it should encourage funds to cooperate in corporate governance and prevent excessive concentration of economic power in the hands of some large IPFs. The limitation was strongly opposed by the then Minister of Finance Václav Klaus who believed (and still believes) that strict regulation also restricts competition.[7]

3.1.2 Later Amendments to the Regulation of Investment Companies and IPFs

One of the prime criticisms of the initial regulation of investment funds was targeted at restrictions limiting funds to owning stakes of no more than 20% of one joint-stock company. Critics argued that corporate governance and monitoring of a company were seriously impaired by this provision. Only by being allowed to attain and hold a larger stake giving funds the option to become majority owners would there be an incentive to actively take control of a company and impose restructuring measures. After extensive discussions, an amendment of the Investment Companies and Investment Funds Act (InvAct) passed in April 1996 was as a consequence written to allow for such majority ownership - although still not for a single fund, but rather by relaxing the prohibition for investment companies. The provisions are fairly straightforward. If an investment company manages several funds, then it can accordingly combine the stakes of different funds in one company to take a majority influence. Yet, investment funds are further restricted to only being allowed to invest up to 10% of their portfolio in one single company (§24(3) InvAct) and barred from owning the stock of companies holding an interest in the fund exceeding 25% (§24(7) InvAct). Figure 3.1 gives an overview of the new regulations on investment companies, investment funds and unit trusts.[8]

Originally, the proponents of the amendment envisioned two classes of investment funds: 'portfolio' funds and 'managerial' funds. The law reflects this distinction by allowing - as mentioned - investment companies to combine funds' shares beyond the original 20% limit. This boils down to a managerial fund, since active monitoring is made possible. In turn, these

Figure 3.1: Portfolio restrictions on financial groups*

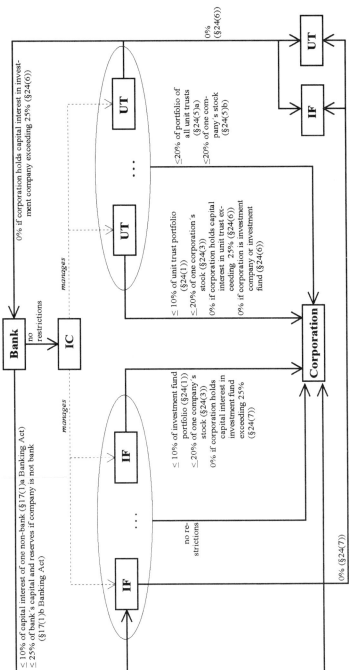

* Regulatory environment after the InvAct amendment of April 1996; IC = Investment Company, IF = Investment Fund, UT = Unit Trust; if not specified, sections refer to the Investment Companies and Investment Funds Act.

funds would be submitted to strict provisions on mandatory disclosure - detailed in paragraph 6.3.2. On the other hand, unit trusts managed by the same investment company may not (singularly or accumulated) exceed the 20% limit.[9] These funds would be acting as passive 'portfolio' funds. This distinction was made somewhat irrelevant by the conversion of funds into industrial holding companies (joint-stock corporations) since early 1996; these entities do not face any restrictions concerning the size of ownership stakes and in addition have to fulfil less strict disclosure requirements.[10]

3.1.3 Regulation of Banks and Proxy Voting

The Czech Banking Act provides for universal banking, permitting commercial banks to hold shares in companies and thus to participate in equity control. This is important in the context of the emerging Czech financial groups as it makes possible joint equity control through both bank-sponsored funds and the founder-banks themselves. However, the law restricts shareholdings of banks to 10% of the equity of non-banks. In addition, no single holding is allowed to exceed 25% of a bank's equity and reserves and a bank must not own stakes in other banks. In turn, to avoid self-dealing and the entrenchment of bank management, unit trusts operated by bank-sponsored investment companies may not hold any stakes in the mother bank if the latter owns more than 25% of the investment company. The same is valid for investment funds in which a bank holds a stake higher than 25%.

Banks can enhance their governance potential through two channels. Firstly, Czech law does not encourage strict firewalls between the banks and their investment company subsidiaries. It only stipulates that board members and employees of investment funds 'are obligated to treat as confidential all facts concerning the business interests' of an investment company or investment fund. In particular, law does not prevent directors and employees of the banks from getting involved in the management of the funds. Banks therefore can (and - as shown in the next chapter - largely do) disregard fire walls between themselves and their investment companies. Of course, this allows banks and their funds to pool information to realize economies of scale and scope in the execution of corporate control. Moreover, personal ties considerably tighten the banks' grip of funds and portfolio companies.

The second possibility is to offer proxy services to their clients. The latter issue has not yet been publicly discussed in the country. The Commercial Code at the beginning of the provisions on the general meeting of a joint-stock company (§184 (1) CCode) generally allows for representation of shareholders:

(1) (...) A shareholder participates in the general meeting in person or through a representative (proxy) holding a written power of attorney. (...)

Analysing the relevant section of the Securities Act, the law would allow for a similar procedure as in Germany - the so-called *Depotstimmrecht*. There, an individual's shares are commonly held by a custodian, usually that individual's bank. Unless the shareholder explicitly instructs the custodian bank on how to vote his stock at the according general meeting, the bank will vote the share as if it owned the securities. This practice has come under increasing criticism in Germany, with criticism focusing on an excessive influence of banks on corporate affairs. Nonetheless, it represents an important tool for large shareholders to consolidate their influence.

The Securities Act provides for the possibility of offering the service of depositing and administering the shares of an individual. The depositary, concluding a contract with the depositor (shareholder), may only be a bank or a securities dealer. Under such a contract, the depositary is empowered (authorized) to exercise the voting right attached to the security. In turn, the depositor undertakes to pay the depositary a fee. The difference from German procedures is the fact that German banks have been benefiting (at least historically) from the physical necessity of share custody. This was due to the sheer physical existence of shares. Frequently, banks thus had virtually no transaction costs attracting customers to deposit their shares with them. As shares of privatized corporations in the Czech Republic are so-called registered shares, there is no need for shareholders to actually deposit their shares for reasons of security. What could, though, possibly evolve from this specific legislation is a proxy service for small shareholders as envisaged for Germany.[11] The legal provision of only banks or securities dealers being allowed to offer this service reduces the possible number of service suppliers, but doesn't make the provision itself impossible. Banks may have incentives to create a good reputation as proxy administrators. This may encourage them (and their funds) to carry out corporate control in the interest of small dispersed shareholders.

3.2 IPF PERFORMANCE DURING VOUCHER PRIVATIZATION

3.2.1 Marketing Strategies of Investment Companies

Different investment companies also ran different marketing and investment strategies to give themselves a clear profile (see Table 3.1). For the biggest banks, Sporitelna (savings bank) and Komercn, it was more or less sufficient to rely upon their extended branch networks and their reputation. Each of them pooled all voucher points attracted in a given wave exclusively in one fund with a quite fuzzy investment strategy.[12] The other two large state-owned banks, Investicní and Obchodní, tried to meet the time- and risk preferences of various classes of investors by diversification of their funds. Obchodní's investment company Kvanto set up both a dividend and a growth fund. Investicní's company PIAS even established an intricate family of 12 funds. Five of them were unit trusts, three closed-end and two open-end trusts.[13] PIAS followed a two-track marketing strategy. On one hand, it set up dividend and growth funds like Kvanto. On the other hand, it also diversified its funds over various branches, establishing sectoral funds for banking, energy, food, commerce and so forth. The strategy proved to be successful at least for the first wave when the funds collected 8.5% of all available voucher points and PIAS was the second most successful investment company topped only by Sporitelna (11.1%) which gained from its unbeatable branch network, its good contacts to the small savers and the highest redemption promise of the big state-owned banks (CSK 12,000).[14] It is striking that the success of the big bank-sponsored investment companies is correlated to the value of their put options. With comparatively similar retail networks, Investicní's promise to pay CSK 11,000 for each fully obtained voucher book was probably decisive in its lead over Komercní which abstained from announcing any buy-back promise and consequently gathered merely two thirds of Investicní's points.

3.2.2 First-wave Performance of IPFs

Most of the small and medium investment companies had been founded by private entrepreneurs or cooperatives. In terms of finance, they could not compete with the big companies sponsored by financial institutions. As they did not have comparable credit lines to cover start-up, operational and advertising costs, they frequently tried to shape a clear profile by focusing on one sector or region. Sometimes they also cooperated with local enterprises and tried to persuade citizens to invest in the funds in order to support 'their' local industry or to gain control over it. Other investment companies attempted to draw investors by cultivating a certain image. They promised to use company stakes to implement an ecologically oriented corporate policy or chose the names of important persons of Czech history like the national Saint Wenceslas (Václav).[15] Some funds used catch words like 'top profit' or 'success 2000' to attract points. The second biggest investment company after the two waves, HC&C, successfully alluded to traditional Czech enthusiasm about America by including 'Harvard' in its name.[16] However, the enormous lead of HC&C over the remaining privately founded investment companies is based upon its bold and innovative overall marketing strategy. They not only invented the put option for voucher investors, but also swiftly built up an effective network of sales agents, often students and pupils directly acquiring customers still before the preliminary round at the filing counters and registration offices where citizens bought voucher books. Interestingly, some private funds benefited from the individual popularity of their founders. For instance, one fund was founded by a former tennis professional, another one by a rock star who concurrently held a seat in the Czechoslovak parliament. The latter fund, Trend, belongs to the most successful medium-sized IPFs of the second wave.[17]

Table 3.1: IPF marketing strategies

IPF families:	*Branches:*
PIAS (IPB group) (12 funds)	Bohemia Crystal
Agrobanka (17 funds)	Pivovarnický IF (Brewers' IF)
Cistá reka (Clean river, 17 funds)	První strojírenský IPF (First IPF of
HC&C (31 funds)	mecanical engineering)
	Stavební fond (Fund of the building
	industry)
Reputation:	IPF energetiky a chemického prumyslu
Sporitelní privatizacní (bank)	(IPF of the energy and chemicals
IPF Komercní banky (bank)	industry)
Trend (managed by musician and	
member of parliament)	*Agriculture:*
Srejber tennis investing (managed by	Agrofond
former tennis star)	Rolnický IF (peasant IF)
	Lesnickodrevarský IPF (IPF of forestry
	and timber industry)
Slogan:	Mlékárenský zemedelský (IPF of dairy
Valuta	farming)
Top profit	
Fond jistoty (Safety fund)	*Regions:*
Profesionální IF Garance (Professional	Proregio
IF guarantee)	První jihoceský IF (First South
Uspech 2000 alfa (Success 2000 alfa)	Bohemian IF)
Harvardský Diamantový IF (Harvard	První budejovický IF (First IF of the city
diamond IF)	of Budweis)
	IPF Obcanu západních Cech (IPF of the
	citizens of Western Bohemia)
Image:	
IF pro ekologii a recyklaci (IF for	*Branches and regions:*
ecology and recycling)	Moravský energetický fond (Moravian
První Václavuv IF (First Wenceslas IF)	energy fond)
Komenius-zelený fond prosperity	Moravskoslezský potravinárský IPF
(Comenius-green fund of prosperity)	(Moravian-Silesian food IPF)

IF = Investment Fund

In sum, several factors were critical for the relative success of IPFs in the first wave. In general banks had great success in collecting points due to their reputation (see Table 3.2). This is also true for foreign banks like

Zivnostenská and Creditanstalt which didn't offer put options. Factors like put options and the size of the branch network positively contributed to the individual results of the state-owned banks. Put options seem to explain to a certain degree, too, the good standing of the private investment company PPF (CSK 11,000) and the insurance company Ceská Pojistovna (CSK 15,000). Indeed, with one of the highest put options, Ceská Pojistovna managed to come close to the results of the big banks without disposing of a similar network of branches. HC&C is the undisputed star among all private companies. Its clever marketing strategy made it in the eyes of the broad public the archetype of all IPFs. Other companies like PPF could copy Harvard's success on a lower level.

Table 3.2: Largest investment companies in voucher privatization

investment company (IC)	over-all rank	founder	voucher pts. acquired (in million) in			% of[a]	
			1st wave	2nd wave	total	IPF pts.	total pts.
SIS (Savings Bank)	1	state bank	950	124	1,074	13	9
Harvard Cap. & Consult.	2	private	639	292	931	11	8
PIAS (IPB group)	3	state bank	724	98	822	10	7
IKS Komercní Banky	4	state bank	466	124	590	7	5
KIS (C. Pojistovna)	5	insurer	334	187	521	6	4
A-Invest (Agrobanka)	6	private bank	111	320	431	5	4
Expandia (Chemapol)	7	holding	-	306	306	4	3
Kvanto (CSOB Bank)	8	state bank	50	198	248	3	2
PPF	9	private	118	130	248	3	2
Creditanstalt	10	foreign bank	166	80	246	3	2
YSE	11	private	70	156	226	3	2
Czech Coupon Invest	12	private	35	152	187	2	2
Zivnostenská	13	private bank	118	60	178	2	1
IS Podnikatelu	14	private	-	157	157	2	1
CS Fondy	15	private	50	94	144	2	1
MorCe IS	16	private	-	113	113	1	1
CSFB	17	foreign bank	n.a.	70	> 70	1	1
Trend	18	private	n.a.	60	> 60	1	1
4 ICs by state banks	-	state banks	2,190	544	2,734	33	22
top 8 bank-founded ICs	-	banks	>2,585	1,074	>3,559	43	29
top 3 ICs[b]	-	-	2,313	918	2,827	34	23
top 9 ICs[b]	-	-	3,626	1,898	5,523	66	45
all ICs	-	-	4,450	3,920	8,360	100	68

a   Data provide for 120 million voucher points transferred from Slovak individuals to Czech IPFs.
b   Refers to biggest investment companies of given wave or of both waves together respectively.

Source: Mejstrík (1994), Roland Berger & Partner, Centre for Voucher Privatization, own calculations. First-wave data for Kvanto, YSE and Czech Coupon are author's estimations based upon Mejstrík (1994).

During the first wave, the bidding behaviour of investment companies was heavily influenced by the amount of attracted voucher points. The priority of most bank-founded companies like SIS and Komercní was to let as few points expire as possible. The quality of firms was secondary. This led to a stampede of bidders in the early rounds and to comparably high share prices. Consequently, sales prices tended to decrease over the bidding rounds. In the fourth and fifth round, they averaged less than half the level of the first round and were even below one third of the average of the second round (cf. Table 2.10). While the bank funds succeeded in minimizing expired points after the five rounds, the actual winners arising from the bidders' stampede were several small and medium-sized 'entrepreneurial' IPFs which had the nerves to wait and place their points in later rounds. This was the stated strategy of the second biggest private investment company of the first wave PPF (117.5 million points) and of YSE, a company managing the eleventh biggest single IPF of the first round with some 70 million voucher points. They both invested the lion's share of their points in the last two rounds. As it turned out after the first wave, the book value of one voucher book completely allotted to funds of the two investment companies was two times or three times the value of books invested with the bank-sponsored funds. The entrepreneurial private funds clearly outperformed their competitors in terms of aggregate book value and net asset value per voucher book.[18]

3.2.3   Second-wave Performance of IPFs

The relative success of private funds made many voucher holders change their investment decisions and place their points with YSE, PPF and other entrepreneurial funds. In relative terms, this caused a reallocation of points from the big state banks to small and medium-sized funds. While most funds issued very low or no redemption promises at all, now the first-wave performance of the funds became the most important decision criterion for citizens who refrained from direct investment. Many investors gave the big bank-sponsored funds the cold shoulder. SIS merely collected 12% of its first-wave points. The 'big three' bank companies (SIS, Komercní and PIAS) all slipped down to between 98 and 124 million points. HC&C suffered somewhat from its protracted share redemptions and mediocre first-wave performance as measured by book value. It gathered slightly less than 50% of the points of the first wave. Nevertheless, with nearly 300 million points, it was the third most successful company.[19]

Viewed as a whole, the distribution of points over funds was clearly more even in the second wave. In comparison with the first wave, two main winners can be identified among the IPFs. The leading company of the second wave was A-Invest, the investment subsidiary of the country's biggest private bank Agrobanka. The company had offered all citizens investing with its open-end trust a CZK 2,000 cash loan. The loan had been advertised and made available already weeks before the beginning of the preliminary round in which individual investors could allocate their points to IPFs. Backed by a portion of the shares purchased through voucher points and thus ultimately by the trust certificates, each loan was linked to the legal obligation to invest the whole voucher book with A-Invest. The whole action reminds one of the marketing success of HC&C in the first wave. Both investment companies started the canvass well before the preliminary round and applied innovative tools to make their investment services attractive to many citizens. Other companies imitated the successful campaigns but mostly couldn't overtake the innovative trailblazers. In the end, both HC&C and A-Invest rendered the voucher programme a great service by essentially increasing its popularity. As for the second wave, it was probably the many times copied marketing strategy of A-Invest that substantially contributed to the high participation rate (beating that of the first wave) and again secured the IPFs the majority of points. The most successful imitator of A-Invest was Expandia, the investment company of the powerful Chemapol group, which attracted as much as 306 million points. The financial support of the mother company enabled Expandia even to outperform the funds of the state banks in the second wave and to become the country's seventh biggest investment company after the termination of voucher privatization.

Yet, as a consequence of the higher amount of points consigned to the IPFs and of their more uneven distribution in the first wave, the second wave results could only slightly affect the overall ranking of the leading investment companies. Five out of the top six investment companies had been founded by financial institutions, four of them by domestic banks. The four state banks assembled roughly one third of all points allocated to IPFs and over 23% of the overall number of points invested in the course of voucher privatization. This demonstrates that they clearly had the capacity to become active owners raising their voice in the boardrooms of Czech corporations. The central meaning of banks for the emerging Czech capital market is also reflected by the fact that the investment subsidiaries of the state banks together with those of four private (both domestic and foreign) banks attracted nearly 43% of all IPF points, respectively 29% of total points. The most important company not founded by a financial intermediary is HC&C, far in front of Expandia, PPF and YSE. This means that, after the termination of voucher privatization, a small oligarchy of some dozen of institutional investors has been equipped with the power to control many big players in the corporate sector.

Table 3.3: Ownership structures of voucher-privatized firms

owner class	Jan. '93 mean	standard deviation	min.	max.	Apr. '95 mean	Feb. '96 mean
IPFs	39.39%	22.22%	0.00%	90.89%	39.65%	28.0%
individuals	36.53%	21.62%	1.56%	96.82%	26.58%	23.2%
public authorities	8.37%	15.38%	0.00%	84.00%	18.21%	18.4%
companies	3.25%	12.51%	0.00%	84.00%	8.71%	9.7%
non-residents	1.34%	8.00%	0.00%	80.00%	5.07%	8.6%
not sold/others*	11.12%	10.40%	1.14%	92.83%	2.52%	6.5%
largest IPF	13.42%	6.26%	0.00%	32.44%	12.20%	9.3%
top-2 IPFs	22.20%	10.86%	0.00%	49.97%	20.48%	16.3%
top-10 IPFs	38.36%	21.32%	0.00%	86.52%	n.a.	n.a.
bank-sponsored IPFs	11.39%	n.a.	n.a.	n.a.	n.a.	n.a.
non-bank IPFs	28.00%	n.a.	n.a.	n.a.	n.a.	n.a.
top-10 owners	62.44%	20.99%	3.18%	98.06%	n.a.	n.a.

* While column 2 presents the average proportion of unsold shares, the last two columns contain the proportion of stock held by other investors (including banks).

Source: Ownership data in columns 2 to 5 are taken from Claessens (1996, pp. 13 and 31) and relate to all 1,491 companies included in the first wave of voucher privatization, i.e. 988 Czech and 503 Slovak companies. The data in the last two columns are from Coopers & Lybrand, Prague. The data of 1995 are based upon a sample of more than 100 joint-stock companies which have participated in large privatization. Most of them were included in the first wave of voucher privatization, some firms have been privatized in the second wave or by methods other than vouchers. The data of 1996 are based upon a sample of 70 joint-stock companies and are estimated by the author in accordance with a bar chart provided by Coopers and Lybrand.

3.3 OWNERSHIP STRUCTURES OF VOUCHER-PRIVATIZED FIRMS

Unfortunately, it is still most difficult to obtain reliable ownership data to assess the pecking order among different classes of owners at the corporate boards more in detail. Table 3.3 drops some hints in this direction. Claessen provides us with some data on the ownership structure of companies privatized in the first wave of voucher privatization. As of January 1993, IPFs jointly held the biggest stakes in Czech and Slovak companies with nearly 40% on average. The margin to the individual investors, however, is quite narrow (< 3%) since the funds tended to buy more expensive shares. The average stake of the public authorities including municipalities and various public funds amounts to less than 9%, with the remainder prevalently in possession of large domestic and foreign investors. The data may slightly understate the size of IPF holdings in the Czech Republic because Slovak investors consigned a smaller proportion of their voucher points to funds than Czech investors (70% as against 73%). Moreover corporate equity is fairly concentrated. The largest fund holds on average over 13%, the ten biggest owners average over 62%. This lets us suppose that cooperation between owners can eventually lead to effective governance in many companies. Amazingly, the average share of bank-sponsored funds is some meagre 11%, i.e. only about 30% of the overall equity stake of all funds together. This underpins the fact that bank funds apparently invested in more expensive shares and in bigger firms. Both can be explained by two facts. Firstly, the high number of points transferred to bank funds in the first wave induced them to bid early to avoid expiring of points even though prices were lower in later rounds. Secondly, because of portfolio limitations (of ultimately 20%) the big bank funds had to turn to large firms. They simply had no chance to use up their points bidding for small and medium-sized companies. We therefore can conclude that, relative to other investors, the governance capacity of bank funds tends to rise with an increase in firm size. In addition, it's striking that the largest fund stake exceeds 32% and two IPFs may jointly hold up to 50% of a company. This demonstrates that the authorities were not too ambitious in enforcing portfolio regulation. As voucher privatization had not yet been finished and the overall success of the programme still relied heavily upon the activities of the funds, the passivity of the supervisory body is not surprising at this early stage.

The funds' capacity to exert corporate governance is corroborated by a study of Lastovicka et al. (1994). They examine the relative power of different classes of shareholders in 949 (out of a total of 988) Czech enterprises included in the first wave of voucher privatization. They report that the single largest IPF holds 20% or more in 102 firms; the two largest IPFs do so in 673 firms. Joint control by four IPFs in possession of at least 40% of firm equity seems possible in 408 companies, hence in almost one half of all cases. Foreign direct investors acquired stakes in 51 firms, domestic ones in 58 companies. They each hold equity stakes equal to or bigger than 20% in 38 firms. Foreign stockholders are in possession of at least 50% of equity in 19 corporations, domestic investors do so in 16 firms.

Furthermore, the authors define the relative power of a given principal shareholder by the proportion of his stake in relation to the aggregate holdings of the 18 largest shareholders. They discover that the single largest fund holds more than 50% of the top-18 shares in 146 joint-stock corporations while the same minimum proportion is commonly owned by the three biggest funds in 669 cases.[20] In 85 out of those 669 cases the three biggest funds dispose of more than 50% of the entire company stock, in another 495 firms they own at least a larger percentage of equity than the remaining institutional shareholders (i.e. overall shareholders minus dispersed individual shareholders). The three largest funds could therefore effectively control 853 out of the 949 Czech companies (89.9%), provided they have incentives to collude. Of course, in most companies their governance power is highly contestable as outside or inside investors contending for corporate governance may acquire additional equity blocks at any time. While the study does not inform about the relative importance of bank-sponsored IPFs, it is quite obvious that, immediately after the end of the first wave, the funds had the capacity to actively control most companies privatized through vouchers up to this date. The question remains whether they have been willing to become involved in corporate policy and, considering the 20% ownership limit, whether they find a way to cooperate.

The two last columns of Table 3.3 convey a picture of the ownership structure of Czech firms after the second wave of voucher privatization. Unfortunately, the reduced size of the underlying samples requires a most careful contemplation of the data (cf. note below table). The samples comprise companies whose equity has been transferred to new owners in the course of large-scale privatization, mostly with the inclusion of vouchers, in rare cases also exclusively by standard methods. As of April 1995, the average proportion of company stock owned by IPFs on aggregate is virtually identical with their stake after the first wave. Many individuals have sold their shares from voucher privatization. Net buyers are domestic companies and foreign investors, i.e. both direct and portfolio investors.[21] At first glance, the expanded public stake is surprising. The explanation is that a higher proportion of the stock of second-wave companies has been reserved for municipalities or retained by the state than in the first wave. The data for February 1996 back up the trends revealed by the previous year's data. Individual investors continue to sell their stock while non-residents and domestic corporate investors go on amassing shares. The group of 'other owners' comprises, among others, banks and insurance companies. The sharp rise of their equity share can be put down to the banks' efforts to increase their stockholdings. The IPFs reduce their holdings, both in aggregate and individually. The latter trend is well documented by a decrease in the average size of the stakes of the biggest funds.

Three reasons may explain the investment behaviour of the IPFs. The first reason is a natural preference of most small funds for passive investment and well-diversified portfolios to minimize non-systemic risk. This is valid all the more in transitional economies whose investment risks dramatically exceed those of established market economies where capital markets are dominated by companies which have, for the most part, a proved track record of economic success in a selective market environment. In rearranging their portfolios obtained in voucher privatization, the smaller funds tend to reduce excessive holdings and to further diversify their assets.

The second reason is that numerous funds have come under liquidity pressure because they must meet the promises given to their owners and begin to redeem shares or investment certificates. If they are not financially backed by banks or other intermediaries, they have no choice and must begin to massively sell their holdings on the stock exchange or over the counter. The general sell-off of shares by IPFs is speeded up by Czech law stipulating adequate liquidity reserves for funds which entered into redemption promises. Furthermore, open-end unit trusts have to gradually accumulate liquid means before they have to redeem certificates after the expiring of the legal protection period of one to three years. One year after the termination of the second wave, most open-end trusts are still 'closed'.[22] One exception is, for instance, an open-end trust run by Credis, the fund management arm of the Credit Suisse group, which opened on 1 March 1996, that is the earliest possible date permitted by law - exactly one year after shares had been handed over into private hands after the second wave of voucher privatization. No wonder, privileged Credis draws from the liquidity of a big foreign bank. The fund belongs to the biggest open-end Czech unit trusts. As of March, the market value of its portfolio came close to one billion crowns. The liquidity pressure resting on Czech open-end unit trusts becomes clear in view of the fact that, well half a year after opening, the fund's assets have shrunk by some 30% despite a considerable rise of the market index over the same period. Some trusts try to alleviate the initial liquidity pressure. An example is the Alpha Effect Fund, one of the biggest second-wave funds with a total net asset value of roughly CZK 1,600 million in end-1996. The fund managed by KIS, the investment company owned by insurer Ceská Pojistovna, will charge a 20% fee to unit holders redeeming their certificates immediately after the opening in January 1998 and decrease it to 3% by the year 2001.

A third reason may be an 'intra-goup levelling-out' of shareholdings in single portfolio companies. Large investment companies like PIAS soon adopted a unitary investment approach for their entire fund family. This included the spreading of big stakes over various funds and other affiliated firms so as to keep constant or increase the governance power over certain bigger companies and at the same time to reduce the size of the largest holdings (of individual funds managed by the investment company) in the enterprises in question. Thereby, the investment companies could diminish the non-systematical risk of the portfolios of individual IPFs, given a constant risk for the group's overall investment portfolio. Such a strategy is clearly in line with the preferences of the funds' small and dispersed investors. The unitary investment policy of major fund families is documented for bank-sponsored investment companies in Tables 3.4 - 3.10. Particularly in the case of an investment company that had set up various

Table 3.4: Industrial holdings of Sporitelna group

company	industry	owner	owning entity % of equity	entire group[a] % of equity	holding by face value (in CZK)	holding by market value (in CZK)
top 100[b]:						
BVV	services	SP ces. IF	10.20	10.20	54.5 mio	190.8 mio
DEZA	chemicals	SP ces. IF	15.89	15.89	408.0 mio	924.1 mio
Elektrár. Opatov.	energy	SP ces. IF	22.42	22.42	255.5 mio	1,180.7 mio
IPS	construct.	SP ces. IF	16.00	16.00	198.0 mio	57.4 mio
Krkonos. papírny	pulp & paper	SP výn. IF	19.65	19.65	31.9 mio	3.5 mio
Metrostav	construct.	SP výn. IF SP ces. IF	12.95 20.62	33.57	162.5 mio	495.6 mio
Mor.slez. Teplárna	energy	SP výn. IF	10.89	10.89	273.1 mio	258.4 mio
Setuza	food	SP ces. IF	18.64	18.64	214.9 mio	399.7 mio
Skoda Praha	engineering	SP výn. IF	14.99	14.99	81.9 mio	87.2 mio
Vodní stavby	construct.	SP ces. IF	15.90	15.90	295.3 mio	452.0 mio
ZKZ	glass	SP výn. IF SP ces. IF	13.25 16.04	29.29	287.4 mio	630.3 mio
ZPS Zlín	engineering	SP ces. IF Sporitelna	15.64 11.92	27.56	583.1 mio	903.8 mio
ZVU	engineering	SP vse. IF	10.98	10.98	7.5 mio	0.6 mio
others:						
Cristal palace	services	2. SP IF SP vse. IF SP ces. IF	17.45 16.16 13.27	46.88	70.7 mio	34.9 mio
Cs. Plav. Labska	services	SP ces. IF	15.89	15.89	408.0 mio	122.8 mio
Janka	engineering	2. SP IF	11.02	11.02	44.0 mio	4.2 mio
Lites	engineering	SP ces. IF 2. SP IF SP vse. IF SP výn. IF	19.98 10.31 10.19 19.93	60.41	173.8 mio	7.9 mio
Vertex	glass & ceramics	SP výn. IF	11.22	11.22	191.4 mio	696.3 mio

a   Total of holdings listed in column 4. Real extent of group holdings in given company may be larger due to undisclosed minor equity stakes ('hidden control reserves'). Market value as of 9 January 1997.

b   The top 100 are the 100 companies listed at the Prague Stock Exchange with the highest sales revenues.

Source: Securities Centre, Prague Stock Exchange; own calculations; all data as of December 1996

Table 3.5: Industrial holdings of Komercní group

		owning entity		entire group[a]		
company	industry	owner	% of equity	% of equity	holding by face value (in CZK)	holding by market value (in CZK)
top 100[b]:						
Elektrár. Opatov.	energy	Komercní IPF KB	11.35 16.16	27.51	227.0 mio	1,049.0 mio
Cechofra.	trade	IPF KB	12.50	12.50	12.8 mio	21.1 mio
IPS Praha	construct.	IPF KB	17.50	17.50	201.5 mio	58.4 mio
JC Mlék.	food	IPF KB	12.92	12.92	97.6 mio	51.7 mio
Metrostav	construct.	IPF KB	12.89	12.89	62.3 mio	190.0 mio
Prazská teplár.	heating	Komercní	17.25	17.25	715.6 mio	1,006.8 mio
PVT	services	IPF KB	17.39	17.39	135.8 mio	550.0 mio
Vodní stavby	construct.	IPF KB	19.90	19.90	368.4 mio	565.9 mio
ZKZ	glass	IPF KB	14.72	14.72	144.4 mio	316.7 mio
others:						
Ambit	construct.	IPF KB	27.01	27.01	20.1 mio	6.2 mio
Cristal Palace	glass	IPF KB	19.91	19.91	30.0 mio	14.8 mio
Frigera	engineering	IPF KB IF KB plus	20.38 19.38	39.76	177.4 mio	8.9 mio
Lázne Teplice	spa	IPF KB IF KB plus	20.96 21.18	42.14	42.2 mio	13.9 mio
Mor. naft. doly	energy	IPF KB	14.52	14.52	121.2 mio	139.4 mio
Mrazírny Praha	food	IPF KB	23.18	23.18	151.3 mio	6.1 mio
Nápoj. technika	engineering	IPF KB IF KB plus	19.29 19.29	38.58	54.4 mio	8.7 mio
Optimit	textile	Komercní IPF KB	29.20 17.78	46.98	286.3 mio	69.0 mio
Rybárství Trebon	food	Komercní IPF KB	28.52 17.97	46.49	174.4 mio	36.6 mio
Sklarny Kavalier	glass	IPF KB	15.21	15.21	110.0 mio	241.5 mio
Velvana	chemicals	IPF KB IF Universum	19.99 19.47	39.46	55.5 mio	14.0 mio
Vertex	fibreglass	IPF KB	18.53	18.53	316.0 mio	1,149.6 mio

Source and notes: See Table 3.4

Table 3.6: Industrial holdings of IPB group

		owning entity			entire group[a]	
company	industry	owner	% of equity	% of equity	holding by face value (in CZK)	holding by market value (in CZK)
top 100[b]:						
Biocel	pulp & paper	RIF	11.16	11.16	370.4 mio	337.1 mio
JC Mlék.	food	RIF	14.74	14.74	111.3 mio	59.0 mio
JC papír.	pulp & paper	IPB Bank	27.57	27.57	673.9 mio	241.4 mio
Milo	food	Domeana	11.08	31.87	258.8 mio	266.0 mio
Mor. slez. teplárny	heating	IPB Bank	16.43	16.43	412.1 mio	389.8 mio
Plzenský prazdroj	brewery	IPB Bank Bankovní Holding RIF	16.50 10.26 29.50	56.26	633.9 mio	1,643.7 mio
PVT	services	RIF	19.97	19.97	156.0 mio	631.8 mio
SC Doly	mining	RIF	15.12	15.12	1,095.2 mio	788.5 mio
Seliko	food	Domeana RIF	21.33 29.09	50.42	201.8 mio	403.6 mio
Setuza	food	RIF	10.83	10.83	12.5 mio	23.3 mio
SVIT	textile	IPB	10.63	10.63	256.8 mio	18.2 mio
Vítkovice	steel	RIF	15.63	15.63	581.3 mio	130.2 mio
ZDAS	engineering	RIF	19.01	19.01	265.4 mio	144.1 mio
others:						
Ambit	construct.	IF bohat. IF rozvoj.	12.60 12.60	25.2	25.2 mio	7.8 mio
Chemapol	chemicals	IPB	10.24	10.24	168.0 mio	208.3 mio
Hotel Panorama	services	Domeana RIF	14.17 20.17	34.34	169.6 mio	26.1 mio
Chlum. ker. záv.	glass & ceramic	IPB	24.78	24.78	129.2 mio	418.6 mio
Janka	engineering	RIF	10.97	10.97	43.8 mio	4.2 mio
Kruznoh. lesy Tepl.	forestry	Bankovní Holding IF bohat. Ifrozvoj.	10.45 10.01 10.52	30.98	108.1 mio	3.0 mio
Obchodní sladovny	malthouse	IPB	31.23	31.23	294.1 mio	147.1 mio
Pivovary Bohemia	brewery	RIF 1. mestsk. banka	15.00 17.23	32.23	79.0 mio	14.8 mio
Post. tisk. cenin	printhouse	IPB RIF	51.01 10.54	61.55	20.4 mio	6.7 mio
Selgen	agriculture	IF bohat. RIF Rent. IF	12.76 20.29 20.14	53.19	58.1 mio	32.0 mio
Velvana	chemicals	IPB	52.78	52.78	74.2 mio	18.7 mio
Vertex	fibreglass	RIF	20.42	20.42	348.3 mio	1,267.1 mio
Zbrojov.	engineering	IF bohat. Rent. IF	15.35 15.35	30.70	457.0 mio	54.8 mio

Source and notes: See Table 3.4

Table 3.7: Industrial holdings of CSOB group

		owning entity		entire group[a]		
company	industry	owner	% of equity	% of equity	holding by face value (in CZK)	holding by market value (in CZK)
top 100[b]:						
BVV	services	Finop	29.12	29.12	155.6 mio	544.6 mio
Cechofra.	trade	Kvanto IF	16.54	44.11	45.0 mio	74.3 mio
		Finop	27.56			
Jablonex	trade	ZLUF	18.42	33.42	46.8 mio	9.4 mio
		Kvanto				
		Finop	15.00			
Motokov Internat.	trade	Kvanto IF	17.76	27.76	119.4 mio	44.5 mio
		Finop	10.00			
Motokov Praha	trade	Kvanto IF	20.00	51.17	318.3 mio	30.7 mio
		Zlatý IF	20.00			
		Kvanto				
		Finop	11.17			
SM plyn.	energy	CSOB	25.62	25.62	293.5 mio	602.3 mio
VC plyn.	energy	CSOB	18.86	18.86	117.4 mio	280.1 mio
ZVU	engineering	Kvanto IF	20.00	48.22	473.3 mio	38.1 mio
		Zlatý IF	28.22			
		Kvanto				
others:						
Agrostroj	engineering	Kvanto IF	19.99	35.24	162.3 mio	22.1 mio
		Zlatý IF	15.25			
		Kvanto				
C. lupk. závody	mining	Kvanto IF	18.42	86.86	183.0 mio	25.6 mio
		Zlatý IF	49.46			
		Kvanto				
		ZLUF	18.98			
		Kvanto				
Chladicí veze Praha	engineering	Zlatý IF	19.97	39.94	44.8 mio	3.2 mio
		Kvanto				
		ZLUF	19.97			
		Kvanto				
Jitex	textile	Kvanto IF	20.57	41.10	300.3 mio	56.8 mio
		Zlatý IF	20.53			
		Kvanto				
Kovofinis	metallurgy	Kvanto IF	19.97	55.10	151.8 mio	4.3 mio
		Zlatý IF	19.97			
		Kvanto				
		ZLUF	15.16			
		Kvanto				
Prago-export	trade	Kvanto IF	22.75	41.56	16.7 mio	16.7 mio
		Finop	18.81			
Tanex	trade	Kvanto IF	19.24	38.48	244.0 mio	9.3 mio
		ZLUF	19.24			
		Kvanto				
Tuzex	trade	Kvanto IF	19.65	71.62	649.8 mio	13.3 mio
		ZLOF	11.49			
		Kvanto				
		ZLUF	10.50			
		Kvanto				
		Finop	29.98			
Zoska	engineering	Kvanto IF	19.99	39.98	99.0 mio	19.8 mio
		Zlatý IF	19.99			
		Kvanto				

Source and notes: See Table 3.4

Table 3.8: Industrial holdings of Motoinvest group

		owning entity		entire group[a]		
company	industry	owner	% of equity	% of equity	holding by face value (in CZK)	holding by market value (in CZK)
top 100[b]:						
Krkonos. papírny	pulp & paper	Agrobank	12.16	12.16	102.7 mio	11.3 mio
Prazská energ.	energy	CA IPF	15.94	15.94	404.9 mio	899.7 mio
Spolchem		C.S. fond energ.	10.65	25.80	750.9 mio	111.9 mio
		C.S. infrast. IF	15.15			
ZDB		AGB IPF	17.09	17.09	355.6 mio	72.9 mio
others:						
KB Likér	beverages	C.S. infrast. IF	20.19	40.38	42.2 mio	2.9 mio
		CA CEIF	20.19			
Koh-I-Noor.	pencils	A-Inv. IPF	16.71	60.27	51.8 mio	4.5 mio
		AGB IPF	43.56			
JM lesy	forestry	C.S. fond kap. výn.	16.58	49.78	240.2 mio	11.4 mio
		C.S. infrast. IF	16.62			
		Rentia plus IPF	16.58			
Lesy C. Krumlov	forestry	C.A.S. 9. holding	18.63	60.39	49.2 mio	24.8 mio
		CA CEIF	20.88			
		C.S. infrast. IF	20.88			
Pivov. a sod. Brno	brewery	3. CS holding	12.68	45.51	79.3 mio	4.4 mio
		C.S. fond kap. výn.	17.21			
		Rentia plus IPF	15.62			
Slovác. Stroj.	engineering	Moto-invest	13.47	35.26	197.6 mio	19.4 mio
		2. CS holding	11.20			
		3. CS holding	10.49			
Texlen	textile	Agrobank	68.27	68.27	427.5 mio	23.3 mio
Ústecké pivovary	brewery	Agrobank	35.03	40.07	40.7 mio	12.7 mio
		Apollón	5.04			
VÚKV Praha	R&D/ engineering	Moto-invest	39.99	85.98	15.5 mio	14.0 mio
		2. CS holding	45.99			
ZVVZ	engineering	AGB IPF	25.61	67.56	393.1 mio	207.2 mio
		Agrobank	21.43			
		CA CEIF	20.42			

Source and notes: See Table 3.4

Table 3.9: Industrial holdings of Zivnobanka group

| | | owning entity | | | entire group[a] | |
company	industry	owner	% of equity	% of equity	holding by face value (in CZK)	holding by market value (in CZK)
top 100[b]:	no top 100 holdings		-	-	-	-
others:						
Bask	food	ZB 1. IPF	19.48	39.29	43.2 mio	33.8 mio
		ZB PF	19.81			
Ceská Zbrojov.	engineering	ZB 1. IPF	19.07	19.07	131.1 mio	230.5 mio
Juta	textile	ZB 1. IPF	20.53	20.53	96.7 mio	209.6 mio
Later	construct.	ZB PF	32.80	32.80	87.4 mio	17.4 mio
První SZ teplárny	heating	ZB 1. IPF	16.79	16.79	169.0 mio	220.0 mio
Rakov. ker. záv.	industrial ceramics	ZB 1. IPF	12.00	12.00	136.4 mio	150.0 mio
Spofa	chemicals	ZB 1. IPF	19.10	37.74	55.9 mio	29.2 mio
		ZB PF	18.64			

Source and notes: See Table 3.4

Table 3.10: Industrial holdings of Ceská pojistovna group

| | | owning entity | | | entire group[a] | |
company	industry	owner	% of equity	% of equity	holding by face value (in CZK)	holding by market value (in CZK)
top 100[b]:						
Adamov. strojírny	engineering	1. PIF	13.11	13.11	121.2 mio	22.7 mio
Skoda-Liaz	engineering	1. PIF	15.04	15.04	288.2 mio	28.5 mio
ZPS Zlín	engineering	Ceská pojistovna	10.26	10.26	217.0 mio	336.4 mio
ZVU	engineering	1. PIF	11.09	11.09	108.9 mio	8.8 mio
ZDAS	engineering	1. PIF	15.12	15.12	211.1 mio	114.6 mio
others:						
KF	services	Ceská pojistovna	60.00	80.10	120.1 mio	38.2 mio
		Thesaurus KIS IPF	20.10			
MSA	engineering	1. PIF	19.77	19.77	177.5 mio	101.0 mio
Radegast	brewery	1. PIF	14.49	14.49	115.1 mio	610.8 mio
Tesla Votice	engineering	Thesaurus KIS PF	22.70	42.42	46.5 mio	2.4 mio
		AAA KIS IPF	19.72			
Unex Unicov	engineering	Alpha Effect IPF	24.64	38.84	220.7 mio	19.9 mio
		KIS spec. IPF	14.20			

Source and notes: See Table 3.4

second-wave funds in addition to its IPFs from the first privatization wave, intra-group diversification produced a sometimes dramatic decline in the size of the group's largest holdings in individual portfolio companies. Likewise, some large funds split up into several successor IPFs. The most prominent example of this was SPAS, the first-wave fund of the savings bank and biggest voucher fund altogether. Its splintering into three smaller IPFs in end-1995 was linked to a splitting up of many shareholdings in major companies, too. This substantially contributed to a decrease in the average size of the equity stakes of the largest IPFs. Of course, the governance power of the investment companies wasn't affected by such rather formal changes.

The decline of the average stake of the largest fund and the top two IPFs is fostered by control premia paid by raiders for large shareholdings or controlling stakes. Those premia primarily induce the small funds to unload their bigger holdings first. In this way, they can reduce the non-systematic risk and hedge more effectively against possible losses from stock price fluctuations in a highly volatile capital market. Besides, they don't have to rely upon the illiquid organized stock markets to provide liquidity. The result is an accelerated split of the IPF community into two groups with divergent investment strategies, managerial funds preferring controlling stakes in companies and active governance ('voice') and portfolio funds which are pursuing passive investment strategies and striving for broad diversification and liquidity of their assets ('exit'). The first group is dominated by well-capitalized, rather large funds while their smaller fellows are increasingly pushed into the second group.

3.4 THE 'THIRD PRIVATIZATION WAVE': CONCENTRATION OF OWNERSHIP

3.4.1 Concentration and IPF Regulation

Initial contemplation of the legislative straight-jacket of funds (most of all the limitation of equity holdings to 20% of a portfolio company) and the lack of majority owners was somewhat quieted by a development dubbed the 'third wave' of privatization. After shares had been distributed to their new owners, heavy trading began amongst IPFs and banks. Not being obliged to disclose their portfolio, it is presumed that several of the big IPFs amassed stakes that were at times beyond the 20% limit. Not only would it have been difficult for the Ministry of Finance to police the portfolio regulation, but also was it reluctant to do so.[23] The argument in favour of the process - including 'inevitable' breaches of the laws - was two-fold. First, a concentration and consolidation was welcome because higher equity stakes would possibly lead to better governance by the new owners. Second, economists argued the initial ownership was inefficient, as the allocation of assets was not by way of a market mechanism but through a (necessarily less efficient) politically designed process.[24] Moreover, the voucher scheme generated an unintentional interdependence of government and IPFs. The government knew too well that the scheme's overwhelming popularity originated from the activities of the funds rather than its own skills in 'marketing' voucher privatization. The funds, in return, could implicitly expect the ministry to be generous in interpreting and, more important, enforcing portfolio regulation. Remarkably, this *quid pro quo* response of the authorities didn't relate exclusively to the bidding process, but was still persisting for a long time after the end of voucher privatization.

The central features of the third wave are the constant concentration of ownership structures of corporations and the attempts of various investors to build up large financial conglomerates. Both developments are inseparable from each other and have been proceeding, for the major part, in strict secrecy. Subsequently, we will illustrate them in the light of events which belong undoubtedly to the most spectacular on the Czech equity market after the termination of the voucher programme.

3.4.2 Harvard's Joint Venture with Stratton Investments

Although secrecy accompanied developments throughout the third wave, its significance was first realized with the emergence of Stratton Investments, an investment vehicle founded by American industrialist Michael Dingman and initiated by Viktor Kozený, head of HC&C.[25] From the beginning, the Harvard funds followed the strategy of a managerial fund group. In spite of the huge amount of points collected primarily in the first wave, they left voucher privatization with a portfolio totalling only about 60 enterprises. In October 1995 it was publicized that Dingman had acquired considerable (even controlling) stakes in seven Czech companies from Kozený for a supposed total of more than $200 million (see Table 3.11). It was quickly realized that Harvard could not have done this without breaching the ownership cap of 20% at some point. Still, officials did not act. The new and very positive light this threw on Czech developments was that for the first time a serious, managerially and financially capable investor had bought into the Czech market through the market (and not through government sale of controlling stakes). Stratton both has the know-how and financial resources to pursue 'deep restructuring' and claimed to be a medium-term investor. The question was whether Dingman's restructuring interest was real.

Table 3.11: Stratton and Harvard Investment stakes in percent of company stock

Company (rank by stock market capitalization)	Branch	Nov. '95			Sep. '96
		Stratton	*Harvard*	total	total
Biocel Paskov (21)	pulp & paper	*22.5*	*13.0*	35.6	33.2
Ceská námorní plavba (38)	ocean shipping	*35.5*	*33.5*	69.0	87.0
Moravské naftové doly (n.a.)	petroleum	*17.7*	*4.7*	22.4	21.7
Plzenský Prazdroj (14)	beer	*0.0*	*30.7*	30.7	0.0
Prazská teplárenská (31)	heating	*13.9*	*13.7*	27.6	43.3
Sepap (15)	pulp & paper	*25.9*	*25.1*	51.0	47.6
Sklo Union (41)	glass	*19.1*	*37.7*	56.8	100.0
Spolana (26)	chemicals	*18.3*	*11.8*	30.1	0.0

Source: Securities Centre, Prague Post (Dec. 6-12, 1995), Prague Post Book of Lists 1996, Prague Business Journal (Sept. 16-33, 1996); n.a. = not available. Rank reflects position among all listed Czech joint-stock companies as of 31 December 1995.

Kozený's coup had been preceded by a further tightening of the Harvard portfolio. During 1995, the company had sold more than 30 portfolio firms. Its two top funds, Harvard Dividend and Harvard Growth, alone had lost nearly one third of their net asset value slimming from CZK 17,280 million down to CZK 12,000 million.[26] From the cash obtained from Stratton, Harvard could rebuild its stakes in the seven companies and expand its holdings in other firms. The deal between HC&C and Stratton was that Stratton would use the voting rights attached to Harvard's stock to control the companies and to carry out active restructuring. HC&C, in turn, would receive 10% of any future capital gains realized by Stratton on the shares it purchased through Harvard. Dingman announced, too, that he intended to increase further the Stratton stakes in all firms where the joint holding of both investors did not reach 50% of company stock.

Stratton underlined its restructuring interest by replacing many board directors and hiring several high-powered executives from the US to put the companies into better shape.[27] In Sklo Union, a holding company with stakes in the country's top 15 glass manufacturers, it decided within weeks that the holding was 100% overstaffed and withdraw the whole workforce of 55 employees, leaving them the options to retire or to be transferred to the subsidiaries. In summer 1996, Sklo Union was split. While its biggest subsidiary Glavunion was entirely sold to a Belgian direct investor, the remainder was merged with HC&C and Stratton to the new megaholding Daventree.

Difficulties arose through the takeover of a 51% majority in Sepap, the largest Czech paper producer. Before the secret raid, Sepap had been governed by the Swedish paper company AssiDomän which held a 36% stake in the company, originally planning to even up its holding by increasing company equity. Taken by surprise by the entry of Stratton, the Swedes threatened to pull out of some lucrative investment projects they were going to launch with Sepap after Dingman had removed the Czech chairman of the managing board and stacked the board entirely with Stratton representatives, excluding the Swedes entirely from strategic decision making. Finally, both sides came to an outline agreement on mutual cooperation and coordination. Meanwhile AssiDomän has taken two seats on the board and both sides contribute to the joint venture, the Swedes by delivering marketing know how and Stratton by taking responsibility for the internal 'reengineering' of Sepap. The cooperation appears to succeed as it has even been expanded to Russia and the Ukraine where Stratton, along with AssiDomän, has acquired a cluster of paper mills and extended tracts of forest. Today the Sepap story possibly is the most successful example for a long-term joint venture between a domestic investment company, an international 'turnaround' specialist and a branch expert. Sepap is undergoing an extensive restructuring programme and may well benefit from its integration into an emerging eastern European pulp and paper group. The group is supplemented by a controlling stake in the biggest Czech pulp mill Biocel Paskov and a 20% holding in Prague-based paper producer Ospap.

Yet, in most other firms, Stratton wasn't quite that successful. The temporary stake of 30% in the chemicals company Spolana turned out insufficient to change the strategic orientation of the company. Dingman couldn't get through its intention to merge Spolana with US-based General Chemicals. As incumbent management obstructed the plan and Stratton couldn't bring the other owners behind the plan, it finally decided to sell its shares, along with stakes in the petroleum company Moravské naftové doly and plastics producer Fatra Napajedla, to the Czech Chemapol group.[28] In the Prague-based heating company Prazská teplárenská, Stratton competed for control with two other major owners, the City of Prague and a German holding company, jointly in possession of more shares than Stratton. In late 1996, Stratton threw in the towel and sold its stake to two other major investors, one of them being Komercní banka. For the country's largest beermaker, Plzenský Prazdroj, Stratton had originally envisaged the implementation of a restructuring programme under the auspices of a former Anheuser Busch executive. But the programme was rejected by the management and several other (domestic) stakeholders. Furthermore, legal complications have seemingly delayed Stratton's purchase of the Harvard stake in the brewery. A five-year agreement among the major shareholders which took effect in 1995 prevents the transfer of shares to outsiders without the consent of the incumbent owners. Harvard thus pulled out of the firm, selling its stock to one of the major incumbent owners, the IPB group which thereby gained a majority stake in Plzenský.[29]

While the results and the length of Harvard's and Stratton's joint investment commitments in the Czech Republic remain to be seen, Stratton clearly demonstrated its intention to instill know-how into the firms included in its portfolio. As those firms each have a dominant position on the Czech market and an above-average development potential, Stratton had to face hard competition in its struggle for corporate control. Nevertheless, where it sold its holdings, it supported the consolidation of ownership structures. To date, there is little information available on the activities of the successor company Daventree on the Czech capital market. As of December 1996, apart from the stakes presented in Table 3.11, Daventree announces only two additional shareholdings exceeding 10% of firm equity. This doesn't mean, however, that Daventree's interest in the Czech market is exhausted since it hides its shareholdings through an extensive net of subholdings to disguise its investment plans. Still, it appears that the major part of the returns realized by the re-sale of shares have flown abroad to be invested predominantly in Russian, Belorussian and Polish firms, with a focus on the pulp and paper industry.

3.4.3 Motoinvest's Secret Takeover Raids

The other main actor on the early Czech takeover scene was the financial group Motoinvest, founded by half a dozen young entrepreneurs with an average age distinctly below thirty. In contrast to the Harvard-Stratton venture, it appeared doubtful whether Motoinvest had the know-how to carry out deep restructuring. Moreover, the origin of Motoinvest's equity capital was widely unknown and it was therefore no wonder that regular accusations of money laundering were heard. The company itself claims to have got hold of cash by the sale of a small start-up bank to the IPB group in 1994 and by preceding foreign exchange speculation on the split of former Czechoslovakia in 1993. Afterwards it used the general initial opaqueness of the Czech capital market to buy quietly into several investment funds and two other banks, the aforementioned Agrobanka and the small Plzenská Banka. By 1996, Motoinvest disposed of a wide net of investment entities with significant links to the industrial sector (see Table 3.12). Having attained a major stake in Plzenská, it completely and overnight changed the small commercial bank into an investment bank serving Motoinvest as a vehicle to accumulate (now openly) large stakes in six mainly bank-sponsored IPFs.[30]

For this purpose, in November 1995, Plzenská mailed buyout offers to millions of citizens who had participated in voucher privatization. The whole campaign was claimed by the bank to be the start of a 'third wave of privatization'. The slogan soon became a popular saying for the process of ownership consolidation proceeding in the wake of voucher privatization. Another, likewise contentious headliner to make the decision to sell easier to the public was the headliner 'Small investors weep!', alluding to weak minority shareholder protection, unfulfilled buyback promises of many funds and a sharp decline of the market index at the Prague Stock Exchange (PSE) in the course of 1995.[31] The sponsors of the raided funds reacted immediately and began themselves to launch buyout offers for their IPFs. Zivnobanka 1st IF, the biggest fund of Zivnostenská banka's investment company, could 'save' control over the fund assets at the last minute by increasing its equity capital after the bank hadn't succeeded in buying sufficient shares in the open market. Zivnostenská took over the entire new share issue.

Table 3.12: Intra-group cross holdings of Motoinvest as of December 1996

company	type of company	owner	% of company equity
Agrobanka	bank	AGB IF II	19.70
AGB investicní fond II	investment fund	Agrobanka	27.74
Apollón holding (former AGB IF I)	holding	Motoinvest	13.20
C.S. infrastrukturní IF[a]	investment fund	Motoinvest	10.79
		2. CS holding	10.61
Creditanstalt CEIF[b,c]	investment fund	Motoinvest	23.83
C.A.S. 5. Holding	holding	2. CS holding	23.54
C.A.S. 6. Holding	holding	Motoinvest	12.14
C.A.S. 9. holding (former YSE II)[c]	holding	Motoinvest	16.90
2. CS holding[c]	holding	Motoinvest	16.82
3. CS holding[c]	holding	Motoinvest	21.55
4. CS holding[c]	holding	Motoinvest	16.09
Portfolio IF OVA	investment fund	Agrobanka	10.76
Kredital IF OVA	investment fund	Motoinvest	14.96
IF Top Profit	investment fund	C.A.S. 6. holding	18.61

a   Former Creditanstalt Czech Investment Fund
b   Former Creditanstalt Czech Infrastructure and Utilities Fund
c   Ownership stake as of 12 September 1996

Source: Securities Centre; Burzovní noviny, no. 184, 19 September 1996, p. I

Komercní Banka even considered abolishing public tradeability of the shares of its investment flagship IPF KB to protect it from a hostile takeover. The Czech National Bank rejected Komercní's application and Motoinvest gained a controlling stake in the fund. Until end-1995, Motoinvest had financed Plzenská's stock market raids with more than $ 35 million and grabbed control of the Kvanto funds of CSOB, IPF KB, the Creditanstalt funds and some private funds like YSE 2, the C.S. funds, Rentia and

Panok.[32] Komercní and CSOB had to buy back the equity blocks in their funds at high mark-ups, netting Motoinvest a cosy $ 8 million profit in the case of Komercní alone. Creditanstalt denied to repurchase the stock of its two funds and withdrew from the fund management in January 1996.

Motoinvest successfully used the initial secrecy of the Czech equity market to attain control of several major bank-sponsored and private IPFs and to rake together enough cash flow to further expand its net of industrial holdings. The reaction of the big Czech banks proves their strong interest in the fund business. It made the banks and some affiliated or cooperating companies the biggest owners of bank-owned IPFs in the legal form of joint-stock companies. The bank holdings in their funds are strategic stakes. After the expensive 'rescue' of the bank funds from the clutches of Motoinvest, they are serving primarily to entrench the banks' investment funds against future hostile takeover bids.

Still, it appears somewhat unclear how far-reaching the restructuring interest of HC&C and Motoinvest is in reality. Representatives of both groups claim to have a strategic interest in firms in which they purchased large equity stakes. Evidence for corporate restructuring is so far rather anecdotal, see the case of AssiDomän. As for Motoinvest, most Prague stock brokers seem to suggest that its primary concerns are basically share trading and asset stripping rather than deep restructuring. One major activity of Motoinvest is obviously the sale of strategic company stakes to foreign investors while the group lacks the people to manage or actively restructure firms.[33] Serious liquidity problems of Agrobanka have recently forced the group to sell part of its shareholdings at the capital market.

A former manager of HC&C even intimated that the company used to apply various practices of asset stripping to the detriment of minority shareholders, mainly the conclusion of contracts on the purchase of assets at extremely low prices from firms controlled by the Harvard funds. This suggests that, while investment companies obviously can exert control over companies and prevent managers from asset stripping to the detriment of individual investors as ultimate corporate owners, the problem arises as to who prevents the funds as trustees from fraud and cheating.

The true extent of the holdings of both groups is largely unknown. While equity stakes exceeding 10% of a company's equity meanwhile have to be made public through the Securities Centre, both HC&C and Motoinvest have split their stakes over a wide net of subholdings and affiliated companies which frequently hold less than 10% of corporate equity or which have a rather informal connection to the given group. Both financial groups are very reluctant to reveal information about their portfolios and strategic companies.

Without doubt, the actions of HC&C and Motoinvest have accelerated the consolidation process of company ownership, in the hands of both the respective group and other domestic or foreign direct investors. In the absence of developed capital and control markets, this may pave the way for swift restructuring and the implementation of fixed control structures in numerous companies. Another important consequence of the takeover raids started by Motoinvest is a significant strengthening of the ownership links between banks and their IPFs and, hence, between banks and the industrial sector.

3.5 ASSET STRUCTURE OF FUNDS AND FINANCIAL GROUPS

3.5.1 IPF Investment Foci by Branches

All else being equal, investment funds face a trade-off between the capacity to actively control portfolio companies and efficient risk diversification. The latter requires scattering of capital over many industries whereas active corporate governance gains from economies of scale if the portfolio concentrates on merely a few key branches. Investment managers can then accumulate insider knowledge and specific branch experience which may enhance the efficiency of corporate control. Subsequently we will take a closer look at the branch structure of the portfolios of major Czech investment companies.

We can generally distinguish between three groups of sectors. The first group comprises highly concentrated sectors like banking, energy and telecommunications (in Table 3.13 classified under transportation & infrastructure). At the time of voucher privatization, companies of those industries had high market shares and were in fairly good condition. Considering their positions as monopolists or oligopolists, they were comparatively safe investments in industries with guaranteed returns. The uncertainties linked to investments in the energy sector or in telecommunications originated from political risks like a lack of knowledge about the future regulatory environment rather than market risks like shifting consumer preferences or enhanced competition from domestic and foreign firms of the same industry. Furthermore, at least in the medium term, the industries in question are tightly controlled by the state, which holds majority stakes in most of the companies at issue. There is rarely any perspective for active corporate control by investment funds. Some of the major private IPFs like Harvard and YSE tried to maximize their stakes in companies with a strong starting position in their industries and heavily

Table 3.13: *Sectoral distribution of funds' share portfolios by market value as of end-1995*[a]

fund sponsor & name	no. of IPFs	highly concentrated sectors			demand-robust sectors			risky sectors				size of share portfolio		
		finan-cial services	ener-gy	infra-struc-ture	food	glass & ceram-ics	con-struc-tion	engi-neer-ing	chem-icals	trade	pulp & paper	by market value (in CZK)	by no. of com-panies	shares/ overall portfolio
domestic bank:														
SPAS (SIS)[b]	1	0	17	3	11	5	12	**26**	6	6	12	17,031 mio	270	79.4%
IKS Komercni banky	2	13	19	5	5	11	7	**14**	9	0	6	9,537 mio	258	95.0%
PIAS	16	**19**	18	10	8	8	3	8	7	n.a.	7	19,000 mio	n.a.	81.5%
foreign bank:														
ZB-Trust	2	1	10	7	**13**	**24**	12	10	8	0	3	2,839 mio	76	85.7%
Creditanstalt IPF[c]	1	0	1	5	**32**	3	**40**	10	4	0	3	2,355 mio	68	68.0%
Credis	1	9	13	**24**	1	2	9	2	**26**	0	0	571 mio	36	n.a.
private founder:														
HC&C[d]	2	**25**	**22**	9	2	14	5	3	7	1	13	10,000 mio	56	58.9%
YSE IF[e]	1	**37**	**27**	5	4	n.a.	6	n.a.	n.a.	n.a.	n.a.	3,332 mio	106	96.5%
I. CCI[f]	1	0	0	0	16	0	10	**26**	0	0	1	253 mio	17	33.9%

a All sector-related data are in percent of overall portfolio of respective fund/group. Top two shareholdings by sector are presented in bold type. Various sectors like services (hotels, computer companies etc.) or mining & metallurgy are not listed. All data refer either to asset portfolios of entire investment company or to major IPFs making up a dominant and representative share in the group's overall portfolio. In all cases, the group's main IPF is included. The exact number of IPFs covered for each group is reported in the second column

b Portfolio of SPAS as of 28 February 1995, i.e. four months before the split of SPAS into three successor funds.

c Data cover Creditanstalt's main IPF (out of two) as of 31 August 1995.

d Data cover both major funds of HC&C, i.e. Harvard dividendový IF (dividend fund) and Harvard rustový IF (growth fund).

e Data refer to biggest YSE fund as of 31 December 1994, last column according to face value of share portfolio.

f I. Czech Coupon Invest placed 42% of its share portfolio in mining & metallurgy. Yet, merely 34% of the fund's overall assets are company shares. The remainder are liquid means (20%) and bonds issued by public authorities (46%).

Source: Annual reports, various financial statements; own calculations

invested in financial institutions and the energy sector. More than half of the portfolio of both is placed in sectors with monopolistic supply structures.

Domestic banks revealed a strong preference for energy companies, too. This clearly contrasts with the reluctance of funds sponsored by foreign banks to place their points or financial means in this sector. The reason for this may be a lack of information about the corporate strategy of the large energy producers and distributors. The management of the Creditanstalt IS, the investment manager of two funds founded by the Austrian bank Creditanstalt, complained about difficult access to information relevant for the evaluation of the economic situation of the energy companies. Reportedly it was difficult for them to obtain fairly accurate information about the relative size of revenues from customers and expenses for the modernization of the capital stock and for the implementation of control systems for the pollution level. Domestic banks had a distinct informational edge over other investors and could probably make more accurate assessments of the economic prospects of the sector. Their privileged access to information is based upon both long-established credit ties to the enterprise sector and good connections to the relevant public authorities as domestic banks still are owned chiefly by the state.

In addition, the biggest electricity producer CEZ is running the country's largest existing nuclear power plant and has taken a leading part in putting up a new plant in Temelín in South Bohemia. The liabilities resulting from two such gigantic projects are not only difficult to assess for outsiders, but may also turn out very big. This may have prevented many IPFs from purchasing bigger stakes in the energy producer. As CEZ is the Czech company with the second biggest market capitalization[34], the well-capitalized fund families of the domestic banks and the major 'entrepreneurial' (and hence less risk-averse) funds like HC&C and YSE may be in a better position to bear the risk linked to significant investment in CEZ.

From a long-term perspective, substantial holdings in the energy sector may be a good base to acquire control over the companies with a dominant market position in the future when the state will withdraw from the industry. The governance interest of the bank-sponsored funds is indicated by the case of Elektrárny Opatovice, the third-highest capitalized utility at the Prague Stock Exchange. The company was carved out and privatized from CEZ. By early 1997, only 13% of the power company was owned by public authorities (three municipalities), while 45% of the capital stock was in hands of two bank-sponsored funds (managed by SIS - 20% - and IKS KB -10%) and of Komercni banka (15%). Both financial groups have been actively involved in running Elektrárny. So far, their engagement is apparently successful. In the years 1995/96, the company paid shareholder dividends of roughly CZK

200 per share with a face value of CZK 1,000 at a time when most listed firms refrained from distributing any dividend or paid just a token amount. Besides, the firm was able to set aside CZK 1,400 million in cash reserves only in 1995. The 'excess cash' was taken to purchase a strategic 44% stake in an area heat distributor (Prague-based Prazská teplárenská) and smaller shares in other utility companies. It has outperformed virtually all other Czech power companies in terms of both operating profit and cash-flow generation. In the view of an analyst of a leading Prague broker house, Elektrárny even 'has the best management in the country - by any standard. The company is clean, efficient, environment- and shareholder-friendly, and future-oriented'. The performance of Elektrárny may be a first hint that both bank-founded investment companies as well as the banks themselves have both an active governance interest and the capacity to carry out efficient monitoring.

Rather remarkable is also the approach of various banks towards investments in their own sector. As already touched upon, according to IPF portfolio regulation, funds sponsored by financial institutions were originally forbidden to purchase stakes in other funds as well as in financial institutions in general. The latter constraint was not valid for IPFs founded by non-financial entities. This should prevent an excessive concentration of the financial sector as most banks and insurance companies had been included in the voucher scheme. While virtually all funds sponsored by foreign banks stuck to this portfolio constraint, the investment companies of domestic banks invented a different interpretation of the law. They claimed that the constraint concerned exclusively funds directly founded by banks. The only fund set up directly by a domestic bank has been SPAS of Ceská Sporitelna. The remaining funds belonging to the financial groups of the domestic banks were founded by management companies which had themselves been set up by the banks. Capital market supervision, exerted by the Ministry of Finance, never interfered with this interpretation even though it clearly contradicted the intention of the regulators. As a result of such a weak enforcement policy, IPFs (indirectly) founded by domestic banks belong to the most important investors in the financial sector. As will be discussed later, this also led to considerable cross-ownership and concentration in the banking sector.

The PIAS funds even revealed an unambiguous preference for the financial sector. Holdings in no more than four financial institutions - IPB (the sponsoring bank), Komercní banka, Ceská sporitelna and the former monopoly insurer Ceská pojistovna - make up 18.2% of the company's overall securities portfolio.[35] SPAS had originally acquired substantial holdings in the financial sector, too. Shortly after the first privatization wave, shares in financial institutions constituted about 15% of its portfolio.

In order not to lose its stakes in the financial sector, Sporitelna's fund management arm SIS established the joint-stock investment fund Sporitelna IF (SIF) which didn't draw from voucher points but from issuing own shares for cash. SIF is a unique specimen in the Czech capital market as it is the only cash fund issuing its own stock instead of certificates. The key investments in the SIF share portfolio were purchases of banking stock. The major reason to set up the fund was apparently to transfer part of the stakes in the financial sector from SPAS to SIF. At the end of 1995, some half of the fund's assets of CZK 659 million were invested in the banking sector. Nevertheless, the overall investment of SIS in the financial sector is significantly smaller than that of PIAS and IKS KB. Interestingly, since July 1996, bank-founded funds are allowed to invest in financial institutions (apart from the sponsoring bank itself). Of course, this institutional relaxation clearly is an *ex post* acknowledgement of results that already had been created by the regulated subjects themselves. That means that, in this specific case, the institutional framework adjusted to a given behavioural reality, and not vice versa.

A second group of industries consists of sectors which are more competitive, but still fairly robust against transition-induced decline of demand. They offer attractive investment opportunities even for investors suffering from a lack of 'insider' or 'private information'. Apart from the food industry, also including beverages of all kinds and tobacco, the construction sector (including construction materials) could be supposed to be rather resistant against the transitional recession since the Klaus government had announced firm plans to undertake extensive investment in public infrastructure soon after the 1989 revolution. Other beneficiaries of increased public expenditures for infrastructural projects are producers of industrial glasses like fibreglass, hence various firms of the glass & ceramics sector. Considering the difficult access to company information, the investment of foreign bank-sponsored funds like Zivnobanka and Creditanstalt in the mentioned sectors is easy to explain. Indeed, ZB trust placed one half of its portfolio in the three sectors, Creditanstalt even three quarters. On the other hand, the Credis trust managed by Credit Suisse invested half of its assets with three companies of the chemical industry and two of the telecommunications sector (15% of its portfolio with SPT Telecom alone). Yet, due to the enormous size of the portfolio companies and the small size of the holdings, Credis cannot really influence corporate policy and must be considered a passive investor, furthermore its major holdings are in very liquid firms ('blue chips').

The third group includes comparatively competitive sectors with very different companies, i.e. those in a good economic and financial condition as well as firms with outdated plants, high indebtedness and pressing liquidity problems. One of the most problematic and heterogeneous industries is engineering, including electrical engineering and machinery. Since companies in this industry have very different future prospects and many of them are on the edge of bankruptcy, any allocation of voucher points or financial means to this sector requires careful *ex ante* screening of firms to reduce investment risks. In the absence of risk-reducing factors like pre-announced public investment programmes or a certain robustness against cyclical trends ensuring some minimum demand for the goods produced in a sector (like in the second group), investment in weakly performing enterprises may quickly lose its value. This is true, though to different degrees, for all sectors of the third group. On the other hand, high risks may generate chances for high returns. Many companies may eventually become winners after deep restructuring. However, heavy investing in the industries of the third group presupposes:

- sufficient *ex ante information* to make a well-balanced assessment of the chances and risks of a specific investment and/or
- entrepreneurial competence and *ex post monitoring* to turn around and restructure companies which are in temporary trouble.

The former favours the domestic bank-sponsored funds, which indeed made substantial investments in the engineering industry as well as in pulp and paper. The latter explains the investment focus of various entrepreneurial funds, e.g. of Coupon Invest in engineering or - less extensively - by Harvard in pulp and paper (see also the SEPAP story above).

In sum, the sectoral distribution of share portfolios reveals some trends for the investment strategies of the various groups of IPFs. Foreign bank sponsored funds largely acknowledged regulatory constraints and abstained from investment in financial institutions. Domestic financial groups didn't stick as much to the constraints aside from SPAS which cleared its portfolio from banks and other financial holdings after voucher privatization. Domestic bank-sponsored funds spread their portfolios more evenly across industries than other IPFs. Considering the huge amount of voucher points collected by the domestic bank funds, this is quite understandable. All other funds tended to concentrate a substantial proportion of their investment in two or three industries. The major foreign bank-sponsored IPFs favoured 'demand-robust' sectors for their investment to minimize portfolio risk given a constitutional lack of information. Domestic funds frequently trusted in companies with a dominant market position and hence placed their investment in sectors like energy and finance. Their groundfloor knowledge of the Czech economy is likewise reflected by investment in risky sectors, especially in engineering.

For the large domestic bank-sponsored groups, the size of their portfolio doesn't allow any sectoral specialization or concentration comparable to that of other IPFs. All the more is it amazing that 42% of IKS KB assets and 37% of the huge PIAS portfolio are allocated to only eight and six companies respectively. Yet, the focus of the big holdings of domestic bank-sponsored funds on highly concentrated sectors like banking and energy doesn't tell us much about their true governance influence in the concerned companies since most of them are not only very large, but also still under state control - like the banks themselves. Nevertheless, provided the state will wither away from those sectors in the future, banks (then eventually under private control) could become the dominant owners in sectors like energy and telecommunication - and possibly also in the banking industry itself!

The allocation of assets into core industries, as practised by the most major investment companies, surely may enhance the quality of active corporate governance. However, it is no proof that the funds are really interested in executing active control over portfolio companies. The existence of a widespread interest of the biggest fund groups - and hence of the major players in corporate control - still is to be evidenced. For this reason, we will inquire into the governance power and strategy of the financial groups in the following section.

3.5.2 Governance Power and Strategy of Financial Groups

The voucher scheme bundled a considerable part of company stock up in the hands of a relatively small amount of funds sponsored by financial intermediaries. After the takeover of Creditanstalt by Motoinvest, there can be identified seven major financial groups. Each group is composed of various investment entities with strong equity links with each other and to the group's core company. The latter may be a bank, an insurance or investment company. Likewise, there may exist equity ties to allied companies which are in a friendly or trust relationship with the core company. A partial list of intra-group ownership connections of some of the main financial groups is presented in Table 3.14.

Subsequently, we will analyse the governance potential and interest of the top 7 financial groups by taking a closer look to their portfolios and strategies. As a rule of thumb, a fund obtains a seat on the board of a portfolio company if it is in possession of an equity stake of at least 10%. Stakes exceeding 18% frequently secure a dominant position among the company owners, rendering possible active control of the affairs of the corporation. With Egerer (1994, p. 20), we may therefore refer to the former as significant and to the latter as controlling stakes. However, in the context

Table 3.14: Intra-group crossholdings of financial groups[a]

controlled company		owning entity		sponsor (group)	
name of company	type of company	name	holding in % of company stock	name	holding in % of company stock
AGB IF II	IF	Agrobanka	27.74		27.74
Apollón holding	holding	Motoinvest	13.20		13.20
C.S. infrastr. IF	IF	Motoinvest	10.79		21.40
		2. CS hol.	10.61		
CA CEIF[b]	IF	Motoinvest	23.83		23.83
C.A.S. 5. Holding	holding	2. CS hol.	23.54		23.54
C.A.S. 6. Holding	holding	Motoinvest	12.14	Moto-	12.14
C.A.S. 9. Holding[b]	holding	Motoinvest	16.90	invest	16.90
2. CS holding[b]	holding	Motoinvest	16.82		16.82
3. CS holding[b]	holding	Motoinvest	21.55		21.55
4. CS holding[b]	holding	Motoinvest	16.09		16.09
Portfolio IF OVA	IF	Agrobanka	10.76		10.76
Kredital IF OVA	IF	Motoinvest	14.96		14.96
IF Top Profit	IF	C.A.S. 6. h.	18.61		18.61
FINOP holding	holding	CSOB	45.74		45.74
Kvanto IF	IF	CSOB	10.12		22.92
		Komenius holding	12.80		
Zlatý IF Kvanto	IF	CSOB	10.75		19.47
		F.B.E. hol.	18.72	CSOB	
FINOP Výnos. IF	IF	FINOP	11,28		11,28
IF Bohemia dopr.	IF	FINOP	54.77		54.77
IF Bohemia ener.	IF	FINOP	40.54		40.54
Zemed. IF Rabbit	IF	FINOP	37.89		37.89
Bankovní hol.[c]	holding	IPB	41.77		49.07
		Domeana	07.30		
Rentiérský IF	IF	Bank. hol.	19.96		83.86
		SP Group	63.90		
Potravin. IF	IF	Bank. hol.	33.22		33.22
Prumyslový IF	IF	Bank. hol.	28.00	IPB	28.00
IF Obchodu	IF	Bank. hol.	38.09		38.09
IF Bohatství	IF	Bank. hol.	21.74		21.74
Kristálový IF	IF	Bankov. holding	30.42		30.42
Restitucní IF	IF	IPB	22.43		22.43
IF energetiky[c]	IF	IPB	11.85		11.85
2. Spor. priv. IF	IF	SIS	22.96		22.96
SP Ceský IF	IF	Sporitelna	25.88		55.88
		Midland Bank	30.00		
SP Vseobecný IF	IF	Sporitelna	65.11		65.11
SP Výnosový IF	IF	Bankers Trust	10.00	Ceská	65.40
		Sporitelna	25.40	spor.	
		Midland Bank	30.00		
Spor. IF[c]	IF	Sporitelna	42.84		42.84

a Ownership structures of IPFs and holdings sponsored by financial groups: stakes of banks and affiliated or cooperating companies as of 5 December 1996

b Ownership stake as of 12 September 1996

c Ownership stake as of 6 June 1996

Source: Securities Centre; Burzovní noviny, no. 184, 19 September 1996, p.I

of the large financial groups, the existence of significant or controlling stakes in the portfolio of individual funds is of rather limited validity. Most groups execute company control through an extended network of IPFs and other holding companies founded and governed by banks. Besides, the banks themselves are allowed to hold equity stakes in the corporate sector and they often use their direct holdings in portfolio companies to support the governance activities of their funds (and vice versa). The governance power of bank-sponsored IPFs can thus be measured most adequately in a group context.

Table 3.15: Holdings over 10% of major financial groups

		CS	KB	IPB	OB	MI	ZB	CP	total
no. of[a]									
- IPFs		5	3	6	4	18	2	5	43
- other investment companies		2	1	3	4	3	-	1	12
Holdings[b]>10%:									
	>10%	146	68	160	50	136	15	61	636
Portfolios	>18%	57	28	83	36	71	8	21	307
of	>20%	16	13	57	23	49	2	16	179
individual	>30%	1	-	16	10	22	1	8	63
investment	>40%	-	-	9	7	12	-	3	37
entities	>50%	-	-	6	4	3	-	2	17
	>10%	112	65	128	30	99	13	56	400
Group	>18%	53	30	87	28	58	6	19	264
Portfolios	>20%	32	14	69	27	46	4	7	222
(cumul.	>30%	17	2	36	22	38	3	5	160
face value)	>40%	2	2	16	16	25	-	3	90
	>50%	2	-	9	10	14	-	2	55
cumul. face value of holdings >10% (in million CZK)		10,005	6,239	11,789	4,977	6,565	931	3,763	43,554
% of overall face value of holdings exceeding 10% of firm equity[c]		4.1% *3.0%*	2.6% *1.9%*	4.9% *3.6%*	2.1% *1.5%*	2.7% *2.0%*	0.4% *0.3%*	1.5% *1.1%*	18.3% *13.3%*

a   Estimated *minimum* number of affiliated IPFs and other entities with holdings over 10% in at least one portfolio company. Former investment funds which have been converted into holding companies are listed as IPFs. Other holding companies include banks.

b   Only holdings in non-banks, data as of 6 December 1996.

c   Only overall face value of large stakes in companies listed at the PSE which are non-banks. As of 6 December 1996, the overall value of large holdings amounts to CZK 353,960 million. The NPF holds large stakes amounting to CZK 89,462 million, that is 25% of the face value of all large holdings. Data in upper row do not include holdings of NPF. The lower row in italics presents the same data including NPF holdings.

Source: Securities Centre; own calculations.

By December 1996, the top 7 financial groups are administering 636 significant stakes (out of a total of about 4,200 significant stakes held in companies quoted at the Prague Stock Exchange). The overall face value of significant stakes held by the top 7 financial groups amounts to CZK 43.6 billion, i.e. 13.3% of the face value of all holdings over 10% in listed companies (see Table 3.15). A considerable proportion of the overall number of significant stakes is still owned by the NPF. Most of them are controlling stakes in strategic enterprises whose privatization methods haven't been decided so far. Deducting all NPF holdings, the proportion of significant stakes held by the financial groups comes to 18.3% (as by face value). These data reflect a distinct interest of most financial groups in active corporate governance. Altogether, the top 7 financial groups hold significant stakes in exactly 400 corporations. Adding up all 636 significant stakes held by the groups' 43 IPFs and 12 other holding companies (including banks)[36], they own controlling stakes in 264 companies and stakes higher than 30% in 160 firms. The groups are hence provided with enormous governance power - especially if they bundle their stakes and cooperate in the execution of corporate control.

The group disposing of the biggest governance power as measured by the face value of significant holdings is the IPB group. At first glance, this fact may be surprising as the group is only in third place as measured by the number of voucher points collected. The main reason for the group's outstanding position is that its investment arm PIAS had obtained the government mandate to manage the Restitution Investment Fund (RIF). Running a portfolio with a market value of CZK 13 billion in end-1995, RIF is the country's largest investment fund. Its portfolio represents some 45% of the overall assets managed by PIAS and contains 66 significant holdings. Considering the originally scattered portfolio of the fund (3% of each company slated for voucher privatization) which was imitating an index fund, meanwhile the fund has substantially reduced the number of portfolio companies. IPB itself directly owns 20 significant stakes in companies which is much more than any other bank. A substantial proportion of IPB's direct holdings comes from sell-backs of unit trust certificates. In March 1995, IPB even had to liquidate one of its unit trusts, the open-end trust Fond aktivních reserv (fund of active reserves), after more than one third of the trust's participation certificates had been returned over the preceding six months. In such cases, Czech law requires immediate liquidation of a trust. To pay off unitholders, IPB bought all assets of the fund portfolio.[37] In end-1995, another PIAS fund, Investicní fond rychlého výnosu (Quick yield investment fund), merged with IPB, thereby providing the bank with sizeable stakes in several companies.[38] Furthermore, the group controls companies through Domeana, a subsidiary wholly owned by IPB with extensive stakes in the corporate sector. Another ally of the group is e.g. První mestská banka, a smaller bank with significant shareholdings in several industrial firms, which is controlled by IPB through a 25% equity stake.

PIAS doesn't tire of publicly announcing that the portfolio of each investment fund and unit trust is built up and managed independently according to a business plan worked out by the fund management and in harmony with the statutes of the individual fund. A look at the portfolio of various PIAS funds is evidence to the contrary. The common approach of the IPB group members to investment and corporate control can be well exemplified by the case of Plzenský Prazdroj, the biggest Czech brewery and the 24th biggest company listed at the PSE. The IPB group jointly owns more than 50% of the brewery. Remarkably, Plzenský belongs to the major portfolio holdings of all 15 IPFs managed by PIAS in June 1996 (excluding the RIF). More concretely, the brewery represents the largest equity interest in the portfolios of five IPFs (four of which belong to the top five PIAS funds by asset value). Besides, it is the second biggest interest in six IPFs, the third biggest interest in three funds and the sixth biggest interest in only one fund (namely in IF energetiky, by far the smallest IPF managed by PIAS). Pure chance? Hardly, all the more as the brewery makes up a major holding of the RIF and IPB itself, too.[39]

There are more examples for concerted conduct of the group. Jointly with PIAS, IPB owns not only a majority of Plzenský, but also several other strategic stakes in the beer industry which belongs by tradition to the most competitive branches in the Czech economy. The IPB group is controlling shareholder of the second biggest Czech brewery Radegast (34% of equity), holds 9% in the third biggest brewery Prazské pivovary (controlled by a foreign investor) and is presently building a strategic position in the fifth biggest brewery Jihoceské pivovary. The group's overall portfolio is more or less symmetrically mirrored in the individual IPF portfolios. The Radegast interests exceed 5% of the fund assets in five IPFs while stakes in Prazské pivovary come to between 3% and 6% of overall assets in four funds.

A similar approach to corporate governance can be observed in most financial groups. The individual members of the groups use their capital links and personal webs to exercise concerted conduct in the control of corporations. Of course, this enhances the efficacy of corporate control because company managers are facing one large and powerful owner rather than several funds whose holdings are constrained by portfolio regulation. However, joint corporate control makes it difficult to evaluate the real governance power of a group. Presently, funds are only obliged to make public interests exceeding 10% of the equity of an individual portfolio company or 3% of the fund's overall assets. Interests of group members acting in concert must be revealed, but the underlying legal norm isn't enforced very strictly due to problems of policing the definition of 'concerted action' (see section 6.4.2). Information about stakes under 10% is not systematically available. The listings of industrial holdings of financial groups presented in this chapter thus have in many cases the character of minimum holdings rather than of accurate portfolio data. The upshot is that the groups have considerable 'hidden control reserves' which are difficult to assess given the secrecy of the capital market. Since group holdings are scattered frequently over several funds and subholdings, the data presented in this chapter still tend to understate the actual governance power of the financial groups in relation to other classes of investors (like e.g. foreign direct investors and 'independent' funds which are not embedded in the web of a financial group).

The consolidation of group portfolios has been logically accompanied by a reduction of the number of companies in the funds' portfolios. Komercni's flagship IPF KB started to operate with a portfolio of more than 250 firms. By April 1996, the portfolio shrank to 180 titles. Going by fund officials, the plan is to reduce further to 100 companies. The group's control power is strengthened by holdings of Komercni's second-wave unit trust IKS KB plus and several direct holdings of the bank itself. Yet, the most prominent example of portfolio contraction is SPAS, the first-wave IPF of Ceská Sporitelna. The largest IPF of the first wave started its activities with a portfolio of as many as 514 firms in 1993. In the following years, it sold off minor holdings and enlarged a strategic core of enterprises in which it holds significant and controlling stakes. In end-1994, the fund portfolio comprised 445 firms and the market value of the 50 largest holdings amounted to 75% of the value of the overall share portfolio. In July 1995, the fund divided into three successor funds managed according to three different investment strategies. The overall portfolio of the three funds consisted of less than 280 companies.

The successor fund with the biggest net asset value (nearly CZK 10 billion in end-1995) is Sporitelni privatizacni-Ceský IF. It contains about 50 highly liquid and large companies with a strong financial performance and a stable position in their industries. The fund's main objective is to take care of the long-term appreciation of its assets. This means that the holdings are strategic. The portfolio of Sporitelni privatizacni-výnosový IF comprises less than 100 medium-sized firms, likewise with a sound financial standing and good growth and dividend prospects. The main goal of this fund is to generate dividend income for its shareholders. The third fund Sporitelni privatizacni-vseobecni IF took over all remaining SPAS holdings, that is predominantly stakes in smaller and poorly performing companies with a low market value. Their stock is to be gradually sold and the revenue should be transferred completely to the fund's shareholders. It is planned that the fund will be wound up by the year 2000.

The policy of SIS is to liquidate unattractive companies which suffer from financial distress and to enter into a long-term commitment with well-positioned and comparatively sound corporations. In this, SIS doesn't differ much from all other financial groups. The strategy mirrors the general willingness of most bank-sponsored funds to get involved in active corporate control in the long term. The limits of this willingness to exert governance are determined by the quality of the individual portfolio company. In most cases, the financial groups do not feel competent to turn around distressed firms. While it may pay to take over the entrepreneurial risk and to try to increase the competitiveness of poorly performing companies because of potentially high upside gains from restructuring, banks so far shy away from becoming providers of venture capital. This risk aversion substantially lowers the chances of many smaller companies to obtain the financial means necessary to start deep restructuring.

Interestingly, similar to PIAS, the SIS officials stick to the alleged independence of their funds.[40] Again, reality looks different. The split of SPAS has permitted the Sporitelna group to increase its shareholdings substantially and accumulate controlling stakes in many individual companies. The SIS funds, including second-wave 2. Sporitelní IF and the smaller cash fund Sporitelní IF, are running a common approach to the control of their portfolio companies. In some cases (e.g. engineering firm ZPS Zlín), their position is strengthened by direct holdings of Ceská Sporitelna.

Similar control patterns occur among the portfolio companies of the CSOB group. However, the major holdings by market value are owned by the bank itself or the former state holding Finop rather than by the bank-sponsored Kvanto funds. Finop was included in the voucher scheme. Today, two thirds of the holding are owned jointly by CSOB and one of its IPFs, Zlatý IF Kvanto. The structure of the group holdings reveals a strong preference for trading companies. On one hand, this is due to the traditional destination of CSOB as financier of Czechoslovak foreign trade. Of course, the bank's insider knowledge about trade firms is an asset which has been widely used for the funds' investment decisions. On the other hand, the strong weight of the trade sector must be put behind the bank's intention to preserve and to stabilize the business relationships with its major clients. In this respect, the holding structure of the group corroborates the bank-firms relationships of the old command system.[41]

Another striking feature of the CSOB group is the high concentration of its holdings. In 28 out of a total of 30 portfolio companies with equity shares over 10%, the group holds controlling stakes exceeding 18% of the firm's equity. In as many as 27 companies, the stake is higher than 20%, in 22 firms even higher than 30%. This high degree of concentration clearly proves the strategic character of the holdings. Moreover, it indicates the group's preference for undivided control instead of cooperation with other owners. The striving for strong and stable control is observable, for instance, in many medium-sized trade companies. Also fairly concentrated are the holdings of the IPB group. 87 out of 128 significant stakes are concurrently controlling ones (>18%). More than 50% of the significant stakes of the Motoinvest group are controlling ones, too.

The investment imperium of Motoinvest has undergone the quickest (and most surprising) expansion of all financial groups. The group's acquisitions on the 'market for fund control' made it a major player in corporate control, too. Motoinvest governs companies through a vast network of funds and holdings. We could identify no less than 18 affiliated funds with significant stakes in portfolio firms. In the course of 1996, the sponsor converted several of the investment funds into holdings to increase their governance power. Holdings are not subject to portfolio restrictions like the 20%-limit concerning the stock of portfolio companies or the 10%-restriction relating to the fund's assets. From a group perspective, considering the huge amount of affiliated investment entities, there was no real necessity for the conversions. Motoinvest could disperse its stakes in individual firms over sufficient funds so as to meet regulation and, at the same time, to entrench control of portfolio companies. It seems therefore that the actual reason behind the conversion of most of the goup's investment funds was to evade capital market supervision and to avoid financial disclosure. In fact, the group is extremely reluctant to reveal data about its funds. The other financial groups didn't follow Motoinvest. While several managers of bank funds favoured a relaxation of portfolio regulation in interviews carried out for this study, most of them were afraid of adverse reputational effects connected with conversions to holdings.[42] Outside the Motoinvest group, Bankovní IF of PIAS is the only bank-sponsored fund which has been converted into a holding (now Bankovní holding, a.s.).

3.6 CONTROL OF LARGE ENTERPRISES: OWNERSHIP OF THE TOP 100

To make a most detailed and true assessment of a group's importance in corporate control relative to other groups and investors, we must consider the size and economic weight of the controlled companies. Therefore, we need a criterion to determine the relative economic importance of a portfolio company. As share prices are still highly distorted because of the segmentation of the Czech capital market and extensive insider trading, mere market capitalization (number of shares issued multiplied by share price at the PSE) is no reliable criterion.[43] The face value of equity likewise isn't based upon an assessment by capital market participants. As matters stand, the best indicator for the economic importance of a company may be its turnover. Under this assumption, a group's relative importance in corporate control depends to a large degree upon the amount of holdings in the top 100 companies by turnover.[44] Table 3.16 presents significant ownership stakes in the top 100 companies of various groups of investors. With a total market capitalization of CZK 323 billion in June 1996, the top 100 make up roughly 55% of the overall equity market. Some half of their equity is held in stakes exceeding 10%. Significant stakes comprise 53% of the face value and 50% of the market value of the top 100. This means that many companies are governed by one or more large shareholders. The far most important shareholder still is the NPF, holding 60% of the face value and 56% of the market value of all significant stakes. Other public authorities, i.e. prevalently municipalities, own only a small fraction of the stakes over 10%.

In the private sector, domestic direct investors (non-financial companies) are the most important owners. They hold 14% of all significant stakes by market value. If one assigns the turnover of each company to its significant shareholders proportionally according to the size of their ownership stakes, it turns out that domestic direct investors control as much as 31% of the turnover assigned to significant stakes in the top 100 companies. Foreign direct investors control roughly 14% of the turnover attributed to large equityholders. The governance power of individual investors is rather low. This is not surprising as a class of powerful individual owners (like the famous 'family companies' in Germany) can develop only in the long run. The concept of large privatization hasn't yet supported this development.[45]

The top 7 financial groups jointly own some 8% of the significant stakes both by face value and market value. This is dramatically lower than their share in the significant stakes of all listed companies (13.34% of face value). The reason for this is that many of the top 100 companies are strategic firms with majority stakes held by the NPF.[46] After deduction of all NPF holdings, the financial groups hold nearly 20% of the remaining significant stakes. As NPF holdings are to be gradually run down in the future, the influence of the financial groups may rise through further acquisitions or dispersions of NPF stakes (especially if stakes are sold off through the stock exchange).

More important, the real influence of the financial groups is stronger than suggested by the data because, in contrast to both direct investors and the NPF, they dispose of hidden control reserves which are frequently invisible to outsiders. For instance, as of December 1996, it is estimated that

Table 3.16: Ownership of significant equity stakes in Czech top 100[a]

	(1) NPF	(2) Other public authorities	(3) Individual investors	(4) Foreign direct investors	(5) Foreign banks	(6) Domestic direct investors	(7) Other IPFs	(8) IPFs of top 7 financial groups	(9) Domestic banks[b]	(8+9) Top 7 financial groups overall	Σ(1…9) All big investors	Signific. stakes as % of total	Overall top 100 (in billion CZK)
no. of holdings	39	8	3	13	10	54	9	47	16	63	199	-	-
proportion by													
- face value	60.1%	2.0%	0.2%	7.1%	1.2%	19.8%	1.9%	5.8%	2.2%	7.9%	100%	52.9%	497.2
- market cap.[c]	56.5%	1.0%	0.8%	5.7%	1.8%	14.3%	4.5%	5.3%	2.3%	7.6%	100%	50.3%	322.9
- asset value	53.0%	3.6%	0.4%	6.8%	1.0%	24.4%	2.2%	7.3%	2.4%	9.7%	100%	53.6%	887.1
- net profit[d]	61.9%	2.3%	0.2%	13.8%	2.0%	4.3%	4.7%	7.5%	3.3%	10.8%	100%	57.7%	25.5
- turnover	44.2%	3.1%	0.6%	13.6%	1.7%	30.8%	2.5%	7.9%	2.2%	10.1%	100%	60.1%	647.5

a The top 100 are the 100 companies listed at the Prague Stock Exchange with the highest sales revenues. Ownership data as of December 1996, face value and market capitalization as of June 1996, asset value as of December 1995, net profit and turnover for 1995.

b Including holdings of Ceská sporitelna, Komercni banka, IPB, Agrobanka and the insurance company Ceská pojistovna, i.e. exclusively holdings of the core banks of the top 7 financial groups.

c Number of issued shares multiplied by share price at PSE as of 10 June 1996.

d Net profit is the residual after deduction of all money costs, that is sales revenue minus wages, salaries, rent, fuel and raw materials, interest on loans, depreciation and taxes.

Source: Sdruzeni TOP 100, PSE; Securities Centre, own calculations

the IPB group controls roughly 44% of the stock of the pulp mill Biocel Paskov, the 44th-largest Czech company by turnover and the second-largest firm in the pulp and paper industry. However, the Securities Centre registers only a 17% direct stake of IPB itself. The rest is scattered in portions smaller than 10% of company stock over various funds and subholdings. This is in accord with the fact that, in end-1995, the PIAS funds alone held a 22% stake in Biocel, with no individual fund disposing of more than 6%. Likewise, at that time, PIAS was in possession of some 16% of the heating company Moravskoslezské teplárny, the country's 55th-largest firm by turnover. Again, the stock was split into small portions and dispersed over various funds. Today, the group holds more than 30% in the heating company, 17% of which is a direct holding of IPB. Together with a 20% stake of SIS, the company is run by two financial groups. The mechanical engineering firm ZPS Zlín is dominated through a 30% equity stake by the Ceská sporitelna group. The ownership of 22% (held by one SIS fund and the savings bank itself) has been disclosed, the rest is scattered over the group's remaining funds. This anecdotal evidence well illustrates that the actual influence of the financial groups is bigger than expressed by the mere ownership data of the table. This is due to both the high amount of investment entities affiliated to most fund families and the common investment and governance strategy run by each group.

Finally, Table 3.17 presents significant stakes of the financial groups in the 100 Czech listed companies with the biggest turnover.[47] The distribution of shareholdings roughly confirms the results already drawn from Table 3.15 above. With 16 significant stakes in 13 companies, the IPB group is slightly ahead of the Ceská Sporitelna group managing 15 stakes in 12 firms. Ignoring the extensive strategic holdings of the NPF, the IPB group controls nearly 8% of the face value and 4% of the market value of all significant stakes in the top 100. This corresponds with roughly 5% of the turnover of the top 100. Striking is the rather low involvement of Motoinvest in the top 100 with significant stakes in no more than four companies. This is in line with the assumption made above that Motoinvest tends to concentrate its industrial shareholdings in medium-sized and small corporations. It is remarkable, too, that Zivnobanka has no significant stake in the top 100. This observation can be attributed to the small size of the group's overall equity portfolio. In December 1995, the net asset value of the two funds managed by the bank's investment company was CZK 3,300 million. This is roughly one third of the portfolios of just the biggest funds of SIS and IKS KB and one fifth of RIF. Concentrated equity holdings in large firms may therefore present too big risks for the group. On the other hand, it might also indicate that Zivnobanka's interest in active corporate control is not as pronounced as that of other financial groups, headed by IPB and the savings bank.

Table 3.17: *Non-bank holdings over 10% of major financial groups in Czech top 100*

	CS	KB	IPB	OB	MI	ZB	CP	total
holdings > 10% in:								
- no. of individual holdings[a]	15	10	16	11	5	-	6	63
- % of all holdings > 10% in top 100[b]	9.4%	6.3%	10.0%	6.9%	3.1%	-	3.8%	39.4%
	7.5%	*5.0%*	*8.0%*	*5.5%*	*2.5%*	-	*3.0%*	*31.6%*
- no. of companies	12	9	13	6	4	-	6	35
proportion by[b]								
- face value	3.9%	3.3%	7.7%	1.5%	2.2%	-	1.0%	19.6%
	1.6%	*1.4%*	*3.1%*	*0.6%*	*0.9%*	-	*0.4%*	*7.9%*
- market capitalization[c]	4.6%	3.1%	3.8%	3.3%	1.7%	-	0.8%	17.3%
	2.0%	*1.4%*	*1.7%*	*1.4%*	*0.8%*	-	*0.4%*	*7.6%*
- asset value	5.0%	2.6%	6.6%	3.1%	1.6%	-	1.2%	18.9%
	2.5%	*1.2%*	*3.2%*	*1.5%*	*0.8%*	-	*0.6%*	*9.7%*
- net profit	7.2%	7.4%	11.2%	1.6%	0.9%	-	0.0%	28.3%
	2.8%	*2.8%*	*4.3%*	*0.6%*	*0.3%*	-	*0.0%*	*10.8%*
- turnover	4.6%	2.4%	4.9%	3.1%	1.5%	-	0.8%	17.3%
	2.7%	*1.4%*	*2.9%*	*1.8%*	*0.9%*	-	*0.5%*	*10.1%*

a Estimated *minimum* number of affiliated IPFs and other entities with holdings over 10% in at least one portfolio company.

b The top 100 are the 100 companies listed at the Prague Stock Exchange with the highest sales revenues. Ownership data as of December 1996, face value and market capitalization as of June 1996, asset value as of December 1995, net profit and turnover for 1995. Data in upper row do not include holdings of NPF. The lower row in italics presents the same data including NPF holdings.

c Number of issued shares multiplied by share price at PSE as of 10 June 1996.

Source: Securities Centre; Sdruzení TOP 100; own calculations.

NOTES

1. Another 5 funds had registered for the first wave and withdraw after the preliminary round in which they attracted, in sum, only about 400,000 voucher points from some 600 individuals.

2. Cf. also Spiska (1993, pp. 13-17).

3. The US equivalent of unit trusts are the mutual funds.

4. Many high-rank fund representatives were and still are former ministries officials (e.g. from the 'founders' of SOEs) contributing with deep inside knowledge about companies to the management of their funds. Kozený, for instance, had aggressively wooed top officials involved in the drafting of and deciding on privatization projects already in the run-up to the first privatization wave so as to get an early information edge for HC&C over other investment companies.

5.   Open-end unit trusts have to publish weekly information about redemptions, sales and the value of their certificates.
6.   Section 24 of the Law on Investment Companies and Investment Funds actually imposes a 20%-restriction on all investment funds and unit trusts of the same investment company respectively. To exhaust the 40%-limit, the company had, strictly speaking, to manage both at least one investment fund and one unit trust.
7.   See also Coffee (1996). Like the other architects of the voucher scheme around Dusan Tríska, Klaus speaks up for competition on free markets wherever possible. If regulatory measures are to be carried out, then he favours reactive regulatory interference after problems have cropped up as against prophylactic *ex ante* regulation which could lead in his view to considerable distortions.
8.   Figure 3.1 doesn't contain a later amendment of the InvAct passed in November 1997 restricting the investment of individual funds to 11% of the equity of each portfolio company.
9.   § 24(5)a InvAct limits the holdings of all unit trusts managed by the same investment company to 20% of their overall portfolio. However, § 24(1) already sets a ceiling for each single unit trust, amounting to 10% of its portfolio. The latter section clearly defines a lower limit, which cannot be exceeded by the joint investment of all trusts managed by one investment company. § 24(5)a InvAct is therefore redundant.
10. The Harvard Funds were the first to merge into non-investment fund 'holdings.' See section 6.2.2 below.
11. See Baums & von Randow (1995).
12. While Sporitelna established two investment funds, i.e. one for each wave, Komercní founded merely one IPF that participated in both waves.
13. One open-end trust had to be liquidated in 1995 in accordance with Czech law after more than one third of its unitholders had requested redemption within six months. One investment fund has been merged with Investicní in the same year.
14. Coffee (1996) notes that diversification over several funds could signal, too, the intent of the founder to actively exert corporate governance. This is valid at least for the funds participating in the first wave. At the time of their establishment, investment companies with more than one fund were still allowed to hold up to 40% of a firm.
15. A curiosity is a fund registered under the name 'Comenius - green fund of prosperity'. Its name obviously tries to combine a bright image (Comenius was a famous Czech philosopher) with an ecological orientation and the promise of wealth.
16. There is no affiliation with Harvard except that the founder of HC&C holds a bachelors degree from this university.
17. Meanwhile, Trend has been subjugated under forced administration by the Ministry of Finance. The founder as well as some other managers have been accused of mismanagement and fraud by the shareholders after the value of the fund had declined by 44% on the Prague Stock Exchange in the first six months of 1996 even though the overall market had increased by almost 30%.
18. The book value per voucher book for the IPF YSE was the highest after the first wave and reached about CSK 48,500; PPF's První Ceský Fond (First Czech Fund) realized a value of CSK 42,000. The book values of voucher books invested with the biggest funds sponsored by state banks ranged from a scanty CSK 18,500 (Rentiérský IF managed by PIAS) over CSK 22,500 (SPAS managed by SIS) up to CSK 25,500 (IPF Komercní Banky). Measured by net asset value on the emerging Czech capital market on 30 June 1994, YSE was still heading in front of HC&C's Dividend Fund (which had collected some 50% of all points allocated to Harvard), Rentiérský and První Ceský while SPAS and Komercní just came to some half of the net asset value of a voucher book invested with YSE. For more detailed data see Egerer (1994, p. 13).
19. The relative strength of HC&C in the second wave must probably be put down to the comparably high net asset value of its shares. See preceding footnote.
20. A foreign investor owns more than one half of the top-18 equity holdings in 33 companies, domestic investors do so in 24 firms.
21. Cablemaker Kablo Kladno (see case study in chapter 4) is an example of a voucher-privatized company in which a foreign direct investor acquired a controlling stake in the course of large-

scale privatization and then increased its shareholding by open-market transactions (purchased from individuals and other investors). In addition, the foreign direct investors carried out a capital increase to further enhance its holding.

22. The largest open-end trust produced by voucher privatization, the Agrobanka unit trust (AGB IF II) managed by A-Invest, opened in January 1998. It's difficult to make a reliable assessment of the net asset value of the fund's portfolio as A-Invest is very sparing with portfolio information. According to the Prague Business Journal (28 Oct. – 3 Nov., 1996, p. 21), the fund controlled assets worth CSK 2,200 million in October 1996. As of December 1996, some 26 Czech open-end unit trusts were redeeming units. However, most of them were cash funds that didn't participate in voucher privatization.

23. See Hospodárské noviny, 15 December 1995, p. 1.

24. Interview with Zdenek Tuma, Chief Economist of the sole Czech investment bank Patria Finance.

25. See The Wall Street Journal Europe, 23 October 1995, and 17/18 November 1995.

26. See The Wall Street Journal, 12 July 1996.

27. To name but the most prominent staff members, Lou Ross (former Ford executive), James Wood (Babcock and Wilcox) and John Susunu (ex-White House Chief of Staff) all belong to the Stratton experts team.

28. Despite the appointment of a US manufacturing expert to its board, Fatra's general director repeatedly criticized Stratton as a mere 'financial investor'. In the end, Stratton had to sell its stake to the Chemapol group which the general director called a 'strategic investor' (Prague Business Journal, no. 35, 16-22 Sept., 1996, p. 12).

29. For the sequel of the story of beermaker Plzenský under the control of the IPB group, see Chapter 6.

30. The raids initiated by Plzenská were opposed by the bank's second largest equityholder, monopoly insurer Ceská Pojistovna. The latter had been in possession of some 25% of Plzenská's equity. The conflict between the two major owners escalated into a split of the bank's managing board. Ceská Pojistovna withdrew its board representatives and appointed a new board. Over some weeks, it was quite unclear who would have the voting majority at the general meeting and it came to the most bizarre situation of two competing boards trying to run the company affairs. In the end, when it became clear that Motoinvest's voting share exceeded the holding of the insurance company, Ceská Pojistovna sold most of its bank stock to Motoinvest which has been in control of the bank ever since. As of mid-1996, Motoinvest holds some 70 to 80% of Plzenská.

31. In his letter to the public from 31 October 1995, the general director of Plzenská banka estimates most pessimistically 'that no changes to the better are waiting for the small shareholder. For this reason, we [Plzenská banka] are presently realizing the third wave of privatization for you. The main objective is to top up the yet fallow potential of shares of small stockholders - to render possible their immediate revaluation'. The start of the campaign had been chosen very cleverly since the stock index had reached its all-time low in the months preceding the offer.

32. Interestingly, Motoinvest made no attempt to acquire controlling stakes in SIS and the PIAS funds. As for SIS, the sheer size of the far biggest Czech voucher fund might have deterred the group from launching a hostile takeover bid. In the case of PIAS, the major reason is seemingly not to endanger a certain degree of strategic cooperation between Motoinvest and the IPB group. This informal cooperation had been reflected in a series of block trades of company stakes between both parties, the most sensational of which was IPB's sale of a big stake in Agrobanka to Motoinvest in autumn 1995 to strengthen Motoinvest's equity interest in the biggest private bank of the country (and the fifth biggest bank overall as measured by asset value). As of December 1996, Motoinvest held some 15 to 20% of Agrobanka. Considering some substantial stakes in the bank administered by allied funds and by other companies cooperating and voting with Motoinvest, this appeared to be sufficient to control the bank. Yet, after the detection of Agrobanka's liquidity crunch in late summer 1996, Motoinvest had to promise to pull out of the banking sector.

33. See Business Central Europe, September 1996, p. 68. This view is implicitly confirmed by a chief representative of Motoinvest who claims the group's intention is to supervise the

management of several 'good' enterprises and to keep a close eye on them to prevent managers from cheating rather than to actively run company affairs. See Motoinvest's general director Pavel Tykac in an interview in Ekonom, no.4, 1996, p. 13.

34. In December 1996, the stock market capitalization of CEZ was CZK 52.1 billion. The equity value of top-ranked SPT Telecom was CZK 99.6 billion. Other major non-financial corporations were Tabák (CZK 17.7 billion), Chemopetrol (CZK 11.5 billion) and Cokoládovny (CZK 10.8 billion). Furthermore there were 13 non-financial companies with a market capitalization between CZK 5 billion and CZK 10 billion. 9 out of the 13 companies belong to the energy sector.

35. The mentioned four holdings in financial intermediaries all belong to the top ten holdings of PIAS which make up 46% of its overall portfolio. The market value only of the four holdings amounts to 40% of the total value of the top ten holdings.

36. Take note that the data presented in Table 3.8 only relate to investment vehicles (funds and holdings) identified by the author. Yet, there are more investment entities allied to or governed by the seven groups under review. For that reason, all numbers in the table are to be regarded as minimum numbers. Furthermore, one should take into account that the actual governance power of the financial groups is higher than reflected by the table due to numerous stockholdings under 10%. Unfortunately, no accurate statistical evidence of such stockholdings is available.

37. In practice, IPB had no choice but to take over all assets of the trust. The illiquidity of the Czech equity market would have permitted a sale of the fund's portfolio only at a prohibitive discount, leaving PIAS with considerable losses from the transaction.

38. In its annual report for 1995, PIAS justified the merger with the negative development of the capital market which allegedly forced the company to seek for the most advantageous way (for the shareholders) how to liquidate the fund. The fund's highly dispersed equityholders, who couldn't prevent PIAS from executing the merger due to prohibitive coordination costs, assessed the action quite differently from the investment company. Many of them complained about the low compensation received from IPB. Indeed, the takeout compensation followed the fund's highly discounted market value rather than its net asset value.

39. In an interview carried out by the author, a PIAS manager confirmed that the IPB group follows a common approach to the control of portfolio companies. Strategic decisions are made on a group level, including the bank itself. The fund managers then frequently only execute the common strategy and compose individual portfolios in accordance with given, binding investment guidelines. With respect to the 'dozens of strategic enterprises' in the PIAS portfolio, their investment decisions are undoubtedly not autonomous.

40. The deputy general director of SIS and chairman of Sporitelní privatizacní - Ceský IF, Václav Srba, emphasizes in an interview in Úspech (no.7, 1995, p.56) that the three successor funds of SPAS are managed independently from each other and their interrelationships are based exclusively upon commercial principles.

41. Without doubt, this is true for all banks split off from the former monobank. Yet, in the case of CSOB, the efforts towards 'conglomeratization' of old command structures are most obvious due to the bank's sectoral specialization which finds its reflection in the group's equity links.

42. All the more after the cropping up of various problems concerning minority shareholder protection in connection with the conversion of private funds into holdings during the first half of 1996, see Chapter 6 below.

43. Indeed, only a small fraction (roughly 20%) of market transactions is executed and reported at organized markets. Most deals are realized directly between the interested parties at the Securities Centre where shares are registered. In the past, the prices at which the transactions were executed were secret so that the official prices at the PSE always reflected but a small part of the deals. Hence, the informational efficiency of the market has been extremely low.

44. The Czech top 100 are established and published each year by the association Sdruzení Top 100 whose members are six independent institutions, among others ING Bank and the Prague Economic University. The list considers exclusively firms quoted on the PSE. It hence doesn't include SOEs like Transgas and the Czech railways, nor privately-held corporations like car maker Skoda-Volkswagen. A list of the 1995 top 100 companies has been published in Hospodárské noviny, no. 121, 21 June 1996, p.19.

45. Of course, that isn't valid for Slovakia where intransparent and dubious privatization methods largely accelerated the emergence of an entrepreneurial elite of domestic individual investors. In the Czech Republic, the rather weak control power of individual owners reflects in some way the consequent renouncement of discriminating ways of property divestiture in large-scale privatization. MBOs have been applied infrequently and not systematically. Examples for MBOs and LBOs in big companies are the cases of the engineering concern Skoda Plzen in which the former and current general director holds a share of less than 10% of the capital stock, and of steelmaker Poldi Kladno whose majority had been sold to a private entrepreneur. While the restructuring of Skoda Plzen so far has made considerable progress, Poldi's recovery plan failed. The company got caught in serious liquidity problems so that the new owner couldn't meet its payments obligations to the NPF from which he had purchased his majority stake. Meanwhile, the NPF has filed for bankruptcy so as to force the owner to withdraw control of the company.

46. 27 out of the top 100 firms by turnover belong to the strategic companies of the NPF. Many of them are well-capitalized and boast high turnovers. For example, the NPF holds significant stakes in 9 out of the top 12 companies by turnover. In five of them, it even holds more than 50% of the equity stock.

47. Table 3.10 hence reveals some details about columns (8) and (9) of Table 3.9.

4 Equity control and restructuring: The governance performance of the financial groups

4.1 BOARD MODEL

4.1.1 The Legal Structure of the Joint-stock Corporation

The structure of the Czech joint stock corporation (*akciová spolecnost*, abbreviated *a.s.*) as modelled by the Commercial Code closely resembles the German *Aktiengesellschaft*. The law intends a dual board structure comprising a management board (*predstavenstvo*) and a supervisory board (*dozorci rada*).[1] The supreme body of the corporation is the general meeting (*valná hromada*). Figure 4.1 models the interrelations between the three company organs and summarises their main duties and rights.

The general meeting is held at least once a year and convened by the management board. Under the CCode, the meeting has a quorum if the attendance matches at least 30% of the capital stock (unless the articles of association require a higher attendance). The general assembly elects and recalls both the management board and the owner representatives at the supervisory board. Yet, the articles of association may determine that the management board is elected by the supervisory board. Here we encounter a major difference to the German model where the management board must be named by the supervisory board, thus entrenching the German *Aufsichtsrat* as an important controlling instance with considerable power over the top executives. The shareholders of the corporation may choose between two constellations, either direct control of the management board by the owners or German-style indirect control through the supervisory board. Direct control tends to enlarge the discretion of the managing directors and to enhance their legitimacy as against the supervisory board.

Nevertheless, the general assembly retains the most important strategic decisions on the corporation. It passes resolutions by majority vote on the distribution of profits, the approval of financial statements and the financial reward of members of both boards. It approves by two-thirds majority vote amendments to the articles of association, increases or reductions of the capital stock, the issuing of bonds, the winding-up of the company in

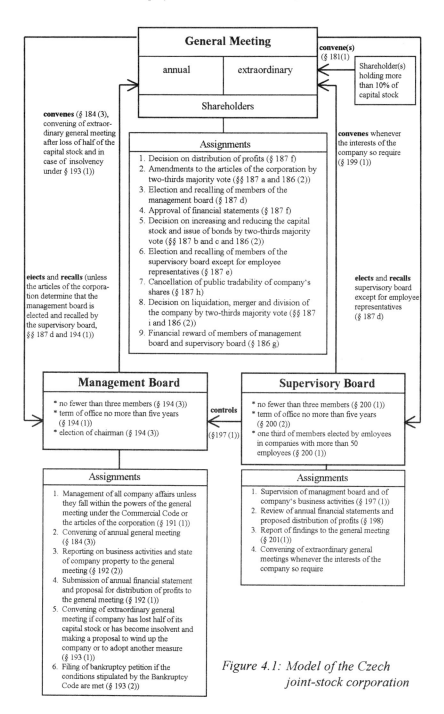

Figure 4.1: Model of the Czech joint-stock corporation

connection with its liquidation and its transformation, merger or division. Finally, the general meeting decides by no less than three-quarters majority of the attending equityholders owning the relevant shares, changes of the class or the type of shares (registered, bearer, to order), changes of the rights attached to a given class of shares, restrictions of transferability of registered shares (i.e. to name) or the cancellation of public tradeability of the company's shares.

The governance power of company owners is strengthened by their right to require the convention of extraordinary general meetings. A shareholder or a group of shareholders holding more than 10% of capital stock may request the management board to convene an extraordinary general meeting to discuss and approve proposals made by such shareholders. The threshold of 10% is double the ratio of 5% prescribed by German corporate law. But in most Czech companies it should be surmountable in times of crisis, while it is high enough to protect the management board from the activism of dispersed minority owners holding only tiny proportions of corporate stock. Clearly, a too low threshold could effect a significant decrease in the efficiency of the management if small shareholders misused the clause to boycott the corporate policy implemented by the controlling majority of company owners.

The management board is responsible for managing the day-to-day affairs of the company and the implementation of the decisions of the general assembly. Any member of the board may act in the name of the corporation in dealing with other parties. The board has to report on business activities and the state of company assets and to submit annual financial statements to the general meeting. Its scope of action in times of distress is tightened by the provisions to convene an extraordinary general meeting after the company has lost half of its equity stock or has become insolvent and to file a bankruptcy petition if the conditions stipulated by the Bankruptcy Code are met (see section 5.1.5.1).

The supervisory board's main task following the CCode and the German model is to monitor and supervise the activities of the managing board. In companies with no more than 50 employees, the supervisory board is elected by the shareholders. In larger firms with more than 50 employees, one third of the board members are to be elected by the employees. This provision closely resembles the German 'consensus model' with workers' co-determination even though the proportion of worker representatives is lower than in the German corporation (50%). A striking difference to the German approach is the triggering of co-determination already from 50 employees as against 2,000 in Germany. This means that virtually no joint-stock corporation can dodge worker participation at the supervisory board. Clearly, in the event of a conflict of interest between workers and owners, the latter will dominate the board due to their voting preponderance. Provided the delegates appointed at the general meeting are acting in concert, worker representatives will rarely be able to block their decisions as the board decides by simple majority vote. In the Czech model of the corporation, the supervisory board may be an effective governance tool of the company's owners as they dispose of at least two thirds of the board seats. Let us briefly remember: In the German case, the governance power of the owners is structurally based upon the board's chairman who is appointed by the general meeting and whose vote doubles in deadlocks. The Czech supervisory board has to elect a chairman, too, but his power is deducted more from his personality and competence then any voting edge. His foremost task is to draw up and sign minutes of the board meetings.

The supervisory board members have to be ordinary individuals and must not concurrently be managing directors, procurators or other persons entrusted to act on behalf of the corporation according to an entry in the commercial register. Independent of the governance approach chosen by the general assembly, the board's duties embrace the reviewing of the financial statements provided by the management board and the reporting of all essential findings to the general meeting. It must also inform the owners how the management board exercises its range of powers and how it conducts, in the opinion of each single member of the supervisory board, the business activities of the corporation. In this respect, the board fulfils an important function as informational intermediary between the company and its equityholders. To this end, its members are entitled to view all documents and records relating to the activities of the corporation. To protect the interests of company owners effectively, the supervisory board can decide to convene an extraordinary general meeting 'whenever the interests of the company so require' (CCode, §199(1)). This allows strategic and personal changes to be initiated before the company will slide into a crisis.

Quite obviously, the legal structure of the Czech corporation is largely inspired by the German dual-board model. The major difference is the higher flexibility of the Czech legal blueprint, leaving owners with considerable discretion in the actual design of the company bodies. This fits the overall approach of Czech large-scale privatization and the evolutionary openness of the emerging property system. Czech lawmakers are very reluctant to give a binding institutional framework - a fact typical for most parts of the property system including privatization and, as we will see later, the overall regulatory framework of the capital market. They intend to shift the responsibility for economic results as much as possible to individual economic agents and to react only to undesirable outcomes after they have appeared. This strategy of step-by-step regulation and improvement, reflecting once more the authorities' huge confidence in the market powers, necessarily accepts temporary inferior or non-efficient results of economic activity. In many respects, individual actors are responsible for finding and selecting efficient institutional arrangements which afterwards can be integrated into the evolving institutional overall environment (see also the emergence of the IPFs). To put it into Hayekian terminology, a constitutional lack of knowledge keeps the authorities away from constructing an elaborated institutional set-up tightly restricting the scope of individual action. Institutions emerge from a selection process making use of the decentralized knowledge of all market agents. In this sense, the Czech regulatory framework provides for a market for institutions and hence for an effective selection mechanism for institutions.

As for the structure of corporations, shareholders are offered the opportunity to try out various institutional alternatives which are centred around two basic models. The first model resembles the original idea of the lawmakers and institutionalizes the dualism between management and control in a German-type dual board structure. The second approach would be more equal to the Anglo-Saxon model combining management and control in one board. The question arising in the latter case is which function is assigned to the supervisory board. In addition, it needs to be established which basic model better fits the specific circumstances of the still emerging Czech property system.

4.1.2   Corporate governance and the real structures of joint-stock corporations: An IPF view

4.1.2.1   Board recruitment

So far, most owners have definitely preferred the 'Anglo-Saxon model' of corporate governance and sent their representatives to the managing boards. This has effected a mix of managers and owners (along with some external consultants) in one company body, thereby boiling down to the Anglo-Saxon board of directors. This trend has been observable especially for the investment funds. In interviews carried out by the author, virtually all major funds expressed a strong interest in occupying as many seats on company boards as possible. Apart from the funds' interest in executing corporate governance and gathering inside information on the performance and development potential of a company, the allowances paid to the members of both boards are a major incentive to enter a panel. The membership at only one management board may easily provide the fund or its delegate with an allowance of CZK 20,000 per month, which more than doubles Czech average income. Considering the monthly five to six hour meetings of the average management board, this is a most attractive salary.

A SIS manager told us that representatives of the biggest first-wave fund SPAS attended 436 annual general meetings as well as another 100 extraordinary general meetings convened in the course of 1994. At these meetings, the fund used its voting rights to nominate its employees or other contracted experts for membership at the statutory bodies. During 1994, some 150 SPAS representatives were involved in performing functions on the managing and supervisory boards of more than 350 corporations. This is astonishing considering the overall number of 445 companies included in the fund's portfolio at the beginning of 1995. Of course, as was clearly spelled out by the fund management, these data do not mean that the portfolio consists virtually exclusively of strategic long-term holdings. They rather indicate that the fund actively exercises its shareholder rights wherever possible to constantly upgrade its overall portfolio. In companies in which the fund appears more as an arm's length investor, the main task of its representatives is to ensure that management runs the firm in the fund's interest and to get through an optimal distribution of cash flow, so that a reasonable proportion is reinvested and, where justified, dividends are paid. Independent of the fund's approach to an individual company, an important aspect is always the privileged access to company information for board members in comparison with owners without board representation.

On the other hand, as indicated above, allowances of board directors help to cover a substantial part of the fund's operational costs. Especially, it enables the fund to contract competent external experts who monitor enterprise management and eventually prepare and implement long-term strategies and specific development plans in cooperation with the in-house staff of the investment company. In the case of SPAS, about three quarters of the board nominees are external experts, e.g. branch experts, independent consultants or university professors. While most IPFs finance their external representatives through board allowances, internal staff members usually have to pass their fees entirely or partially on to the investment company or the fund. This had been the case for Creditanstalt's Czech investment fund before its hostile takeover by Motoinvest. According to Creditanstalt, the fund had board nominees in 35 managing and 17 supervisory boards in 1994. Most of the board positions were occupied by employees of the Creditanstalt investment company. Its chairman, a former university lecturer and Czech native, was a member of the management board of seven companies of different industries. In addition, he sat on 'several' supervisory boards. All directors and many higher employees of Creditanstalt investment company held six to eight board positions in portfolio companies. As a result, Creditanstalt showed a very lean management and administration structure. The fees collected by the representatives of Creditanstalt were recaptured by the fund and allocated to its shareholders in form of higher dividends. This means that the fund couldn't use its board seats to increase the profit of the investment company. This is, however, an exception as most fund administrators financially benefit from their board activities.

In general, bank-sponsored funds make extensive use of employees of the mother bank. Usually they (have to) send senior managers of the bank to the boards of major strategic portfolio firms. As a result, it is not uncommon for even the CEOs of the big banks to occupy seats on the boards of portfolio firms of their investment companies. In addition to the top officers of the headquarter, regional branch managers of the bank are often delegated by the funds into the board rooms of local firms. The latter is justified by the in-depth firm knowledge of local managers who have often been in contact with the respective portfolio firm for many years and thus are in possession of considerable inside knowledge. One typical example for the extensive personal entanglement of banks and their IPFs are the PIAS funds of the IPB bank. In an interview carried out by the author, one PIAS manager reported that the funds' board representatives are recruited from a pool of experts coming from the investment company as well as the headquarter and local branches of the bank.

4.1.2.2   The management board as central governance tool

Most funds, including the bank-sponsored ones, prefer the Anglo-Saxon model to position their nominees in the managing boards of their portfolio companies. In our interviews, Zivnobanka trust was the only major fund administrator with a clearly stated preference for the German model. Nevertheless, in most portfolio companies, the ZB funds are not the dominant shareholders and hence have to adopt the Anglo-Saxon model. PIAS told us that its preference for management board representation is rising proportionally to the size of the IPB *group* stake in a portfolio company and hence to the group's interest in the execution of active control in a given company.

There are three important reasons why most funds holding significant equity stakes in a company like to be represented at the management rather than supervisory board. Firstly, they are closer to the activities of the senior management and thus get a more detailed impression of the quality of the company and its top management. This is of utmost importance for funds whose nominees are in touch with a firm for the first time and suffer from a lack of information about the firm's technological and managerial capacity.

Secondly, as management boards bring owners into constant contact with firm managers, they are most appropriate to 'bring them into line' with the plans and preferences of the equityholders. Under the command regime, managers had to deal with state bureaucrats who frequently had neither the information and competence, nor a real motivation to control companies efficiently. During the preparation and implementation of large-scale privatization, management enjoyed again substantial discretion. Even a privatization programme as comprehensive and rapid as the Czech one couldn't entirely avoid a temporary lack of corporate governance in many enterprises. In the aftermath of voucher privatization, many managers had difficulties in coping with the fact that they couldn't freely dispose of company assets any longer and had to run the firm on behalf of the new owners rather than their own. Under such circumstances, the steady and direct contact with the management in one company body appears to be essential to 're-educate' managers and make them accept a new system of norms with the objective of profit maximization at the top.[2] After the firm has reached a stable market position and management has adopted a profit-oriented long-term strategy in line with the preferences of the new owners, most funds are prepared to 're-engineer' the governance structure of the corporation and to eventually go over to the German model. The fund manager of a private investment company and chairman of the management board of railcar manufacturer Moravskoslezská vagónka Studénka explains that

> in the future we would like to have the German model of corporate governance, with the management board composed exclusively of the company's management. At present, however, this is not possible because neither the top management nor the product development of Moravskoslezská is as yet stabilized. For now, [we have] one representative on the management board and one on the supervisory board.[3]

A third reason for circumventing the supervisory board when it comes to strategic decision-making is co-determination. In this respect, the situation resembles very closely that in many German companies where owner representatives on the supervisory boards complain that the decision-making process is sometimes essentially blocked or delayed by employees and trade unions. For that reason, the nominees of the owners are frequently not willing to discuss the most important problems of the firm in the presence of employee-representatives. On one hand, conflicting interests between owners and employees require mechanisms rendering possible the finding of a consensus between both sides. The supervisory board is one major tool to this end. On the other hand, a consensus brings about costs for both sides. During the restructuring period, many Czech owners try to evade those costs and exclude employees from corporate governance.[4]

4.1.2.3 Cooperation between owners
At present, the major owners of the typical Czech corporation are represented on the management board. In fund-controlled companies, the

biggest two or three IPFs (or financial groups respectively) are frequently in control of the management board and hold the majority of seats while managers make up some third of the seats, with the remainder held by smaller investors or the NPF. Fund managers largely confirm that joint governance by several cooperating IPFs is executed in many firms where no single fund family has a controlling stake. Funds pool their voting rights to get elected to the boards. Interestingly, bank-sponsored funds appear to favour cooperations with their fellows more than with private funds. For example, PIAS revealed to us that it would explicitly prefer cooperation with other bank-founded IPFs over groups like HC&C whose activities are, in the opinion of the PIAS managers, intransparent and unpredictable: 'You never know what they are going to do tomorrow.' This view presupposes that bank-sponsored funds have a common long-term interest in certain firms. Therefore, it ought to be comparatively easy to reach an agreement on a joint long-term strategy among bank funds. The view assumes, too, that the common interest largely guarantees that all parties stick to - possibly implicit - contracts concerning their individual duties. For instance, they may implicitly settle not to sell their stakes to outside investors without the consent of the co-owning bank IPFs.

The fund manager of the lead fund of Zivnobanka trust confirmed this view. She added that it is easier for bank-sponsored funds to care for the long-term prospects of the firm than for private funds because the bank funds have better access to finance. Backed by great financial reserves, they are prone to put more weight on the long-term development of their portfolio firms while private IPFs are subject to dividend pressure and are often reluctant to reinvest corporate profits in promising projects. Different types of owners seemingly have different time preferences. This can lead to conflicts in the board rooms and thus to an enhancement of coordination costs of equity control.

Cooperation between bank-sponsored IPFs or financial groups isn't restricted to the joint execution of corporate control. In some cases, it may boil down even to mutual (implicit) arrangements on the delegation of corporate control to one or two lead funds or groups which are to act as guardians on behalf of other (mostly bank-centred) financial groups. This may be the case especially in companies where one or two funds own controlling stakes, while IPFs of other financial groups hold minor equity interests. Some evidence for the supposed evolution of such mutual monitoring agreements is presented in section 4.1.3.

A fund manager of SIS, however, suggested that the nature of the sponsor wouldn't be very important in deciding whether to enter a collusion agreement. According to him, the personality and competence of the respective individual representing the co-owner is more decisive than mere group affiliation. His statement is evidenced by the case of ZDAS, a major engineering company. While the company is completely under control of three major financial groups[5], the chairman of the management board is the representative of a small entrepreneurial fund managed by the (likewise rather small) private consultancy firm Consus. A fund manager of Consus reported to us that the branch expertise of the chairman was decisive in electing him to this job. With his long work experience in the engineering and consulting industry, his task is to actively design and carry through the restructuring programme of the company. Of course, in an environment where qualified managers are very scarce even on the guardian level, the readiness for mutual cooperation and the use of human resources supplied by fellow stakeholders must necessarily be high. In the case of ZDAS, the large financial groups also sent their own nominees to the board and can thus easily monitor whether the chairman's restructuring policy conflicts with their interests. However, the case demonstrates that small owners can participate in corporate governance provided they can contribute the necessary competence or branch expertise.

4.1.2.4 The 'pecking order' on the management board: Responsibilities and decision power of owners and the senior management

As stated in section 1.4.4, the central figure on the Anglo-American unitary board is the CEO. In fact, the Czech equivalent is the general director, that is the top senior manager of the firm. During the communist era, the general director embodied a patriarch who was in control of all company affairs. His hierarchical position within the firm and his informational edge over the central planning committee provided him with enormous power both internally and on the outside in relation to the state bureaucracy. *De facto*, he concurrently decided on the strategic course and controlled the day-to-day operations of the company. Many interviewees reported that this traditional concentration of power still is the norm in many Czech companies where the general director often also chairs the management board. They also suppose that the self-image of most general directors still is the same as under the command regime. General directors typically expect to run the company both strategically and operationally. This arrangement is very similar to the Anglo-American model where the CEO is also the chairman of the board of directors in many companies.

A separation of both functions is most likely in firms with a direct investor, especially if the latter is a foreign investor. For instance, after the takeover of the leading Czech paper producer SEPAP by HC&C and the American direct investor Stratton, the first action taken by the new owners was to release the Czech general director from the post of chairman of the managing board. According to Stratton officials, 'we liberated him from the bureaucratic proceedings of the board of directors. So he will have the opportunity to do what he does best - manage the company'.[6] Clearly, the 'liberation' effected a shifting of the balance of powers between owners and managers and made it easier for the former to implement a new corporate policy and to take over strategic control of the firm, leaving the senior management headed by the general director in charge of the operational business. However, this approach presupposes, in addition to financial means, sufficient knowledge and human resources of the direct investor so as to be able to take over the sole responsibility for active restructuring. As IPFs suffer from a lack of capable managers and branch know-how, they frequently depend upon the general director and his capacity to draw up and implement a restructuring plan ensuring the survival of the firm. As a consequence, the general director may then concurrently chair the management board where strategic decisions on corporate policy are commonly made.

According to inquiries carried out by the Prague office of Coopers and Lybrand in 1995, the general director chaired the management board in 39% of the companies. In 15%, the board was chaired by another senior manager of the firm, in 32% by an IPF nominee and in 14% by an appointee of another (strategic) investor. The results indicate that management may still set the tone in some half of the Czech corporations. Nonetheless, many companies appear to be under tight control of the new owners and IPF representatives play a crucial role in strategic decision-making at the management boards.[7]

A frequent remark made in our interviews was that IPFs and senior management share corporate governance in many corporations. The fund nominees feel that they have no real competence in the production sphere. Therefore they leave it to the management to organize the production process. For the same reason, management's influence is great when it comes to the introduction of new products. On the other hand, IPF nominees usually have the final say in corporate finance and marketing. They decide on capital increases, dividends and the raising of investment loans. They argue that they have more expertise in the field of corporate finance as a substantial proportion of their representatives are former or current bank managers. Moreover one of their major tasks is to re-educate company managers from production specialists to market-oriented sales managers. Most of them still haven't any real sense of the laws and functioning of the market. Thus, the funds must support the transformation from production firms to sales companies by providing the boards with marketing expertise.[8]

In addition, funds cooperate with the management in the designing of strategic plans for the companies. Provided they have the necessary expertise, they take over responsibility for finding a strategic orientation fitting the market conditions and hence giving firms a good chance of surviving in increasingly competitive markets. The better and more competent the general director or the company's senior management (in the view of the IPFs), the more passive is the funds' participation in strategic decision-making. In the end, funds representatives may confine themselves to periodical monitoring of managerial plans and activities. In the event of dissent on managerial performance or policy, 'passive' IPF-owners tend to exchange the general director along with the whole management crew rather than to actively intervene and re-design corporate strategy.

Funds reportedly have the last word on important investment projects like joint ventures or the formation of a new subsidiary. They control the major sales transactions, too. If the management plans to sell company assets exceeding a certain value, the funds generally scrutinize whether the transaction is really in the best interest of the owners (at least of the IPF owners). Of course, such compulsory approval procedures for transactions of major importance for a company are essential in order to minimize managerial self-dealing. Finally, the funds are usually involved in the firms' recruitment and payment policy. While senior management is mostly responsible for the recruitment and wages of low- and medium-rank employees, the funds decide on top management positions, particularly on positions linked to board representation.

4.1.2.5 Role of the supervisory board
Smaller funds without nominees on the management board are normally represented at the supervisory board. There is no fixed threshold as to how great a percentage of firm equity is required to obtain one seat. Like the management board, it depends upon the specific ownership structure of the individual company. On average, the proportion of IPF representatives on supervisory boards is clearly smaller than on management boards. The majority of company supervisors consists of employees and external experts. As co-determination is triggered from as little as 50 full-time employees and there is rarely any corporation employing fewer people, virtually one third of all members on the boards are employees. Finally, the supervisory board is a melting pot of various external experts and stakeholders. Frequently one can find scientists or lobbyists. On many supervisory boards, one seat is reserved for a banker, representing the biggest single creditor of the firm.[9]

The supervisory boards meet about once every two months for approximately three hours. Normally, no owner with a long-term strategic interest in the firm is represented on the board. Shareholders holding board positions are typically portfolio investors. There are very few fund-dominated companies where the management board is elected by the supervisory board. In fact, the supervisory board is the body with the smallest influence on firm policy. Its influence on financing, corporate strategy or the hiring and remuneration of top management is negligible. In fund-dominated companies, the board generally doesn't even have the discretion to select the auditor. Contrary to its name, it is not the body responsible for monitoring and controlling the management.

Therefore the question is legitimate what then is the function of the Czech supervisory board. Its foremost function is to serve as an information platform for non-strategic shareholders and creditors. Minority shareholders represented on the supervisory board are provided with information about the long-term strategy and current affairs of the company. Yet, they have no right of veto regarding the corporate policy approved by the strategic owners through the management board. But a certain amount of inside information helps them to make an assessment of company performance and to decide whether to keep the firm in their portfolio or to sell their equity stake (exit).

Creditors, i.e. primarily banks, need inside information to check whether the company violates existing implicit or explicit agreements made in the context of loans. Besides, they evaluate the performance of the company from the viewpoint of a fixed claimant. The information gathered at the board has a major impact on the future credit policy towards a debtor company. This is of special relevance for banks which have no indirect board representation through their investment companies. Finally, the NPF has a strong informational interest in companies sold to strategic investors. If the NPF still holds a minority share in the company, it may use its board representation as a tool of contract management, i.e. to control whether the strategic investor fulfils all requirements of the sales contract. Board nominees provide the NPF with information on whether the owner has invested some agreed minimum capital in the firm, sticks to certain employment targets and so forth.

Supervisory boards are also 'sounding boards' bundling up industrial and academic expertise. The function of branch experts and academics is, as with the Anglo-American model, to give advice to the management and the owners of the corporation. Especially in big companies, some board members may also be hired lobbyists trying to find political support for the objectives of the company.[10]

4.1.3 Present and Future of the Czech Board Model

Members of the management board are trustees. They stand in a commercial law relationship to company owners, i.e. they are fully responsible and personally liable to the shareholders for the consequences arising from their managerial activity. Senior managers additionally stand in a labour law relationship to the firm as legal entity. From a legal viewpoint, the latter clashes with the commercial law relationship as it may exempt management from the responsibilities and duties anchored in the CCode.[11] This means ultimately that an imbalance could arise between factual power and responsibility on one hand and legal liability on the other hand. In this way, labour law may draw a dividing line between the active drafting and executing of a corporate strategy and the fiduciary responsibility for the strategy and the operations of the firm.

Inconsistencies do exist, too, on the part of the owner representatives. The responsibility linked to a position at the management board requires an adequate commitment to the job. The German experience suggests that a full-time commitment should be the norm to commensurably fulfil the fiduciary duty. The problem in the Czech Republic is that '[management] boards have so much responsibilities and not enough time. This needs full-time attention but investment funds [can't give] it'.[12] It is highly questionable as to whether a person who is occupying three or more seats on management boards and, in addition, is possibly in charge of managing an IPF portfolio is capable of executing this task in a satisfactory manner. Similar concerns are expressed by both fund managers and company managers, as well. Yet, considering the cardinal lack of managerial competence and the necessity of giving firms a strategic direction fitting the goals of the shareholders, they can hardly think of any other solution than to bundle up scarce managerial competence in the major IPFs and to allocate it via the management boards into the portfolio firms until the latter have adopted a more market- and profit-oriented course.

Furthermore, the *de facto* lack of a clear dividing line between control and management leads to the classical inconsistencies linked to the Anglo-American model. The representatives of the owners (the IPF nominees) have to take over management tasks and responsibilities, e.g. to arrange corporate finance and to draw up and implement a marketing strategy. But they likewise have to control their own performance as the supervisory board has limited authorities and is not usually as well informed about the performance of individual members of the management board as the members themselves. This may cause considerable damage if IPF representatives want to disguise their own failure or are even captured by the firm management.

Shareholders increasingly recognize that the Czech model of corporate governance is loaded with several inconsistencies. The result is that, while the strategic orientation of many companies is stabilizing and the competence of the senior management in finance and marketing is increasing, more and more funds are going to switch the model. Frequently, the Anglo-American model appears to be a temporary means of tightly controlling the restructuring period. As soon as the long-term strategy and the current market position of a firm have been stabilized and the enterprise has been brought on a course that is in harmony with the long-term profit-interest of the owners, more and more companies tend to go over to the German model where owners monitor the management through the supervisory board. Besides, a crucial precondition for the switch is a significant reduction of the informational asymmetry between managers and new owners in the post-privatization phase when shareholders suffered from a lack of knowledge about the capacity and integrity of management or the current state of the firm. The importance of the supervisory board as a tool of equity control hence will increase with the qualification level of managers and their willingness to stick not only to legal, but also (the only evolving) ethical norms of the economic system.

Interestingly, a gradual switch to the German model can recently be observed even for the IPB group which expressed in our interviews a strong preference for management board representation. An example is the case of Obchodní sladovny Prostejov (OSP), a malt house which is governed through a 31% equity stake directly owned by IPB (presumably complemented by some smaller holdings of the PIAS funds) and belongs to the strategic companies of the group's extensive beer empire. After reportedly good restructuring progress which has found its expression in the company's establishment as leading European malt producer and largest Czech malt exporter, IPB switched the board structure and adopted the German model in January 1997. The stated assignment of the new supervisory board is to formulate the basic business strategy of OSP and to control and elect the management board which is now composed exclusively of senior managers.[13]

As touched upon above, ZB trust has revealed an unambiguous preference for the German board model. Its management considers the 'Czech approach' superior exclusively in companies 'which are in trouble'. Vendula Klucková, manager of the company's investment flagship ZB 1. IF, occupies two seats on boards of portfolio companies. One is on the management board of Vodní stavby Praha (VSP), one of the country's biggest construction firms. As she told us, the firm hasn't yet experienced deep restructuring. Her task is therefore to draft, together with the general director, the nominees of two other bank-sponsored IPFs and one representative of a private fund, a comprehensive restructuring programme and a clear long-term strategy as guiding line for the management. Restructuring includes radical changes in the senior management which, in part, lacks both competence and willingness to vigorously address the measures necessary to give the company a chance to survive in the long term. The role of the funds in VSP appears to be mainly to carry out crisis management and initiate the turn around of the company through personal and policy changes. For this purpose, IPF nominees meet twice a month, which is significantly more frequently than the sessions of most Czech management boards. Moreover, the board members reportedly have to allocate a considerable part of their working time ('and most of the weekends') for their assignment to turn around the company. This lets us assume that effective restructuring puts a tight limit on IPF representatives concerning the number of board appointments one individual may reasonably accept.

Mrs. Klucková is optimistic that new executives will soon be recruited, capable of running the firm more independently in the interest of the owners. Afterwards, she would prefer to switch the board structure and to merely control the management board. She does so already at the supervisory board of the Prague-based Hotel Inter Continental which is owned chiefly by ZB trust (approximately 25% held by two IPFs) and the investment arm of the Czech insurance company (20%) and is operated by an experienced and professional management team. Given the hotel's good profitability and clear strategic orientation, ZB trust could get the German model accepted by the other owners, too.

Both examples demonstrate, once more, that there is a close link between the quality of the management and the financial situation of the company on one hand and the board structure implemented by the funds on the other hand. At present, the Czech board model boils down to the Anglo-American rather than the German model, meaning that the supervisory boards are of clearly less significance than the management boards in the decision-making process. Yet, the German model is increasingly gaining in importance and may well dominate the Anglo-American model in the long term.

4.1.4 Summary

Largely following an evolutionary approach, Czech regulation is rather permissive and guarantees enough discretion to implement the best board model given the firm's individual ownership and governance situation. The dominant board model applied by the funds is the Anglo-American model. However, companies with a good restructuring performance and a clear strategic orientation have been switching increasingly to the German dual-board model. In the absence of regulatory measures to design a politically desired board model, the future Czech board model will be a hybrid (on the macro level). Control through the management board is more expensive due to the more frequent meetings of the board in comparison to the supervisory board and a far-reaching entanglement in the operative affairs of the company. Moreover, there are some inconsistencies concerning the separation of management and control and the fit between legal liability and managerial responsibility and discretion. There are some preconditions on the macro and micro level with a critical impact on the switch to the dual board model:

- On the firm level, the initial informational asymmetry between IPFs and incumbent management must have been lowered and a clear restructuring policy must have been drafted and implemented.

- Likewise on the micro level, managers must have been re-educated so as to accept their fiduciary duty towards company owners. The process of re-education is accelerated by the swift emergence of a young and competent managerial generation contesting many older and inflexible managers.

- Ultimately, on the macro level, behavioural norms conform to a market environment and a new principal-agent relationship of managers and owners only need to evolve. New and firmly established norms will add to more stable trust relationships between management and IPFs/owners. Similarly important, the enforcement of the new norms effectively establishing the management's fiduciary duty has to be supported by the legal environment and the courts. So far, few managers have been punished for having violated their fiduciary duty or having robbed a firm to the detriment of the owners. Of course, in an environment still largely marked by normative and legal uncertainty and weak enforcement of rules, there may be a considerable lack of trust between owners and managers which drives owners onto the management boards. While they clearly have a tighter grip on company affairs from the management boards, they have to accept higher monitoring costs, too.

4.2 BANK GROUPS AND EQUITY CONTROL

4.2.1   The Governance Performance of IPFs: A Managerial View

In interviews, we asked managers of privatized firms for their opinion about the control performance of IPFs. Subsequently, we will discuss three main areas of managerial criticism, namely the governance competence of the funds, the duration of their investment commitment and their contribution to corporate finance.

(i) Competence of IPF nominees
As could be expected, the managerial assessment of the IPF governance performance is rather heterogeneous. A gradually fading minority of managers still criticizes the mere fact that the governance activities of new owners unduly restrain managerial discretion. This type of critic has its 'cultural' roots in the communist era when the senior management led by the general director essentially determined the course of the company.

Subsequently we will sketch three main areas of managerial criticism. Afterwards, we will inquire into the dedication of different owner classes in the execution of corporate governance (as viewed by Czech managers) and draw some careful conclusions for the incentive structure underlying the cooperation of IPFs in the control of portfolio companies.

Serious complaints are brought forward sometimes concerning the competence of fund delegates. Apart from problems connected with excessive accumulation of board representations, managers criticize the fact that some IPF nominees have neither the know-how, nor the will to contribute to corporate governance and are seemingly only interested in gaining some 'perks' from their jobs on the boards. Hardly surprising, this view isn't confirmed by the investment companies (at least concerning the performance of their own IPF representatives). Going by Tomás Kopriva, spokesman of PIAS, the investment arm of IPB has developed an internal trainee programme ensuring that all appointees have sound know-how in the field of finance and marketing.

Managers acknowledge some improvement of the situation after an amendment of the Commercial Code in mid-1996. Members of the management board are now directly responsible for their activities to *all* shareholders. The threat of shareholder suits allegedly has driven some of the most incompetent directors out of the boardrooms. The smallest common denominator of most managers today is that the funds are better 'than some faceless bureaucrat in a ministry'.[14] This mirrors a widespread consensus that IPFs are at least more capable and motivated to intervene in corporate policy and to give advice for restructuring, than state officials. If this is true, the Czech approach to privatization not only gains some additional legitimacy, but also corroborates the common assumption that most private owners are more suited to running a company than the state.

In some cases, the funds' expertise is even regarded as an indispensable input for the company. Calbreath (1995, p. 48) quotes the general director of a medium-sized engineering firm with 1,150 workers. After voucher privatization, the company was virtually free of IPFs. More than 80% of equity were scattered over thousands of individuals and another 15% over a group of small funds, while the biggest investor held as little as 3.5%. The management expressed serious doubts whether the company could draft a market-oriented long-term strategy without external support. The complete absence of funds with a strategic interest in the firm was considered a significant competitive disadvantage. Going by the director, the main function of funds is to provide consultancy services to the firm in order to ensure its survival in a market economy.[15]

(ii) Speculative intentions

Independent of the economic situation of companies, managers prefer stable ownership relations. The general director of the engineering company ZVVZ Milevsko reports that the firm has made good headway in the restructuring even without external help.[16] Over some five years, state-owned ZVVZ has dismissed one third of its workforce (originally about 3,000), rearranged the production process, reorganized the distribution structure after the break-up of the Comecon, and drastically reduced its heavy debts such that it could pay its first dividend in 1996. After 1995 (i.e. the year when 88% of ZVVZ stock was transferred into private hands in the second wave of voucher privatization), the 'third wave' of privatization has been spilling over the company, leading to various changes in the ownership structure. By spring 1997, 68% of ZVVZ was in the hands of the Motoinvest group, 15% was owned by SIS. According to the general director, frequent changes in the ownership structure and uncertainty about the identity of the major owners has largely impeded the restructuring process in the last two years. At some stages, it was far from clear for the management whether the current (unknown) owners would agree on the strategic direction of the company. In the view of the general director, it was also strenuous and time-consuming to detect the identity of new owners, to enter into negotiations on corporate policy and to find a consensus.

This case, surely not singular given the secrecy of the process of ownership concentration during the third wave, exemplifies the difficulties of management in companies without firmly established shareholder structures. The problem for the management arises from the fact that IPFs may gain a quite substantial (controlling) part of firm equity allowing them to interfere with corporate policy, but only have a short-term or medium-term investment horizon. This is, to some degree, true for all IPFs as their portfolios generally consist not exclusively of strategic companies, but also of stakes acquired for speculative purposes which may be sold off very quickly if a nice trade profit can be realized.

(iii) Contribution to corporate finance

While most managers acknowledge the positive role of the funds in cutting costs and finding a fit between production and market demand, the role of the funds as providers of finance is more controversial. The smaller IPFs in particular normally do not have sufficient financial reserves or credit lines to back their portfolio companies. In times of financial distress (which have been quite a normal condition of many companies so far), they often even enhance the pressure on the management to distribute high dividends so as to cover the operational costs of the funds.[17] In fact, a major problem that couldn't be resolved by the voucher scheme is the chronic lack of fresh capital in privatized firms.

One way to satisfy the needs of financially depressed companies with the assistance of the funds has been to find a well-funded (chiefly foreign) direct investor to cooperate with. The most prominent example for this is the joint venture of Harvard and Stratton. Contrary to original expectations, the example hasn't yet been copied too frequently. Rather, funds support foreign investors trying to obtain controlling stakes in companies[18], but afterwards themselves refrain from the given firms. The majority of Czech companies, however, cannot hope to find a financially sound direct investor within an adequate period of time when firms are most badly in need of cash injections.

Several managers emphasize that companies controlled by bank-sponsored IPFs (or, even better, by the banks themselves) have privileged access to bank finance. The general director of Královopolská, the eighth-biggest engineering company by sales revenues, laments a two-tier society composed of firms with equity links to the banking sector and those not affiliated to banks.[19] In his opinion, affiliated companies can be sure of full bank assistance, 'no matter whether a project is actually good'. As for his firm, unfortunately, the financial groups so far didn't signal any interest in a significant stake. The restructuring programme of Královopolská has therefore experienced several delays as the company found no real doorway to debt capital. As a consequence, no major investment project has been financed through bank loans for five years. On the whole, many managers expressed a strong affinity to bank-sponsored funds due to their financial strength and, as compared to private IPFs, their alleged long-term commitment to firms. In the field of corporate finance, the big financial groups undoubtedly have a decisive edge over other investors and may come up with a positive contribution to the restructuring of firms.

4.2.2 Level of Governance Activity

In a 1995 inquiry, Coopers & Lybrand separately requested general directors and other members of both management and supervisory boards to assess how actively different owner classes were executing corporate governance in Czech companies. The inquiry covers the opinions of 67 general directors and 227 other board members of altogether more than 100 corporations. The respondents were to decide whether a given owner category showed, in their view, a rather passive, mediocre or very active interest in corporate governance. In this way, Coopers & Lybrand could find out which proportion (percentage) of the respondents assigned a certain activity level (out of the three levels) to a given owner category.

Figure 4.2: Relative activity levels of various classes of investors

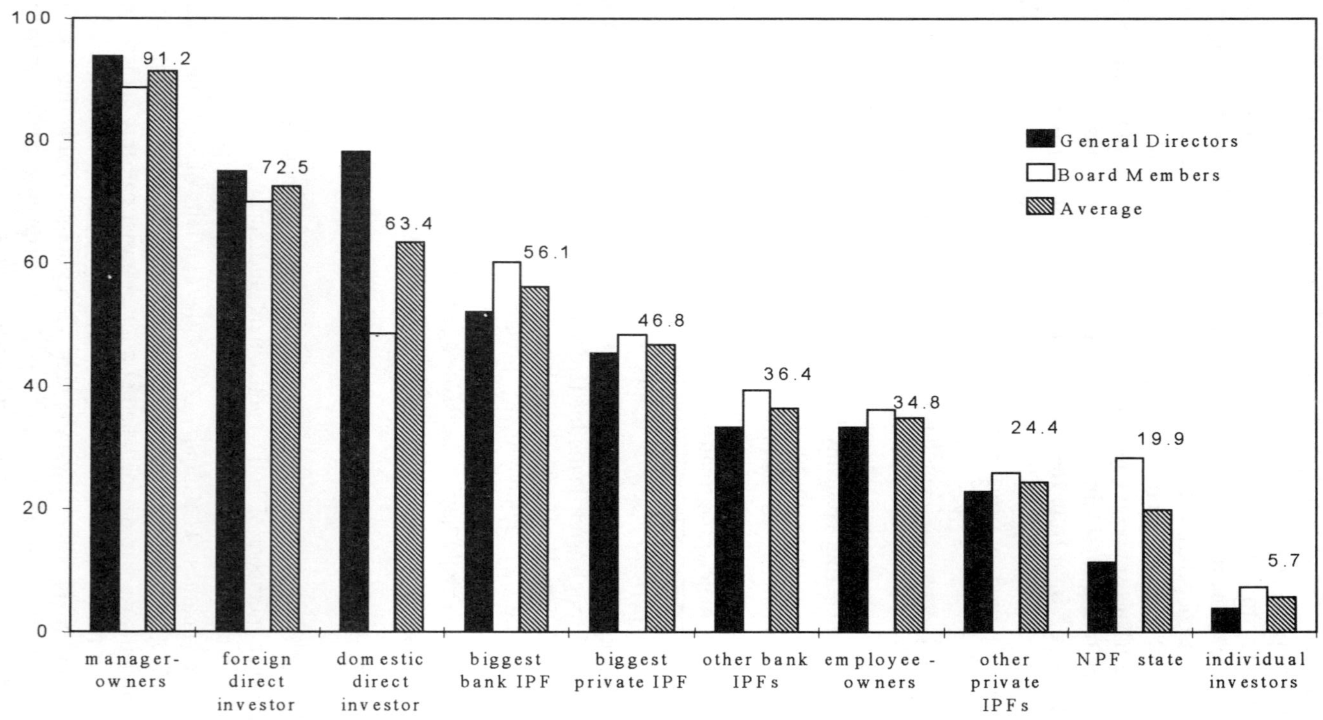

Subsequently we try to quantify the assessments made by the respondents by transforming them into index numbers, thus making possible a comparison of the activity level of the different owner classes. For this purpose, we have linked each assessment to an 'activity number' measuring the level of governance activity in absolute terms. We took the value 0 for 'passive', 0.5 for 'mediocre' and 1 for 'very active' governance. By simply multiplying the respective percentages of each owner category with the corresponding activity numbers and adding up the three products, one obtains an index value reflecting the weighted average level of activity on a scale between 0 and 100. The weighted relative activity level (RAL) of each owner category is defined by

RAL = percentage of respondents deciding for 'passive' governance $\cdot$ 0
     + percentage of respondents deciding for 'mediocre' governance $\cdot$ 0.5
     + percentage of respondents deciding for 'very active' governance $\cdot$ 1.0.

Of course, the higher the RAL index, the higher is the activity level of the respective class.[20] The comparison of index numbers allows us to make judgements about the relative activity level of each owner category. Figure 4.2 presents the results of our transformation separately for both groups of respondents, general directors and other board members, as well as an unweighted average RAL based upon the assessments of both groups.[21] The figure ranks the different owner categories according to their average RALs.

General directors and board members agree that the most active owners are managers with equity stakes in their companies. In general, managers have acquired holdings in their own companies on the open capital market rather than in the course of voucher privatization itself. Their average RAL reaches as much as 91.2. Thereby, the overall assessment of general directors (93.75) slightly exceeds that of other board members (88.69). Considering the incentive effects of managerial stock holdings, the result corroborates the experience of western economies like the US. The figure likewise suggests high RALs for foreign and domestic direct investors. Remarkably, the appraisal of the governance activities of domestic investors made by general directors is most different from that made by other board members. While the general directors rank them even higher than foreign direct investors (78.13 versus 75.00), the latter evaluate their governance performance with 48.65 much lower than that of their foreign fellows (70.00). Astoundingly, going by the other board members, a higher index level is even attributed to the biggest bank-sponsored fund (60.10). In the inquiry, 62.5% of all general directors shared the opinion that domestic direct investors execute very active governance while only 6.25% judged that they played a passive role. The assessments of other board members were far less homogeneous. With 37.84% describing their governance activities as mediocre and the rest split almost evenly over the remaining two activity categories, opinions were distributed most equally over the three activity categories.

Measured by the RAL value of 56.1, the biggest bank-founded IPF appears to be, on average, the most active fund owner in the board rooms. Both general directors and other board members confirm that the biggest bank-sponsored fund tends to have a more active governance interest than the biggest private fund, averaging 46.8. Besides, the smaller bank funds are more active than their private fellows, too (36.4 as against 24.4). Somewhat surprisingly, the smaller private IPFs are still ranked behind employee owners (34.8). This assessment may reflect the frequently tiny proportion of corporate equity held by small private funds (which use to be passive risk-diversifiers). To a significantly higher extent than the bank funds, they concentrate on portfolio management rather than active corporate control. As for the IPFs, the bank-sponsored funds are clearly the main players in the field of corporate control.

The most passive investors are individuals and the state (in most cases represented by the NPF). The stated passivity of (non-managerial) individual investors complies with the fact that their holdings are very dispersed in nearly all companies which have undergone voucher privatization. The NPF leaves the implementation of corporate governance to private owners in most enterprises where it still holds significant stakes. Its behaviour is more active, however, in strategic companies. Interestingly, general directors tend to emphasize the passivity of the NPF even more than other board members (11.38 as against 28.40). Employees holding equity in their firms show generally more interest in corporate governance than the state and individual shareholders. They may influence corporate policy through their owner-representatives on both boards of the corporation as well as, probably to a smaller extent, through employee-delegates on the supervisory board.

4.2.3 The Lead Group Function

The IPFs are ranked in the middle of the scale. According to the majority of the respondents, the biggest funds (by the proportion of equity held) are the most active ones. Most respondents assess them as executing either very active or at least mediocre corporate governance. The activities of the 'other' IPFs (bank-sponsored as well as private funds with smaller equity stakes) were described predominantly as passive. Considering the high proportion of companies owned jointly by two or more IPFs, this could in many firms indicate a kind of 'lead function' of the biggest bank-sponsored fund in the execution of corporate governance. The lead fund then has to bear the major responsibility for the policy and restructuring of the company.

The concept of a 'lead player' in corporate control is commonly associated with the role of the main bank within the Japanese *keiretsus*. The latter are bank-centred industrial groups with strong financial and trade links among its members. The main bank is both principal shareholder and lender of the group members. Its average loan share is typically some 25% of the member firm's total loans (Sheard, 1989, p. 402), its equity share approaches frequently the legal limit of 5%. Interestingly, in comparison with independent firms, keiretsu companies go seldom broke. The reason is that the main bank is regularly and probably implicitly committed to rescuing and reorganizing failing firms. It is even willing to bear the bulk of restructuring costs thereby suffering from disproportionate losses. Clearly, the existence of one major and liable creditor strengthens the bargaining power of debtholders as against management and reduces their coordination costs. One explanation for the effective commitment of main banks to debt control is that main banks behave like cooperative players in a repeated game (Sheard, 1994). Opportunistic *ex post* behaviour of a main bank does not arise as the bank's reputation as delegated guardian is at stake. The main bank will always bear the residual loss of clients' default, even if the costs exceed its loan stake. If it reneges, it might be excluded from future arrangements of reciprocal delegation of firm control.[22] That's also the reason why banks enter into main bank relationships. A tentative thesis could be: The more main bank positions a bank holds, the higher the number of delegation arrangements it can passively participate in without bearing the downside residual risk, i.e. by supplying virtually riskless loans to firms. Provided this agreement is valid for Japanese banks, it gives us an explanation why at least the big main banks cannot simply free-ride on each other's monitoring efforts.

In the boardrooms of Czech companies, the lead fund has to represent the interests of other (at least major) IPFs or financial groups. If it breaks this implicit commitment and over-emphasizes its own interests at the expense of the co-owners, the other IPFs may punish the lead fund, e.g. by kicking its representatives out of the boardrooms, running a policy that harms the interests of the lead fund in other corporations or excludes the sponsoring bank from syndicated loans. A concrete example for the credibility of such a 'punishment mechanism', which may well contribute to the maintenance of implicit governance arrangements among IPFs, is the case of IPB's investment arm PIAS. PIAS reportedly had (mis)used its representatives on various company boards to induce the management to finance current investment projects largely through loans from IPB. Other bank-sponsored funds viewed this behaviour as a violation of their interests (i.e. actually of the interests of their sponsors). As a consequence, IPB was temporarily denied access to the interbank market, causing a serious deterioration of the bank's liquidity situation. As IPB is a net borrower on the interbank market and thus largely dependent upon the short-term liquidity provided by the market, it had to restore the accessibility of the companies to other providers of debt finance. In a number of cases, the IPB group thus failed to shift the housebank relationships of portfolio firms even though it might have disposed of a controlling stake.

The case in point demonstrates well the functioning of implicit sanctionary mechanisms which are creating strong incentives to lead funds to stick to implicit obligations and not to misuse their governance power to unduly restrict the competition between the financial groups. Clearly, the mechanism works best between funds or groups with a common long-term interest in a given firm. For this reason, the lead fund conception may be a most effective device to stabilize governance cooperations in particular among the bank-centred financial groups. The incentives underlying the 'delegated governance commitments' of the lead funds are basically similar to those in the Japanese main bank system: Opportunistic *ex post* behaviour of individual lead funds - or better: lead groups - is minimized as the group's reputation as delegated guardian is at stake and the costs incurred by the triggering of punishment actions will normally exceed the short-term gains from breaking the implicit agreement. The major difference from the Japanese system is that the Czech arrangement relates more to equity control executed by bank-affiliated IPFs while Japanese delegated monitoring is based upon the debt control power of the banks. While Japanese banks shift the residual risk of debtor's default onto the shoulders of the responsible main bank, Czech banks have to bear the default risk on loans for themselves. Mutual delegation arrangements, as far as they occur, only help to minimize the costs of equity control. In particular, like in Japan, they reduce coordination costs and avoid the duplication of monitoring costs. Furthermore, considering the dilemma evoked by the still pervasive lack of governance competence and the concurrent need of active restructuring by company owners, a certain degree of governance delegation seems to be inevitable. Where it occurs, the role of the board representatives of other funds is primarily to monitor the governance activities of the lead group.

Clearly, we have to be careful with our thesis about a Czech lead group conception, all the more ownership structures are still far from stable in the country (in contrast e.g. to Japan). But the judgement of the respondents and especially the significant difference between the activity level of the biggest bank-founded IPF and the other bank funds let us assume that delegated guardians may govern a part of the companies dominated by bank-centred financial groups. As far as delegated monitoring does exist, the responsibilities and duties connected with the lead group function apparently create incentives to carry out fairly active corporate control.

Let us now turn to the restructuring performance of concrete voucher-privatized firms and analyse how different types of owners can and do contribute to corporate control and restructuring.[23] Thereby, we will focus on bank-sponsored financial groups (funds and banks), but also examine the performance of private IPFs and foreign direct investors.

4.2.4 Restructuring Performance under Different Ownership Structures: Five Cases in Point

4.2.4.1 Joint restructuring by bank groups: Janka Radotín

Janka Radotín, established in 1872, is the world's oldest producer of air technology. It produces and installs a wide range of goods like air conditioning and ventilating systems, heating coils and air pipes. Before 1989, the firm had been integrated into the big engineering combinate ZVVZ Milevsko and holding a monopoly position in its branch for decades. 77% of company stock was privatized in the first wave of voucher privatization, the remainder was included into the second wave. As of June 1995, briefly after the end of voucher privatization, some 55% of stock was in hands of individual voucher investors. The rest was held by various IPFs, including the RIF and some remaining stock from the second wave still left with the NPF. Already since 1993, Janka has been controlled by three financial groups, namely CS, IPB and CP, each holding between 7 and 10% of company stock in mid-1995. As of January 1997, the major owners were 2. sporitelní privatizacní IF (11.02% of equity) and PIAS-controlled RIF (10.97%). Going by Janka's management, the concentration of Janka's equity stock is still continuing in April 1997 and the controlling shareholders have boosted their stakes up to some 40% (PIAS-IPB) and 20% (SIS-CS) respectively.

So far, the new owners have been running a rather passive approach to corporate governance. Four seats out of five on the management board have been occupied by the top three owners (chairman from PIF-CP, two members from SIS, one from PIAS). One seat has been given to the general director. The board meets once a month and its main tasks are to assess and to decide on the restructuring plans presented by the management. It doesn't draft its own strategic plans but rather lays down the strategic orientation of the company based upon the management's proposals. The supervisory board consists of three members. Two of them are owner representatives (from SIS and a smaller IPF) and one is elected by employees. The board now meets once every three months (before 1996, it met at shorter intervals, in the early phase of restructuring even once a month). In the view of the management, the board's main function is to evaluate and control the past performance of both management board and senior management.

In end-1993, Janka was experiencing the most dramatic crisis of its company history. Losses reached astronomical CZK 121 million and the firm was technically insolvent.[24] In addition, Janka had virtually no sales network and, after decades as monopoly producer with delivery periods stretching over several years, most of the 700 employees didn't reveal much dedication to customers. Labour productivity was extremely low and Janka's market share was constantly shrinking in favour of aggressively penetrating western competitors. This also effected a continuing decline of output and employment (from some 2,500 workers in 1989 down to 658 at the end of 1993). On the brink of collapse, the new owners recognized that the turnaround of Janka could be achieved only through a comprehensive restructuring programme. As a first important step, they replaced the entire senior management which they deemed responsible for the decline of the firm.[25] On recommendation of a western consulting agency, they appointed a new general director, who was 23 years old when entering the company.[26] He was given a free hand to get together a completely new senior management. Furthermore, together with the new management team, he took responsibility for the drafting and implementation of a strategic plan to rescue the company from going broke. The IPFs restricted themselves to sending nominees to the boards whose main task was and is merely to approve the policy drafted by the management and ensure *ex post* monitoring of its restructuring performance. As for restructuring, the main attention was turned to three objectives: to the improvement of the competence and motivation of employees, the building of a sales network and regaining of customers' confidence and, last but not least, the reorganization of the corporate structure and re-engineering of production processes.

Looking back, firm management reports that changing the mentality of employees has been the most urgent, yet also difficult task in the restructuring process. It was crucial to gradually create a corporate identity, to give workers a vision of the firm's future development. Besides, Janka implemented a trainee programme obligatory for managers of all hierarchical levels. On weekend workshops, the executive teams of the individual divisions had to deal with case studies simulating concrete managerial problems in their respective fields of activity. The firm paid the expensive trainee programme while the managers' contribution was their free time. Workers and managers not actively supporting the policy of the new management were replaced. As qualified and experienced staff is hardly available on the Czech labour market, the management's policy was to recruit young and highly-motivated employees, even though they couldn't produce work experience in the respective field. According to the management, the strategy turned out right and today Janka is run by a young and motivated management crew. An essential tool to increase the motivation of all employees was a radical switch of the payment system. At present, each single worker has a variable component in his wage. As for the sales staff and the top management, more than one half of the salary is performance-related. Because of the positive incentive effects resulting from this wage policy, the increase in labour productivity could entirely compensate for the firm's dynamic growth of the average wage, amounting to some 25% annually in the years between 1993 and 1997.[27]

As for customer relations, Janka successfully refurbished its damaged image by building up a qualified nation-wide sales network, granting quick delivery of spare parts and carrying out of maintenance services. Moreover, the new field service is an indispensable acquisition tool in times of increasing competition. Yet, considering its bad reputation as not-customer-oriented company, Janka had to convince its industrial clientele of its new technical standard. As early as 1994, it entered the market with a new generation of products whose technical parameters were fully comparable to those of western European competitors.[28] To prove the high and reliable quality of the new air-conditioning systems to the customers, Janka more than doubled the guarantee period to 42 months, which is longer than any competitor on the Czech market.

Table 4.1: Restructuring indicators for Janka Radotín

indicator[a]	1991	1992	1993	1994	1995
assets	1,185.5 m	839.7 m	634.6 m	660.4 m	725.2 m
short-term receivables[b]	257.5 m	338.7 m	196.7 m	189.0 m	176.1 m
equity[c]	477.2 m	452.6 m	321.7 m	354.4 m	452.2 m
debt-equity ratio	1.48	0.86	0.96	0.85	0.58
bank loans	195.5 m	137.2 m	108.1 m	111.4 m	110.7 m
long-term bank loans	n.a.	n.a.	68.1 m	77.4 m	95.7 m
bank loans/overall debt	0.28	0.35	0.35	0.37	0.42
number of employees	1,296	787	658	541	408
overall payroll costs[d]	68.7 m	54.8 m	65.6 m	61.2 m	60.7 m
payroll costs/employee	52,999	69,632	99,696	113,124	148,775
output/employee	n.a.	n.a.	339,944	406,895	689,603
value added/employee	n.a.	n.a.	91,793	148,983	215,931
production output	n.a.	n.a.	223.7 m	220.1 m	281.4 m
value added	n.a.	n.a.	60.4 m	80.6 m	88.1 m
net profit	64.2 m	11.0 m	-121.1m	33.0 m	-24.3 m

a   all data end of period or result for period; all balance sheet and P&L items in CSK/CZK
b   Janka does not hold any long-term receivables
c   including share capital and reserve funds
d   including wages, fees paid to board members, social security contributions and social
    expenditures

Source: Janka a.s., own calculations

On the other hand, the new management also adopted a new approach to non-performing receivables, trying to come to out-of-court agreements with defaulting customers. Furthermore, it broke off the business relationship to those buyers with the worst paying habits and ability. The approach has significantly hardened the budget constraint of many customers. Since 1993, no reported problems with new payment arrears have emerged. Clearly, the consequent policy towards overdue buyers has also strengthened the firm's financial soundness.

One major problem of Janka had been the fact that some of its customers had been concurrently competitors of its supply division. As a consequence, the company had lost numerous contracts to foreign competitors. Therefore, in early 1995, owners and senior management decided to hive off all installation services ('turnkey services') to the newly established subsidiary Janka Final. Subsequently, the latter has been sold to Asea Brown Bovery, a major customer of Janka. According to estimations of the management, the whole operation blessed the firm with a 30% increase in sales contracts. It also completed Janka's transformation to a pure production company. In 1996, Janka additionally became exclusive representative for the Czech and Slovak market of HCF, a leading European producer of cooling systems.

In the production sphere, the management's aim was to streamline production. In 1993, Janka had still been producing in three separate plants, situated at a distance of approximately one kilometre from each other. Frequent transports of input materials between the plants had been generating excessive production costs. In the following years, the new owners reorganized the production process of the firm and merged the three plants in one production area, thus significantly cutting overhead costs (particularly for transportation and personnel) and reaping higher benefits from economies of scale and scope. In addition, the re-engineering of the production process led to a marked shortening of the firm's delivery periods and an ongoing reduction of the workforce from over 700 in the beginning of 1993 down to 340 in mid-1997.

The implementation of lean production and the enhancement of product quality have been requiring high investments in machinery (between 10 and 26 million crowns per year between 1994 and 1997). In part, the investments could be financed through depreciations and retained earnings. A considerable part has been financed through bank loans. Janka has a typical *Hausbank* relationship to Komercní banka which has so far been the only provider of bank finance. This contrasts with its ownership structure with PIAS and SIS as major shareholders. Janka's major owners apparently do not put the screws on the management to rearrange its credit links and to take (possibly at excessive costs) loans from Investicní and Sporitelna. We may carefully suppose that the lead group concept contributes to their readiness to renounce from undue pressure. According to the management, Janka's credit line at Komercní has been constantly expanding due to the good restructuring performance. Therefore, the firm could substantially increase the share of long-term bank credit granted for more than four years. In fact, unlike many other privatized companies, Janka has no problems gaining access to investment finance.

In 1996, Janka underwent drastic organizational changes. The production of air conditioning and industrial cooling systems was transferred to a joint venture with an American producer of air-technical systems, the previously loss-making production of coils was moved to a joint venture with a French competitor. [29] This effected Janka's conversion into a holding. More important, the new strategic ties have brought the company a promising foothold for sales activities on foreign markets and access to western know-how. The latter is important since, in spite of all progress made after the management switch, Janka's labour productivity still amounts to no more than some fifth of that of its western competitors.

Meanwhile, the bulk of restructuring is done. The Janka group has gained a consolidated profit of CZK 10 million in 1996, most of which will be reinvested. The overall volume of the 1997 investment programme is planned to be CZK 26 million. A substantial part of it will be channelled into R&D to enlarge the firm's range of products. Janka has regained a strong standing on the Czech market. 10% of the production is sold abroad, e.g. in Austria, Germany and Poland. In 1997, the company plans to forge ahead onto new export markets like France, the Baltic states and Japan.

4.2.4.2 Restructuring by a single bank group: Elektro-Praga Hlinsko

Elektro-Praga Hlinsko (ETA) is the leading Czech producer of electronic household appliances. In former Czechoslovakia as well as in other Comecon countries, ETA was a brand name. Its high technical standard allowed the company to enter into a joint venture to develop and produce vacuum cleaners with the western multi Philips in the early 1980s. This cooperation has been surviving until today. Nonetheless, when ETA's management tried to find a strategic investor in 1990, Philips and several other western contenders rejected the invitation to invest in the firm. Subsequently, 80% of ETA's capital stock was given to voucher privatization in which it was entirely auctioned off in the first round of the first wave at the introductory price of 100 voucher points for three shares. 20% was distributed among restitution claimants, local authorities and the NPF. After the first wave of voucher privatization, the firm's equity was fairly dispersed. Some 40 IPFs had acquired 72% of company stock, with four bank-sponsored investment companies holding stakes of around 10% (SIS, IKS KB, PIAS and the investment arm of the Slovak VÚB bank). The absence of a dominant owner turned out to be rather damaging for the firm's development. Dissension and conflicting interests among owners caused substantial delays in the decision-making process and the drafting of a long-term restructuring plan. High coordination costs obviously increased the passivity of the guardians of the corporation. Over the following years, share ownership was concentrating increasingly in the hands of the IPB group and in end-1995, the group along with some allies had accumulated a majority stake and took over control of ETA.

Soon after its privatization, ETA had adopted the Anglo-American board model which has never been modified essentially since that time. The four major owners each sent one representative to the management board. The representatives' attachment to and function within their respective investment groups was quite different. The range extended from the external consultant of Komercní banka over the fund manager (VÚB) and the member of the management board of the investment company (SIS) up to the general director of PIAS (which may have already reflected a particular strategic interest of the IPB group). The board was completed by three ETA managers, among them the general director who took up the post of the chairman. The management board met once a month and ought to decide the strategic orientation of the firm. The senior management had to carry out the board's decisions. Reportedly it enjoyed considerable discretion in doing so. The management board was controlled by the supervisory board consisting of six members, namely two employee representatives, two managers of smaller IPFs, a professor of the Prague Economic University and a private entrepreneur. Yet, according to the management, the board's control activities were rather formal. In praxis, the supervisory board served primarily as information conveyer for smaller funds and 'to comply with law'.

Since the takeover through the IPB group, the management board has been composed of two company managers (one of them the general director), two PIAS representatives (one of them the general director of the investment company), one banker from IPB and one external consultant (a senior manager of another producer of electrotechnical equipment) appointed by the group. The supervisory board has been scaled down to three members, two of them from PIAS. In comparison to the old board, the new majority owners have been running a markedly more active approach to corporate governance. After the coordination problem of the previous owners had ceased, IPB could largely speed up the decision-making process and quickly clarify the strategic orientation of the firm. For instance, the former owners had for some years been discussing the closure of one of the firm's six production plants without reaching an agreement. The IPB group decided immediately after the takeover to shut the plant down, thereby realizing savings of about CZK 18 million per year. The plant closure along with the sale of other (from a commercial view redundant) production facilities allowed for a reduction in the workforce of more than 10% during 1996. The restructuring programme passed by IPB envisages further drastic reductions both in production facilities and workforce. Besides, after the firm's bad financial performance in 1995, IPB fired the general director and most senior managers or transferred them to lower posts within the firm hierarchy. The new top management, including the new general director and chairman of the management board, was recruited exclusively from second-tier managers of ETA. The top management is still responsible for the drafting of restructuring measures which then are to be discussed, modified and decided by the management board. In the view of the management, the owner representatives on the board are now 'nearly too active', looking after all details of corporate policy. They monitor 'even the sponsoring and donation activities of the firm'. This stands in remarkable contrast to the habits of the paralysed old board whose main area of activity was the monitoring of financial data and the distribution of dividends. The supervisory board's function today is chiefly that of a mere 'sounding board'.

In the first year after its appointment, the new management was concerned predominantly with the design and implementation of a long-term restructuring programme. It put the focus on three main areas, i.e. the reorganization of the production sphere to cut costs, the lookout for both foreign and domestic cooperation partners and the extension of the sales network. As for the production, under the former owners, Eta's strategy had been to reduce costs by throttling down all production capacities more or less simultaneously. The company used to sell or rent assets of all production units instead of winding up single plants (including a painful reduction of the workforce). IPB agreed with the management rather to cut down entire plants which are not working at full capacity. The production programme of the shut-down plants was not completely cancelled, but for the major part redistributed over the remaining plants to have them run to capacity. The result is a better use of production facilities and manpower. In fact, labour productivity as measured by value added has increased by some quarter in 1996.

Furthermore, ETA is going to move part of its production programme abroad. For this purpose, it is also trying to reactivate old contacts from the Comecon era. In Russia, the company has a former cooperation partner for the assembly of several appliances. Meanwhile, the Russian partner has been gradually recovering from years of payment difficulties and is going to get into shape so that business ties can be re-established. The cooperation with western multis is already at a more advanced stage. Over some 15 years,

ETA has been manufacturing vacuum cleaners for Philips. As the volume of orders has been slowly, yet constantly going down, the management had to find additional partners. In 1996, ETA entered a joint venture with Bosch-Siemens and is presently producing deep fryers developed by Siemens. The management stresses that the company is too small to progress with such a wide range of products as in the past. Because of growing competition, triggered by the rapid opening of the Czech economy, customers make increasingly greater demands on the quality of goods. Forced to keep a high technical standard and faced by ever shorter product and innovation cycles, ETA has to concentrate on fewer goods than before to remain competitive and control its R&D expenditures. Joint ventures are important to get access to western technical know-how, but also to attain a foothold on foreign markets. Indeed, a substantial proportion of ETA's revenue is realized abroad.[30] Only 25,000 out of more than 300,000 deep fryers manufactured with Bosch-Siemens are going to be sold on the domestic market. The remainder goes into export.

Table 4.2: Restructuring indicators for ETA

indicator[a]	1992	1993	1994	1995	1996
assets	1,578 m	2,002 m	2,309 m	2,216 m	2,062 m
short-term receivables[b]	256 m	447 m	621 m	429 m	482 m
equity[c]	769 m	842 m	1,196 m	1,042 m	1,050 m
debt-equity ratio	0.987	1.337	0.868	1.075	0.916
bank loans	360.6 m	398.0 m	346.4 m	674.9 m	538.1 m
long-term bank loans	167.8 m	136.6 m	108.7 m	123.5 m	75.7 m
bank loans/overall debt	0.475	0.353	0.334	0.575	0.560
number of employees	4,358	4,583	4,376	4,298	3,871
overall payroll costs[d]	201.8 m	341.1 m	402.8 m	418.8 m	486.2 m
payroll costs/employee	46,306	74,427	92,048	97,441	125,601
output/employee	504,377	524,888	522,654	557,043	668,300
value added/employee	136,829	162,666	155,027	153,653	201,671
revenue	2,177 m	2,482 m	2,351 m	2,398 m	2,587 m
export[e]/revenue	0.497	0.485	0.508	0.473	0.475
value added	596.3 m	745.5 m	678.4 m	660.4 m	780.7 m
net profit	40.4 m	80.6 m	23.3 m	-130.0 m	1.8 m

a   all data end of period or result for period; all balance sheet and P&L items in CSK/CZK
b   ETA does not hold substantial long-term receivables. As of June 1996, they amounted to CZK 15.9 m which is some 3% of overall receivables at that time.
c   including share capital and reserve funds
d   including wages, fees paid to board members, social security contributions and social expenditures
e   including Slovakia

Source: ETA a.s., own calculations

In 1996, Eta intensified, too, the cooperation with its domestic partner Mora, a producer of stoves and electrical appliances. The partners agreed to split up their manufacturing programmes where both companies have similar product groups. Moreover, they plan to make mutual use of sales agencies of both firms abroad. On the domestic market, they are going to build up a joint network of agencies, beginning with joint sales representations of Eta and Mora in the cities of Prague and Brno.

To further strengthen its position on the Czech market, Eta set up several subsidiaries in 1996 with the only assignment to distribute the goods of the mother company. In the management's view, the subsidiaries are not yet operating efficiently and will still need some time to break even. Nonetheless, they represent a promising basis for the development of the company's sales structure. In addition, Eta has established a sales subsidiary in Russia and is going to set up more subsidiaries in Kaliningrad and the Ukraine. With the help of a British consulting firm, it is carrying out some market research in Romania in order to find joint venture partners for manufacturing and distribution.

In the past, the lion's share of investments was made in the acquisition and overhauling of machinery. The investment programme has been financed from various sources like depreciations, a bond issue in 1993 and a capital increase undertaken with the help of the bank-sponsored owners in 1994. Since 1995, the focus has been more on R&D with the aim of catching up their western competitors in terms of quality and technical standard. For that purpose, the firm has spent nearly CZK 100 million annually on R&D in the past two years and plans to do so also in the near future. The relevant investment has been financed chiefly through medium-term bank loans allowing ETA's house bank to tightly monitor the firm's restructuring performance through regular loan renewals. The financial restructuring has significantly enhanced the share of bank loans in overall debt. While the company has current accounts with a number of banks, the far biggest portion of loans comes from Komercní. Reportedly, the IPB representatives have been exerting some pressure on the management to change the house bank and to receive loans from IPB. So far, the management has been successfully opposing, pointing to the better terms of interest at Komercní. Nevertheless, the conduct of IPB confirms the actual non-existence of firewalls between banks and their investment subsidiaries and reveals the natural wish of the banks to use their funds so as to boost their own business.[31]

Like in many other firms, the financial stability of ETA is most seriously threatened by the growing volume of dubious receivables. After the takeover, IPB forced the management to exchange the auditor, i.e. to hire an established western auditing firm instead of the previous Czech auditor. The new auditor applied international criteria and recommended ETA to sell its overvalued useless inventories at prices below book value. Moreover, he induced the corporation to dramatically enhance its reserves on dubious receivables. Both largely contributed to the huge loss incurred in 1995. By mid 1997, the extent of non-performing receivables has declined, but is still a serious problem. The management mostly tries to renegotiate the terms of payments or to net out circle arrears affecting ETA, its suppliers and customers. Moreover, it has filed about 100 bankruptcy petitions against defaulters. Of course, most of the overdue receivables must be written off.

As of today, the company's restructuring programme is well underway. First results of successful restructuring are observeable in the form of increased productivity and revenues. Besides, in 1996 ETA has reached break even and has been chosen the most popular brand name in the country (rising from 10th place in a random sample of Czech consumers in 1995 to first place in the 1996 poll). The main contribution of the IPB group to the recovery was to speed up strategic planning as well as decision-making and to press for prompt implementation of restructuring measures. The story of ETA thus emphasizes the potential dangers linked to dispersed ownership and conflicting shareholder interests in times when a firm is badly in need of a new strategic orientation. Yet, it also hints at the funds' capacity to push for quick and successful restructuring provided they can install a capable management.[32]

4.2.4.3 Joint restructuring by bank groups: Inženýrské a prumyslové stavby Praha

The construction firm Inženýrské a prumyslové stavby (IPS) was founded in 1953 as part of the big construction conglomerate Zemstav. The conglomerate, supplying a large range of different services, grew quickly and soon became the country's biggest construction company. In 1988, it consisted of nine sub-enterprises and employed some 20,000 workers and administration staff. IPS was the biggest sub-enterprise with a workforce of 6,000. Its main domains were the construction of industrial buildings and of supply networks like sewage or district heating systems.

In the early nineties, Czechoslovak building conglomerates were subject to 'wild break-ups'. The high degree of concentration of that particular industry drove the bureaucrats of the then still existing construction ministry to dissolve the big conglomerates without much consideration of the consequences in terms of synergy losses and diseconomies of scale. IPS was separated from Zemstav and, in compliance with a privatization project drafted by the ministry, 86% of its equity was inserted into the first wave of voucher privatization. 5% was set aside for employees, the remainder went to public authorities like the NPF and the RIF. Soon after privatization, a majority of company shares was held by five investment groups. The major owner was HC&C with 17%, other investment groups like PPF and the CS group owned some 11% each. Between 1992 and 1997, the firm's ownership structure underwent slow, but constant change. For instance, HC&C completely left the firm in 1995, PPF reduced its holding to a mere 3.85% in spring 1996. As of spring 1997, three bank-centred financial groups control more than 40% of the capital stock. The biggest investors are the CS and KB groups with stockholdings of more than 15% each.[33] The ZB group disposes of more than 7% of the capital stock. Employees still hold some 4% while nearly 40% is in hands of foreign portfolio investors who all own stakes of less than 6%. This means that three bank groups are effectively governing the company and holding the vast majority of all IPS stock in hands of domestic investors.

Constant changes in the firm's ownership structure have been mirrored by drastic changes in its board structure. In early 1993, when private IPFs still were the most influential owners of the company, IPS adopted the 'Anglo-American board model'. Four out of nine seats on the management board were occupied by the new senior management,[34] the board's chairman was the chief executive (general director). Five seats were held by representatives of the five biggest owners. Interestingly, until summer 1996, the holdings of the CS and KB groups were owned for the most part directly by the banks rather than the IPFs. Therefore, both group representatives on the management board were bankers, not fund managers.[35] The supervisory board had three members, one of them an employee representative. The remaining two seats fell to the major owner, HC&C, and to IKS KB, the investment arm of the firm's house bank Komercní. The decision of the firm owners to take seats at the management board and to make it thereby the central strategic decision organ was made chiefly to gather information. It should help them to be closer to the company affairs (and the top management) so as to get a clear picture of the state of the corporation.

Nevertheless, the restructuring programme and the basic direction of firm policy were designed by the top management. In the view of the current management, the former owners never really had the competence to reorganize a big construction firm like IPS (today the second biggest company of its industry) and monthly board meetings simply didn't fill this gap of information and competence. In the end, the restructuring work so far has been done nearly exclusively by the senior management while the owners' function was to carry out some *ex post* monitoring. Thus, shareholders haven't been able to adopt an active entrepreneurial approach towards the firm. Besides, the role of the sporadically meeting supervisory board was rather vague as no clear dividing line had been drawn between the two boards concerning their responsibilities and rights. Since all major investment groups wanted to be represented in the firm's most important decision body, the supervisory board was not permitted even to elect (let alone effectively to control) the management board. In the eyes of the management, its main function was probably to provide the employees of the two investment groups represented with some nice perks. It therefore rather benefited the fund management teams of Harvard and IKS KB than the corporation or its ultimate owners, most of which were small voucher investors.

The current major shareholders acknowledged this fact in mid-1996 at a time when the restructuring programme was already well under way. They reorganized the board structure and left the management board which has been made up of the firm's five senior managers ever since. The board now meets three times a month to develop and to decide on corporate policy. The owners have moved to the supervisory board where they occupy six out of nine seats. Three seats are for workers representatives while each of the three bank-sponsored groups holds two mandates. The company model now largely corresponds to the German board model with a clear institutional division of management and control.

Table 4.3: Restructuring indicators for IPS

indicator[a]	1993	1994	1995	1996
assets	3,472.0 m	3,482.7 m	5,834.7 m	8,375.3 m
financial investments	102.0 m	227.7 m	744.2 m	753.9 m
short-term receivables[b]	931.3 m	1,073.4 m	1,130.8 m	1,742.8 m
equity[c]	1,132.9 m	1,556.5 m	1,838.2 m	1,915.2 m
debt-equity ratio	1.79	1.04	1.91	3.06
bank loans	347,6 m	352.4 m	762.1 m	1,030.6 m
long-term bank loans	n.a.	90.5 m	52.4 m	52.4 m
bank loans/overall debt	0.17	0.22	0.22	0.18
gross capital investment	177 m	204 m	477 m	495 m
number of employees	4,658	4,299	4,333	4,400
overall payroll costs[d]	696.6 m	735.6 m	864.5 m	1,121.4 m
payroll costs/employee	149,549	171,110	199,515	254,863
output/employee	0.739 m	0.976 m	1.215 m	1.537 m
value added/employee	0.240 m	0.267 m	0.310 m	0.368 m
revenue	4,078 m	4,910 m	6,130 m	9,300 m
value added	1,119.1 m	1,146.5 m	1,342.8 m	1,618.7 m
net profit	128.8 m	137.4 m	168.1 m	78.6 m

a   all data end of period or result for period; all balance sheet and P&L items in CSK/CZK
b   IPS does not hold substantial long-term receivables. As of end-1996, they amounted to CZK 43.2 m which is some 2% of overall receivables at that time.
c   including share capital and reserve funds
d   including wages, fees paid to board members, social security contributions and social expenditures

Source: IPS a.s., own calculations

However, the reorganization of the board structure doesn't mean that the owners intend to run a more passive approach towards corporate governance. On the contrary, in early 1997, they tightened their grip on management through two measures. First, they gave the sack to almost the entire senior management including the chief executive accusing it of weak leadership and, as a consequence, a deteriorating corporate performance. They blamed the management board for the dramatic profit decrease in 1996. Of course, a management board can be held responsible for its performance and decisions much more easily than top managers who stand in a labour-law relationship to the firm. The three investment groups appointed a new chief executive and gave him free hand to pick out the new board members. Through their intervention, they clearly enhanced the pressure on the new management to care for the profitability of the firm. The second measure was the setting up of an additional monitoring committee to gather more information on managerial performance. The committee consists of a handful of employees of the three main investment groups, CS, KB and ZB. Its task is to collect, process and evaluate information about the state of the firm and the policy of the management board, and to report its findings directly to the supervisory board. The committee meets more frequently than the supervisory board, which has its meetings once a month, and is supposed to contribute to a more effective supervision of the senior management.

Interestingly, the reorganization of the boards was accompanied by transfers of most of the IPS holdings from the funds to the banks within the CS and KB investment groups. This gives strong evidence for the funds' dependence on the sponsoring banks and indicates that the investment policy of IPFs is made on the group level under the 'coordinating aid' of the bank rather than by individual fund managers. As already mentioned, personal links between banks and funds are revealed through the composition of the boards, too. As of summer 1997, the supervisory board of IPS consists of one IPF manager and one delegate of the sponsoring bank of each investment group. The composition of the supervisory board of IPS teaches us that the 'institutional origin' (fund, investment company or mother bank) of the board delegates seems to be largely detached from the question as to which group member (IPF or bank) is currently owning the stake in the relevant company, i.e. here in IPS.

The restructuring programme, started off still under the former management, aimed at a radical reorientation of corporate policy in three areas. Firstly, the company should acquire a strong position in new market segments. To accomplish this most quickly, the management ran a most expansive acquisition policy including the purchase of controlling stakes in many construction companies. Secondly, the management adopted a new entrepreneurial approach, leading *inter alia* to the acceptance of higher project risks. Finally, it enhanced the firm's flexibility to react to changing market conditions by initiating closer cooperation with subcontractors.

Persistently unfavourable market conditions in the fields of industrial buildings and supply networks forced the new owners basically to change, jointly with the senior management, the company's production profile. For this purpose, IPS displayed busy acquisition activities and purchased step-by-step majority stakes in dozens of construction companies with a good and stable position in their industry segments. Between December 1993 and the same month in 1995, financial long-term investments thus rose from CZK 102 million to CZK 744 million, meaning that their growth ratio was much higher than that of total assets. Besides, the firm invested heavily in the building of new construction plants as reflected in the swiftly growing amounts of gross capital investment. The major reason for building up a large construction group was to get immediate access into more lucrative market segments like house building and the expansion and overhaul of the railways. Another strategic consideration was that large construction concerns have an edge over smaller firms in attracting large-scale orders.

During the past years of feverish acquisition activities, senior management concentrated entirely on drawing up the basic strategic goals of the group. Individual plants and subsidiaries under the control of IPS were organized as profit centres and enjoyed considerable discretion concerning e.g. the range of products and services or personnel matters. According to the firm's financial director, the strategy was right. Customers are increasingly preferring large and stable suppliers like IPS. In the end, the expansionary acquisition policy was also a means of regaining some of the economies of scale and scope which had been lost through the disintegration of the old Zemstav conglomerate before voucher privatization.

As of end-1996, the previous domain of the company, industrial construction, represented a mere 8% of the group's production. The main reason was a general drop in buildings investments in the industrial sector. The overhauling of outdated machinery and investment in the building of sales networks apparently have a higher priority on the investment agenda of the industrial sector. Similarly the building of supply networks makes up no more than 15% of firm output. The management is hopeful that demand for them will rise again after the privatization of companies administering such networks, especially in the power-supply industry. Today, the lion's share of production represents residential and municipal construction. For example, IPS was involved in the reconstruction of several historical palaces of the Czech parliament on Prague's Little Side (Malá Strana). On the whole, municipal construction amounted to 38% of the company's construction work in 1996. Another new area where IPS is expanding its services is the building of transportation infrastructure. After the takeover of the railways construction company Zeleznicni stavitelstvi Praha, IPS could attract two major assignments (each running over three years) with a total volume of almost CZK 5 billion in this field.

IPS didn't change only its orientation towards certain market segments, but also its entrepreneurial strategy. One of its main areas of interest is the building of apartment houses (*panelaky*). In the Prague region, the company isn't only responsible for the construction of apartment houses financed by the town council or individual investors. In addition, it appears more and more as developer, that is as investor responsible concurrently for the planning, financing and realization of house building projects. Going by the management, the developer activities are even the most profitable business of the firm. They are the main reason for the progressive growth of revenues since 1994. In the beginning of 1997, the company entered into a joint venture with one of its major owners, the Czech savings bank, to set up an enterprise specialized in developer activities, hopeful of merging the technical competence of IPS with the financing experience of the bank.

Finally, the management is now searching more actively for strategic cooperation with subcontractors. Up to now, IPS has executed most projects single-handedly. Recently, subcontractors have contributed approximately one half of the firm's revenue. The new strategy allows the company to adapt its capacity more flexibly to varying volumes of orders.

The enormous capital and financial investments undertaken in 1995/96 have been financed predominantly from the firm's own resources like depreciations and reinvested net profits. In addition, the firm relied on external sources of finance, that is the capital market as well as bank loans. Two new share issues effected an increase of registered share capital by some 20% between 1994 and 1996. Thereby, the company benefited from its above-average performance in the stock market which had created reasonable demand for IPS stock.[36] A part of the restructuring programme was financed by medium-term bank loans and a bond issue in 1995 due to mature in the year 2000. The rapid increase in the firm's debt/equity ratio after 1994 must be attributed chiefly to advance payments received for accomplished construction work. This kind of short-term liability thus suggests a rise in the firm's order volume rather than financial instability. Most of the loans have been extended by Komercni banka, i.e. by the firm's house bank which is also directly represented on the supervisory board and well-informed about the economic situation of IPS. The bank was the underwriter of the bond issue, too. As reported by the management, after a series of insolvencies of small and medium privatized and start-up businesses, the big banks have been increasingly contending for the financing of large enterprises, like IPS, with a strong standing in their respective industries. Moreover, the management candidly admits that personal ties between the senior management (management board) and bank representatives (supervisory board), intensified through periodical meetings of both boards, proved to be helpful in obtaining good access to bank finance.

The biggest problem in the financial sphere so far has been non-performing receivables coming up to nearly one third of overall receivables in December 1995.[37] The management usually tried to enter into renegotiations with the defaulter, aiming thereby at interest rescheduling or in-kind compensation. If renegotiations are not successful or the defaulter doesn't stick to the new payments schedule, IPS files for bankruptcy. In those cases, the firm can normally save only a tiny fraction of its claims due to the lengthiness of insolvency procedures. In 1996, write-offs and value adjustments to overdue receivables (along with three loss-making construction projects) significantly added to the unexpected decrease in net profit and, thus, turned out to be the decisive stumbling block for the management.

As of 1997, IPS has finished the expansion phase and entered the consolidation phase. Despite the mediocre performance in terms of profitability in 1996, the company has attained an essentially sound and stable position in the market for construction services. Positive restructuring results are reflected by constant increases in labour profitability, in terms of both production and value added per employee. IPS has become the biggest construction group by assets and takes second place as measured by revenue. For the future, the focus should be on internal reorganization rather than net investments in plant equipment or in new ownership interests. In particular, the management plans to cut back the independence of the single profit centres (plants and subsidiaries) and to play a more dominant role in the coordination of their activities. This should generate additional synergies and help to attract more large-scale orders requiring the cooperation of several plants and subsidiaries.

4.2.4.4 Restructuring by a private investment company: Armabeton Praha

The SOE Armabeton (AB) was established in 1951. Its original aim was to participate in the construction of thermal and nuclear power stations. In 1991, the enterprise merged with a smaller construction company and was transformed into the joint-stock company Armabeton a.s. At that time, the company belonged to the five biggest firms of the construction branch. Its main fields of activities were industrial buildings in the energy, engineering and chemicals sector and laminated timber structures. For the latter, it held a quality certificate in accordance with the German DIN 1052 norms.

In harmony with the privatization project drafted by the construction ministry, two thirds of AB's equity were included in the first wave of voucher privatization. The remainder was earmarked for a direct sale to a strategic investor and a public tender offer. As investors' demand turned out to be very modest, the stock was simply transferred to the second wave of voucher privatization. The firm ended up with a dispersed ownership structure. After the second wave, two Harvard funds jointly owned 18% of AB; two big bank-founded IPFs each were in possession of 10% equity blocks. The private YSE fund had purchased roughly 5%, the rest was in hands of small IPFs (26%), individual voucher investors (30%) and the RIF (3%). In the meantime, the performance and market position of the company had considerably deteriorated and AB had dropped out of the group of privatized firms which were attractive for strategic investors. While the bigger funds sent their representatives into the boardrooms, they didn't show any interest in designing a comprehensive restructuring programme or getting involved in active corporate governance. Between 1992 and 1996, the composition of both boards wasn't subject to any personal changes.[38] Neither was a single member of the senior management replaced (of those who had been appointed by the ministry in 1990).

Table 4.4: Restructuring indicators for Armabeton

indicator[a]	1993	1994	1995	1996[e]
assets	1,517.8 m	1,526.9 m	1,471.6 m	2,310.8 m
tangible fixed assets	572.8 m	521.3 m	514.3 m	795.3 m
financial investments	429.9 m	421.6 m	391.2 m	5.5 m
short-term receivables[b]	169.5 m	214.4 m	134.2 m	580.4 m
long-term receivables[b]	0.2 m	-	-	41.0 m
equity[c]	1,068.5 m	1,086.0 m	1,089.1 m	1,380.3 m
debt-equity ratio	0.42	0.40	0.34	0.59
bank loans	316.0 m	304.5 m	264.9 m	290.1 m
long-term bank loans	86.1 m	47.2 m	104.9 m	130.9 m
bank loans/overall debt	0.71	0.70	0.71	0.36
output/employee	n.a.	835.000	1,050,000	475.000
revenue	339.6 m	252.7 m	344.6 m	767.4 m
value added	129.8 m	98.4 m	152.1 m	162.8 m
realization of hidden reserves[d]	9.7 m	48.4 m	22.0 m	12.7 m
net profit	8.1 m	19.2 m	17.4 m	-48.0 m

a   all data end of period or result for period; all balance sheet and P&L items in CSK/CZK
b   without intra-group receivables
c   including share capital and reserve funds
d   surplus of revenue from sold investment assets over book value
e   In November 1996, AB was merged with its five subsidiaries. The merger caused an increase in firm assets and employees.

Source: Armabeton a.s., own calculations

During this period, the firm was drawing solely from its capital and tradition. The management failed to set up any long-term restructuring plan, failed to build up a functioning marketing department and largely lost the contact to the technological development in the field of construction. AB fell behind its main competitors and dropped to the tenth rank in its industry as measured by revenue. Nevertheless, the owners didn't tighten up control over management. Their focus was more on short-term dividend earnings than on the long-term viability of the firm. They even arranged for the sales of investment assets and real estate in order to realize a net profit and, hence, to make possible the distribution of dividends also in view of a miserable economic performance. Since 1993, yields from the realization of hidden reserves have been (sometimes substantially) higher than net profits. This shows that the firm yet hasn't carried out appreciable restructuring which is essential on order to survive in competition with recovering and expanding construction companies like IPS.

In the first half of 1996, the YSE funds accumulated a majority stake in AB and took over control of the company. YSE is one of the bigger private investment companies and known for applying an active approach to the governance of most of its portfolio companies. Its flagship, the first-wave fund IF YSE, meanwhile has been converted into a holding company to sidestep all restrictions concerning the maximum size of equity stakes in individual portfolio firms. As stressed by the general director and chairman of the management board of the investment company, all investment entities act in concert and try to accumulate controlling stakes in the group's portfolio firms. As a consequence, the group's overall portfolio is limited to some 20 to 30 strategic holdings, mostly majority stakes. In the view of the general director, this approach is the only way to successfully execute active governance as 'five or seven representatives of different owners will never come to an agreement'. YSE prefers the Anglo-American board model and aims at occupying the majority of seats at the management board with its own employees or delegated external experts. In September 1996, YSE became an integral part of the Stella Group, a financial holding controlling an extensive net of investment companies, industrial (mainly construction) and commercial firms.

After the takeover of AB, YSE immediately dismissed the entire senior management. A former, 'pre-revolution' general director of AB was asked to come back and temporarily administer firm assets until the appointment of a new general director. In May 1997, the latter was finally found and charged with getting together the new top management. Furthermore, the new owners reorganized the boards. The management board now consists of the general director and four top managers from other Stella subsidiaries. The very composition of the board demonstrates the group's effort to adopt a very active governance approach from the beginning and to transfer managerial know-how from other (predominantly better-performing) group members to the firm. The supervisory board is made up of two YSE managers and one employee representative. The management board meets every month and decides the strategic orientation of the company. The personal entanglement with other Stella subsidiaries allows easy coordination of the policies of all group members and the creation and exploitation of synergies. The supervisory board meets only once every three months, but the YSE delegates usually participate in the meetings of the management board. This provides them with detailed information on corporate affairs and a good grip on both the top management and the managing directors. Of course, as in virtually all fund-dominated firms, the ultimate responsibility for the restructuring of the company is borne by the general director who is also the main link between managers and owners.

Since 1990, AB has been organized as a radial holding, comprising five wholly-owned subsidiaries and the mother company with its two plants in the centre. The decentralized group structure didn't turn out to be advantageous for the firm. Expected benefits from enhanced flexibility and nation-wide representation were drained by shortcomings in the communication and coordination between the centre and the subsidiaries. The old management failed to develop effective governance mechanisms between the mother company and the subsidiaries. Besides, there was no comprehensive marketing concept that could give the AB group a uniform look in the public. The group didn't appear as one big integrated entrepreneurial entity in the construction market. In times when customers' preferences were shifting towards big and stable construction conglomerates with a complex range of services, this inevitably led to a competitive disadvantage. The company had no longer a real chance to acquire lucrative large-scale orders. Even in its traditional domain, the building of power plants, it used to become the mere sub-contractor of more integrated domestic and foreign construction groups with a more complex range of services like IPS or Asea Brown Bovery.

To strengthen the internal governance structure and to pave the way for better access to profitable contracts for large-scale projects, YSE decided to merge the mother company with its subsidiaries immediately after the takeover in summer 1996. According to the new general director, the actual restructuring of the firm began only after his appointment in May 1997. His first task was to draft a long-term strategic plan. So far, he could identify three main areas with an urgent call for restructuring. Firstly, the company has to enlarge its product range to become a competitive general contractor. This will require considerable investment in new plants and probably the acquisition of construction firms supplying complementary products and services. In the long run, this should let the firm expand significantly. Secondly, as for the technological state of the firm, AB must quickly catch up with its major competitors. As of now, it has the lead exclusively in the field of timber constructions. However, the volume of orders of this segment is too small to boost the firm's revenue and profitability decisively. For that reason, R&D expenditures must largely increase in the next few years. Finally, the firm suffers from an excess of white-collar workers. The administration staff will be reduced by some hundred employees in the near future to increase the labour productivity of the firm.

In the past, AB's investments have been made more in the maintenance of its plants than in new equipment. Between 1993 and 1995, the book value of overall assets as well as of tangible fixed assets declined despite an annual inflation rate of some 8-10%. This hints at a reduction in machinery and investment assets in real terms. The former owners were not interested in providing the company with external finance through share (capital increase) or bond issues. Consequently, investments had to be financed chiefly through depreciations and bank loans. AB's house bank is Komercní banka, the biggest commercial bank of the country. So far, the management hasn't complained about insufficient access to bank finance. It intimated, however, that companies governed by bank-sponsored funds might be in a better position as banks are better informed about the economic state of the firm. Moreover, availability and costs of bank finance may become a problem if a company is in direct competition with a firm in which a bank-sponsored IPF is holding a strategic stake. Banks then tend to give preferential treatment to 'their' enterprises and thus, in absolute or relative terms, to raise the price of bank finance for the competitor. From this perspective, AB could have a substantial competitive disadvantage as against its branch fellow IPS, whose three biggest owners are bank-centred financial groups (one of them Komercní). AB's final owner Stella Group is therefore trying to set up a working in-house-banking system to allocate financial resources immediately to the most profitable investments. Management is optimistic that the firm can draw extensively from expected intra-group resources to finance a part of its planned future investments.

A constantly high volume of non-performing receivables has been putting a heavy financial burden on the group. As of end-1995, overdue claims amounted to CZK 58 million, which is equal to 65.7% of all claims on customers. CZK 15 million or 45.2% of all claims on customers were overdue more than one year. Paradoxically, the biggest overdue debtors of the group are public authorities like the city of Prague, which didn't settle payables frequently still stemming from the late 1980s. While the old management tried to sell part of the receivables at a vast discount or to initiate netting out schemes for mutual arrears with various customers and suppliers, a large proportion of non-performing receivables had to be written off and contributed to the negative net profit of 1995.

Table 4.5: Dubious receivables of Armabeton group

	end-1994		end-1995	
claims on customers	CZK 70.9 m	(100.0%)	CZK 97.1 m	(100.0%)
overdue claims on customers	CZK 67.9 m	(69.7%)	CZK 58.0 m	(65.7%)
of which overdue > 12 months	CZK 42.3 m	(36.1%)	CZK 15.0 m	(45.2%)

Source: Armabeton and Hospodárské noviny, 2-8-1996, stock market supplement, p. VI

4.2.4.5 Restructuring by a foreign direct investor: Kablo Kladno

The cable producer Kablo Kladno was founded in 1865 for the manufacturing of steel ropes. From 1918, the company has been producing and installing cables with oil-filled paper insulation, communications cables and related instruments. Before 1990, it was an integral part and 'lead firm' of a big conglomerate containing all Czechoslovak cable manufacturers. 66% of Kablo's equity stock was distributed in the second wave of voucher privatization. Another 30% was sold directly to the German producer of energy-technical equipment Felten & Guilleaume Energietechnik (F&GE). In accordance with the privatization project drafted by Kablo's management in cooperation with the German direct investor, F&GE increased Kablo's equity by 43% in December 1994, thereby transferring some CZK 500 million to the cablemaker. The transaction secured F&GE a 51% stake in the firm. After further stock market operations, the holding grew to 56% at the end of 1996.[39] The original intention of F&GE was to obtain a 67% stake. However, due to the Commercial Code amendment of summer 1996, stipulating a mandatory bid after the acquisition of a two thirds majority of company stock, it isn't sure whether the German owner will stick to its target. Of course, if he does, the transaction costs of the purchase may rise considerably. Soon after the acquisition, F&GE started a comprehensive restructuring programme, running over three years from 1995 to 1997. The ambitious goals of the investor were to make Kablo the industry leader in the Czech Republic and a cable producer of European calibre.

F&GE so far has adopted an active, yet cooperative approach to corporate governance. It didn't replace any member of Kablo's senior management after the takeover of the firm in late 1994. F&GE's delegates control both company boards. Three of five members of the management board represent the German investor, two seats are occupied by the senior management. The general director also holds the function of the board's chairman. The board meets ten times a year and is the central strategic decision organ. It is responsible for specifying the basic targets of Kablo's commercial, financial and investment strategy. The senior management, consisting of five directors, is responsible for the implementation of the resolutions of the management board and has considerable scope for drafting its own policy proposals. If they are of strategic importance (like e.g. the acquisition of strategic stakes in other companies or changes of the product line), they must be adjusted to F&GE's concern policy and passed by the management board. The supervisory board, consisting of two representatives of F&GE and one member elected by Kablo's employees, meets only twice a year and has so far devoted most of its attention to changes in the production sphere of the company. At the end of 1996, for example, it initiated the transfer of production facilities from a Berlin factory of F&GE to Kablo.[40] Thus, the supervisory board at the same time controls and complements the work of the management board.

Table 4.6: Restructuring indicators for Kablo Kladno

indicator[a]	1993	1994	1995	1996
assets	853.5 m	838.4 m	1,309.8 m	1,489.1 m
short-term receivables[b]	157.7 m	123.2 m	106.8 m	140.7 m
equity[c]	595.9 m	558.0 m	1,056.9 m	1,137.8 m
debt-equity ratio	0.432	0.503	0.239	0.236
bank loans	59.6 m	149.3 m	88.5 m	32.0 m
long-term bank loans	n.a.	n.a.	11.6 m	23.3 m
bank loans/overall debt	0.231	0.532	0.393	0.098
gross investment	91 m	142 m	228 m	348 m
number of employees	n.a.	795	761	780
overall payroll costs[d]	89.9 m	100.3 m	130.3 m	164.7 m
payroll costs/employee	n.a.	126,163	171,222	211,154
output/employee	n.a.	1.360 m	2.014 m	2.142 m
value added/employee	n.a.	n.a.	0.367 m	0.448 m
revenue	1,211.3 m	1,088.5 m	1,370.1 m	1,688.5 m
value added	n.a.	n.a.	279.1 m	349.1 m
net profit	114.6 m	-32.6 m	80.7 m	83.4 m

a   all data end of period or result for period; all balance sheet and P&L items in CSK/CZK
b   Kablo does not hold any long-term receivables.
c   including share capital and reserve funds
d   including wages, fees paid to board members, social security contributions and social expenditures

Source: Kablo Kladno a.s., own calculations

At the time of its privatization, Kablo's weak spots were its rather outdated machinery and products and, in part as a consequence, a rather poor export performance. In 1994, exports made up 11.7% of the firm's overall turnover. The restructuring programme jointly designed by the incumbent management and the new owners includes extensive investment over four years (ending in 1997) which is to be financed predominantly from the firm's own resources and those of F&GE, i.e. from the money attracted by the capital increase and the profits of both firms. In harmony with the privatization project and a follow-up agreement with the NPF, Kablo will consistently reinvest its retained earnings for the time of the investment programme. One effect resulting from both the privatization method and the financing approach chosen for Kablo has been the constant decline of the company's debt/equity ratio. As early as 1996, the firm is financially very sound and virtually independent of bank loans.[41] After 1997, Kablo is expected to finance its ongoing investment activities for production lines, overhauling of machinery and further improvement of the administration independently of F&GE. As soon as possible, it should be able to pay dividends.

Since 1995, Kablo has been undergoing dramatic switches in its product range. In the beginning of 1996, the manufacturing of the formerly most dominant product, cables with an antiquated oil-filled paper insulation, was cancelled completely. Instead, the firm started to produce power cables with a polyethylene insulation. The switch-over was accompanied by a record investment amounting to some CZK 282 million (i.e. 83% of the 1996 overall investments) in a new line for manufacturing cables with plastic insulation and sheath. In 1996, the new product only made up 6% of the firm's overall revenue. Since it is produced mainly for the energy sector, this share is expected to rise swiftly after the privatization of several Czech energy producers. Going by the company's strategic plan, the output of polyethylene wires will double in 1997 and subsequently become the main pillar of Kablo's future production programme.

According to estimations by the management, Kablo has boosted the export share in overall revenues within two years by 15 percentage points to some 25% in 1996.[42] In absolute terms, this means nearly a quadrupling of exports as the overall turnover has grown by more than one half in the same time period. [43] The sales volume in the ex-Comecon states, especially Russia and Ukraine, as well as in some EU countries like Germany and Austria has been constantly growing. The main reason for the improvement of the export performance is the successful implementation of German and international quality standards (DIN VDE, ISO 9001) which are indispensable preconditions to deliver e.g. into the European Union. Only after Kablo proved they could meet the German quality norm DIN VDE, did they acquire a large-scale order from Iran, making up CZK 130 million and 8% of its revenue in 1996. As emphasized by the management, the access to the technological know-how of F&GE was crucial for the rapid improvement of Kablo's quality assurance system. The direct investor hence contributed not only financial means, but also technological competence to spur restructuring and increase the competitiveness of the company. Furthermore,

Kablo benefits from sales assistance by F&GE on the German and other western markets and cooperation in the selling of cable accessories for jointing and terminating cables in the Czech and Slovak Republics. In December 1996, Kablo purchased a strategic 25% equity stake in Hagard Hall, a Slovak wholesaler of electrotechnical products with a vast sales network all over the country. The explicit reason behind the acquisition is to quickly double exports to the neighbour country. In 1996, Slovakia already absorbed 39% of Kablo's exports.

As of end-1996, most indicators suggest a positive development and successful restructuring of the company. Despite temporarily high depreciations caused by the high investment made in 1996, the firm's net profit didn't decline, but even went up slightly in comparison with the preceding year. Kablo's recovering performance is based substantially upon the financial and technological support and the sales assistance provided by its majority shareholder, making possible the quick overhauling and extension of the firm's machinery, a radical switch of the production programme and the implementation of internationally accepted quality norms as an essential tool to boost revenues on both domestic and foreign markets. At first glance perhaps surprisingly, the post-privatization restructuring programme didn't lead to any reduction of the workforce. However, redundant manpower (particularly in the administration) had already been cut under the current management in the period between 1990 and 1994, effecting a shrinking of the workforce from 1,200 down to some 800 employees. For that reason, a 57% increase in labour productivity between 1994 and 1996 could be achieved at a steady employment level and even compensate for the high rise in payroll costs during the same period. Today, Kablo has a market share of approximately 30% in the domestic market for power cables and is, according to its management, the largest and most modern Czech company in this industry.

4.2.5 Summary

In the Czech Republic, powerful bank-centred financial groups have arisen spontaneously from voucher privatization. Notwithstanding various portfolio limitations, the banks and their funds are both interested and involved in the execution of equity control. The banks' governance power is based both upon indirect stakes in the enterprise sector (i.e. holdings in their own privatization funds and in other investment vehicles) and direct equity stakes in portfolio companies. Their extensive direct and indirect equity involvement in the enterprise sector helps banks to realize economies of scale and scope in the execution of corporate control and, at the same time, brings their governance interest more in line with that of dispersed shareholders, thereby reducing incentives to run a too cautious policy (satisficing).

In the IPF industry, the most active players in corporate control are the bank-sponsored funds and some four or five private investment groups like HC&C, PPF and YSE-Stella. Virtually all funds with an active control interest are affiliated to financial groups with sometimes a high number of investment entities.[44] Most other funds are simply too small to exert a noticeable influence on the industrial sector. The tiny private IPFs have a much smaller financial scope than the bank-centred groups, which makes active restructuring difficult. The small funds' natural interest in risk-diversification will spur their development towards passive investment vehicles. With increasing liquidity of the capital market, they will specialize in securities trading (exit) rather than long-term investments. However, the large funds are not purely managerial funds, either. Usually they have their portfolio divided into strategic firms and small passive holdings to diversify risk. Over the past three years, one could observe an increase in the weight of the strategic part (in relative terms, not by number of strategic companies).

There is some evidence that the bank groups made efforts to draw up and implement effective monitoring structures in portfolio companies like the set up of additional monitoring committees to support the owner representatives in the boardrooms. In a number of cases, group representatives have participated actively in drafting restructuring plans for portfolio firms. Their major contribution has been marketing and financial expertise while the senior management, headed by the general director, has been mostly responsible for the production sphere. In the end, however, the general director bears the key responsibility for turning around ailing companies. Therefore, the choice and exchange of the general director has become the most important means of active IPF control. At the same time, the threat of management exchanges has increasingly been disciplining incumbent managers. It ensures that the managerial labour market is a fairly effective control mechanism in spite of low unemployment and a still chronic lack of managerial expertise. This is valid for companies under IPF control as well as firms with (still) scattered ownership structures whose management is in danger of suddenly falling prey to an IPF raider (or another investor) who has accumulated a controlling stake on the open market.[45]

As for the bank groups, a main area of restructuring so far is financial restructuring. This includes both the adoption of a more active and consequent receivables management and the attraction of badly needed external finance through loans or new share issues. The injection of fresh capital is often supported or prepared by the banks which stand in the centre of the financial groups. Other fields of restructuring are the drafting of a new marketing and sales strategy (including the opening up of new markets), the reengineering of production processes and the implementation of a new quality management. The cases of Janka and ETA prove that the bank-centred financial groups are ready to initiate and carry through (together with the management) deep restructuring, even if it is linked with painful measures like a dramatic downsizing of the workforce. Many firms are entering into joint ventures, preferably with foreign partners actively supporting the restructuring process. Sometimes, the investment companies and financial groups initiate joint ventures of two or more portfolio companies or (exceptionally) enter into common projects for themselves (see e.g. the development company set up jointly by IPS and the savings bank). Given the still persisting lack of qualified and financially capable direct investors, the bank groups have done an important job in spurring restructuring in many companies.

Firewalls between funds and banks mostly do not exist. Banks hence have a leverage to get their interests in the boardrooms accepted and, in practice, they also make use of it. While this in itself isn't necessarily bad, in some cases banks reportedly try to influence corporate policy in order to boost their business volume at the debit of the portfolio company. However, management usually can resist the pressure of the bank groups if another bank is offering loans at better terms (see e.g. the case of ETA). In our interviews, most managers favoured bank-sponsored funds over private IPFs not only for their supposed long-term interest in the firm, but also for better access to finance and lower interests on loans (see e.g. the statement of AB). This points to fairly efficient debt/equity finance with the banks letting the enterprise sector participate in reduced agency costs.

Incentives for implementing a corporate policy with a detrimental impact on other stakeholders are weakened by implicit rules of cooperation among the bank-centred financial groups. In some cases, this may even lead to mutual delegations of guardian functions, e.g. to benefit from the expertise or personal network of individual IPF representatives. Furthermore, implicit, but obvious rules of cooperation have arisen which are also binding for non-bank funds. They primarily concern claims to board seats and active participation in corporate control. Of course, rules of cooperation are only evolving and yet have to be learnt by many players. The process of learning isn't free from flops and failures, effecting delays in the restructuring process (see the post privatization performance of ETA before the takeover by the IPB group). Cooperation is going to improve with an ongoing improvement of its normative environment and with a further increase in ownership concentration (setting incentives to invest in the development of mechanisms of cooperation). Due to the similarity and long-term nature of their interests, bank-sponsored funds show a very tight cooperation. While mutually aligned interests of bank-centred groups enhance the efficacy of corporate control and economize on monitoring costs, the quality of the whole system of corporate control crucially depends upon the incentive schemes of the banks themselves. The latter, in turn, are made up of the banks' own asset and governance structures and the degree of competition in the banking industry. They are analysed in the following chapter.

NOTES

1. In the literature, the term management board is often replaced by the terms executive board or board of directors. The Czech term *predstavenstvo* is the literal equivalent of the German *Vorstand*. The same is valid for the Czech phrase *dozorčí rada* and the German *Aufsichtsrat*.
2. As intimated by several interviewees, the greater the success of managers in mastering the difficulties inherent to transition, caused e.g. by the loss of the former COMECON 'markets' or a cutback in subsidies, the less was their willingness to cede corporate control to new owners. In contrast, the management of poorly performing companies was clearly more open to interference 'from outside', expecting outside investors to effectively support corporate restructuring.
3. Quoted from Prague Post, July 3-9, 1996, p. 9.
4. Today, the situation in the Czech labour market still supports employees' interests. Due to over-employment, employers are in strong competition with each other to attract labour. This considerably strengthens the bargaining position of employees as against the employers and ensures a high wage level even in absence of well-organized and strong trade unions. From this viewpoint, one can interpret the Czech board structure as an attempt by the owners to weaken the strong market-induced bargaining position of their employees.
5. The major owner is the IPB group (RIF alone holds some 20%; other PIAS funds dispose of smaller stakes). Insurer Česká Pojistovna's biggest fund 1. PIF owns 15% of company equity. Some 10% is held by a Slovak bank-sponsored IPF.
6. Quoted from Prague Post, 6-12 December, 1995, p. 5.
7. It should be stressed, however, that the position of the chairman of the management board in itself is not formally linked to power privileges like double voting rights in deadlocks in Germany. Nevertheless, the filling of the position is a good indicator for the balance of powers between owners and management.
8. According to the marketing director of IKS KB, fund representatives do not have to be branch specialists. This should be the task of the firms' technicians and production directors: 'Our people have a deep understanding of management, marketing and finance. Companies are in urgent need of exactly such experts.' Mladá Fronta Dnes, 21 August 1996, p. 12.
9. Following a 1995 inquiry by Coopers & Lybrand, Prague, representatives of creditor banks chair the supervisory boards in some 5% of the companies reviewed. Yet, in many cases, they may have been elected on behalf of the bank's investment company. A clear assignment of bank representatives to the firm's debt or equity holders is therefore not always possible. However, considering the broad scope for debt/equity finance through the big bank-centred financial groups, a separation between both groups of stakeholders may be pointless anyway. IPF representatives head 38% of the supervisory boards. 17% of the chairmen are even company managers. The CCode stipulates that they must not be authorized signatories of the firm.
10. Lobbyism is an extremely widespread phenomenon in the Czech Republic. In its intention, it does not lag behind Western societies. Lobbying isn't restricted to political behind-the-scenes activities. Well-organized interest groups are constantly actively trying to influence public opinion. For instance, each group of institutional investors like banks, investment funds and pension funds, is organized in its own association (with high-profile full-time staff including

prominent branch experts) that uses its political channels as well as mass media to get its way. Of course, both the impact and marginal utility of lobbyism is much higher in societies experiencing massive institutional changes than in countries with an established institutional environment that allows only gradual changes. Czech ministry officials told us that lobbyism is a serious problem for state supervisory institutions whose performance is severely affected by the political pressure generated by various lobbying groups. Frequently supervision isn't executed by politically independent entities, but by special departments of the ministries. We will discuss this problem later in the context of enforcement of capital market regulation.

11. This point has been stressed emphatically by Jiří Marek, chairman of the supervisory board of energy giant CEZ, at the conference on 'Správa a řízení akciových společností' (governance of joint-stock corporations), Prague, June 1995. As Mr. Marek reported, this legal contradiction is the main reason why CEZ applies the German board model where members of the management board are in no labour law relationship to the corporation.

12. Quotation of a Coopers & Lybrand consultant in the Prague Post, 5-11 July 1995, p. 6.

13. IPB executes its control only through one board seat. The remaining seats at the supervisory board are occupied by two smaller institutional investors, by employees (two seats) and by a company manager (by law no senior manager). On one hand, this arrangement clearly reflects the governance approach of the German banks which dominate the boardrooms of many large corporations by the dispatch of just one or two representatives. On the other hand, it proves that IPB has successfully built up a trust relationship both with the co-owners sitting at the supervisory board (and hence co-deciding on OSP's business strategy) and with the company management.

14. Opinion of a factory director as cited by King (1995, p. 24).

15. The general director seemingly doesn't realize, however, that valuable consulting services must usually be paid for in market economies: 'There is no free lunch!' Zdenek Bakala, founder of the first Czech investment bank Patria Finance, remarks that consulting services were free under the communist regime. This is why managers are only gradually going to understand that professional advice can be inevitable to reduce business risks or cut costs. See Cook (1995b, p. 60).

16. Interview in Ekonom, 1/1997, pp. 9-11.

17. In the past, several funds reportedly got their portfolio firms to fork out liquid means so as to meet their redemption promises from voucher privatization or to pay off unitholders after the opening of unit trusts.

18. Funds accumulating controlling stakes in portfolio companies on behalf of anonymous direct investors have become quite a common appearance on the Czech capital market.

19. Interview with Zdenek Pánek, general director of Královopolská Brno, in Hospodárské noviny, no. 252, 30 December 1996, p. 7.

20. For example, 22.92% of the general directors interviewed valued the governance behaviour of the biggest bank-sponsored fund as passive (= 0), 50.00% as mediocre (= 0.5) and 27.08% as active (= 1). Going by the general directors, the weighted RAL of the biggest bank-sponsored fund hence equals $22.92 \bullet 0.0 + 50.00 \bullet 0.5 + 27.08 \bullet 1 = 52.08$. The corresponding RAL for the assessments of other board members is 60.09. The average RAL is the rounded (unweighted) average of the two preceding RALs. For the biggest bank-sponsored IPF, the average value is $(52.08 + 60.09)/ 2 = 56.1$ (cf. Figure 4.2).

21. The latter is the average of the index numbers of both respondent groups for a given owner category.

22. In practice, a free-riding bank can be excluded by explicit contracts between main banks and client firms which keep debtors away from any business with the excluded bank. The exclusion could also be put down to an implicit cultural norm which does not require explicit agreement (but on the contrary excludes it!). Indeed, implicit commitments are neither 'informal' nor 'hand-shake' agreements, but agreements which are valid without ever having been made. This clarification seems worthy of notice, as - especially in the context of the Japanese and German economic systems - informal agreements are frequently mixed up with implicit contracts (see e.g. Kester, 1992). While we can plausibly consider the economic system of the US to be predominantly based upon formal and rather complete contracts, the Japanese system surely is grounded to a higher degree on informal and more incomplete contracts and on trust. Implicit

contracts in the sense of cultural norms which have evolved over time are probably playing an important role, too. But so far, we know little about the way how and whether contracts are made to establish reciprocal delegated monitoring arrangements among banks. Nor do we have much information on the way that other stakeholders like state authorities or debtor firms are integrated into such arrangements.

23. The case studies are based upon interviews with managing directors (in some cases complemented by interviews with second-tier managers), company information like annual reports and press releases.

24. Overdue receivables which had to be written off in 1993 contributed to the exorbitant loss considerably.

25. In the view of the owners, the biggest deficit of the old management was its lack of capacity to draw up a comprehensive business plan and a marketing strategy for the firm.

26. The track record of the new chief executive were studies of law and business administration in the Czech Republic and Germany and one year of work experience as managing director for the Czech subsidiary of a German food producer.

27. The steep rise in wages is also due to Janka's geographical position in the Prague region where unemployment virtually doesn't exist and employers' competition on the labour market hence is very hard.

28. Still in 1994, the new products have been awarded the label 'Czech made'. This label is awarded to products of any branches fulfilling well-defined quality norms and enjoys considerable prestige in the Czech public.

29. Janka's contribution to the joint ventures consisted of machinery and real estate while the foreign partners prevalently contributed financial means and more liquid assets.

30. Including the revenue realized in Slovakia, some half of the overall revenue is made abroad.

31. Provided the loans are at market terms, the resulting debt/equity finance is efficient as it avoids the duplication of information and monitoring costs. It gives rise to inefficiencies, however, if companies have to accept loans at above-market prices.

32. Interestingly, the firm's turnaround has not been reflected in share prices on the still largely non-efficient Czech equity market. ETA stock was trading in the range of CZK 800-1,000 in the summer of 1996 shortly after IPB had acquired majority control of the company. ETA's stock was quoted at below CZK 400 at the beginning of September 1997.

33. Exact data are not available. According to data released by the Securities Centre in March 1997, IPF KB and SPIF Ceský own 13.81% and 15.04% of IPS, respectively. The real size of the group holdings may be substantially higher due to additional equity stakes in the portfolio of the banks themselves or other funds of both groups. Unfortunately, data about shareholdings below 10% are not available.

34. The old senior management, which had already been running the firm under the old regime, didn't find the trust of the private owners and was dismissed. The new senior management consisted of former second-tier managers of the company.

35. The delegate of KB was the bank's deputy director for investment banking. Sporitelna's strategic interest in IPS was well reflected by the fact that it sent into the boardroom no less a person than its own general director and chairman of the management board Jaroslav Klapal. As of spring 1997, both bankers have still been representing their banks at the supervisory board of IPS.

36. In 1995, the price of IPS stock went up by 12% at the PSE while the stock index PX 50 dropped by 24%. In the first half of 1996, the price of IPS soared again, growing by another 49% as against a 28% increase of the index.

37. More than one half of the non-performing receivables were beyond 90 days overdue. The payment due period normally used by IPS customers in 1995 was 17 days.

38. During this period, the management board was composed of four owner representatives and three senior managers while the supervisory board contained two fund delegates and one member of the workforce.

39. As of end-1996, 17% of the the remaining stock is held by five IPFs and four foreign institutional investors who own more than 1% of equity. 27% is in hands of individuals and institutional investors owning less than 1% of equity.

40. In summer 1996, increasing unit costs forced F&GE to wind up the Berlin plant. Part of its machinery was transferred to Kablo.
41. Kablo has only one long-term loan with the due date in 1999 with Konsolidacní banka and a current account with Komercní banka. As of December 1996, the amount of overall bank debt was roughly equal to the firm's long-term commitments to F&GE. It must be added, however, that Kablo had already produced a comparatively strong financial performance before 1994. After serious liquidity problems generated prevalently by overdue receivables in 1990/91 (when the firm had been reportedly on the brink of liquidation), the management initiated a netting-out programme of mutual arrears with its main debtors. The programme ran over three years from 1991-93 and freed Kablo's balance sheet from overdue receivables of some CSK 250 million. As a consequence, the company could drastically reduce its indebtedness. Besides, Kablo broke off business connections to several customers with a bad record of payments. Of course, only the capital increase carried out by F&GE ultimately relieved Kablo from all financial problems.
42. The exact share is difficult to determine as Kablo frequently sells to Czech trading companies which resell the goods to foreign customers. Thus, the true export share may be even bigger than the assessments presented above, due to indirect exports.
43. As the management of Kablo remarks, a high export ratio is important to hedge against currency risks because the company buys 80% of its input materials (like copper and aluminium) abroad.
44. Several funds converted to holding companies in 1996 - *inter alia* in order to evade restrictive portfolio regulation and acquire bigger equity stakes in companies. Most of them are allied to one of the three private groups mentioned above, but some bank-sponsored funds like the Bankovní fund of PIAS have followed this trend, too.
45. In a small number of companies, management has bought a sufficiently high proportion of company shares so as to get entrenched against hostile takeovers. Managers regularly benefited from high discounts on the stock of their companies permitting them to undertake leveraged buy-outs. The necessary bank loans have been collateralized through company assets (mostly real estate) whose aggregate value could sometimes be substantially higher than the market value of the discounted stock.

5 Debt control in transition: Banks, enterprises and the rule of law

5.1 BANKS AND DEBT CONTROL

5.1.1 The Banking System at the Outset of Transition

The emergence of a two-tier banking system dates back to the year 1990 when the former Czechoslovak mono-bank was divided into a central bank and three newly created commercial banks (Komercní banka, Investicní banka and the Slovak Vseobecná úverová banka). The banking scene was completed by Ceská sporitelna and Slovenská sporitelna (the two institutes in charge of collecting the savings of the population under the command regime), Ceskoslovenská obchodní banka (the former monopoly supplier of foreign trade) and Zivnostenská banka (previously the monopoly provider of foreign exchange services for private households). According to the new Banking law, the central bank enjoyed far-reaching independence and commercial banks were allowed to offer universal banking services. Hence, commercial and investment banking services can be supplied by one institute and don't have to be separated by firewalls.

In the course of privatization, banks commonly used their regulatory freedom to build up equity links to the industrial sector both by purchasing shareholdings amounting up to 10% of the equity of a non-financial company (the limit stipulated by law) and indirectly through the foundation of investment companies running privatization funds. On the other hand, the banking sector was expected to support the functioning of the emerging market-based economic system through the allocation of loans and the execution of the monitoring and control services connected with debt finance. In the absence of developed bond markets, banks (along with trade creditors and public authorities like e.g. the tax offices) are responsible for initiating a hardening of firms' budget constraints. In times of transition, efficient debt control depends upon three crucial preconditions:

1. Bank balance sheets must be sufficiently sound such as not to get caught in a creditor trap.
2. Budget constraints are not softened by trade creditors or the state.

3. Creditors have to be provided with effective legal tools to enforce their debt claims.

One may add another precondition, namely that banks must have access to relevant company information in order to cut agency costs of debt control. While a lack of information clearly is a serious problem in times of transition, it is somewhat reduced by the stated equity links between banks and the industrial sector. Subsequently, we will analyse whether and how far the listed three criteria are fulfilled in the Czech Republic. Sections 5.1.2 and 5.1.3 relate to the quality of the banks' asset portfolios. 5.1.4 deals with the problem of interenterprise arrears and 5.1.5 with an analysis of institutional devices of debt control. Section 5.2 then deals with the governance structures of banks.

5.1.2   Bank Assets: The Stock Problem

5.1.2.1   Dealing with 'old' bad debt

The major problems of the banks split off from the mono-bank were their weak capital structures and a heavy burden imposed upon them by bad loans inherited from the old system. The reasons for their initial financial weakness are of systemic nature. In the past, bank managers couldn't make independent decisions about the allocation of credit. Banks were mere executive bodies of the central planning agency. Moreover, as money was 'passive', they couldn't even put sufficient pressure on enterprise management to ensure the 'profitability' of their clients and thus the amortization of loans. This 'stock problem' of bad loans can easily be translated into a 'flow problem' of credit misallocation (Dittus, 1994, p. 16). Banks are caught in a creditor trap if their financial fragility puts them under pressure to prolong bad loans in order to avoid a further deterioration of their balance sheets. Likewise they may try to disguise the true quality of their loan portfolio through the extension of new credits to defaulting debtors. As a consequence, they prolong lending to distressed customers, rolling over loans and accruing unpaid interest, while access to debt finance is barred for sound enterprises, e.g. promising start-ups of the emerging private sector. Besides, there is no hardening of the budget constraints for the (former) SOEs if the banks' position as creditors is too weak to stall financial support of inefficiently operating enterprises or to raise the credibility of debt control by occasionally choosing the 'exit' option for badly performing clients. For those reasons, in 1990 the Czech authorities (like other governments in the region) decided to implement a comprehensive restructuring programme to strengthen the financial health of the banking sector.

At the outset of transition, the authorities tried to overcome the financial fragility of the banks basically by two sub-programmes. One aimed at the clearing of classified loans on the banks' balance sheets. It should, at the same time, support the enterprise sector whose stability was heavily threatened by a sudden rise of interest rates. Thus, it should also help companies to become financially more sound and avoid a chain effect of insolvencies in the enterprise sector. The second programme focused exclusively on the recapitalization of banks.

In the early phase of transition, most bad loans were credits on so-called permanently revolving inventories (*úvery na trvale se obracejíci zásoby-* TOZ loans), coming up to more than 40% of the balance sheet of e.g. Komercní banka in 1990. Before 1989, the TOZ loans had been granted to the enterprise sector at interest rates of only 6% p.a. After price liberalization in the banking sector in January 1991, they were converted into standard short-term and medium-term credits at considerably higher market prices (20-24% p.a.). As the TOZ loans, like other credits, had been distributed by bureaucratic rather than allocative criteria under the old regime, most companies were not financially sound enough to cope with this heavy interest burden. In 1991, the government decided to set up Konsolidacní banka, a 'loan hospital' charged with dealing with bad loans of the banking sector. It took over TOZ debt to the amount of CSK 110.8 billion (CSK 30.4 billion of which was coming from Slovak enterprises) of some 6,000 bank clients along with the corresponding liabilities of the balance sheets of Komercní, Vseobecná úverová, Investicní and CSOB.[1] The instalments on TOZ credits were stretched over eight years at a unitary preferential rate of 13% p.a. (from 1997 14% p.a.), i.e. four percentage points over the discount rate.

In end-1991, the government started a second mass programme to clean up the balance sheets of the former state-owned banks. Komercní, Investicní, CSOB and Konsolidacní banka received bonds at a value of CSK 22 billion from the NPF to write off an equivalent amount of 'old' bad loans of highly indebted, yet economically prospective SOEs. However, since the banks could decide for themselves which companies to include in the programme, they were not free from perverse incentives and sometimes simply wrote off the loans of weakly performing rather than promising enterprises. The bonds were redeemed in end-1996. Later on, the fund distributed a smaller amount of bonds to write down company debt on a more individual basis.

Individual programmes to reduce bad loans were also triggered at two banks, namely Investicní and CSOB. The latter suffered from a serious imbalance between a high amount of foreign debt denominated in convertible currencies on the liability side and a high proportion of dubious 'Comecon receivables' denominated in non-convertible currencies on the asset side of the balance sheet. The government took over a substantial part of both, thereby shortening CSOB's balance sheet and significantly decreasing the bank's interest, currency and liquidity risk. The transaction was financed by an increase in government debt. The restructuring of CSOB's balance sheet was resumed in end-1993 by the foundation of two additional loan hospitals, the Czech and the Slovak collection agencies (*Ceská inkasní* and *Slovenská inkasná*) for bad loans. Both companies are owned by the ministry of finance of the respective republic. Until end-1996, dubious claims amounting to CZK 26 billion (as well as the corresponding liabilities) were transferred from the bank's accounts to Ceská inkasní while another CZK 11 billion were taken over by the Slovak agency. CSOB, in turn, has to guarantee the long-term refinancing of both agencies to an extent equal to the value of the transferred dubious assets. The bank's advantage from the entire transaction is the guarantee of both governments for the repayment of the loans extended to the collection agencies. Again, both the interest and liquidity risk has been shifted to the state authorities.[2] In the case of Investicní, the Czech and Slovak Ministries of Finance took over bad loans amounting to CZK 13 billion, which previously had been backed by the state as a measure to support investment projects in member countries of the Comecon.

In 1992, Konsolidacní banka purchased classified loans of a nominal value of CSK 15 billion at a discount of 20% from the banking sector. Despite the discount, the transaction contributed to a strengthening of the banks' balance sheets as the banks already had depreciated part of the loans. The banks, in turn, helped to finance the whole operation and deposited CSK 12 billion with Konsolidacní banka. In 1994, the Czech government decided to spend CZK 7 billion of the NPF's privatization revenues to clear the old debt of agricultural businesses which have been restored to their former owners. This led to a further improvement of the banks' balance sheets, thereby sparing the old-new owners the repayment of debt generated in the communist era under state ownership.

5.1.2.2 Recapitalization of banks

The second component of the restructuring programme is the recapitalization of the credit institutes. The programme was started in 1991, when the Czech (then still entirely) state-owned big banks (i.e. Komercní, Investicní, CSOB and Ceská Sporitelna) had a capital injection of CSK 12 billion, paid by the NPF in form of zero-bonds which were exchanged for the stock of privatized companies after five years. The measure was aimed at increasing the capital adequacy of the banking sector. Since recapitalization was tightly connected with privatization, it also strengthened banks' equity links to the enterprise sector.

Other actions carried out to increase the banks' capital base were grounded on a more individualistic approach, picking out single credit institutes. In 1993, the capital base of CSOB and Konsolidacní banka was strengthened through NPF bonds with a value of CZK 1 billion and CZK 3 billion respectively. The Ministry of Finance and the NB contributed an additional CZK 2 billion for the capital increase of CSOB. In 1994, the NPF issued two more tranches of bonds. The bonds worth over CZK 30 billion strengthened the general reserves of Konsolidacní banka. They can be used only after the depreciation of old debt, but on no account to finance the bank's current operations.

A non-standard approach to recapitalize banks was applied by the NPF in 1992. The fund issued bonds for CSK 23 billion and deposited them as subordinated debt with Komercní and Investicní. As the priority of the deposit was very low, close to equity, it boosted the banks' capital base. The bonds were transferred as a guarantee for the repayment of old enterprise loans for companies earmarked for the first privatization wave. However, as the previously expected wave of bankruptcies didn't occur until the end of the first wave, the bonds were re-transferred to the NPF in 1993.

In the end, the recapitalization programme didn't only give banks a fair chance 'to make a new start'. In a more indirect way, the enterprise sector gained from the recovering of the banks' balance sheets, too. While companies didn't take direct advantage from write-offs like in the 'old debt' programme, they benefited from an increase in the banks' credit capacity and a reduced pressure on banks to extend the interest spread in order to build up reserves on classified loans. In 1990, the capital-to-assets ratio (as defined by the CNB) of the big banks was under 1.5% and did increase substantially up to 6% in 1991. Nevertheless, banks were still under considerable pressure to gradually enhance reserves until end-1996, when they should have reached a risk-weighted capital ratio of 8% as requested by the Basle accords.

5.1.2.3   Other approaches to the restructuring of bank balance sheets

The government has still applied various other approaches to restructure bank balance sheets. Many of them have been anchored in the enterprise sector. When, in 1990, the crown experienced a sharp devaluation before it was linked to a currency basket, the government spent CSK 10 billion to cover losses and debt which had emerged as a consequence of the devaluation (Horcicová, 1996b, p. 17). By this means, the authorities effectively shifted part of the currency risk away from the enterprise sector to the state budget. Likewise, the government subsidized several industrial sectors seriously hit by transition-induced or policy-induced changes in the demand structure. For instance, still in 1990, it allocated about CSK 3 billion to companies of the arms industry which was undergoing a dramatic conversion to the production of civil goods. Another CSK 1.5 billion were earmarked to cover corporate losses resulting from the freezing of receivables due to be repaid in countries subject to international trade embargoes.

Finally, Investicní and Ceská sporitelna were compensated for long-term credits at very low interest rates which had been granted before 1989. This concerns, above all, loans for the construction of individual and cooperative flats (housing loans) and preferential loans for newly-married couples. As those loans used to be extended at interest rates substantially below the post-1989 discount rate, the banks were compensated for the balance through yearly payments of CZK 2 to 3 billion. While these differential payments are not high enough to make the low-interest loans lucrative for the banks, they help to lower the opportunity costs of commercial loans and thus spur the capitalization process of the banks.

To sum up: the overall restructuring programme for the banking sector significantly helped to curb the stock problem of 'old' bad loans and to raise the capital adequacy of the big state banks. The programme has been financed through public means, primarily through privatization proceeds (usually future proceeds transferred by means of NPF bonds), to a smaller extent also through the government budget. Nonetheless, a drastic increase in public debt could be avoided due to the synchronicity of bank restructuring and privatization. Restructuring was to support the conversion of the former executive bodies of the planning bureau (united in the monobank system) into independent banks adhering to commercial principles rather than perpetuating their dependence on public subsidies. For this purpose, the government emphasized the unique character of its measures. It put a clear dividing line between old bad debt inherited from the command system and new bad debt generated by the banks' independent decisions on credit allocation in a market environment. Finally, the banks were actively involved in the restructuring of their balance sheets. They participated in deciding which loans to write off or to sell to the consolidation bank. The taking of co-responsibility for the solution of the stock problem should have sharpened their awareness that they have to take full responsibility for their future performance and a further improvement of their balance sheets. Of course, in the post-restructuring period, the government's foremost task must be to set clear incentives for both the old state banks and the new private banks to run an efficiency-oriented policy and not to rely on eventual further bail-outs by the state.

5.1.3 Bank Assets: The Flow Problem

5.1.3.1 Problems of the 'small banks'

(i) Adverse selection
In the early phase of transition, the Czech National Bank pursued a most liberal licensing and supervision policy. Indeed, during the years 1990-92, when the banking sector started to expand, there was no adequate institutional framework regulating the activities of banks and the supervision department of the CNB. The relevant law on banks and savings banks had been passed in 1989, under the old regime. Given the lax regulation and easy access to banking licenses, the banking sector grew quickly from 6 institutions in early 1990 up to 38 in December 1993. 22 out of the 38 banks were without foreign capital participation.

Table 5.1: Lending rates for the 3rd quarter of 1994

maturity of credits	banks without foreign participation (small domestic banks)	banks with foreign partici-pation in equity capital up to 50% (big state banks)
short-term loans	15.29%	13.87%
medium-term loans	16.01%	15.11%
long-term loans	15.24%	14.22%

Source: Czech National Bank, Capek (1995, p. 26)

Most of them were weakly capitalized small banks, often founded with the sole objective to financially support the entrepreneurial activities of their owners. Their position in competition with the big state banks was quite difficult. Their branch networks were limited and their reputation was low in comparison with the established big banks which were, in addition, implicitly backed by the state. Yet, as the CNB was reluctant to open the 'discount window' and the big banks (above all Ceská Sporitelna) offered them only limited and expensive credit lines on the interbank market, they tried to enlarge their own deposit base. To pull investors away from the established big banks, they had to offer above-average interest rates on deposits. Until June 1992, this didn't affect their lending rates because the NB had imposed tight interest rate ceilings on loans to the enterprise sector. After the liberalization of the lending rates, the small banks tended to raise their rates over the level of the big banks (see Table 5.1). They did so to produce a spread sufficiently high to cover all operational costs and losses from credit failure of customers and to strengthen their capital base. Given the constitutional uncertainty about the creditworthiness of customers and the quality of projects, their behaviour closely resembles a debtor's gambling for resurrection in financial distress. This is not amazing considering their high debt/equity ratios and imminent solvency problems. The problem is that the higher the lending rates, the less solvent are, on average, also the customers attracted by the bank and the riskier are their projects (usually combined with an inferior risk/profit mix justified, in the view of the debtor, by the possibility of shifting a relatively high part of the entrepreneurial risk to the bank). In the end, the gambling of the small banks was self-reinforcing: The extension of risky high-interest loans accelerated the growth of 'new' non-performing loans in their balance sheets and, hence, set incentives to get involved in even riskier credit operations.

Table 5.2: Selected balance sheet items of banks

in percent of overall assets, end of 1993	3 big banks[a]	3 small domestic banks	2 problem banks[b]
deposits of the population	23.6	11.9	3.9
deposits of firms	14.5	37.0	10.1
deposits & loans from other financial institutions	10.4	27.6	56.0
deposits & loans to other financial institutions	16.7	11.5	0.4
credits to SOEs	19.5	8.5	3.0
credits to private firms	19.5	64.5	75.7

a selected from the top six banks
b small domestic banks with liquidity problems in 1993

Source: Capek (1995, p. 30)

The competitive disadvantage of the small banks and the connected risks are well reflected by Table 5.2. The large banks have better access to cheaper sources of refinance. Because of extended branch networks, some quarter of their liabilities are deposits collected from the population. As of 1993, the amount of loans to and deposits with other financial institutions clearly exceeds the amount borrowed from the interbank market by 6.3 percentage points (16.7% - 10.4%), i.e. by 61%. Small banks are heavily relying on the interbank market to refinance their lending businesses. The financial means borrowed from the market surmount the credits granted to the market by 16.1 percentage points (i.e. 140%). For the problem banks, i.e. small domestic institutions with liquidity problems in 1993, deposits and loans from other financial institutions make up as much as 56% of overall liabilities whereas their own claims towards other banks are virtually non-existent (0.4% of liabilities). Of course, given the financial fragility of the small start-up banks, their interbank refinance is charged with substantial risk premiums. The same is valid for deposits of firms. On the asset side of the balance, the small banks have a less diversified loan portfolio (as for the classes of debtors) than the big banks. While the latter have scattered their loans evenly over SOEs and private firms (including privatized companies as well as start-ups), the small banks depend heavily upon private firms. The problem is that many private start-ups have no financial track record helping banks to evaluate the credit risk of the given debtor. Thus, the risks of loans granted to private firms are on average higher than those of loans distributed to SOEs. This assumption is evidenced by the high proportion of loans to private companies in the balance sheet of the problem banks, amounting to more than 75% of overall assets.

(ii) Unlawful actions
The deterioration of the balance sheets of various small banks was accelerated by risky and often unlawful actions of their shareholders and weak supervision of the CNB. Many small banks were set up exclusively to channel financial means from the bank accounts to intransparent shareholder groups so as to cheaply finance their entrepreneurial activities. Those shareholder groups commonly were a mesh of physical persons and firms with frequently changing company names and headquarters. In many cases, they were linked to the banks additionally as both directors and debtors and misused their governance power to channel bank assets through loans to the allied firms (*tunelování*). The debtor firms then transferred the money to other companies linked with the bank's shareholders and defaulted. The helplessness and passivity of the CNB against the machinations of such owners was revealed for the first time when the small AB Banka was caught up with a credit crunch in late 1993. The CNB's only measure was to let AB Banka survive on emergency credit thus enabling the bank to continue with orgiastic lending to its own shareholders who were already bearing responsibility for the previous looting of the bank.[3]

In January 1996, Ekoagrobanka, one of the bigger 'small banks' (but with a market share still below 1%), ran into financial distress. It appeared that the bank had lent money to some dozen companies owned by its owner-managers. The amount of classified loans granted to shareholders was estimated at CZK 2.5 billion while the bank's capital stock was as low as CZK 600 million. Like in many other cases, the CNB should and could have interfered much sooner with the banks' operations as they clearly violated exposure rules. By law, banks were and are barred from extending loans exceeding 25% of the capital stock to individual customers. Furthermore, since 1994 the CNB has at its disposal a wide range of measures to intervene early in banks' policies if they carry out transactions in a way 'that impairs the interests of their depositors or threatens the security and stability of the banking system'.[4] Reluctance to take action against unlawful behaviour hence must be put down to both weak off-site supervision and the idea of deliberate non-intervention of the state, boiling down to *laissez-faire* liberalism in banking.

(iii) Restructuring of small banks

As Ekoagrobanka was the sixth bank going under in three years and public confidence in the banking industry was therefore drastically declining, CNB decided to start a consolidation programme for the small banks. Its goal was to purge the industry from insolvent banks and to head off crashes where possible. Essentially, shareholders should take the hit and bear the financial costs of insolvency. NB was going to slash the capital stock (in the case of Ekoagrobanka from CZK 600 million down to CZK 1.2 million)[5] and force shareholders to raise it again so as to cover problem loans. If shareholders refused to cooperate or were not able adequately to strengthen the bank's capital base, the ailing bank would be put under forced administration by Konsolidacní banka. The latter would then replace the management and exert all ownership rights until it found a financially sound investor, i.e. either a foreign investor or a more healthy domestic bank. The task of the new investor would be to restructure the distressed bank. Unfortunately, as the cases of AB Banka and Ekoagrobanka demonstrate, the gaps in funding in problem banks were often several times the share capital. Therefore, the programme has been implemented too late to give the owners the incentive to care for the financial health of the banks. Meanwhile, the value of control over bank assets has become too low to justify expensive balance sheet restructuring by investors who established banks to use them as personal money machines rather than to carry out efficiency-oriented banking.

By the end of 1996, six banks have gone bust and are either subject to a bankruptcy procedure or even in liquidation. Another five institutes with solvency problems are under forced administration by Konsolidacní banka and CNB.[6] Ekoagrobanka has been sold to another domestic bank, the rapidly expanding Union banka which has also taken over two other small banks (Evrobanka and Bankovní dum Skala) and, meanwhile, built up the country's sixth biggest banking group by asset volume. As for CNB governor Josef Tosovský, all banks now have sufficiently high reserves to cover all problem loans.[7] The price for cleaning the balance sheets of the problem banks was the launching of another restructuring programme exclusively designed for 13 small domestic institutes whose assets do not exceed CZK 30 billion per bank. Konsolidacní banka has offered to purchase non-performing loans from them up to an extent equal to their (paid) capital stock plus 10%. The overall volume of the programme is about CZK 14 billion.[8] The loans sold by the banks are to be exchanged for zero bonds with a maturity period of five to seven years. Once again, it's the NPF which has to reimburse Konsolidacní for eventual losses arising from the transaction.[9]

It may turn out that the CNB's reaction came too late. Many investors have lost their trust in the private domestic banking sector. An obligatory deposit insurance, established in 1996 and covering 80% of the value of all deposits up to a limit of CZK 100,000, is seemingly not sufficient to prevent small investors from withdrawing their savings from the high-interest accounts of the small banks and to transfer it to the big banks which are supposed to be more stable and - in case of imminent insolvency - 'too big to fail' (all the more as the state is still holding big equity stakes in them and is seemingly not willing to reduce them under 10% in the future).[10] Encouraged by the CNB, several smaller banks have merged in order to raise their liquidity. Likewise, the big banks have capitalized parts of their bad loans given to smaller banks. This is true above all for Ceská Sporitelna which has allocated a considerable portion of its huge deposit base to the interbank market. Whether the consolidation programme will produce long-term benefits or is just a flash in the pan can be evaluated only in the long-term and depends primarily upon the quality of the CNB's future supervision. In the past, a lack of effective control instruments along with both weak competence and willingness to execute strict supervision have largely contributed to a quick increase in 'new' bad loans in the banks' asset portfolios.

5.1.3.2 Lack of expertise

It would, however, be too simple to put the problem of newly emerging bad loans exclusively down to fraudulent behaviour and adverse selection problems of small banks. Especially in the early phase of transition, incompetence and non-existent risk-management systems were crucial for the distribution of bad loans. Of course, this problem concerned both the newly-founded small banks as well as the old large banks. Yet, as the informational asymmetry between banks and debtors was more serious in the case of the new banks than of the old banks (which possessed more information about individual companies due to both the past relationship between mono-bank and enterprise sector and because of their extensive IPF networks), the negative impact of incompetence turned out to be more drastic in the case of the small banks. Nevertheless, a sizeable portion of bad loans must be attributed to a constitutional lack of company information rather than incompetence since classical 'western-style' evaluation methods (even if applied right) are not very reliable in times of transition. It simply is most uncertain whether previously well-performing SOEs can maintain their position in competitive markets.

5.1.3.3 Political pressure

The rise of new bad loans on the balance sheets of the big banks must be partially attributed to political pressure exerted by the government and the public in the early phase of privatization. In 1990/91, the large banks were running a fairly prudential lending policy. To meet the timetable for the increase in capital adequacy (originally, they should reach a capital-asset ratio of 6.25% in the end of 1992 and one of 8% by 1994), they called off loans (e.g. by refusing to prolong them) and halted their lending activities.

Another reason for the curbing of lending activities were the mentioned interest rate ceilings imposed upon bank loans before June 1992. Frequently the ceilings prevented banks from marking up the interest rates to offset the higher risks of loans to the private sector. For this reason, the banks refrained from many venture loans to private entrepreneurs. As a consequence of the credit ceilings, real deposit and (temporarily in 1991) also lending rates became negative in the early phase of transition. This effected a redistribution of financial means from the individual depositors to the enterprise sector and was intended to encourage some initial pre-privatization restructuring and to cushion some of the shocks generated by the hardening of the budget constraints. Of course, the price of the redistribution policy was a declining savings inclination of the individuals. In the end, the ceilings ensured cheap finance for the SOEs but hampered the development of the private sector because of both the banks' disability to charge adequate risk premiums and the decrease in overall savings which could be distributed to the enterprise sector.

Prior to 1992, the expansion of the private sector was hampered by the banks' conservative lending policy and the restrictive monetary policy of the CNB which tried to nip in the bud the eventual danger of an inflation spiral after far-reaching price liberalization. Both factors together threatened to put brakes on the approaching privatization process. Small-scale privatization began in 1991 and its success was crucially based upon the willingness of banks to finance the sales of businesses. Therefore, it was in the interest of the state and the just emerging entrepreneurial class to overcome the banks' reluctance in providing loans. Both groups put great pressure (e.g. by launching campaigns in the mass media) on the state banks to support the development of the private sector more actively and enhance their credit involvement in the privatization process. In the end, the banks couldn't stand the pressure and, according to the needs of small-scale privatization, expanded mainly the allocation of medium-term loans. Banks began to participate actively in the financing of small-scale privatization and new start-ups, thereby accepting the high risks connected with venture capital. Most of the debtors were not well-equipped with equity or property for collateral and their businesses suffered, from the beginning, from an extremely high debt/equity ratio. In many cases, these leveraged buyouts (LBOs) were not able to repay their loans or did so with considerable delays. Insolvencies of start-ups and newly privatized firms led to a serious deterioration of the quality of the loan portfolios of the large banks by end-1992.

Table 5.3: Non-performing loans as a proportion of total loans

end of year	1991	1992	1993	1994	1995	1996	1997	1998
nonperforming loans/total loans	2%	19%	24%	38%	36%	29%	27%	27%
total loans in billion CZK	494	579	672	776	877	880	997	996

Source: CNB, own calculations

The lifting of the interest ceilings in 1992 additionally motivated the banks to get engaged in large-scale privatization and the financial restructuring of large enterprises. Along with an enhancement of their discretion to adjust interest rates to the supposed quality of the borrower, banks also raised their readiness to finance more risky projects. They had to pay for it through a further rise of non-performing loans until end-1994.[11] Finally, it's an open secret that state representatives at the supervisory boards of the large banks occasionally have exerted pressure on the management to allocate loans according to political rather than economic criteria. While this modus to allocate scarce financial resources is clearly non-efficient, it has an adverse impact upon the banks' asset portfolios only if the loans are not backed by government guarantees (some 'political' loans reportedly have been backed).

Table 5.4:   Balance sheets of big banks

data as of end-1996	Komercni	C. sporitelna	CSOB	IPB
total assets (CZK)	446 bln	358 bln	203 bln	219 bln
loans to companies (CZK)	259 bln	163 bln	103 bln	146 bln
capital adequacy	10.7%	9.1%	12.3%	8.2%
non-performing loans/ total loans	0.26	0.19	0.24	0.19
reserves/non-performing loans	0.29	0.42	0.74	0.24
(reserves+provisions +government guarantees)/ non-performing loans	0.38	0.62	1.43	n.a.

Source: Annual reports, various press releases, Thompson Bankwatch, own calculations

As of end-1998, the balance sheets of the big banks are still quite fragile (with the only exception of CSOB). High proportions of non-performing loans (most of which are so-called 'lost loans' which are overdue more than 360 days) along with still modest reserve ratios demonstrate that, in contrast to the stock problem of 'old' bad debt, the flow problem of 'new' bad debt could not be solved effectively for the top three banks Komercní, Sporitelna and IPB. Weak supervision, a lack of expertise and experience and political pressure contributed to the deterioration of the balance sheets after 1990. As will be shown later, another major reason was the absence of effective legal tools to enforce debt claims.

5.1.4 Interenterprise Arrears

An important factor relaxing the budget constraints of the industrial sector are interenterprise arrears.[12] To a certain extent, they can be considered as inheritance of the command system. The vast majority of arrears has emerged, however, in the period after 1990. There are two forms of interenterprise indebtedness. The first one is *primary* arrears, that is the overhang of a company's overdue payables over its overdue receivables. The second form is *secondary* arrears. They consist of a firm's total overdue payables (including also the proportion of debt which could be hypothetically covered by its overdue receivables) minus its primary arrears. Secondary arrears hence emerge from the failure of the firm's customers to pay their trade debt in due time.[13] As can be seen from Table 5.5, the secondary arrears of Czech (and Slovak) firms exploded after 1990 and peaked in December 1991 when they made up 16% of the gross domestic product and some quarter of all bank credits to the enterprise sector. They dropped slightly, together with the total amount of arrears, only in 1992. At the end of 1993, the arrears of Czech companies amounted to roughly CZK 100 billion, representing some third of total interenterprise credits.

What are the causes for this unfavourable development? One is surely the credit crunch produced by the CNB's restrictive monetary policy in the early 1990s. Together with the cautious lending policy of the big banks in 1990/91 and their refusal to prolong the cheap TOZ credits, this policy brought many firms into liquidity trouble. Used to quasi-automatic credit alimentation by the state, enterprises looked for alternative tools to soften their budget constraints. The easiest way to cope with insolvency turned out simply to ignore it - along with the trade bills obtained from suppliers. The failure in paying trade debt in due time quickly became a self-reinforcing mass phenomenon, generating large networks of mutual indebtedness and threatening to reinstall the passivity of money well-known from the previous system. The only difference was that the softening of companies' budget constraints was not effected by the state (through the mono-bank), but by the inability and unwillingness of the enterprise sector itself to enforce a better financial discipline.

Table 5.5: Interenterprise arrears*

end of period	Interenterprise arrears (in billion crowns)			yearly nominal increase (%)	yearly real increase (%)	% of firms
	total	primary	secondary			
Czechoslovakia:						
1989	6.6	3.2	3.4	-	-	30.2%
1990	47.8	20.0	27.8	624.2%	500.4%	34.2%
1991	170.7	37.8	133.0	257.1%	61.4%	42.8%
1992	154.6	35.3	119.3	-11.8%	-20.7%	n.a.
Czech Republic:						
1993	100.0	n.a.	n.a.	-	-	n.a.
1994	110.4	n.a.	n.a.	10.4%	0.4%	n.a.
1995	123.2	n.a.	n.a.	11.6%	1.0%	n.a.
1996	132.5	n.a.	n.a.	13.4%	-1.6%	n.a.

* Yearly real increases (i.e. real changes in percent as against end-December of previous year) have been calculated using the producer price index of the given year. Data for 1992 (Czechoslovakia) are for end-September, data for 1996 (Czech Republic) for end-June. Nominal and real increases for both years are extrapolated by the author. Data for 1993 are based upon CSÚ estimations of arrears as presented by Capek (1995, p. 11).

Source: Hrncír (1994), Czech Statistical Office (CSÚ), own calculations

In the absence of an effective exit mechanism for insolvent companies, most managers didn't feel any urgent need to improve the financial situation of their enterprises. In the period before 1992, when most companies were still in an interim phase between fading state control and approaching privatization and managers enjoyed considerable discretion, the relaxation of solvency pressure caused delays in restructuring in many SOEs. The situation was aggravated by the demand shock produced by the disintegration of the Comecon and the resulting breakdown of existing sales networks. On aggregate, Czech enterprises were net creditors of companies from other countries of the former Comecon. Amazingly, many of them didn't even break off business contacts after the defaulting of their trade partners abroad. Instead, they further delivered goods, knowing that payment of their receivables would be more than dubious. This behaviour reflects a high priority for the technical going concern of a firm and a strong commitment to the (short-term) maintenance of jobs rather than a market-oriented policy. Still in mid-1996, overdue receivables of Czech industrial companies exceeded their overdue payments by 50%. A constant increase in overdue receivables furthermore indicates the secondary nature of growing indebtedness. Not surprising, the same indifference towards the creditworthiness of customers came into play in deals with domestic enterprises. As a consequence, already in December 1991 some 43% of Czech companies suffered from secondary arrears.

Originally the government didn't foresee any 'constructivistic' intervention to stop the ongoing accumulation of arrears. But it had to recognize soon that the market forces alone didn't incentivize the enterprise sector to stop their rapid expansion. The authorities thus initiated a mutual netting out of overdue payments arrears through the state banks.[14] The programme effected a slowing down of the real growth of arrears during 1991 and a real reduction of roughly 21% in 1992. The high inflation rates of 1990 (17.1%) and particularly 1991, caused by a 'liberalization shock' after far-reaching price deregulations, put an additional brake upon the real increase in interenterprise arrears while arrears were rising swiftly in nominal terms. Of course, inflation as a tool to slow down the expansion of arrears has largely vanished as inflation rates have stabilized below 10% after 1992.

During and after privatization, part of the companies have changed their policy towards defaulters and discovered various tools to encourage customers to fulfil their payments obligations in due time. The most simple form of exerting pressure on customers is just to actively start renegotiations of the payments schedule. Besides, several firms are now discriminating against defaulters, granting superior payments conditions and preferential prices to reliable clients. The higher a customer's backlog of payments, the higher is also his individual risk premium added to the product price.[15] In some cases, creditor enterprises with a strong market position have even cut their trade relationship to non-paying debtors. Other companies charge special collection agencies with the collection of overdue receivables.[16] Various firms, however, complain that they cannot put effective pressure on a customer who holds a strong market position. If they depend upon one or a few such customers and hence do not have a sufficiently well-diversified customer portfolio, they are - similar to banks - in a (trade) creditor trap. If the worst comes to the worst, the monopoly customer has himself a well-diversified supplier portfolio and he may feel no pressure to pay as long as suppliers are (paradoxically) possibly even standing in intensive competition for delivery contracts. The high bargaining power of the monopolist may then cause serious cash flow problems for the whole supplier industry.

On the whole, the success of the government in combating the problem of interenterprise arrears has been limited. The netting-out programme has undoubtedly dissolved some chains of mutual arrears in the industrial sector. Nevertheless, as shown in Table 5.5, arrears have stabilized at a high level.[17]

Since the split of Czechoslovakia in 1993, low inflation rates have been preventing an erosion of the real value of arrears. Moreover, companies had hardly any opportunity to write off bad trade credits as the authorities were frightened of losing tax revenue if they approached the problem of bad trade credits by changing the tax laws (priority of a balanced budget). Today, there is rarely any firm not affected by the problem. For many companies, especially the loss makers, payment delays still represent a comfortable way of financing operative costs. For those enterprises, arrears have become the 'third tier of the banking system'. On the other hand, economically viable companies are increasingly adapting their behaviour and trying to improve their solvency through *ex ante* evaluations of their customers' mode of payment. In the long run, this will effect a selection of 'bad' trade creditors and trade credit may fulfil the function it plays in most market economies: to lower both transaction costs and the costs of debt finance. Yet, the most important precondition for this is the implementation of an effective bankruptcy law. The government's cardinal mistake thus was to have delayed the institutionalizing of exit for a painfully long time (cf. next section) and, instead, to have addressed the symptoms rather than the systemic causes of enterprises' soft budget constraints. This proves, once again, the importance of credible and powerful institutions for the efficient function of corporate control.[18]

5.1.5 Institutional Tools of Debt Control

5.1.5.1 Bankruptcy

(i) Institutionalizing debtors' protection
Under the communist regime, enterprises were insured against bankruptcy by an implicit long-term contract with the state (Kornai, 1993, p. 316). A working bankruptcy law as major tool of credit-based enterprise control had only to be constructed in the course of transformation. The first version of the Bankruptcy and Composition Act (BCA), launched in August 1991 still before the split of Czechoslovakia, reflects serious political concerns of mass bankruptcies in the enterprise sector, mainly due to the unexpected explosion of interenterprise arrears. The government supposed that the implementation of an effective and creditor-oriented bankruptcy law early in the transition could cause an economic 'domino effect' and ultimately also interfere with the mass privatization programme. Therefore, the law allowed the courts to trigger bankruptcy procedures only for companies overloaded with debt (without specifying the criteria for such an over-indebtedness). Moreover, the issuance of a bankruptcy order for SOEs and corporations held by the state was conditional upon the approval of the founding body of

the creditor after a hearing of the founder of the debtor. Finally, insolvent enterprises undergoing privatization were automatically protected against bankruptcy in order not to endanger voucher privatization. These provisions made bankruptcy a political rather than market-driven process. Indeed, in 1992, a mere 350 petitions for bankruptcy were submitted at the courts and as few as five bankruptcy orders were issued.

Table 5.6: Results of bankruptcy proceedings between 1992-96

	1992	1993	1994	1995	1996*
submitted petitions for bankruptcy	350	1,098	1,816	2,393	2,296
of which:					
issued bankruptcy orders	5	60	288	480	479
submissions for voluntary com-					
position	-	1	2	2	6
increase in no. of pending pro-					
ceedings	+234	+688	+937	+1,312	+1,171
rejected petitions	111	349	589	599	638
issued bankruptcy orders: Austria	1,583	2,043	1,999	2,043	-
Germany	3,714	4,684	6,899	27,000	-

* As of 30 September 1996

Source: Ministry of Economy of the Czech Republic and Hospodárské noviny, 1 February 1996, p. 2

On the other hand, the government started with the liquidation of so-called remnant firms (*zbytkové podniky*). Those are SOEs which remained as parts of former bigger SOEs after the privatization of other parts. The emergence of remnant firms can be put down to e.g. unresolved restitution claims or unclear ownership rights. Frequently, the remnant firms have taken over most of the debt burden of the old SOE to make possible a separate privatization of the remaining assets. The revenues of the asset sales could be re-channelled to the remnant firm. Nonetheless, many of the hundreds of remnant firms left after privatization had zero property and were closed without liquidation. Firms with positive book value were to be privatized or liquidated after the resolution of ownership questions. Firms with negative book value had to file for bankruptcy. Besides, the state began with the liquidation of SOEs which had taken part in the privatization process, but for which no privatization project had been approved, and of some SOEs constantly operating at losses. Provided the SOEs' book values were positive, the firms entered the liquidation procedure. Companies with a negative value likewise had to file for bankruptcy. Considering the problems of asset valuations occurring in the course of privatization, the strong reliance on the firms' book values in choosing a means of exit (liquidation or bankruptcy) appears somewhat dubious. The treatment of both remnant firms and part of the SOEs yet demonstrates the will of the authorities also to trigger an exit mechanism for public enterprises and thereby to make possible the divestiture of resources to more efficient applications. 376 remnant firms and 71 SOEs have been closed only till the end of 1994. Their liquidations, operated by the founding ministries, can be regarded 'as a substitute to the bankruptcy procedure and as an integral part of the restructuring process' (Tuma & Dotson, 1995, p. 3).

Since April 1993, SOEs have been subject to the BCA, too. However, the BCA has been complemented concurrently by the introduction of a protection period. Debtors may submit for a protection period of three months in which the courts mustn't issue a bankruptcy order for the firm. After the expiry of the period, they may submit for an extension of another three months. The protection period should enable the debtor to improve the company's financial performance, to reorganize the firm and to renegotiate its relationship to its debtholders. In practice, this protection period has been frequently abused (Nesnídal, 1996b, p. II). Creditors complain that, in a series of cases, the asset value of the distressed firm has significantly declined after the protection period so that bankruptcy couldn't be triggered for a lack of assets.

The strong institutional protection of debtors was the main cause for the rather gradual increase in the number of bankruptcy processes before 1996. Given the financial weakness of many companies, the number of bankruptcy orders issued was remarkably low during the first years after the implementation of the law. Various additional institutional deficiencies contributed to the reduction of the efficacy of the BCA and the weakening of the creditors' position. For instance, the debtor was not obliged by law to petition for its own bankruptcy. In standard market economies, the majority of petitions is submitted by the debtor itself. In Germany, the management of financially distressed firms has to file for bankruptcy within three weeks when the firm becomes insolvent in order to grant timely triggering of the bankruptcy process and to protect the interests of creditors. In the Czech Republic, creditors had not only to file for bankruptcy regularly for themselves. They had to document, too, that the debtor was really insolvent. As the creditor's access to information on the debtor's financial situation is commonly limited, he was in a difficult position and in danger either of submitting the petition too late or of having insufficient proof of the debtor's insolvency.[19] Furthermore, there was no protection of the bankruptcy estate between filing and the issuance of an order. The debtor could further dispose of company assets more or less without constraints. He often abuses his discretion in order to reduce the value of the estate considerably.

(ii) Progression of the bankruptcy proceeding

According to the BCA, the progression of bankruptcy proceedings logically comprises up to six stages and may end with the termination of the firm or its reorganization (see Figure 5.1).[20] The proceeding starts with the submission of the petition for bankruptcy. The debtor may then file for a protection period (and later for its extension). Before the issuing of a bankruptcy order, the debtor can submit a proposal for voluntary composition (*vyrovnání*). In his proposal, he must state how to satisfy all debt claims against him and which reorganization measures to take. The court may accept the proposal only if the latter respects all rights of preferential and secured creditors and if the claims of non-preferential creditors are repaid at least by 45% within two years. Provided the court has confirmed the plan, creditors are going to vote on it. The composition proposal is accepted if it is approved by a simple majority of all unsecured creditors participating in the voting procedure and by a majority of more than 75% of the firm's overall volume of unsecured claims. If the proposal is passed by the creditors, the debtor can reorganize the firm according to his plan and with a reduced and/or rearranged debt burden. If the proposal has been rejected either by the court or by the creditors, the next stage is the issuance of a bankruptcy order by the court (provided it recognizes the debtor's insolvency).

It turned out to be a major problem that the BCA didn't provide a clear definition of insolvency. Debtors were considered insolvent if they couldn't meet their financial obligations due to several creditors over a 'protracted period of time'. The courts had to decide on a case-by-case basis without any guiding lines for their judgements. This lack of definition of insolvency reportedly gave rise to considerable legal uncertainty. If the court finds sufficient evidence for insolvency and triggers bankruptcy, it immediately appoints a receiver to take control of the debtor's assets. However, as mentioned above, until recently it has been only from this point that the estate has been protected. Under court administration, all claims against the firm crystallize and interest stops accruing. If there are more than 15 creditors, they must elect their own committee of three to nine members to oversee the receiver.[21] It is striking that, even if insolvency has been recognized by the court, most petitions are rejected for a lack of estate to cover the administration costs of a bankruptcy process. This fact (rather than the stated solvency of the respective debtors) explains the high proportion of rejected petitions in Table 5.6.

Under receivership, the debtor has another chance to save the firm from liquidation. The bankrupt may propose to terminate bankruptcy through an involuntary composition (*nucené vyrovnání*). The procedure is very similar to voluntary composition. Again, all preferential creditors must be paid in full and secured claims must be respected. Moreover, unsecured creditors must get repaid at least one third of their claims within one year. The debtor has to detail the method of settling debts. After hearings on the composition, the reorganization plan designed by the debtor must be accepted by the court and find majority support of the creditors analogous to the voting procedure in voluntary compositions. So far, the settlement criteria for the acceptance of a reorganization plan in both types of in-court composition procedures have proved to be too demanding to give debtor-initiated reorganization a real chance. Until the end of 1995, only five composition proposals had passed the institutional hurdles set up by the BCA. This is in line with the intention of Czech lawmakers to place the satisfaction of creditors above the going-concern of the debtor. This basic principle puts the BCA close to the German insolvency law.

If the procedure ends with the termination of the firm, the bankrupt's estate is realized by either auctions or other sales methods. Other sales methods must be approved by the court and the creditors' committee. The realized revenues are distributed to the creditors according to priority.

(iii) The BCA amendment of 1996

After the termination of the voucher programme in 1995, the government recognized the necessity of accelerating and simplifying bankruptcy proceedings. Its attempts to increase the efficacy of the BCA led to an amendment of the law which took effect in June 1996. In fact, the amendment was successful in correcting some of the law's major drawbacks. The new law stipulates that a debtor who becomes insolvent is obliged to file for bankruptcy. The legal obligation concerns all persons authorized to file petitions for the opening of judicial proceedings, especially the debtor's management board.[22] If the directors fail to do so, they are jointly and severally liable to the creditors for any damage caused to them. The provision clearly strengthens the position of creditors as against the management and sets strong incentives to the latter to reveal timely solvency problems. Ultimately, this obligation is likely to increase both the number of bankruptcy petitions and the protection of creditors' claims.

Figure 5.1: Progression of bankruptcy proceedings according to the BCA

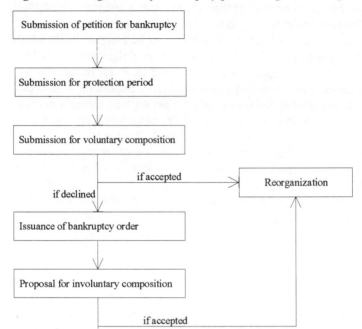

The amendment also provides for a more concrete definition of insolvency stating that a debtor is insolvent 'also if he is overburdened with debts'. This is the case if he has more than one creditor and his due payables exceed the value of his assets. Nevertheless, the law leaves considerable scope for interpretation, thus diminishing legal security. For instance, the debtor's assets comprise expected future revenue from business activities, if the income of the business is supposed to exceed its expenses. Lawyers object that it will take years to find a generally accepted definition of insolvency through the judiciary as the BCA still doesn't specify the terminology sufficiently. As a consequence, they argue, many distressed debtors do not know when to submit for bankruptcy. On the other hand, even if they supposed the criteria to be fulfilled, they might protract the petitioning to keep their discretion and positions as long as possible. Considering the still prevailing inclination of Czech judges to interpret law in a most literalistic manner, they may easily evade their liability explaining that they made a positive prediction of the firm's future prospects. Thus, while the introduction of debtor's liability will undoubtedly enhance the efficacy of the law, the definition problem still isn't resolved in a satisfactory manner. Despite an increase in filings and procedures, the actual numbers of both will probably be lower than the numbers which are optimal from the lenders' viewpoint.[23]

Another important institutional change concerns the protection period which has been used by debtors often exclusively to delay the triggering of bankruptcy rather than to care for an improvement of financial performance and the preparation of reorganization (as originally intended by the law). A legal redefining of the protection period should help to change the situation. Firstly, court protection is now limited to companies with at least 50 employees. Secondly, debtors applying for protection now have to provide detailed information about the financial situation of the company and to sketch a proposal as to how to settle creditor claims and which measures to take to improve corporate performance. This means that, in contrast to the previous practice, protection is not granted more or less automatically any more, but is conditional upon the debtor's serious intention to satisfy creditors' claims as far as possible. If the courts do not see any chance for a company to recover within the three-months protection period to a degree rendering possible adequate satisfaction of creditors claims, it must not trigger protection. Equally important, if the debtor doesn't stick to his *ex ante* announced recovery proposal or if company information handed out to the court does not correspond with the actual economic situation of the firm, the court may terminate the protection period prematurely and issue a bankruptcy order. The amended law hence sets strong incentives for the debtor not to abuse court protection to further damage creditors. Again, the question is to which extent the judges are willing and able to enforce the intended enhanced creditors protection in practice.

One major drawback of the old law was the lack of protection of the bankruptcy estate between petitioning and the issuance of an order. The amendment introduces a list of legal transactions carried out by the debtor which may eventually harm the interests of creditors, like e.g. the transfer of assets from the debtor firm to other entities or persons for free or at remarkably low prices, the taking of inadequate liabilities or the acquisition of interests in other companies. All transactions of that kind which turn out harmful to creditors and which have been carried out within the six months prior to triggering of bankruptcy now are declared null and void. The obvious intention of this provision is to tighten up on asset-stripping and other actions committed by the debtor in order to line his pockets at the expense of the lenders. While this provision will surely lower agency costs between owners and lenders in times of financial distress, its ultimate effect remains unclear due to considerable scope of interpretation for the assessment of real transactions. In practice, the courts' interpretation of 'remarkably low prices' and 'inadequate liabilities' is still far from clear.

(iv) Remaining deficiencies

The 1996 amendment of the BCA reflects the authorities' intention finally to implement, in practice, the law's formally already existing creditor-orientation. Apart from some definition gaps and inevitable scope for judicial interpretation, the lawmakers were successful in strengthening the position of creditors in financial distress. Most observers agree, once again, that the core problem is enforcement of both law and legal intent. Besides an inevitable lack of experience and training of judges in bankruptcy issues, there is a dramatic lack of capacity in the court system. At the end of 1995, as few as 167 judges were working for the business sections of the Czech district courts, the courts of the first instance (while there should be 208 according to the plan of the Ministry of Justice).[24] The lack of manpower is one major reason for the chronic backlog in the settlement of bankruptcy petitions. The amendment is not complemented by any solutions to this problem like additional training and staffing.[25] Still, the bankruptcy procedure is very lengthy. According to lawyers, it usually takes at least one year until an order is issued. But only a reduction down to less than six months could ensure a certain protection against asset stripping and related fraudulent actions by the debtor since this corresponds with the reservation period for damaging debtor transactions as defined by the new law. The lack of legal infrastructure thus threatens to drain potential benefits from enhanced creditor protection.

In addition, the lengthiness of the procedure is not very conducive to an increase in legal certainty. As the law leaves problems of interpretation, the jurisdiction by the courts is crucial in developing the institutional framework of bankruptcy. Yet, in practice the termination of a bankruptcy procedure may easily take some three to five years. As verdicts are reached only with considerable delays, interpretational gaps are vanishing most slowly. The outcomes of procedures are quite unpredictable for creditors. The resulting uncertainty about the 'rules of the game' is aggravated by the fact that the 1996 amendment already is the eighth modification overall (and the second extensive one) of the BCA.

Further complaints relate to the position and quality of the receivers of the bankruptcy estate. Although their payments are linked to the proceeds from the realization of the estate, they are widely believed to be inadequately remunerated.[26] On the other hand, receivers carry unlimited personal liability for their actions. Moreover, this liability never ceases and there is no professional liability insurance available (Deloitte & Touche, 1995, pp. 5 and 22). The resulting risk/remuneration mix effectively lowers the attraction of the receiver job and is the main reason for a lack of professional receivers in the country (and hence an additional cause for the protraction of bankruptcy procedures). In particular, it deters the best-qualified candidates from taking over this job. Furthermore, receivers are neither certified nor obliged to attend any training courses. In fact, there is no fixed qualification profile. Not amazingly, many creditors regard receivers as generally incompetent. According to one Czech lawyer, most of them still haven't developed a basic understanding of economic problems and 'have serious deficits in reading a balance sheet'. The qualification of receivers may, however, improve in the future, following to a new provision of the BCA allowing the courts to freely choose a receiver instead of selecting one by rotation like under the previous law. This sets incentives to candidates to specialize in certain industries, forms or sizes of companies.

Finally, a new institutional device enhancing the agency costs of debt is the provision, added by the amendment, that creditors entitled to separate satisfaction may not receive more than 70% of the proceeds from the realization of the pledged assets if the proceeds from the sale of the bankruptcy estate do not cover all costs of bankruptcy. The provision imposes considerable uncertainty upon secured debt claims. Secured lenders cannot reliably calculate the costs imposed upon them in the event of the debtor's default. Firstly, the formulation 'no more than 70%' renders possible even complete confiscation of the proceeds from pledged assets. At the limit, separate claimants would be effectively unsecured. Secondly, while the law foresees that any remainder of the 'confiscated' proceeds after the payment of the bankruptcy costs is used first to pay unsettled parts of the claims of preferential and secured lenders, the law offers no clear distribution key.[27] Dependent upon the distribution scheme chosen by the courts, this may cause substantial redistributions between the various separate claimants. If secured creditors lose from this 'confiscation' by the courts, they will impose higher interest rates and require more collateral for their loans, thereby raising the costs of debt capital.

5.1.5.2 Collateral

Besides bankruptcy, another means of collecting overdue debt is to secure loans by collateral and, in the event of non-performance, to foreclose on the encumbered asset. Czech law allows security over both real estate and moveable assets.[28] Mortgages as securities over real estate are registered with the land registry. The credibility of the registry is still somewhat undermined by a lack of recording of transfers in the past, especially before 1964. As a result, the efficiency of mortgage lending suffers from sometimes quite unclear property rights. Another serious drawback of mortgages concerns distortions on the Czech housing market due to restrictive tenancy practices. Pledged real property is difficult to sell as it is mostly encumbered by other liens like tenant's rights. Tenants can be evicted only if they are offered alternative housing of equal quality and price. Yet, rents are still tightly regulated and are normally insufficient to cover any more than the maintenance costs of the buildings. Restrictive tenancy practices considerably lower the marketability of real property. Nevertheless, real estate is the usual form of collateral for bank loans. Because of the uncertainty concerning its realizability, banks usually require real estate representing some 150 to 200% of loan value. Liens on moveable property cannot be registered centrally. The lack of evidence of the encumbrance of assets let arise multiple claims on the same property. Therefore, like in the case of real estate, banks secure their loans regularly by assets whose value is far higher than that of the loans. Furthermore, the efficacy of liens on moveable property is diminished by thin markets for the frequently outdated machinery of Czech firms.

Other problems relate to the practical realization of secured and overdue claims. Creditors can try to get their claims settled through the courts. In this case, it is up to the chairing judge to decide whether a loan is indeed due. If he decides in favour of the creditor, the latter will obtain an executory title (*platební rozkaz*) to the debtor's property. The procedure is fraught with uncertainty and may be very lengthy since the debtor may appeal the order without specification of reasons. The title is then withdrawn and the court triggers a standard procedure without a legally binding deadline when it has to be terminated. The simple filing of an appeal is thus sufficient to completely eliminate all effects of an execution title and the related advantages of a shortened court procedure. In addition, the suing creditor has to pay up front large legal fees of 4% of the claim amount up to a maximum of CZK 500,000. Most observers agree that the tremendous transaction costs do not correspond to the usually meagre results of the inefficient procedure. Western market economies usually have more efficient tools to foreclose overdue claims. In Germany, for instance, such claims are executed in an automated procedure. In some federal countries, creditors may even file their claims at a central specialized court so that they can get their titles within a few weeks. Appeals by the debtors must be well founded. Claims are then speedily foreclosed by bailiffs (*Gerichtsvollzieher*).

In the Czech Republic, there is a substantial shortage of bailiffs to foreclose claims confirmed by the courts. As such claims can be realized by law exclusively through auctions which consume lots of time and efforts, there is an enormous backlog in the execution of confirmed claims. It can easily take years to foreclose on pledged property. The government is therefore considering to allow out-of-court auctions of pledged assets trying to make the auctioning procedure more effective and to impose a real threat of foreclosure upon defaulters.[29] Banks are meanwhile making increasing use of a peculiarity of Czech law, namely the opportunity to choose another method of foreclosure (e.g. sale of a pledged asset at a price estimated by a chartered accountant). They can do so provided the method of realization has been exactly defined *ex ante* in the loan contract.

As already mentioned in the previous paragraph, in cases of bankruptcy secured creditors can be burdened with part of the administrative costs. This means that their right to separate satisfaction may be restricted and their secured claims may be only partially satisfied from the bankruptcy estate. The proportion of their claims which is not covered by the proceeds of the realization of collaterals is downgraded to unsecured claims.[30] Moreover, the right of a (secured) creditor to separate satisfaction in respect to the debtor's assets becomes invalid if it is acquired by the creditor within two months prior to the submission of the bankruptcy petition. Of course, all these provisions downgrading the claims of secured lenders raise the agency costs of debt control.

5.1.5.3 Extra-judicial debt workouts

The only method of settling disputes out-of-court is to appeal to an arbitrary board. The procedure is similar to that in most Western countries. The conflict parties may appoint one *ex ante* fixed arbitrator each. The arbitrators (or another *ex ante* specified appointing institution) determine a chairman who makes a binding judgement. As an alternative to this *ad hoc* board, the conflict parties may turn to the permanent arbitration court of the Czech Economic and Agricultural Chamber.[31] Arbitration boards are frequently viewed as the only means of saving both time and transaction costs arising from the use of the public court system. Considering the delays and backlogs in the official judicial system, their contribution to the evolution of legal norms and certainty may in the near future even outweigh that of the public courts.

Czech law fails to provide a basis for extra-judicial debt workouts. In the enterprise sector, Czech tax laws are even setting clear disincentives for the out-of-court reorganization of defaulting debtors. In contrast to banks, trade creditors can write off their nonperforming receivables only after the issuance of a bankruptcy order by the courts. Trade creditors hence cannot diminish their taxable profit through debt relaxation while debtors face a taxable extraordinary gain on such an action. On the other hand, the issuance of court orders often takes a year or more until credit losses can be offset by tax reductions. If the creditor is not operating profitably, he might have very weak incentives for taking any action against the insolvent debtor at all. One could expect a higher engagement of trade creditors in debt control if the tax regime was improved (so as to allow for a reduction of the taxable profit after debt relaxation in order to encourage the participation of trade creditors in the reorganizations of insolvent debtors) and the efficiency of the courts was increased (so as to speed up write-offs in cases of court-led liquidations/bankruptcies to encourage timely petitioning).

It pays for the Czechs to take a look at other transitional countries. Poland, for instance, is far ahead of the Czech Republic in developing its extra-judicial workout system. Under its 1993 bank conciliation agreement, power is shifted from the courts and trade borrowers to the banks (Baer & Gray, 1995, p. 26). If a bank gets approval of creditors representing more than 50% of a debtor's overall outstanding debt, it obtains a 'lead bank' status and is empowered to draft a workout agreement on behalf of all borrowers. While the resulting restructuring plan is binding for all creditors (in absence of appeals), the lead bank becomes liable for any losses incurred by the other borrowers if it neglects its monitoring and control duties after the implementation of the plan. The Polish approach has led to a more active role of banks in the restructuring of defaulting debtors. It provides banks with an additional and fairly effective tool to execute debt control over companies and broadens the range of possible outcomes of active debt control (while the Czech insolvency law has a quite one-sided orientation towards liquidation).[32] The Polish experience shows that bank-led conciliation may help to reduce substantially the transaction costs and time requirements of debt control. Given the imponderabilities concerning the proceeding from liquidations in times of transition, a procedure rendering possible the going concern of insolvent firms may also reduce creditors' losses from debtors' insolvency. Moreover, Polish law reduces the coordination costs of creditors. It gives them a strong incentive to develop a restructuring plan and afterwards to stick to it since most state claims are downgraded under bank-led conciliation (provided the plan is successfully implemented). Provisions analogous to the Polish law would most likely enhance the efficacy of Czech debt control and reduce the costs of bank-led restructuring. Furthermore, the Polish approach would have harmonized well with the Czech philosophy of smooth restructuring, as it favours the going concern of the debtor firm.

In Poland, bank-led reorganizations frequently ended in debt/equity swaps of bank debt. While Czech law generally permits them, it sets some limits through the regulation of equity holdings of banks (≤ 10% of company equity, ≤ 25% of bank's capital and reserves). So far, banks haven't swapped debt claims on a large scale. But some banks, like Komercní and Konsolidacní, executed a limited number of swaps ending sometimes even with holdings higher than 10% of the debtor's equity. This is legal if the bank intends to sell its holding within two years of the acquisition (swap).

5.1.6 Summary

To date, the balance sheets of the four big banks are still rather fragile and the consolidation of the small domestic banks is only beginning. Due to the high concentration of the banking sector, the big banks will be the major executors of debt control in the foreseeable future. So far they have been rather reluctant to tighten credit control. Komercní banka, the bank with the most extensive credit links to the enterprise sector, initiated only 50 bankruptcy proceedings in 1995 (and participated altogether in 360). Sporitelna filed for bankruptcy in 38 cases (and participated in 75 proceedings). Agrobanka submitted more than two dozens proposals (and participated in 62 others).[33] This indicates that the banks haven't yet taken a leading role in enforcing hard budget constraints through the courts. Most bankruptcy petitions have been filed by financially fairly sound private companies which successfully diversified their client base and thus are not critically dependent upon the going concern of one or a few of their debtors.

The banks' passivity in the execution of debt control is due to various reasons. Firstly, the efficacy of debt control so far has been largely reduced by serious institutional deficiencies. Bankruptcy legislation has been implemented only late in transition due to political concerns of mass bankruptcy. Likewise, the position of the creditor has been strengthened only gradually. As of today, there are still problems with definition gaps and a wide scope of judicial interpretation of the law, both leading to weak enforcement of creditor rights. With inexperienced judges and an overburdened court system, lengthy bankruptcy proceedings with unpredictable outcomes are generating a high degree of legal uncertainty. Besides, bank managers complain that court receivers and bailiffs have weak incentives to maximize the proceedings of liquidation and foreclosure and to cooperate with the banks. Considerable transaction costs of foreclosing are adding to a weak institutional environment of debt control. Thin markets for industrial goods, for instance, represent a strong disincentive to foreclose on pledged assets.

Secondly, out-of-court procedures to collect overdue debt are evolving only gradually and are still applied rather infrequently by both banks and trade debtors. However, arbitrary boards are becoming more and more significant for the settlement of business disputes. But due to a lack of experience with their functioning, domestic creditors are still cautious with their use. Creditors are increasingly drafting *ex ante* contractual agreements automatically transferring property rights of debtor's assets to them in the event of default. The performance of such contractual hedges is mixed. As for real property, it is within the discretion of the responsible land registry whether to recognize the validity of the claim or not. In practice, the registries proceeded differently making the use of this spontaneously evolving extra-legal institutional device a rather risky affair.

A third reason for the banks' reluctance to put more pressure on debtor firms is the extant influence of the state on both the banking and the enterprise sector. One major means of the authorities to maintain the social consensus and public support for the transformation process was to give full employment a high priority. This included *inter alia* the conservation of many big enterprises. Triggering the bankruptcy of a large firm would not only have evoked political and social tensions, but in the view of the government could have had a destabilizing effect on the whole economy. Therefore, lax debt control and an only gradual hardening of the budget constraints of large enterprises were implicit elements of the political utility function. While direct political interference with the banks' operations has reportedly only occurred exceptionally, the management of the large banks knows very well the political preferences of the government. The far-reaching renunciation of bankruptcy (especially with large enterprises) underlines that the banks have been largely adhering to the political limits of their operational discretion. In fact, there has been virtually no large company going bust before the bankruptcy of steelmaker Poldi ocel in March 1997. Poldi's bankruptcy was petitioned, however, by the NPF in 1996 after the private majority owner had failed consistently to repay his debt to the fund and other creditors. Banks were not actively involved in the triggering. The political and institutional pressure on banks to renounce from debt control clearly increased their interest in equity control over the enterprise sector. One can view the great influence of the bank-centred groups as an attempt by the banks also to pursue their interests as fixed claimants in absence of effective debt control.

On the other hand, the state still holds significant stakes in many large strategic corporations. They have repeatedly enjoyed subsidies and tax reliefs that were not accessible for small and mid-size companies. The banks hence may assume an implicit guarantee that the state will also care for the strategic firms in the future and refrain from taking any action to liquidate those companies. The government's discriminatory approach in favour of larger enterprises is still evidenced today by the provision of the amended BCA stipulating that protection periods can be granted exclusively to firms with more than 50 employees. This clearly puts small start-up firms in a disadvantageous position as against bigger established companies. Besides, banks know that the large corporations, split off from the huge conglomerates of the command economy, may belong to their major future clients once they have undergone successful restructuring. For those reasons, they may adopt a more patient approach to them than to smaller companies.

Furthermore, banks are frequently caught in creditor traps caused by the large amounts of loans granted to single debtors and the weakness of their own balance sheets. Over the last few years, under-reserved banks have focused more on strengthening their capital adequacy through high spreads (after the CNB had loosened interest rate regulation on deposits and loans) than on the revelation of losses in aggressive debt collection actions at defaulting clients. If a failing debtor can meet at least the payment of high penalty interest, this could be more attractive for a bank than to wait a long time for an uncertain share in the company's bankruptcy estate.

5.2 GOVERNANCE STRUCTURES OF BANKS

5.2.1 Debt Control of Banks: Prudential Regulation and Supervision

Before 1992, there was virtually no legal framework for prudential regulation and supervision of banks. The Czechoslovak National Bank executed sporadic and nonsystematic *ad hoc* supervision. Likewise there was a serious lack of binding requirements for getting a bank licence. As a result, it was quite simple to found a bank at this time. Most of the small private domestic banks having experienced a liquidity crunch in later years started their operations in 1990/91 under weak regulation. Rather astonishing, even the restructuring programme to clean the balance sheets of the old banks was started before the implementation of effective regulation and supervision. Delayed implementation of debt control over banks has contributed to the fast accumulation of new bad loans in the banking sector. Moreover, it reflects the Czech approach towards free banking in the early phase of transition, aiming at channelling sufficient debt capital to the enterprise sector so as not to threaten the smooth functioning of privatization and the priority of private ownership. The central bank set up a separate supervision department only in late 1991. A first 'toothless' version of the Law on Banking took effect in February 1992. Its main drawback was a lack of instruments for the central bank to fine-tune its actions against the commercial banks. The supervisory department could impose fines up to CZK 5 million (no more than 'pocket money' for a bank) or withdraw a licence or impose forced administration only in the event of clearly identified illegal actions by the bank. They couldn't intervene on the grounds of financial instability alone.[34] The limited power of the supervision along with weak bank reporting systems led to a constant deterioration of the balance sheets of many banks.

The supervision reacted and halted the issuing of new bank licences in 1993. Whilst accepting a slow down of the increase in competition within the banking sector, the CNB wanted to give the operating banks a fair chance to improve their financial performance. A more active approach towards supervision was possible only after the amendment of the banking law in July 1994. The new law considerably strengthened the control function and legal power of the central bank. It allows the supervision to apply a broad range of measures to control the commercial banks and to intervene in their policy early if banks carry out transactions impairing the interests of their depositors or threatening the security and stability of the banking system. In particular, it may reduce the book value of a bank's equity capital if the latter has experienced a loss of more than 20% of its equity. The capital reduction puts pressure on the bank's shareholders to increase equity to meet capital adequacy requirements or to fuse with another bank, and thus helps to enhance the stability of the banking sector and of the given bank. Moreover, the CNB now can impose fines up to CZK 50 million, require policy corrections which must be implemented within a certain period of time, limit the range of permitted banking activities, exchange directors and top managers and enforce the building of adequate reserves. Nevertheless, the CNB didn't accept the role of a watch dog immediately after the amendment. Before 1996, it rather played the 'fire man' (Ekonom 45/1996, p. 83) and interfered with the policy of troubled banks only *ex post*, i.e. after information about problems of single banks had become public through the mass media. The supervision seemingly saw its foremost task in the avoidance of a panic among depositors rather than in the implementation of effective *ex ante* measures to enforce a more efficient policy of the banks.

This stance has been changed only recently after an increase in staff and a tightening of off-site supervision. One measure was, for instance, to approve exclusively western auditing firms (belonging to the 'big six' of the auditing branch) for the audit of banks to improve the methodological consistency of audits and the quality of balance sheet data. Likewise, the CNB tightened on-site supervision and significantly increased the number of checks at the banks. Meanwhile the supervision has become an emancipated partner of the banks and appears to fulfil effectively its task to monitor and control banks on behalf of dispersed creditors. To reduce conflicts of interest and to boost the credibility of the banking system, the CNB has even begun to push shareholders out of the banks if they turned out incapable of operating them efficiently or if there was any suspicion that they ran a policy which was not conducive to depositors. For example, Motoinvest had to quickly sell its stake in Ceská Sporitelna and to promise to leave the banking sector after the liquidity crunch of Agrobanka and some suspicion that the bank had been largely (mis-)used in financing the risky acquisitions of its main owner.

Comprehensive prudential regulation has been implemented with the introduction of the new banking law in 1992 and since then gradually tightened up to meet the Basle accords and the relevant European Union directives. Banks had to achieve a capital adequacy of 6.25% of risk-weighted assets by the end of 1993.[35] However, most small banks failed to match the ratio. All banks have to meet a ratio of 8% since end-1996. In July 1994, the CNB released strict binding provisions for the classification of risk loans and the creation of reserves (Mejstrík, 1995, p. 118).[36] The provisions dramatically reduced the banks' discretion in the classification of dubious assets. As a consequence, the book value of classified loans granted to clients was boosted by 61% from CZK 158 billion in June up to CZK 254 billion in September 1994. The sudden rise of bad loans emphasizes the limited informational content of banks' balance sheets concerning the quality of the loan portfolio and capital adequacy prior to summer 1994. Another recent tightening of the accounting and reserve provisions also added to the protection of depositors. New central bank rules mean that banks must reassess the value of collateral held against bad loans. The general assumption is that previous assessments were optimistic and banks will therefore have to raise their reserve funds once again.

A cluster of provisions regulates the banks' credit risk exposures. Loans granted to one individual client or to a group of economically connected debtors must not exceed 25% of the bank's equity capital (125% if the debtor is a bank). The overall amount of loans extended to the ten biggest debtors may not surmount 230% of equity. Furthermore, banks are required to meet certain liquidity standards and to limit their open foreign exchange positions.

As of today, Czech supervision is fairly tight and the regulatory framework is broadly in line with western laws. The problem is that, in the past, recovery programmes for the banking sector were triggered well before the emergence of comprehensive prudential regulation and its (even more delayed) enforcement through a strict banking supervision. Under conditions like that, the accumulation and persistance of bad loans must be put down mainly to incompetence, inexperience with professional evaluation methods, political pressure to pursue an expansive credit policy and outright fraud (*tunelování*). Meanwhile, at least the big banks have gradually improved their evaluation procedures, the successful termination of mass privatization allows banks to run a more conservative credit policy to recover their balance sheets and fraudulent or incompetent shareholders have been increasingly pushed out of the banking sector. This paves the way for a more credible and effective debt control of banks in the future. The new political will to enforce the interests of bank depositors has been underlined by recent extensive triggerings of forced administration and closing-down of ailing banks.

The efficacy of debt control over banks is also enhanced by the design of the deposit insurance scheme which has been introduced in 1994. Banks have to transfer a fee amounting to 0.5% of their collected deposits to a joint insurance fund. In the event of insolvency, the fund covers 80% of the losses of natural persons up to a deposit volume of CZK 100,000. The scheme thus strikes a balance between the security of deposits, thereby avoiding bank runs, and remaining incentives for depositors to critically monitor the performance of bank management (and owners). It puts the screws on the latter to run a well-balanced policy taking regard also of depositors' interests, e.g. to maintain sufficient liquidity and to diversify credit risks well. The drawback of the scheme is that contributions to the fund are not risk-dependent, but the insurance fee per deposited crown is equal for all banks. This lowers the incentives for managers of distressed banks to improve their performance because increased balance sheet risks do not effect higher fees. The comparatively sound banks, in turn, have to pay for the bad performance of their fellows, thereby boosting not only the security of deposits in the wobbly banks but likewise their attraction for small investors.

5.2.2   Equity Control of Banks: Privatization and Ownership Structures

Apart from CSOB, all former state-owned banks of the country participated in the first wave of large-scale privatization. Yet, only Zivnostenská was privatized entirely. A controlling 40% stake was sold directly to the German BHF bank, 12% were purchased by the International Finance Corporation and 48% were slated for voucher privatization. The three biggest banks by asset value were privatized merely in part with the state retaining strategic stakes between 45% and 66%. Together with golden shares, guaranteeing a veto right to the state for certain strategic corporate decisions, the big state holdings effectively ensured the government control over the most powerful players of the banking sector.

There are several reasons for the government's refusal to privatize the financial sector more quickly and sweepingly. Firstly, banks' balance sheets were rather weak in the early phase of transition. The authorities therefore argued that banks should undergo comprehensive restructuring before their ownership was to be transferred entirely into private hands. After a recovery of the banking sector, banks were supposed to fetch substantially higher prices than they would in immediate sales. The authorities failed to recognize that privatization and restructuring of banks are separate items. Their partial and only cursory privatization didn't produce incentives to carry out a profit-maximizing policy. A considerable part of the deficiencies in the behaviour of the banks revealed after the implementation of various recapitalization and debt clearance measures must be ascribed to disincentives set by enduring state ownership. Considering the mere size of the state banks, bank managers were well aware of both the political and economic importance of their institution. State ownership has been a serious obstacle to overcoming their bail-out expectations even though the government didn't start any restructuring programme for the big banks after 1993. In order to make managers adopt a profit-oriented policy more swiftly, the state has to completely cut off its ownership ties to the financial sector. This would be the measure most appropriate to force banks to redefine their relationship to the enterprise sector so as to harden the budget constraint of their industrial clients and, provided there are corresponding incentives on the asset side of the banks' balance sheet, to control companies more efficiently.[37]

Another important reason for postponement of banks' privatization has been a deeply rooted distrust of an eventual increase in the influence of foreign investors in the banking sector and consequently in the whole economy.[38] Of course, a foreign strategic investor might well be motivated to turn around the policy run by the state. Given the huge influence of the banks on several key industries, the state hasn't yet been willing to abandon the banking sector as a tool of political intervention. For instance, it appears most dubious whether completely privatized big banks would have been ready to acquire substantial equity stakes in smaller problem banks to strengthen the capital base and reputation of the latter.

Furthermore, with privately-owned big banks, the authorities wouldn't have been in control of the decisive tool to delay the triggering of bankruptcy after 1993. The opportunity costs of state entanglement in the banking sector are still considerable. Foreign investors, especially if coming from the banking industry, can provide Czech banks with both know-how and financial resources to carry out deep restructuring. The complete separation from public resources and the entry of hard-nosed owners would clearly accelerate the behavioural adaptation of the incumbent management to a market setting. An important task of foreign investors is to dissolve the still existing personal networks between bankers and enterprise managers. The cutting off of those links is an inevitable precondition for the introduction of market-conforming behaviour.

The state's ownership rights in the banks are executed after consultation of the CNB by the NPF. On the whole, NPF control doesn't seem to be very active and the management enjoys far-reaching discretion in running the bank. However, it knows very well the political preferences of the government and must see that the bank's policy is broadly in line with them.

The state representatives sit on the banks' supervisory boards and, in normal circumstances, rather passively monitor the performance of the management. When they had the power to replace top managers instantaneously, they didn't make use of it for a long time. As late as 1998, after the fall of the Klaus government, an interim government headed by the former central bank governor Tosovský made some changes in the management board of Komercní banka.

Nevertheless, the presence of state representatives on the banks' supervisory boards so far has been sufficient to broadly align the preferences of management and government. For instance, as of January 1997, 5 out of 15 members of the supervisory board of IPB, the large bank with the smallest equity stake of the state, were state representatives (among them the chairman and his deputy).[39] If one adds another three representatives sent by two firms under majority control of the state (the Czech Post and the petroleum holding Unipetrol), the number of state delegates rises to a numerical majority of 8. The dominance of state representatives on the board is a powerful threat for the management to adhere to the strategic objectives of the government.

Active state interference with the policy of the large banks could be observed e.g. at the 1995 general meetings of Komercní, Ceská sporitelna and IPB when the NPF blocked the dividend proposals of all three banks and forced them to drastically reduce them (by 15-30%) and to retain a higher proportion of profits to increase their capital base. It was hardly surprising that the NPF's intervention found a negative feedback among the dispersed shareholders of the banks. Afterwards the fund decided 'to coordinate' subsequently all managerial and state proposals in the run-up to the shareholder meetings in order to avoid discontent of small investors that eventually could undermine the political support of the government. As a consequence, state intervention has become even more invisible. It is therefore difficult to evaluate whether strategic measures taken by the bank management are initiated by the government (through the NPF) or by the management board. According to CNB vice governor Pavel Kysilka, who is also a member of the NPF presidium, active state control of banks is very sporadic and - if executed at all - aims at the extension of 'politically acceptable' loans rather than the profitability of banks.[40]

IPB was the first bank out of the 'big four' to be privatized in September 1997. In the run-up to the sale of the NPF holding to the Japanese investment bank Nomura, the government surprisingly dropped its former scepticism about a foreign strategic investor, after three reputable foreign banks had revealed a sudden interest in acquiring the NPF's stake in IPB. Still in January 1997, the confirmed liberal Klaus himself had announced that 'he would like to give preferential treatment to the yet not existing

Table 5.7: *Ownership structure of financial institutions*

As of January 1997:

Komercni banka	Ceská sporitelna	Investicni a postovni banka[c]	Ceskoslovenská obchodni banka	Agrobanka (under forced administration)	Ceská pojistovna	Zivnobanka
49% NPF	45% NPF	32% NPF	26% Czech National Bank	99.9% Konsolidacni banka	27% NPF	47% BHF-Bank
10% Bank of NY[a]	15% local authorities[b]	11% *Bankovni hol.*	24% Slovak National Bank	0.1% other investors	23% IPB	10% IFC
4% RIF	1% RIF	10% *Charouz holding*	20% NPF		20% PPF	
4% IPB	15% Motoinvest group	9% *Vojens. stavby*	20% Ministry of Finance		14% CSOB	
3% IPF Kom. banky	19% other portfolio investors	5% Ceská posta	1% C. pojistovna		10% Kom. banka	
2% C. sporitelna	5% individuals	3% 1.PIF	1% employees			
1% 1.PIF		2% VÚB Kupon	8% other investors			
1% employees		6% *PIAS funds*				
4% Slovak investors		22% other investors				
22% other investors						

As of June 1999:

Komercni banka	Ceská sporitelna	Investicni a postovni banka[c]	Ceskoslovenská obchodni banka	Agrobanka	Ceská pojistovna	Zivnobanka
49% NPF	45% NPF	44% Nomura	66% KBC Bank	100% GE Capital	30% NPF	50% Bankgesellschaft Berlin
18% Bank of NY[a]	15% local authorities[b]	13% *Bankovni holding*	24% Slovak National Bank		32% IPB group	10% IFC
3% RIF	12% EBRD	10% C. pojistovna	4% IFC		22% PPF	13% Czech IFs
3% C. pojistovna	9% C. pojistovna	7% *RIF*	5% other Czech investors		10% Kom. banka	18% other corporate investors
2% PIAS funds	2% Agrobanka	2% Fintop	1% other Slovak investors		6% others	9% individual investors
2% Bank Austria	2% Spor. Priv.	1% *IF Bohatstvi*				
1% 1.PIF	Výnosový IF	23% other investors				
22% other investors	15% other investors					

a Bank of New York holds GDRs without voting rights.

b Stock without voting rights

c Entities in italics are controlled or at least influenced by IPB bank.

Source: Hospodárské noviny, 3 December 1996, p.8; 12 August 1996, p.2; Ekonom No. 49, 1996, p.2; No. 51, 1996, p.75; No. 7, 1997, p.67; No. 7, 1997, p.65; Securities Centre; information provided by banks and own calculations

Czech capital' when it comes to the privatization of the remaining state banks.[41] Considering the mediocre recovery performance of the state-governed banks, the government apparently recognized that domestic investors are not able to channel the necessary finance and expertise to the Czech banking industry.

Interestingly, there is some evidence that the buyer of IPB was chosen by the bank's incumbent management rather than the government. Prior to the sale, the management had been quite successful in entrenching itself against outside control by private investors. In the end, more than 36% of the bank's equity stock was held by funds managed by the bank's investment subsidiary PIAS or companies which were controlled or at least influenced by IPB itself (see entities in italics in Table 5.7).[42] A potential investor hence had to cooperate with the bank's management or to face a battle for control with uncertain results. One can therefore suppose that the takeover was of a friendly nature. This is confirmed by the fact that, by January 1999, no member of the old management board has been replaced. Besides, the strong position of the IPB management is a strong indicator for the past failure of the state to control the bank's operations effectively. As of early 1999, Nomura holds something below 50% of the bank, but has only four persons on the powerful 12 member supervisory board and no representatives at all on the management board. In fact, one may only guess who is controlling the affairs of IPB. At the time of the sale of IPB to Nomura, a confidential deal was struck between the two banks. Most likely, Nomura promised that the incumbent management would keep its senior posts, although the details are kept secret.[43] This indicates a perfect entrenchment of the management which still owns far more than 20% of IPB, either directly or through 'friendly' companies. It would mean, too, that the real privatization of IPB is still to be triggered in the near future when Nomura will probably sell its equity stake to a real strategic investor.

On the whole, the government has preferred a constructivistic rather than spontaneous approach to the development of ownership structures of financial institutions. For instance, when IPB wanted to sell its 23% stake in insurer Ceská pojistovna to the private fund family PPF in autumn 1996, the government forbade the transaction pointing to a shareholders' agreement that each owner can sell his stock only after he has obtained the approval of the insurer's supervisory board. The latter is dominated by the NPF and followed the 'recommendation' of the authorities not to permit the deal. Of course, after the transaction PPF would have significantly enhanced its influence in the insurance company and have a good chance of gaining a majority after an eventual sale of the NPF's 27% stake. Obviously, the government doesn't consider PPF - a major domestic investment group - to be the ideal strategic investor to take over control of a big financial group.

The timetable for the privatization of the remaining banks has been cancelled after the overthrow of the Klaus government and the installation of a provisional government in end-1997.[44] In April 1999, the new government headed by the Social Democrat Zeman sold its 66%-stake in CSOB to the Belgian KBC bank. The privatization of Komercní banka and Ceská sporitelna - supposedly also to foreign strategic investors - is to follow until the end of 2000. Of course, possible further delays will cause further protractions of bank restructuring and diminish the incentives of the banks to execute efficient corporate control. A speedy completion of the privatization of the banking sector thus is also central to the acceleration of the restructuring process of the enterprise sector.

Besides, it is pivotal that the government will stick to its commitment to privatize the banks to foreign direct investors. If active foreign investors are precluded from purchasing significant stakes in Czech banks, the major buyers might be the bank-centred financial groups themselves. Not only are they failing to deliver both the finance and expertise badly needed to implement a successful restructuring programme. Their active involvement in bank privatization would also lead to a high degree of cross ownership within the financial sector and set strong incentives for the privatized institutions to collude. The result is then a mutual entrenchment of bank managements (similar to the shirking equilibrium in the core of the German control system). Another possible scenario would be the participation of some large industrial enterprises in the privatization of the financial sector. Considering the general lack of capital, most companies must be financially sponsored by the banks themselves to have a fair chance of acquiring a significant equity stake in a bank. In the end, this may lead to a more indirect form of cross ownership where the guardian (industrial company) is controlled by the guarded (bank). Again, this suggests collusion and entrenchment rather than powerful equity control. This is not to say that a small degree of cross ownership in the financial sector couldn't be efficient. However, it must strike a balance between lowering coordination costs for guardians through enhanced incentives to cooperate (e.g. in the joint execution of equity control through several bank-centred financial groups) and increasing entrenchment against outside control. For example, in the case of Komercní, it may be efficient for some 10% of the bank's equity to be held by other financial groups. Yet, this presupposes that the 49%-stake of the state will be sold to a strategic investor outside the domestic financial sector who is not governed by Komercní or another domestic bank.

5.2.3 Competition between Banks

Competition within the banking sector is essential to give banks incentives to carry out efficient control over companies. Provided banks are subject to both effective equity and debt control, the selection power of high competition accelerates the adoption of market-oriented behaviour at the side of the bank managers. But even if management is entrenched and supervision and prudential regulation are lax or not sufficiently enforced, competition may impose considerable discipline upon banks and increase managerial efforts to effectively monitor companies with debt or equity links to the banks.

After the split of the mono-bank in 1990, the different segments of the banking market showed a high concentration. The assets of the mono-bank were distributed to six successor banks, but very uneven in the individual market segments. Still in summer 1991, the Czech and Slovak savings banks controlled some 60% of household deposits (Müller, 1993, p. 102). Enterprise credits had been transferred to just three banks and foreign exchange transactions were settled more or less exclusively by the CSOB. In addition, branch networks had been established according to geographical criteria, making the savings banks quasi-monopolists in their parts of the country. Komercní and Vseobecná úverová banka kept similar positions in the Czech and the Slovak credit market respectively. The partition of the country in January 1993 consolidated the dominant market positions of the four institutes and further diminished competition by drawing a clear dividing line between the Czech and Slovak financial services markets.

The increasing number of banks starting to operate in the Czech market in the early 1990s somewhat mitigated the problem. Nonetheless, the 50 private banks competing with the big state banks in end-1995 still couldn't really challenge the market position of the state-owned banks. As of December 1995, they merely controlled some 15% of the deposit market and 29% of the loan market. The licence moratorium after 1992 prevented a quicker growth of the private banking sector and thus more competition. As already depicted, many small domestic banks gambled and extended risky loans to boost their transaction volume. Therefore, their balance sheets were burdened with bad loans and many banks were hit by liquidity crunches or even went into liquidation. Despite fusions and financial aid by the state, the private banking sector still has to recover and its competitiveness will be limited in the near future. Besides, the large banks actively participated in the recovery programme through the purchase of significant stakes in small domestic institutes, thereby effecting a further concentration of the market.

On the credit market, competition has also been reduced temporarily through the reported pressure exerted by some large banks on individual enterprises to take out loans predominantly or exclusively from one bank. Due to their strong bargaining position as lenders, banks could sometimes force (mostly small and medium-size) companies into contracts forbidding them to turn to another lender.[45] In the case of some large corporations, banks seemingly tried to use their own shareholdings and those of their investment subsidiaries to become prime lenders of the companies. However, at least for large enterprises, the banking sector meanwhile has developed punishment mechanisms deterring banks from such behaviour and driving them to accept a kind of 'fiduciary duty' (see the lead group function under section 4.2.3) towards their competitors (as well as towards the financial groups in general). No doubt, the implicit rules of cooperation between the financial groups are an effective insurance against the emergence of monopoly credit links.

Nonetheless, in spite of a grown number of competitors, the large banks have maintained their outstanding position in the banking industry. Further opening to foreign competition and above all privatization of banks will inevitably enhance competition and induce bank managers to behave in a market-conforming way and to execute efficient corporate control.

Table 5.8: Market shares of banks

as of 31 Dec. 1995	overall assets		deposits		loans	
	bln. CZK	%	bln. CZK	%	bln. CZK	%
Komercní banka	407.2	22.0	237.7	25.0	227.2	25.9
Ceská sporitelna	367.8	19.9	295.0	31.0	119.3	13.6
CSOB	201.6	10.9	88.1	9.3	80.3	9.2
IPB	201.4	10.9	106.7	11.2	120.1	13.7
Konsolidacní banka	123.3	6.7	73.8	7.8	73.1	8.3
Agrobanka	69.5	3.8	49.5	5.2	43.0	4.9
top 5 banks	1301.3	70.4	801.3	84.3	620.0	70.7
other banks	546.9	29.6	149.3	15.7	257.2	29.3
total	1848.2	100.0	950.6	100.0	877.2	100.0

Source: Patria Finance, own calculations

end of year	no. of banks		overall assets (in %)		deposits (in %)		loans (in %)	
	1996	1997	1996	1997	1996	1997	1996	1997
top 5 banks	5	5	68.9	65.6	76.6	74.2	74.3	73.3
foreign banks	13	14	12.4	14.6	7.4	9.7	9.9	12.8
other banks	35	31	18.7	19.8	16.0	16.1	15.8	13.9

Source: Czech National Bank

5.2.4 Summary

In the early phase of transition, weak regulation and supervision of banks contributed to a quick accumulation of new bad loans. The institutional power of the supervision department was strengthened only in 1994 when it was provided with a broad range of instruments to interfere with a bank's policy if the latter was acting against the interests of dispersed depositors or threatening the financial stability of the banking system. A proactive approach to bank control has been observable from 1996. Since that time, the supervision has triggered forced administration or even closed down various ailing small and mid-sized banks, among them the biggest private bank Agrobanka. Likewise, prudential regulation has been tightened, e.g. the accounting and reservation provisions. As of today, the supervision does dispose of effective *ex ante* measures to enforce a more efficient policy of the banks and regulation is broadly in line with western economies. However, effective debt control was implemented too late, thus seriously reducing the positive effects of the balance sheet restructuring of the big banks and permitting risky and unlawful actions of small banks.

Delayed privatization of the state's 30-50% stakes in the big banks along with veto rights confirmed by golden shares have been entrenching the state as so far major guardian of the banking sector. While, at least on the surface, state representatives are reluctant to interfere dramatically with the day-to-day operations of the banks, bank management is well aware of the political preferences of the major owner. This effects inefficiencies in corporate control as well as misallocation of scarce capital. The entry of foreign direct investors is essential in order to quickly transfer both capital and know-how to the banks, to finally wipe out the bail-out expectations of bank managers and to accelerate the process of behavioural adaptation, including the adoption of certain ethical norms and the destruction of remaining 'old boys networks' between the banks and the industrial sector. Only after the complete withering away of the state from equity control of banks, can one expect banks to pursue a profit-maximizing policy rather than to adhere to political (and managerial) goals. In sum, both weak equity and debt control over the banking sector has reduced the banks' incentives to care for efficient debt control over the enterprise sector.

So far, competition couldn't fill the gaps produced by weak equity and debt control over banks. Deposit as well as credit markets show high concentration ratios. Some minimum degree of competition is granted by the evolution of implicit rules of cooperation between the bank-centred financial groups. As for debt finance, the lead function places a fiduciary duty upon the biggest bank-sponsored owner of a company. The fiduciary duty obliges him to bear in mind the interests of other bank groups and thus prevents the emergence of quasi-monopolistic credit relationships.

The Czech approach to debt control is fraught with various inconsistencies. While the extensive measures taken in 1990/91 to resolve the stock problem of inherited dubious loans were successful and largely contributed to the low proportion of non-performing loans in 1991 (below 3% of total loans, see Table 5.3), a lack of political will to tighten up debt control and supervision of banks subsequently led to a re-deterioration of the banks' asset portfolios. Most of the big banks are only slowly recovering and realistically will need the aid of foreign investors in financial and 'deep' restructuring. The lesson is that the quality of debt as a control device in transition economies depends heavily upon the simultaneity of the measures taken. A minimum requirement for effective debt control is the simultaneous triggering of financial restructuring, the implementation of tight supervision over banks and the creation of working institutional tools to impose the discipline of the bottom line on debtor enterprises. Furthermore, private direct investors (at best foreign ones) could strengthen the credibility of debt control by additional financial restructuring and the contribution of expertise. A consistent approach to quick and effective debt control hence cannot be based upon Czech-style sequencing of the four steps, financial restructuring - implementation of supervision - design of institutional tools - privatization, but must aim at a big bang.

NOTES

1. Konsolidacní banka took over about 80% of all TOZ claims against industrial enterprises and 50% of those against trade organizations. The TOZ credits transferred to the bank represented some 16% of the overall loan portfolio of the banking sector. Konsolidacní banka draws from a redistribution credit granted by the National Bank, revenues from the NPF and deposits from Czech banks and insurance companies. See Horcicová (1996b, p. 16).
2. Since most of the former foreign debtors of CSOB could redeem only part of their debt and the collection agencies therefore couldn't repay all due loans, the Czech and Slovak property funds had to repay part of the loans given to the collection agencies. For instance, in 1995, the NPF contributed CZK 3.4 billion to the replenishment of Ceská inkasní's sources. See National Property Fund, Annual Report for 1995, p. 15.
3. For example, tram and train manufacturer CKD Praha, owning a 16% equity stake in the bank valued at some CZK 200 million, turned out to have outstanding loans of CZK 500 million. See Business Eastern Europe, June 6, 1994, p. 6.
4. Law on Banks, §26 (3) c)
5. See Alex Friedrich, Huge Share-Capital Reduction Aids Ekoagrobanka's Survival, Prague Post, 24 – 30 January, 1996, p. 7.
6. Among others, the two biggest private banks have been hit by credit crunches, too. Agrobanka is under forced administration, while the second-biggest bank by assets, Kreditní banka Plzen, is even in liquidation. As for Agrobanka, the CNB has completely written off the capital stock and thus called to account the bank's shareholders (mostly companies allied to Motoinvest). The viable parts of the bank are to be sold in a tender to a reputable investor willing to invest

in the bank's recovery. As of late 1997, the only bidder left is General Electric. After the crash, Motoinvest was accused of having used the bank unlawfully as a vehicle to finance its widespread acquisition activities on the Czech capital market. While several senior managers of Motoinvest were temporarily on remand or fled from the country, nobody had to take legal responsibility for the crash (like in other banks).

7.   This means that all banks are disposing of the amount of reserves recommended by external auditors at the end of 1995. See interview with Josef Tosovský in Hospodásské noviny, 9 September 1996, p. 4.

8.   See Hospodárské noviny, 18 October 1996, p. 1.

9.   Other public authorities are paying, too, for the government's attempts to support the private banks. From 1993, the government has increasingly 'recommended' them to deposit liquid means with the smaller banks to enhance both their liquidity and competitiveness. The state has lost billions of crowns when banks went broke on a large scale in 1996. For instance, it lost some CZK 2 billion in the collapse of Kreditní banka. Customs authorities (under the auspices of the Ministry of Finance) had charged the bank with the administration of liquid funds and kept the money in the credit institute even when the ministry knew that Kreditní was getting into solvency problems. They did so assuming that other small banks would have eventually survived if large clients wouldn't have withdrawn their funds. Besides, the ministry considered such a withdrawal as unfair because of its access to inside information.

10. The payments of the deposit insurance come from a fund jointly supplied by all commercial banks (each institute has to pay 0.5% of its overall amount of insured deposits to the fund). If a bank goes bust, individual depositors are compensated from resources of the fund, the NB and the Ministry of Finance (see e.g. Mladá fronta Dnes, 12 July 1996, p. 14). So far, it is still unclear how many percent of the insured deposits have to be paid by the three institutions. It appears that the contributions of both public institutions depend to a large degree upon the situation of their overall budgets. The depositors of the four banks which went bust before 1996 were not compensated for their losses. Several debtors of Ceská banka, which crashed in 1995, largely benefited from the panic of the bank's depositors when they successfully made them an offer to buy up their claims at a discount of 70% (Hospodárské noviny, 21 February 1996, p. 3). Interestingly, it was the bank's liquidator who encouraged the institute's debtors and creditors to enter into common contracts. The bank itself supported the action by netting out its debts and receivables, thereby getting its debtors' rents to the tune of hundreds of millions of crowns. The new deposit insurance scheme aims to prevent such actions which are harming savers and lowering their confidence in the banking system.

11. It should be stressed, however, that the sharp increase in non-performing loans in 1994 as mirrored by Table 5.3 is in part the result of a formal reclassification of loans (see section 5.2.1).

12. Another cause of soft budget constraints, anchored in the enterprise sector, are government subsidies. In the past, large Czech companies (not only state-owned) have used their economic and political power to attract subsidies or, more often, government guarantees to extend their credit lines with the banks. Usually they have pointed to their significance as local employers or their strategic importance for the country (calling themselves the country's 'family silver' or the 'backbone of the economy'). The government has supported them frequently for political rather than economic reasons, e.g. to avoid an increase in unemployment in sensitive regions. See Tuma & Dotson (1994, p. 4).

13. If a firm's overdue payables exceed its overdue receivables, the amount of secondary arrears is equal to the overdue receivables and the firm shows primary arrears. If overdue receivables top overdue payables, the amount of secondary arrears is equal to the overdue payables and the firm doesn't show any primary arrears.

14. Especially through Komercní which had the closest links to the industrial sector due to its huge amount of enterprise credits inherited from the old mono-bank.

15. Capek & Mertlík (1996, p. 59) outline the case of a dairy company differentiating among customers with regard to the terms of payment. Each individual customer is classified on a scale between 1 (poor payment record) and 9 (no payments defaults). The system allows the firm to apply nine different payment regimes to its customers. Of course, this sort of 'fine

tuning' of payment regimes sets strong incentives for the clients to meet their payments obligation in time and is a useful tool to improve the company's own solvency.

16. At present, agencies specialized in the collection of overdue debts are experiencing a boom. Their performance is reportedly mixed.

17. According to a high-ranked Czech banker, overdue receivables represented more than 15% of the capital stock of Czech companies in mid-1996.

18. Meanwhile, arrears have become a serious threat for the survival of basically viable and otherwise financially sound companies without primary arrears. For instance, at the end of 1995, the construction holding Armabeton Praha (see case study 4.3.4) was depressed by overdue receivables amounting to Kc 458 million, Kc 315 million of which were overdue for more than one year and, hence, of low real value. Overdue receivables represented roughly 66% of the firm's overall receivables and were stemming without exception from orders made by former SOEs. At the same time, Armabeton's capital stock was Kc 1,445 million while the pre-tax profit of 1995 made up a modest Kc 37 million. Both facts emphasize the dimension of the problem and the relevance of bad receivables for the financial performance of the holding.

19. Interview with Lukás Sevcík, lawyer with Nörr, Stiefenhofer & Lutz.

20. The author is grateful to Tom Schorling and Lukas Sevcík for helping him to develop an understanding of the working of the BCA. The subsequently depicted progression scheme also draws in part from a survey of the Czech BCA by Deloitte & Touche (1995).

21. If there are no more than 15 creditors, they may appoint one joint representative whose duties and rights are analogous to the committee.

22. See also KPMG Praha, newsletter 4/1996, p. 4.

23. Of course, the latter are not necessarily efficient from the point of view of the whole economy. For example, risk-averse creditors might block reorganization even if the firm's going-concern value is higher than the liquidation revenue. Apart from risk aversion, they might reject composition proposals because, as fixed claimants, they do not (or not sufficiently) participate in the upside gains of reorganization. In composition procedures, debtors are not normally given any incentive to leave all upside gains with the debtholders as they must bear at least part of the reorganization costs. Therefore, debtholders do not consider all upside gains when voting on reorganization. The resulting number of reorganizations tends to be too low.

24. See Nesnídal (1996a, p. 30). Like in most Western countries, business affairs are basically handled by the common district courts (*krajské soudy*). There are specialized district commercial courts (*krajské obchodní soudy*), however, in big towns (Prague, Brno and Ostrava) where commercial activities concentrate. The three specialized courts settle some quarter of all business-related cases of the first instance. Higher courts (*vrchní soudy*) are located in Prague and Olomouc, the Supreme Court (*ústavní soud*) is in Brno.

25. See also Kim Chipman, 'Muddy Bankruptcy Rules Still Mucking up Wheels of Justice', in: The Prague Post, 26 February – 4 March 1997, p. A5.

26. There is a strong degression in their share in the realized proceeds. They receive, for example, 10% of the first Kc 10,000 realized through the liquidation of the estate (with a minimum compensation of Kc 400). But they obtain merely 0.25% of all proceeds above Kc 1,000,000 (see Deloitte & Touche, 1995, p. 22). It is widely believed that such a strong degression is not in the best interest of the creditors as it weakens the receivers' incentives to maximize the value of the estate.

27. See Evan Z. Lazar and Donald P. Augustino, 'Bankruptcy and Composition Act Bandaged but not Fixed', The Prague Post, 16 – 22 October 1996, p. C10.

28. There is no specific law dealing with collateral and the rights of secured creditors. The subject is covered through several sections of the Commercial and Civil Codes.

29. The government plans to charge qualified legal and natural persons with carrying out the auction process in order to ease the burden of the bailiffs and to enhance the liquidity of creditors' claims. See Jan Wagner, 'Drazby jako duraznejsí ochrana veritelu' (Auctions as more effective protection of creditors), in: Hospodárské noviny, 14 February 1996, p. 13.

30. Claims are satisfied from the bankruptcy estate in the following order: (i) bankruptcy administration, (ii) non-satisfied claims of secured creditors who had to contribute to finance the costs of bankruptcy administration, (iii) employees (unpaid wages and benefits), (iv) tax arrears, public fees, social security contributions and claims of the NPF, (v) other claims.

31. According to one observer, the chamber's arbitration court is 'almost as bad as the public courts'. In his view, the court is staffed with members of the former communist nomenclature and decision-making is a most lengthy process. Foreign investors in particular steer clear of the chamber's court as it would tend to judge 'against their interests'.

32. In Poland, banks signed about 200 conciliation agreements with nonperforming borrowers only within one year after the adoption of the new procedure in February 1993.

33. See Hospodárské noviny, 1 February 1996, p. 2.

34. See Julian Duplain, 'Banking Law to Get Small Amendment', in: Business Eastern Europe, 6 June 1994, p. 6.

35. Banks established after 1991, had to meet a ratio of 8%.

36. Before July 1994, risk loans had been classified in three categories as temporarily illiquid, dubious and nonperforming. According to the new provisions, they are categorized as followed loans (sledované úvery: overdue between 30 and 90 days), nonstandard loans (nestandardní úvery: overdue between 91 and 180 days and uncertain repayment), dubious loans (pochybné úvery: overdue between 181 and 260 days and unlikely repayment) and lossmaking loans (ztrátové úvery: overdue more than 360 days and no chance of repayment or bankruptcy of the debtor). The reserve creation requirements on classified loans are 5%, 20%, 50% and 100% respectively of the amount of the loan.

37. The asset structure of the big banks sets strong incentives for efficient corporate control due to extensive direct and indirect equity stakes in the industrial sector. Those stakes are a result not only of acquisitions of holdings in companies or in own investment funds, but in part also of bank recapitalization. As already mentioned in section 5.1.2.2, in 1991 the capital base of the large banks was strengthened by NPF bonds which were exchanged for the stock of privatized companies in 1996.

38. However, on 12 February 1997, the Czech newspaper Hospodárské noviny observes 'an exceptional general consensus that foreign financial institutions shouldn't step as strategic investors into the four Czech banks in control of about three quarters of all deposits and extended loans. Portfolio investors and among them especially pension funds are considered to be the optimal investors. Thereby it is not that important whether they are foreign or domestic funds. It's more essential that they ought to be passive investors.' (p. 3)

39. The chairman of the supervisory board is consultant to the prime minister, the deputy is sent by the Ministry of Finance. Other delegates represent the NPF, the CNB and the office of the prime minister.

40. See Hospodárské noviny, 29 April 1996, p. 1.

41. Quoted from Hospodárské noviny, 26 March 1997, p. 2. As for private/privatized banks, an institutional barrier for foreign investors to step into domestic banks is set up by Czech banking law stipulating that foreign entities and persons may acquire equity stakes in Czech banks only after they have obtained the approval of the CNB. Domestic investors need approval only for stakes exceeding 15% of the bank's equity stock.

42. The table shows shareholders owning more than 1% of IPB stock. Bankovní holding, IF bohatství and Rentiérský IF are run by PIAS. The IPB group also controls the construction company Vojenské stavby. The car importer Charouz holding is known to have obtained extensive loans from IPB - allegedly to finance its acquisitions of the bank's stock (while the IPB maintains that they extended exclusively operating loans to the company). The real volume of stock controlled by the IPB management or its allies was probably higher than 36%. One shareholder owning 'roughly a 5% stake' (IPB spokesman Jan Rezek in: Prague Business Journal, 17 - 22 February 1997, p. 4) refused to disclose his identity as well as the size of his holding. One may speculate that the unpublished owner is chemical giant Chemapol which held some 3% of IPB stock in November 1996 (see Hospodárské noviny, 3 December 1996, p. 8) and is known to have tight credit links to the bank. The successful entrenchment of the IPB management was also confirmed by Roman Ceska, then chief executive of the NPF, who stressed in December 1996 the necessity to rapidly privatize IPB: '... the state isn't able to react quickly enough while executing its ownership rights [in IPB] and it seems that it is slowing down [the bank's] activities (Hospodárské noviny, 12 February 1996, p. 1).

43. See Business Central Europe, February 1999, p. 30.

44. In the case of Agrobanka, which ran into financial distress and was put under forced adminstration by Konsolidacní banka, the authorities separated most of the dubious assets from the bank's balance sheet and sold the viable rest to a strategic investor (General Electric Capital).

45. In the event of contravention of the contract, the bank threatened to terminate all business with the debtor. In some cases, it also used bills payable on demand to enforce obedience.

6 The performance of the capital market and the legal framework of equity control

6.1 BANK-BASED OR MARKET-BASED SYSTEM? THE IMPORTANCE OF CONTROL TRANSACTIONS

In the preceding chapters, we could state a strong initial tendency toward an insider regime of corporate control in the Czech Republic. Nevertheless, as argued in sections 1.4.2 and 1.4.3, from a theoretical viewpoint there are also some powerful arguments endorsing the (parallel) development of institutional elements characteristic of a market-based system. Important issues to be dealt with in a transitional economy are:

- There is a substantial lack of professional competence in both the management and control of companies. Governance capacity can only grow slowly and in many corporations, the current owner(s) may turn out uncapable of implementing 'deep' restructuring to ensure the viability of the firm. As long as the 'best' owner with the most promising business plan hasn't been found, the firm is benefiting from the 'openness' of the system concerning the ownership structure. The chance of attracting a better owner is enhanced by a legal framework enabling a transfer of control at minor transaction costs. That calls for a financial environment with deep and liquid stock markets.

- As finance itself is scarce, transparent and liquid capital markets spur restructuring as they increase the attraction of a country for international portfolio investors.

- Last but not least, in the presence of sometimes rather passive monitors and an underdeveloped 'work ethic' of many managers, financial incentives and the threat of hostile takeovers may considerably enhance the willingness of managers to do their best.

Subsequently we will analyse the performance of the emerging Czech capital market and its institutional environment. Hence we will focus on the substantial amendments of market regulation taking effect in July 1996. Reading this chapter, one should take into account that most legal institutions discussed concern the efficiency of both insider and outsider control in the Czech Republic. This is valid especially for the norms regarding minority shareholder protection.

6.2 MINORITY SHAREHOLDER PROTECTION

6.2.1 The Pre-reform Performance of the Capital Market

6.2.1.1 Unethical actions against minority shareholders

The problem of minority shareholder protection ultimately relates to the creation of institutions ensuring proper incentives for controlling shareholders (direct investors) to pursue an efficient corporate policy. Such institutions are inevitable for the enhancement of portfolio investors' confidence in the stock market. In the emerging Czech capital market, controlling shareholders and investment funds have been applying various tools to enrich themselves at the expense of small investors. Some examples will be presented in this section. In the following section, we will point briefly to the problems attached to the conversion of investment funds into holding companies.

One favourite tool used by controlling shareholders in order to extract control rents at the expense of minority shareholders was asset stripping. Large shareholders, frequently investment companies, forced controlled companies to sell their assets (goods, realties or machinery) to them at artificially low prices. Likewise, controlling shareholders exploited firms through transfer pricing or entered into contracts with controlled companies ensuring them services for symbolic or far-under-market prices. Given the opacity of the market, dispersed minority shareholders normally had difficulty in detecting such deals. If they did, it turned out to be even harder, if not impossible, to get protection by the courts.

A common tactic, most popular among the funds, was to sell shares to an allied brokerage or company at the price officially quoted at the PSE, and then have the ally resell the stock off the exchange at a high premium in a prearranged trade. Of course, the IPFs were taking advantage of the secrecy and duality (organized market versus unregulated free market) of the stock market. Effectively a serious breach of the fiduciary duty, such deals were hard to identify and Czech laws didn't provide for any penalty to deter the IPFs from robbing their shareholders and owners. While the investment companies or their allies respectively were busy pocketing gains from their secret deals, minority investors lost out.

But not only were the funds involved in the dubious game. Other investors, too, made hay as long as the sun was shining. The German producer of construction material Heidelberger Zement (HZ) belongs to the group of investors which has disregarded the interests of minority shareholders.[1] After the purchase of a 40% stake in the cement factory Pragocement Radotín in 1991, HZ increased the company's equity stock in 1993, thereby levering its own stake up to 76%. Afterwards, it stalled Pragocement's public tradeability and delisted it from the exchange. Given the lack of information about corporate policy and financial performance (which increased even after the de-listing) and the significant rise of transaction costs for selling company stock off the organized market, subsequently the liquidity and share price of Pragocement went down dramatically. The case is typical of the actions taken by large shareholders in the period of loose regulation after mass privatization. Minority shareholders were not usually compensated for the losses they suffered (e.g. by a mandatory bid by the controlling shareholder). Restrictions of public tradeability were not implemented exclusively to protect large investors against stock purchases by competitors or hostile takeovers. Often, it was a simple yet effective tool to exert pressure on minority shareholders to sell their stock to the controlling owner at a very favourable price. This especially concerns conversions of bearer to registered shares. Here, tradeability is extremely restricted as each market transaction - purchase and sale - has to be okayed by the firm management and, hence, by the controlling shareholder.

Another widely-applied method of squeezing minority owners out of a company was to decide a capital decrease for a company by the votes of the controlling shareholder, but to place the obligation to sell part of one's shares only on the minority owners. This was exactly the way chosen by the major owners of the construction company Stavební podnik Zlín. The firm had been transferred into private hands in the second wave of voucher privatization. Shortly afterwards, in May 1995, the general meeting decided to decrease the firm's capital stock, determining that all shareholders owning less than 1000 shares had to sell their complete holdings for a certain price per share to the company. The reportedly very low price of the yet unquoted company was arbitrarily determined by the controlling shareholders. Small shareholders were given less than four weeks to comply with the decision of the meeting. Indeed, the company made more or less a Mafioso-type bid to the dispersed owners. If they had turned it down, their stock would have been declared null and void by the company and erased from the register of the Securities Centre.[2] A minority shareholder's objection that the company would deprive him of his property, was countered by the chairman of the management board, pointing out soberly 'that [the company] cannot deprive him of his property since, according to the Commercial Code, he doesn't own any property of the corporation'.[3]

The two cases in point give strong evidence for both a serious lack of legal protection of minority shareholders and the lack of incentives for many controlling shareholders to run a corporate policy in the long-term interest of all owners. They hint not only at a weak regulatory environment after voucher privatization, but likewise prove our thesis, put forward above, that the development of social norms and work ethics in transitional economies falls behind that in established market economies.

6.2.1.2   Conversion of investment funds into holdings

Another obvious phenomenon on the Czech capital market was the conversion of investment funds into industrial holdings. As of mid-1996, 59 converted funds could be registered. There are several reasons for their transformation into holding companies. Firstly, unlike the funds, holdings are not subject to portfolio restrictions. They are 'normal' joint stock companies and may acquire stakes of any size in portfolio companies. A conversion might therefore increase the governance power of the funds. It is somewhat strange, however, that the wave of conversions took place predominantly in the second quarter of 1996, shortly before the amendment of capital market regulation. It is therefore plausible to assume that most funds hastily converted to flee from the strict disclosure requirements imposed by the amended Investment Act. This is confirmed by the fact that the biggest converted funds are part of large financial groups (see Table 6.1). Since the new Investment Act (after the amendment of April 1996) allows fund families running several investment funds to accumulate large stakes in portfolio companies, good governance is a bad justification for the conversion of funds managed by groups such as Harvard, PIAS or PPF.[4]

Table 6.1: Converted funds

(Data as of May 1996) Holding	Manager (financial group)	Net asset value (in million CZK)	ranking among funds[*]	discount
Harvardský prumyslový holding	HC&C	6,533	4	-62.35%
Harvardská financní spolecnost	HC&C	5,054	7	-65.02%
PPF investicní holding	PPF	3,506	8	-62.55%
Bankovní holding	PIAS (IPB)	2,908	11	-43.13%
YSE	LinhArt	2,591	14	-47.62%
Top 6 holdings	-	-	-	-57.56%
Top 6 IFs	-	-	-	-36.61%
Top 6 closed-ended unit trusts	-	-	-	-52.44%

* including funds converted into holdings

Source: Právo, 8 June 1996, p.8; Hospodárské noviny, 23-5-1996, stock market supplement, p.VI; own calculations

Another reason for the conversions is better access to debt finance. Unlike the funds, holdings may issue obligations. They also may initiate 'equity/debt swaps', that is the conversion of equity into debt. Fund investors may prefer fixed interest yields as against dividend payments as they lower the pre-tax profits and hence the tax burden of portfolio companies (while the rate of the withholding tax on dividends and on yields from fixed-interest securities is identical).

Figure 6.1: Decline of the IPF industry*

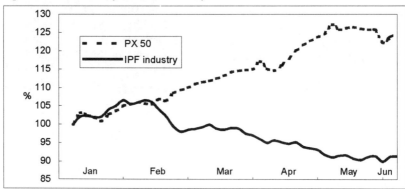

* Indices for period January - June 1996

Source: Právo, 8 June 1996, p.8; Hospodárské noviny, 23-5-1996, stock market supplement, p.VI; own calculations

The tax burden of holdings can also be diminished by registering the company in a tax haven abroad. This is precisely the strategy chosen by the converted Harvard funds. Once again, Harvard chief Viktor Kozený was the trend-setter for many fellow funds. His flagship Harvard Dividendový IF was the first fund transforming itself into a holding, thereby setting off a domino effect among other funds. The conversion came at a little publicized extraordinary general meeting, convened in great haste in a small Moravian village. The meeting's early starting time (at 9 a.m.) and remote location attracted no more than some dozens of shareholders so as making it quite easy for the fund managers to get through the transformation. Later on, Kozený also converted HC&C's second largest fund Harvard Rustový IF (Harvard growth fund) and merged it with Dividendový and the glass-industry holding Sklo Union into the Harvard industrial holding. The holding was, in turn, merged with Stratton Investments into the super holding Dawentree which is registered in the tax haven of Cyprus. What makes the whole transaction somewhat dubious is that the fund's shareholders had no opportunity to influence the process because of both high organization costs and the unconventional way the general meeting was convened. On the other hand, it is doubtful whether the conversion is in their best interest and consistent with the management's fiduciary duty.[5] Holdings have the same legal status as normal joint stock companies and do not fall under the supervision of the Ministry of Finance. For those reasons, they have even smaller incentives to care about the transparency of their portfolio and investment policy than investment funds. Of course, this doesn't increase the security of investments, nor does it enhance the accountability of the former fund managers. It is no surprise that the value of the converted funds sharply declined relative to the market index. Moreover, a series of conversions significantly lowered investors' confidence in the fund industry and thus triggered relative losses on the exchange even for funds not planning to swim in the wake of Harvard. Figure 6.1 depicts the decline of the investment funds industry caused predominantly by the conversions. It is striking that the differential between both indices has been constantly growing from March, i.e. from the beginning of the transformation wave. Clearly, the shareholders of the investment funds - most of all those of the converted ones - were heavily damaged by the whole process.

6.2.2 Reform Measures

Non-transparency of the market and weak minority shareholder protection gave rise to a political discussion about the need for a reform of capital market regulation. Two factions can be identified in the controversy on reforming laws regulating financial markets and subsequently control transactions. The government argued alongside traditional free-marketeer lines, saying basically that the free and unregulated transfer of control in firms is the best assurance for a market process to take place and thus to guarantee the most efficient resource allocation. Regulating this market for corporate control (not to be mistaken with the developed and transparent market for corporate control in the US) would mean losses in efficiency. Critics of these practices - pointing to the increasing number of minority shareholder squeeze-outs - challenged this position as allowing for the 'Wild East' to proceed a rule-of-law and civilized society.[6] The persisting illiquidity and non-transparency had the immediate effect of investors, who were desperately needed for 'deeper restructuring', hesitating or turning instead to the much more liquid and tightly overseen Warsaw Stock Exchange or to Budapest.[7]

Tomás Jezek, one of the architects of voucher privatization and later head of the Prague Stock Exchange, was and is the most prominent advocate of effective shareholder protection and measures to decisively increase market transparency. In his view, minority shareholder protection is best achieved by regulating control transactions to the degree that outside (minority) shareholders have to be offered adequate compensation if they decide to exit the firm and would risk - as a consequence of a control transaction and a possible decline of the share price - a loss of assets. Therefore, takeovers ought to be regulated by introducing mandatory bids and market players should be forced to disclose their portfolio and intentions. It is unclear which of these crudely sketched positions actually is the more appropriate for the still nascent Czech market. Both parties agree on the necessity of control transactions, but very plainly disagree on their terms. As we have argued above, it seems plausible to assume the position of Tomás Jezek. The need for capital and foreign know-how will not be met if investors are unsure of the safety of their investment. Only if there is a reliable and somewhat calculable institutional environment including the set of laws under which activities have to take place will there be the highest possible foreign engagement in the region.

After intense bargaining in the Czech parliament, substantial amendments came into power on 1 July 1996. The remainder of this section takes a detailed look at some changes resulting from the recent amendments. It presents the most important changes to the legal norms for corporate control and tries to give an assessment thereof.[8] Perhaps the most prominent element of the financial market reform is the introduction of mandatory bids. This was and is deemed in particular by Tomás Jezek to be a decisive instrument in protecting minority shareholders from being squeezed out of a given corporation. The respective provisions of the Commercial Code are, above all, a reflex to the frequently observeable going-private actions (de-listing from the stock exchange) after an investor had acquired the necessary controlling stake to achieve this. Outside shareholders found themselves with no compensation and commonly could only sell their shares over-the-counter at considerable discounts.[9] The new law therefore is aimed at ensuring outside (minority) shareholders a fair price for their stake if they wish to sell their shares upon announcement of an imminent takeover.

The law stipulates the following requirements (§183b (1) CCode). If a shareholder acquires a holding in publicly tradeable shares carrying voting rights which amounts to, or exceeds one half, or two-thirds, or three-quarters of the total nominal values of all such company's shares carrying voting rights, then he is obliged to make a public offer to purchase that company's remaining shares carrying voting rights not yet under his control. The offer has to be made within 60 days of the day when the shareholder acquires or exceeds any of the mentioned holdings. The same provision is applied for changes of the type or restrictions of the tradeability of shares. If the general meeting decides such measures, it must compensate all shareholders, who didn't vote for the changes or restrictions or didn't participate in the meeting.[10] The calculation of the minimum price to be offered to minority shareholders by the acquirer is stipulated in §183c (3) CCode:

(3) [T]he price per share must be determined as at least the weighted average of prices quoted on the basis of trading in them on public markets in the six months prior to the day when the duty to make a public proposal ... arose.

Quite obviously, the problem with this compensation price is its calculation basis.[11] As it is determined by the price development exclusively on public markets, i.e. the PSE and the over-the-counter market RM-System (RMS), and most of the deals are made behind the scenes directly between purchaser and seller of a stock, the calculation formula cannot preclude the acting parties from manipulating share prices. For instance, they may flee from the organized markets to the off-market if the purchaser is willing to pay a control premium for the shares. Thereby, he can effectively avoid an increase in the compensation price for minority shareholders. His savings may be quite substantial as indicated by the enormous price differentials between transactions on the organized markets and off-market deals. A side effect of this additional incentive, created by the mandatory bid, to transfer transaction volume to the off-market is a further decline of liquidity and therefore informational efficiency of share prices.

There still is another distortion triggered by the formula of the compensation price. Suppose the price of a stock has been increasing over six months. In this case, the bid price is below the current share price. Apparently, price increases are leading to a significant dilution of minority shareholder protection. More important, they give rise to perverse incentives. Raiders may press minority shareholders to sell for a price lower than the market price if the latter is afraid of being exploited by the majority shareholder if they don't sell. The motivation to launch a takeover is then frequently to make a quick buck from this kind of 'arbitrage' instead of benefiting from long-term restructuring or turnaround management. Likewise, given a decline of the market price over the past six months, an excessive compensation price may deter efficiency-oriented investors from buying 50% or more of a potential target as the mandatory bid dramatically enhances the transactions costs of taking over the majority of the target stock. On the other hand, for an owner disposing of less than 50% of the equity stock, the implementation of a restructuring programme may be too expensive due to the free-riding of minority shareholders. In the end, this dilemma may seduce him to (mis)use a controlling stake to transfer assets or funds from the firm to himself. For the reasons mentioned in this section, it appears at least dubious whether mandatory bids are an appropriate means to protect minority shareholders in transitional economies with underdeveloped and inefficient stock markets.

Finally, there is no central recording of mandatory bids. Law merely stipulates that the bids must be made public in at least two nation-wide newspapers. Minority investors hence have to follow up virtually the complete daily press to be sure not to miss an eventual mandatory bid. Of course, central registration would considerably lower the costs of such a time-consuming procedure and therefore enhance the efficacy of the protection of individual shareholders.

The amendment also provides some protection for shareholders of investment funds converting into holdings. First of all, from July 1996, two thirds of *all* shareholders have to vote for the conversion. Before the amendment, it had to be just a simple majority of the voting stock present at the general meeting. A shareholder who didn't agree on the conversion may require the new holding to buy his stock for an amount equal to the stock's net asset value at the day of the general meeting when the conversion was decided.[12] The advantage of this provision over a compensation at market prices is that the shareholder is not cheated of the discount of the fund.[13]

6.2.3 Remaining Legal Deficiencies and Economic Problems

6.2.3.1 Definition of 'controlling shareholder'

The amendments leave considerable latitude for interpretation - to put it favourably. Considering the main aims of protection of minority shareholders and transparency, it can clearly be said that these have not been fully achieved. The remaining loopholes are indeed astonishing and have led a prominent Czech lawyer to speculate cynically on whether the new law isn't in fact a conspiracy of controlling shareholders to finish off definitively minority shareholders.[14] Although numerous aspects and scenarios are touched upon, the phrasing and definition of important legal circumstances are - even through the eyes of an economist - grossly incomplete. In addition, the enforcement of the laws poses problems not only because of some loopholes but also for lack of sophistication of deciding courts, lack of manpower in the Ministry of Finance and lack of an independent overseeing body such as the American Securities and Exchange Commission (SEC). This chapter will mark some of the most evident problems. They are in part derived from two general problems: the definitions of 'concerted action' and of 'controlling shareholder'.

Crucial for the protection of minority shareholders is an adequate definition of 'control'. This definition is the departing point for several other provisions in the Commercial code, that come into force as soon as a 'controlling shareholder' (single or group) is identified. This is especially important for contracts on profit transfer, usually struck between a subsidiary and a parent company: as will be discussed further on. Shareholders are entitled to be compensated in the event of a controlling shareholder transfers profits from its subsidiary to himself. The passage devoted to the definition of control is §66a CCode. The section runs as follows:

(1) A controlled person (*ovládaná osoba*) is a company in which another person has a majority share of voting rights, based on this person's ownership interest or this person's ownership of company shares to which is attached a majority of the voting rights, or based on this person's agreement with other persons entitled to vote, so that such a person is capable of exercising a majority of voting rights ...

(2) A controlling person (*ovládající osoba*) is the person having the status in a controlled person according to subsection (1).

What is striking about this definition is the fact that while already setting a very high threshold for the definition to be relevant at all, it is solely linked to the objective criteria of owning or commanding by way of proxy over 50% or more of the voting rights in a corporation. The common working definition in the West, e.g. in the US, leaves much more room for a jury or judge to ascertain the existence of a controlling position, analysing whether one party has the power to direct the day-to-day affairs of another party.[15]

The definition will not be fulfilled in the event of an ownership stake of 49%. Thus if the attendance at a general meeting is not more than 74% - which from first experiences doesn't seem to be too uncommon - then obviously this specific shareholder would even command a two-thirds majority enabling him to change the articles of association of the corporation. This would be possible without even legally being a 'controlling' shareholder.

It remains unclear what the initial evaluations were concerning the fixing of this threshold. Tomás Jezek in his original proposal had clearly set a 30% limit beyond which the status of 'controlling shareholder' would lie.[16] This definition has important effects on other laws, not only the arrangements concerning mandatory bids, but also implicitly on the definition of 'concerted conduct' and fighting or having leverage over problems concerning transfer-pricing or transferring profits from subsidiaries to parent companies. This will be dealt with in the following articles.

6.2.3.2 The definition of 'concerted action'
In order to circumscribe groups of shareholders acting as one body and both to be able to apply the mentioned mandatory disclosure provisions and to identify potentially controlling stakes when aggregating individuals' shares,

the term 'concerted conduct/action' (*jednání ve shode*) was added to the Commercial Code. The relevant section for concerted action is §66b CCode in conjunction with §66a CCode (definition of controlling person). The term concerted conduct is to be understood as such action aimed at attaining the same objective (goal). It can be undertaken by

(a) a legal entity and its participants (partners, members, shareholders), statutory bodies, members of statutory bodies and supervisory bodies, employees of the legal entity being in the direct controlling sphere of the statutory body or its member, ...

(b) persons who concluded an agreement on identical exercise of voting rights in one company in matters relating to its management, irrespective of the validity or invalidity of this agreement (CCode §186d);

(c) the controlling person and the controlled person, or among the persons controlled directly or indirectly by the same controlling person.[17]

This set of definitions would seem to be sufficiently drawn if it weren't for two things. First, as mentioned in the preceding section, the term 'controlling person' is too loosely defined. Second, the 'agreement on identical exercise of voting rights' mentioned in CCode §66b (b) is obviously very difficult to police. A recent example for this is the case of the influence of Investicní a Postovní Banka (IPB) on the biggest Czech brewery Plzenský Prazdroj, the 24th largest company by market capitalization listed at the Prague Stock Exchange (see Table 6.2). There was considerable surprise in the financial community, when IPB disclosed its holdings in Plzenský Prazdroj to the Securities Center in accordance with CCode §183d (1) (reporting duty). The percentage of capital interest disclosed was merely 23.55%[18] although the entire IPB group - including the funds managed by IPB's wholly owned investment company PIAS - was known to command 53.2% of voting stock[19] at the last general assembly of Plzenský Prazdroj in June 1996. The question was not only why it hadn't made an official bid for the remaining 47.7% of the brewery's shareholders in accordance with CCode §183b (1) (mandatory bids) but also why IPB hadn't fully disclosed its interest in Prazdroj in the first place. The answer was that IPB did not include any of the investment funds' shares, as these entities were neither controlled by IPB in the legal sense (no interest of 50% or above) nor – according to a spokesman - had IPB 'concluded an agreement on identical exercise of voting rights' as stated in CCode §66b (b).[20]

A look at the ownership relations among IPB group members doesn't confirm this view. The bank holds a strong position as controlling shareholder in virtually all of the investment funds. In fact, IPB owns 20%

to 40% stakes in most of the PIAS funds. The fact that all funds are investing major parts of their portfolios in Plzenský, gives further evidence of the group's concerted conduct. The brewery represents the biggest capital interest in the portfolios of five funds, four of which are investment funds. In addition, it is the second biggest holding of six funds and the third biggest of another three funds. The data suggest that, concerning Plzenský, the strategic orientation of the group is determined by IPB.[21]

Table 6.2: The IPB group's joint control of Plzenský Prazdroj

	Equity stake in investment entity held by IPB (as of 28-8-1996)	Shareholdings in Plzenský Prazdroj (as of 30-6-1996):		
Entity		Rank in portfolio	% of fund's portfolio	% of company equity
Investment funds:				
Bankovní Holding*	41.83	1	7.91	
Rentiérský IF	29.55	1	7.10	
IF Bohatství	29.60	1	7.20	
Kristálový IF	25.22	2	7.59	
IF Obchodu	25.23	1	10.70	Σ = 29.65
Potravinárský IF	34.24	3	7.96	
Prumyslový IF	33.67	2	7.83	
IF Energetiky	13.51	6	7.26	
Rozvojový IF	n.a.	2	8.60	
RIF	11.51	n.a.	n.a.	
Unit trusts:				
Cesky Fond	-	2	9.62	
Moravskoslez. Fond	-	1	9.46	
Fond Majetku	-	3	7.70	Σ = 9.82
Fond Pravid. Príjmu	-	2	9.30	
Fond Prosperity	-	3	7.95	
Fond Zaruc. Odkupu	-	2	8.52	
Domeana s.r.o.	100.00	-	-	5.17
IPB (direct holding)	-	-	-	8.56
Entire IPB Group	-	-	-	53.20

* converted IF

Source: PIAS, Securities Centre

The problem was and is the definition of 'controlling person'. Its sole reliance on the objective criteria of having a consolidated interest in a subsidiary or an affiliated entity of 50% or more is as mentioned the crucial point. IPB wholly owns its investment company, but has no majority stakes in the funds managed by PIAS. Obviously, the amendment fails its goal to protect shareholders in this respect. As of today, the legal recognition of 'concerted action' of several owners depends *exclusively* upon their voluntary disclosure of the state of affairs.

6.2.3.3 Contracts on profit transfers

Of the possible damages that can be inflicted upon minority shareholders, a contract on transfer of profit (*smlouva o prevodu zisku*) is definitely one of the most obviously damaging. The amendment therefore provides for a procedure aiming to ensure appropriate compensation for outside shareholders. Again, current legislation has gaping loopholes leaving outside shareholders rather unprotected if the party extracting profits by having concluded such a profit-transfer contract is aware of certain provisions.

Generally, two scenarios have to be distinguished: one, there is a controlling shareholder in the sense of §66a CCode (disposing of more than 50% of the voting stock), or, two, there is only a *de facto* controlling shareholder with less than 50% of voting stock. If the former is the case ('controlling' in accordance with §66a CCode) then §190a CCode becomes effective. This section runs as follows:

> When a controlling person and the controlled person conclude a contract on profit transfer in favour of the controlling person, and the general meeting of the controlled person approves a distribution of profits in accordance with the said contract, the controlling person is bound to provide the other share-holders with a settlement equal to the average dividend for the last three years, but if no dividend was paid in the last three years, then in an amount equal to the dividend usually paid by companies with identical or similar objects of business activity on making a comparable profit.

First of all it has to be stressed again that this section only comes into effect if there actually is a 'controlling shareholder' in the legal sense. If not, then there is no provision in the Commercial Code as to if and how outside shareholders should be compensated. The problems with the given section are again obvious. The latitude for manipulating dividends and thus manipulating pay-outs to outside shareholders is considerable. If a controlling shareholder manages to reduce dividends to a minimum, then outsiders are left with nothing. The commercial code at no point introduces a really binding fiduciary principle that would let managers think twice about treating minority shareholders badly. Furthermore the law does not stipulate who it is that actually assesses the 'amount equal to the dividend usually paid by companies with identical or similar business activity'. How should this be determined in a rapidly changing economic environment?

The problem becomes more complicated if the shareholder controlling the company holds less than 50% of the voting stock. Then §190a CCode is not effective because there is no 'controlling person' in the sense of §66a CCode. It is unclear what the options for minority shareholders would be in order to secure their proportional share of the corporation's profits as principally guaranteed by §178(1) CCode. What happens if they receive a part of the profit, yet not a proportional one? How can the profit be policed?

This points back to the case in favour of promoting the liquidity of the capital markets. If corporations need to or become aware of the possibility to finance themselves through the stock exchange (enhanced perhaps by bank loans becoming comparatively more expensive), then there would be an *ex ante* incentive for managers and majority owners to ensure a favourable reputation towards shareholders. Apart from inevitable exceptions, this leads to a kind of self-enforcement of minority shareholder protection, where legal sanctions would only be needed infrequently.[22]

6.2.3.4 Insider dealing

The Czech Securities act covers the problem of inside trading only roughly. Section 81 defines inside information as non-public information concerning the economic or financial situation of an issuer 'which, if published, could significantly influence the price of the relevant security.' Furthermore, a person who has access to such information due to his profession or function is not allowed to trade in this security or to make use of such information for his personal benefit. This imposes a certain fiduciary duty upon managers of industrial corporations as well as of both investment funds and unit trusts. The problem is that Czech law fails to define any concrete penalties for breaching fiduciary duties. This stands in a remarkable contrast to Western legislation, in particular US company law which imposes heavy criminal sanctions on inside trading.

The amended Investment Act provides fund managers, paradoxically, with a very elegant tool to reap enormous windfall profits at the expense of minority owners by making use of confidential information. According to the new § 35h InvAct, investment companies may decide to transform closed-end unit trusts into open-end unit trusts. Given the huge discounts of closed-end trusts (which are generated by the general secrecy of the stock market and the fund managers' refusal to disclose portfolio information), it is frequently most lucrative for the trust management to buy a big stake in the trust, to open the trust and finally to cash in the full net asset value of the participation certificates. The first ones to discover this possibility were the managers of two closed-end unit trusts of the investment company Expandia.[23] They were mailing buy-out offers to their unitholders in April 1996, exactly four days after Parliament had passed the new legislation.

Many trust owners decided to sell their certificates to the investment company, thereby obtaining slightly more than the funds fetched on the market. Market analysts estimate that the owner-managers could raise Expandia's stake in both funds to as much as 70%.[24] The catch to the action was that management had started planning to open the trust long before it sent the letters to the trust owners. The chairman of Expandia's management board candidly admits that the opening plans did exist roughly in early 1995. This proves that the management made use of its inside knowledge, thereby seriously violating its fiduciary duty to the unitholders. Hard to imagine that so many investors would have sold their units, if they had known about the opening plans of Expandia. In the US, the action would have been a clear breach of the 'disclose-or-abstain rule', stipulating that insiders are allowed to trade (i.e. buy the certificates) only after complete disclosure of all material non-public information (here the future opening of the trust).[25] After the licensing of the transformation process by the Ministry of Finance in late 1996, the management could start to redeem its units at full net asset value, thus making cosy windfall profits. The damage to the former unitholders is considerable as both trusts had a discount of some 60% prior to the opening.

Ministry officials agreed that the conversion is no violation of law, hastening to add: 'It only concerns ethics'.[26] This seems to be, however, only half of the truth. Apart from the fiduciary duties in the context of inside trading spelled out above, the behaviour of Expandia conflicts with § 14 (1) b, stipulating that investment companies must protect the interests of unitholders. Expandia's action runs clearly counter to their interests. The question hence is whether, apart from mentioned loopholes that can be legally used, there is the additional problem of enforcing the provisions of the amendment. Does the Ministry, responsible for the supervision of the capital market and the funds, dispose of effective instruments to control and sanction the market participants and, if it does so, does it enforce the provisions of the law?

6.2.3.5 Problems of enforcement
A major criticism of the old market regulation was the weak authority of state supervision as against all capital market participants. The amended InvAct, however, provides the Ministry with far-reaching sanctionary powers against both natural and physical persons breaching the law. The supervisory department disposes of a wide range of instruments making possible efficient fine-tuning of fines and penalties. If it ascertains shortcomings in the activities of any market participant, it may, for instance, simply order rectification of such shortcomings, impose fines of up to CZK 10 million, exchange individuals in the bodies of investment funds and

investment companies, or even - in the event of grave offences - reduce the registered capital of an investment fund, withdraw the licence of an investment fund or unit trust or impose forced administration. Ultimately, it can even order the liquidation of an investment fund or investment company. This broad catalogue of sanction measures guarantees the Ministry a potentially strong position as watch dog over the Czech capital market and, in particular, over the funds.

To date, the Ministry of Finance is the only institution responsible to oversee a stock market with some 2,500 companies. It employs no more than about 60 people (including clerical and support staff) to fulfil its mission.[27] This lack of manpower isn't the only obstacle for enforcement of shareholder rights. The ministry's capital-markets supervision department has repeatedly stated publicly that it is not convinced of the necessity and is prepared to regulate every aspect of the capital market.[28] It argues alongside other government officials that the capital markets haven't yet stabilized and tight regulation would cripple the ongoing process of ownership concentration and thus hamper the overall speed of economic development.[29]

This *laissez-faire* attitude is well documented in the ministry's reaction to the conversion of investment funds into 'industrial holding groups.' It could have successfully prohibited the conversions and thus protected minority shareholders by insisting that the 'new' holding groups were nothing else than re-named investment companies. The law clearly defines what the business of such an investment fund is (§7 (1)-(2) InvAct):

(1) An investment fund accumulates pecuniary means by issuing shares.
(2) An investment fund uses means acquired under subsection (1) to purchase securities, real estate or movables, to invest under a silent partnership contract or to make deposits into a special bank account.
(3) An investment fund manages its portfolio either on its own or by entrusting such a portfolio to an investment company on the basis of a management contract.

If this is the business of a company, then the approval of the Ministry of Finance is necessary (§8 (1)-(2) InvAct):

(1) Approval [i.e. a licence] is required to establish an investment company or investment fund ...
(2) A licence is granted (or not) by the Ministry on the basis of an application by the founders.

Holdings being re-packaged investment funds and therefore theoretically in need of a licence and prone to regulatory provisions for investment funds, the Ministry would very likely have succeeded if it legally challenged e.g. Harvard Industrial Holding. It didn't and thus sanctioned the conversions.

A fairly independent Securities and Exchange Commission was set up at the Prague Stock Exchange as late as 1998.[30] Even Jan Veverka, head of the capital market supervision, underlines that such a politically independent institution should be more suitable for carrying out the watch dog function than the ministry which is, in his view, highly vulnerable to strong lobbying from various interest groups including the IPFs. So far, the impact of the 'Czech SEC' has not been substantial. The key question will be whether the body will be in the long run really independent from political decisionmakers. If not, it will clearly lack credibility. Without a supervisory institution free from political incentives and robust against lobbyism, nothing will change substantially. Some yet unresolved problems concern the manpower and financing of the institution. A sufficiently high number of well-trained experts must be found to monitor hundreds of funds and companies with a sometimes still rather dubious attitude towards the compliance of rules - no matter whether laws, self-regulation or social norms.

Nevertheless, public pressure has recently induced the capital market supervision, for the first time, to deviate significantly from its laissez-faire approach and to withdraw the licences of 13 smaller investment funds of the second wave which still haven't issued their own shares. At present, all 13 funds are waiting for liquidation.[31] Besides, the supervision has set three funds under forced administration. In two of them, managed by the same investment group, the management is accused of having transferred illegally and without adequate compensation major parts of the portfolio, invested in blue chips, to the investment company (*tunelování*).[32] The funds suffered a heavy decline of net asset value and were traded, in mid-1996, at no more than small fractions of their market value at the beginning of the year. The management of the third fund (AGB II), which is part of the Motoinvest empire, has allegedly damaged shareholders by consciously purchasing large, yet worthless stakes in two banks tightly affiliated to the Motoinvest group. The net asset value of the fund has been decreasing considerably since management started to accumulate large stakes in Agrobanka and Kreditní banka. At the time when the fund made its purchases, both banks were running into a liquidity crunch. In both events, the fund management should have known about the critical financial performance of the banks. Meanwhile, the viable parts of Agrobanka were sold to General Electric's GE Capital, whereas Kreditní had to be liquidated. Motoinvest had held large equity stakes in both banks.[33]

6.2.3.6 Judicial system and 'legal culture'

It has repeatedly been stressed in interviews undertaken for this book, that apart from the mere lack of human resources in the Ministry of Finance, possible adverse incentives directed against shareholder interests and the delayed establishment of an independent Czech version of the American Securities and Exchange Commission, there is a considerable and rather sobering lack of judicial sophistication and skills.

The Czech legal system, of course, is based on the continental European civil law tradition as opposed to the Anglo-Saxon conception of common law. The trade-off characterizing the two systems is to be seen in finding an equilibrium between immunization of the law against abusive reinterpretation (triggered possibly by short-lived fashionable public views) on the one hand and, on the other, ensuring that courts can decide freely according to the specific circumstances of a given case. The common law regimes of the west have had centuries to evolve and pass on both legal expertise as well as institutionalized norms of judicial conduct. A simple transplantation of a common law system into eastern societies thus had never been an option. In an environment of central-planning and loosely defined responsibility structures, one effective way to defend one's action against accusations of misconduct was to adhere to the very literal sense of laws. Therefore, the vast majority of judges adhere still today to something described vividly by one insider as 'slavish literalism'. The legal provisions that were relevant in the cases brought to courts thus far have been interpreted by judges in a most literal manner. The legal intent of a specific law is seldomly taken into account. The more complicated a law and its implications, the less likely it was and is that there will be an 'interpretative' ruling, taking into consideration the specific circumstances of a given case. In addition, judges are not trained to actually assess the economic bearing of cases brought in front of them. Even in Germany with its tradition of civil law, judges on commercial issues consider very much so the circumstances and implications of a case. In the Czech Republic, there is as yet a serious lack of sophistication and skills among judges dealing with commercial issues.

This obviously doesn't make things easier for minority shareholders fighting abusive conduct of majority shareholders. If an outside shareholder decides to file a law suit on such suspicion, he will only stand a chance to win the case if the accused party objectively violated an explicit legal provision. Thus everything that is not explicitly prohibited must be considered to be allowed. The loopholes in the existing law can only be effectively eliminated if courts begin including 'legal intent' - that is the spirit of a given law - in their deliberations.

6.2.4 Summary

After painful experience with controlling shareholders exploiting companies at the expense of minority shareholders, the Czechs have finally made their choice and implemented the mandatory bid as central tool to protect small and naive shareholders. The obligation to extend a mandatory and equal bid to all target shareholders after the raider has acquired a certain percentage of the target stock is a simple institutional device to prevent the devaluation of minority shareholder stock. Yet, it increases the transaction costs of takeovers. Another and more efficient approach would be to make controlling equityholders effectively liable for the policy of the corporation and to punish all actions taken at the expense of minority shareholders. Of course, such a fiduciary duty requires a most sophisticated legal system in which all kinds of oppression are immediately fined by the courts.

For the time being, the Czechs are already having enough problems with the handling of the new law, see e.g. the loose definition and difficult policing of 'concerted conduct'. Besides, small shareholders who do not 'exit' the company after a takeover still face a high probability of being exploited by controlling owners. This is mainly due to the courts' inclination to interpret laws in a very literalistic manner and to ignore their legal intent. Of course, weak minority shareholder protection has reduced the quality of corporate control. This is valid in particular for companies controlled by private funds or non-bank investors whose actions were not guided by reputational concerns.

This points to a cardinal problem of the Czech economic transformation, namely the insufficient enforcement and policing of existing rules (even more than a real lack of regulation). Law-makers need to realize the importance of legal principles in establishing legal intent. Ultimately, the courts have to shift their interpretation from literalistic to a more case-based analysis, which means a dramatic turning off from the legal tradition forged during the communist decades. In the end, a more sophisticated legal system making judgements based upon legal intent and the evaluation of individual cases, doesn't have to rely primarily upon mandatory bids to protect investors. The introduction of a 'fiduciary duty' of investors would not only make controlling owners effectively liable for their actions without unduly restricting their discretion. Moreover, this would ease the pressure on the legal system to constantly fill gaps in the legislation in order to keep abreast of the creativity of impure investors in evading the law.

The problems of insufficient sophistication are certainly intrinsic to the transition processes all over central and eastern Europe. This certainly doesn't represent a breathtakingly new finding. It is nevertheless important to identify crucial focal points where lack of knowledge has important implications for and effects on the overall development. Therefore, it seems justified to call for increased government effort to accordingly promote and support the judiciary.

6.3 INFORMATIONAL EFFICIENCY

6.3.1 Market Transparency

6.3.1.1 Company information
An organized Czech capital market came into being through the foundation of the Prague Stock Exchange (PSE) in November 1992. Founding members of the exchange are 14 Czech and foreign banks and five brokerage houses. The organized market is complemented by the Registracní místo system (RMS), a fully computerized system of periodical auctions, disposing of a nationwide branch network. It comprises most of the registration places for voucher privatization, linking them to a central algorithm matching supply and demand. The basic idea was to set up an alternative market-maker to guarantee easy and cheap access to share trading for all the small investors holding stock from voucher privatization. In February 1996, the Ministry of Finance conferred a licence to run an organized securities market on a third operator, the Right Time Price system (RTPS). RTPS will be a rival, above all, for the RMS since it plans to carry out periodical Dutch auctions through on-line terminals. So far, it has not started to operate. However, most of the deals made on the Czech capital market have been accomplished through direct trades on the off-market and only registered at the Securities Centre, that is the central register of all dematerialized equity stock that had undergone voucher privatization.

After voucher privatization, the young Czech capital market was quite loosely regulated. This led to rather low market efficiency. The main reasons for this were a lack of market transparency and high transaction costs of securities trading. We will analyse both in this section. The lack of market transparency was based upon scarce company information, weak trade disclosure, insufficient processing of deals into prices and multiple prices on separated markets.

Company information was rare and fragmentary. By law, publicly traded companies were required to publish the results of their financial performance only once a year. They published the demanded financial data frequently incomplete and with considerable delay so that relevant up-to-date company information was hardly available. The ownership structures of most companies were opaque. The PSE tried to enhance transparency through the creation of their own additional disclosure rules like the duty to immediately reveal price-relevant information. Besides, it divided the market into three segments. The main market (*hlavní trh*) was and is open for issuers with a market capitalization of no less than CZK 200 million[34], who are offering at least 20% of equity stock to public trading. The firms have to provide quarterly financial statements covering the complete balance sheet and profit and loss accounts. Companies listed on the side market (*vedlejší trh*) or secondary market must have a minimum capitalization of CZK 100 million[35] and 15% of outstanding stock offered to public trading. Financial statements have to be published, however, only biannually. Finally, all other corporations may enter the largely unregulated free market (*volný trh*). All in all, the self-regulation of the PSE turned out helpful in giving traders and investors a better view of the management performance and financial positioning of tradeable companies. However, the limits of the regulation become visible if one takes a look at the distribution of issuers over the three market segments. In January 1997, only 36 out of some 1700 traded companies were listed on the main market, another 46 on the side market. Those companies, many of them liquid blue chips, have learnt that information disclosure is essential to gain the confidence of portfolio investors. In part, they have already made use of increased confidence and financed part of their restructuring through public share offerings and the issuing of obligations.

However, the majority of firms don't reveal a strong interest in the disclosure of information. Many companies are simply too small to benefit from such a policy. The benefits of disclosure, like an enhanced interest of investors, are more than outweighed by the costs of permanently updating financial data. Besides, a lack of willingness to disclose information is a rather reliable indicator for the strong position of banks in enterprise finance. Banks cannot be interested in revealing relevant inside information to outside investors. Their comparative advantage in the field of corporate finance is privileged access to the information of client firms. Of course, due to the growing power of the bank-centred financial groups, banks have a grip on large parts of the enterprise sector. Their interest is to tie companies to themselves by providing them with loans rather than to lose them to outside investors on the capital market.[36]

Because of the unwillingness of most companies to reveal relevant information, trading has been focusing on a very small group of firms, which pursue a more open information policy and are under permanent screening by the Czech community of brokers and investment bankers. The result is that, in 1996, 200 out of 1,700 listed companies made up 94% of the overall transaction volume on the PSE (see Table 6.3). Concurrently, the prices of the illiquid issues were drastically sinking. In general, their market capitalization amounted to no more than a tiny fraction of their book value.

In March 1997, the PSE began to contract the market. Until the end of June, the 400 stocks with the lowest liquidity were to be withdrawn from the exchange.[37] The policy to gradually reduce the number of listed issues is also to be continued in the future. Its long-term goal is to increase market transparency and reserve the organized market exclusively for issuers willing to comply with all information requirements set by law and self-regulation.

Table 6.3: Volume structure of PSE transactions in 1996

Number of stock issues	% of turnover on central market	% of total PSE turnover	% of stock market capitalization
100	83.28	85.93	88.03
200	92.78	94.32	94.06
300	96.01	97.12	96.61
400	97.57	98.39	97.66
500	98.42	99.08	98.31
1,000	99.76	99.94	99.63
1,500	99.98	99.99	99.97

Source: PSE

Nevertheless, for a long time, the hesitant stance of both the state authorities and the exchange officials concerning the enforcement of disclosure rules has been an incentive for many companies to ignore the rules set by law and the PSE. Since Spring 1996, the PSE has seemed to follow a more consequent enforcement policy. In April, a holding company managed by PPF was excluded from the exchange. Previously, the investment company had got through the conversion of the former investment fund into a holding company at a general meeting. When PPF officials refused to reveal any background information about the purpose of the conversion, the holding company was temporarily suspended from PSE trading until the release of the required information.

Another important determinant of the quality of company information is the accountancy system. While Czech accountancy principles are constantly getting closer to international norms, there still are some differences to Western systems (especially to the very transparent US system). One difference is, for example, the accounting for future receivables as taxable profit which may give investors a distorted picture of a Czech company.[38] Another difference is the accounting for the value of leased property. Czech rules are based upon the principle of 'to whom the property belongs' rather than 'who is using it'. This means that leased property is not shown in the balance sheet of the leaseholder. Likewise, outside investors may understate liabilities as the balance sheet doesn't present payments still to be made for leased property.[39] Most Western audit firms generally confirm that the major problem with Czech accountancy principles is their application and the supervision of this application. Legislation is rather vague, thereby enabling interpretation of the rules to vary widely. Czech auditors often care more about good relationships with the management than about strict supervision.

6.3.1.2 Trade disclosure

While the segmentation of the market helped to increase company information, it has not improved trade disclosure. In fact, weak trade disclosure was a major reason why prices at the PSE were more arbitrary than informationally efficient. While most deals (according to brokers, more than 80% by value of all deals) took place in the form of block and direct trades off the exchange registered only at the Securities Centre, only the small remainder of the transactions was settled at the PSE. With the 'third wave' still under way, most deals will be made off the exchange in the next few years, too.[40]

In the beginning, neither the volumes, nor the prices of the deals handled behind the scenes had to be disclosed. Clearly, stock prices couldn't reflect weighted investors' expectations and were easy to manipulate. From January 1995, the Securities Centre has been publishing the volumes and average prices of the deals made off the exchange. In addition, nine major brokerage houses made an agreement to voluntarily report all over-the-counter deals.[41]

The expectation that the agreement would generate a vortex effect and attract other traders to join the group, didn't come true. The banks are especially more than reluctant to support the agreement and thus to increase market efficiency. Essential improvement of trade disclosure was decided only at a meeting of government representatives (including Klaus and Jezek) with capital market experts in December 1996. As a consequence, the Securities Centre started in February 1997 to publish daily all traded shares, including the volume and price per share.[42] In addition, the PSE now requires all its members to report all off-market deals within five minutes when they are made ('real time' reporting duty).[43] All measures considered, trade disclosure has effectively enhanced transparency and has brought the market closer to Western standards.

6.3.1.3 Block and direct sales

The small fraction of deals made in organized markets is split up between the PSE (ca. 80%) and the RMS (ca. 20%). The structure of these deals presents an additional obstacle to market efficiency. On the PSE, only some 7% of the total volume of business is settled in the central market (11.5% of share trading). Direct sales and block transactions make up some 93% of all deals (see Table 6.4). They are reported, but not instantaneously processed into market prices. Indeed, prices are based upon merely 7% of the overall transaction volume of the PSE. At the RMS, the proportion is less than 16%, that is the proportion of transactions made in the permanent auctions. This means that only a small part of the expectations of trading investors are weighted in share prices. Needless to say that this fact isn't very conducive to market efficiency.

Table 6.4: Structure of transaction volume of PSE and RMS in 1996

Market Segment	Type of security	Share of central market/ permanent auctions	Share of direct sales	Share of block trades	Transaction volume (in million CZK)
PSE:					
main market	shares	9.8%	77.6%	12.5%	148,446
	obligations	0.1%	98.3%	1.7%	112,676
side market	shares	8.4%	59.8%	31.7%	36,572
	obligations	0.0%	100.0%	0.0%	1,775
free market	shares	17.2%	51.3%	31.5%	63,174
	obligations	0.1%	99.1%	0.8%	28,476
entire PSE	shares	11.5%	68.3%	20.2%	248,192
	obligations	0.1%	98.5%	1.5%	142,927
	overall trade	7.3%	79.3%	13.3%	391,119
RMS:					
entire RMS	shares	9.8%	89.8%	0.4%	97,407
	obligations	0.2%	99.9%	0.0%	2,695
	overall trade	9.5%	90.1%	0.4%	100,102

Source: Own calculations based upon data presented in Hospodárské noviny from 31 December 1996, capital market supplement, p.VI (for PSE) and 7 January 1997, capital market supplement, p.VI (for RMS).

6.3.1.4 Multiple prices

The existence of two organized markets effects a further split of the already meagre liquidity. The problem will be aggravated after the start of the third market RTPS. While the existence of three separate markets may ensure low transaction costs of trading due to increased competition, the overall efficiency of the stock market may, nevertheless, decline and investors will have to cope with three different prices for each issue.

So far, the price differentials between PSE and RMS have turned out to be sometimes substantial. Critics put their existence back to the respective price algorithms providing for too sluggish adaptations of share prices. The problem has been ameliorated partially by the introduction of the continuous trading system KOBOS at the PSE in March 1996. However, only the most liquid issues are included in the continuous trading regime and thus subject to permanent price adjustments. Before the start of KOBOS, all issues had been traded exclusively in daily or half-weekly auctions (according to their liquidity) at prices that were fixed for each trading session.[44] One may reasonably assume that the transition to continuous trading has a positive effect on market liquidity (at least for the liquidity of some titles) as investors can trade non-stop and thereby benefit from price differentials emerging during one trading session.[45]

6.3.2 Transaction Costs of Securities Trading

One major institutional obstacle to an increase in market liquidity, raising the transaction costs of trading, are Czech accounting rules. They are the cause of strong disincentives to trade shares whenever the price of a stock falls below CZK 1000. In voucher privatization, all shares were arbitrarily given a book value of CZK 1000, independent of the evaluation made by millions of investors in the various bidding rounds. If IPFs now sell a share at a price below CZK 1000, it has to book a loss to the amount of the difference between book value and sales price. This loss arises even if the share's cash cost in privatization had been below CZK 1000. As the majority of issues have been trading below book value, funds are reluctant to sell shares through the organized markets. They simply would incur heavy losses weakening their ability to pay dividends. Funds commonly rather concentrate on 'swaps' of shareholdings to consolidate and adjust their portfolios. Those swaps are regularly done at prices exceeding book value thereby enhancing the theoretical profitability of the funds. The problem thus is that the Czech accountancy system channels liquidity from the organized markets to the off-market.[46]

Other impediments to boosting market liquidity can be found in the Czech tax system. For physical persons (households), dividend income as well as interest yield on corporate bonds are taxed at a rate of 25%. However, their tax on interest income from bank deposits is merely 15%. This discrimination creates a clear incentive to invest with the banks rather than in securities and, hence, a distortion in favour of the money market. In the corporate sector, the taxation rate of income from both securities and bank deposits is 25%.[47] Nevertheless, the taxation of capital gains may constitute a disincentive to invest in the capital market for Czech corporations. As there is nothing similar to the German *Schachtelprivileg* for large shareholdings (currently for stakes equal to or higher than 10% of a company's equity stock), dividends paid to Czech companies are effectively subject to double taxation, i.e. normal corporate tax at the level of the portfolio company or subsidiary and the withholding tax on profit distributed as dividends at the parent-company level. Such a high tax burden may deter large corporate shareholders from investment in securities or, even worse, induce them to reap their return on investment through methods like transfer pricing rather than through dividend payments. In the long run, this could reduce dividends and cause serious damage to minority shareholders. As argued by a Czech broker, a lower dividend taxation could therefore contribute not only to market liquidity, but also to the protection of the interests of minority shareholders.[48]

Finally, Czech VAT law (*Zákon o dani z pridané hodnoty*) provides some discrimination of industrial companies entering the capital market as portfolio investors. Section 28 of the VAT law presents a list of financial services exempted from value-added tax. It stipulates that securities deals have to be done by financial institutions on their own account to be exempted from the tax. The interpretation of 'financial institutions' is rather broad and covers, among others, entities whose revenue from financial services does not exceed 10% of the overall revenue of the calendar year or CZK 10 million. The law in combination with a decree of the Ministry of Finance (*metodický pokyn MF D-130*) determines that the exemption right may be removed from or at least curtailed for industrial companies not coming under the mentioned definition. Bonds have to be held until the expiry of the repayment period. Otherwise, the company must accept a higher tax burden. It is striking that the law explicitly refers to the revenue instead of the capital gain realized through market transactions. Consequently, the handicap remains even for companies selling their securities at a loss! Once again, we encounter a major incentive for companies to invest free cash flow with the banks rather than on the capital market.[49]

6.3.3 Reform Measures

The 1996 reform package also contained some measures to make the Czech stock market less secretive and to gain investors' confidence through increased transparency. Those measures affect joint stock corporations, investment companies and investment funds. First of all, the new Securities Act (§80 (1) SecAct) obliges issuers of publicly tradable securities to publish once a year, no later than three months after the end of a calendar year, a report providing information about their financial results and financial situation ('annual report'). Furthermore, no later than one month after the end of the first half of a calendar year, an issuer must publish a report on the company's financial results in the first half of such year. This report must contain data in the form of a profit-and-loss account and balance sheet for the period.

Secondly, Commercial Code stipulates in §183d (1) that an entity acquiring 10% or more of the voting rights attached to shares of a company whose shares are publicly traded must announce this to the company and the Securities Centre. If an entity, after having made such an announcement, subsequently increases or reduces its voting rights by 5% it must again notify the Securities Centre and the company concerned. These notifications have to be undertaken within three days of when the voting rights were acquired (§183d (2) CCode). If the acquiring entity does not comply with these provisions, it may not acquire further shares in its company, unless the required notification is dispatched to the Securities Centre.

(2) It shall also be impermissible to exercise voting rights while in default of the reporting duty and for a further year from the day the reporting duty was breached, unless the general meeting complies with the request of such shareholder(s) that the prohibition on their voting be cancelled.

This is clearly a very strong measure to be taken in the event that the regulations are breached. The problem, though, is legal enforcement. While owners disposing of between 10% and 50% of voting rights are obliged to announce the size of their holdings of themselves, stakes of 50% or more are automatically published by the Securities Centre. It is quite difficult, frequently impossible, to detect delays or omissions of mandatory disclosure. In practice, this is only possible if an owner disposes of - yet undisclosed - voting rights exceeding 10% at the general meeting. To avoid this problem, it would have been better to charge the Securities Centre with the automatic and immediate disclosure of stakes of 10% and more than to choose the threshold of 50%. Admittedly, even this solution isn't 'waterproof'. Nobody prevents companies from issuing 'physical' bearer shares (or converting existing de-materialized shares into physical ones) whose owners cannot be registered.

Concerning mandatory disclosure specifically directed at investment companies and investment funds, the commercial code obliges them to disclose in their reports any investment that is in value 3% or more of its (the fund's) portfolio.[50] Apart from that, the funds are obliged to comply with the same disclosure provisions as joint stock companies in general. Yet, as already mentioned, numerous investment funds had already evaded the new regulations by converting into the so-called 'industrial holding companies' and thus not falling under the stricter provisions for investment funds, but under those for joint stock corporations.

6.3.4 Summary

So far, low market transparency and high transaction costs of securities trading have been keeping the informational efficiency of the Czech capital market rather low. There are various reasons for that. Initially, companies used to publish their financial statements incomplete and with considerable delay. Both the PSE and the state authorities reacted and tightened disclosure regulation. As a consequence, many small firms were delisted at the exchange or had to change to the free market. While the overall situation may have slightly improved and listed companies are largely meeting their disclosure requirements, the biggest companies still know how to keep within the letter of the law without revealing too much. In many cases, even for large companies ownership structures are still uncertain. Omissions are difficult to detect and not always punished. That is not particularly a fault of legislation, which while far from perfect is now adequate. It rather mirrors the need for a shift in corporate and financial culture that will take many years to achieve. Other causes of a lack of market transparency are the still rather high share of block and direct trades off the exchange and multiple stock prices due to the existence of two organized exchanges splitting the already meagre market liquidity.

Besides, high transaction costs of securities trading are lowering market liquidity. Firstly, unconducive accounting rules are setting strong disincentives for funds to trade on organized markets (at least as long as share prices are lower than book values). Secondly, a discriminating taxation approach toward dividend yields, which are disadvantaged to interest yields from bank accounts, is preventing many investors from entering the stock market. The authorities still haven't taken any measures to reduce the transaction costs of securities trading.

6.4 TRANSACTION COSTS OF TAKEOVERS

6.4.1 Tender regulation

In the Czech Republic, two waves of voucher privatization initially produced rather dispersed ownership of former state-owned enterprises. Meanwhile, a concentration process is under way, frequently referred to by Czech media as 'third wave of privatization'. But while most companies will find long-term investors actively involved in their strategic decisions, a considerable part will be owned passively by dispersed investors. Therefore, market-based control might become a substantial component of the Czech system of corporate control. Moreover, takeovers are the driving force in the process of ownership concentration. However, the concentration process is in itself a transitional phenomenon. It follows, quite paradoxically, that the relevance of market-based control for the Czech economy will decline with a temporary increase in the number of takeovers of formerly widely-held companies. Nevertheless, Czech takeover regulation deserves a consideration due to the importance of takeovers as both a transitional phenomenon and a precondition for outsider control of widely-held companies (i.e. companies with a dispersed ownership structure) in an emerging system of corporate control.

Interestingly, the reform package of 1996 contains some regulation of public tender offers that reveals distinct parallels especially to the London City Code of Takeovers and Mergers. The most striking similarities are the equal and obligatory bid rules. Like British rules, Czech legislation forbids raiders from discriminating among stockholders by paying different bid premiums for shares. Legislation thereby aggravates the freerider problem of target shareholders as it precludes raiders from launching coercive *two-tier bids* which are an important component of the American market for corporate control.

Czech law allows partial bids but requires obligatory bids after the raider has acquired more than 50% of the target stock.[51] This provision indirectly restricts the scope for *partial offers* as the raider cannot freely determine the size of the stake he wants to buy. He may make a partial bid only for at most 50% of the target. Otherwise he must extend the offer and make a full compulsory bid at a pre-specified minimum price.[52] Especially in a transitional economy where raiders have only restricted access to finance, this may constitute a serious barrier in the market for corporate control and slow down the process of ownership concentration. While the provision on obligatory bids is to protect the interest of minority shareholders, it also considerably raises the transaction costs of takeovers.

The discretion of the raider in structuring the bid is extended by the opportunity to launch *conditional bids* where the buy offer is binding only if the number of shares tendered reaches a minimum number specified by the raider. Thereby, the latter may shift the risk of a failed offer to the target shareholders. However, on the whole the discretion of raiders to structure bids according to their preferences is at best limited. Of course, this means that, in general, takeovers are connected with considerable transaction costs that are reducing the efficiency of the market for corporate control.

6.4.2 Managerial entrenchment, cross ownership and circular voting

One of the deficiencies surrounding the problem of managerial entrenchment is the problem of self-dealing. What is meant by this is that a parent company or a *de facto* controlling company forces (induces) its investment company or fund subsidiary to buy shares of the parent or controlling shareholder by certain means. This action would distort the price of shares and hence contradict the declared aim of lawmakers to increase transparency and market efficiency. Moreover, by amassing their own company shares, managers can effectively entrench themselves against takeovers from outside investors. Self-dealing was intended to be prohibited with the new amendment through the inclusion of InvAct §24(6),(7) in the Investment Companies and Investment Funds Act:

(6) The investment company may not buy for the unit trust's portfolio any participation certificates of other unit trusts or shares of investment companies and investment funds, or shares of joint stock companies whose capital interest in this investment company exceeds 25 per cent. No investment company may have a capital interest in another investment company.

(7) The restrictions under subsection (6) apply *mutatis mutandis* to any investment fund.

The intention is clear: no investment entity should be unduly influenced or even forced to invest in companies simply by way of giving in to pressure by an entity exerting control on that investment entity. Yet as clearly phrased as these provisions seem at first glance, again there is a considerable loophole due to the ill-suited definition of the controlling shareholder.

Consider the following, not excessively complicated arrangement: A joint stock company wholly owns an investment company which in turn manages five investment funds. It is then possible for each of the investment funds to hold 9.9% of the stock of the joint stock company. This in effect means that the joint stock company through the investment company controls 49.5% of its own stock and can induce funds to vote accordingly at its general assembly. This set-up does not conflict with §24 (6),(7) InvAct although 'Part Six' of the law, of which §24 is a part, is titled 'Protection of shareholders and participation certificate holders'.

The law does not recognize the fact that there is a possibility for an entity X to exert control over entity Y through an investment company and the investment funds managed by that investment company. Ultimately, if funds of an investment company are able to deny any allegations of contractually fixed 'concerted conduct' (§66b CCode) then funds could in aggregation acquire even beyond 50% of their investment company's parent company without being legally obliged to buy out the remaining shareholders. The protection of minority shareholders would and actually does turn out to be a 'farce'[53], while the management of the parent company is perfectly entrenched.

The problem is even more evident in the case of cross-ownership between non-bank companies, where no restrictions concerning the percentage of interest apply (except for disclosure and mandatory bids). Cross-ownership can be used for so-called circular voting: a parent controlling a subsidiary also controls the subsidiary's stock in its parent company. Circular voting of a parent's stock is allowed to an unlimited extent, whereas limitations for example in US laws are given. The problem with circular voting is that it may be conceived as a potential defence tactic against (hostile) takeovers and thus the parent's managers can entrench themselves with their own company's resources. Most US jurisdictions are therefore barring majority-owned subsidiaries from voting parents' stock. But this is a similarly narrow provision as the Czech definition of 'controlling person'. A party can easily take majority-control of a corporation even with considerably less than 50% of the voting rights. Black et al. (1994) propose to set the threshold at a 30% interest of a parent in a subsidiary, triggering prohibition to vote the parent's stock. They argue that a limit to circular voting is desirable since it increases costs for potential control transactions. Yet cross-ownership should not be barred completely, as the authors see some advantage in possible co-operative schemes.[54]

In the Czech Republic, the case of Ceská Zbrojovka Strakonice (CZS) well illustrates the entrenchment problem. The company, one of the country's leading supplier firms for the car industry, has been governing two subsidiaries through majority stakes of 70% to 80%. In Summer 1996, the general meeting of widely-held CZS decided to increase considerably the firm's equity stock. The new issue has been completely absorbed by the two subsidiaries, which now hold some 17% and 32% respectively in the mother company.[55] Their joint holding of nearly 49% is just large enough to safely control the mother, thereby avoiding the triggering of a mandatory bid. With another 42% of the CZS stock being in the hands of some 60,000 individual investors, company management is effectively entrenched against all external governance influences and, above all, hostile takeover bids. A further damaging effect of the control transaction has been revealed by the fact that both subsidiaries had to finance their investments predominantly through loans provided by the mother holding.[56] In the view of CZS's former general director, Jirí Rasek, this seriously threatens their restructuring as both were already in a bad financial condition before the deal and must now bear an additional financial burden in the form of the debt capital. CZS's current spokesman defends the manoeuvre, arguing that it was the only feasible measure to ensure the continuity and 'compactness' of the engineering company: 'The swift development and going concern of the firm couldn't be guaranteed by scattered ownership, when 62% of equity was in the hands of 60,000 individuals ... and 10% to 15% of the shares were sufficient to obtain a voting majority at the general meeting. You can make the best and quickest decision on [the firm] if you have some influence on it or if you own it.'[57]

The problem in Czech legislation is that cross-ownership is not limited. As argued above, transitional economies are very dynamic and anything but stable concerning ownership structures and the allocation of know-how. If incestuous cross-ownership is tolerated by law-makers on a large scale, in effect making takeovers artificially costly, then not only are minority shareholders bound to suffer disadvantages but the whole of the economy.

6.4.3 Summary

The transaction costs of takeovers are enhanced by bid regulation as well as by obvious legal loopholes allowing the management (or minority shareholders) of a company effectively to entrench themselves against outside investors. Mandatory bids lowering the scope for partial bids and the non-admittance of coercive two-tier bids significantly reduce the discretion of the raider to structure a takeover bid in harmony with his own financial and risk preferences. Too restrictive regulation hence increases the costs of takeovers.

More serious, legal gaps open a latitude of possibilities to the management of banks and industrial enterprises to buy and control their own shares through affiliated funds or subsidiaries so as to entrench themselves against hostile bidders or raiders from outside. We must assume that a considerable part of Czech companies make use of the scope offered to them by imperfect laws and build protection walls against foreign and domestic direct investors. If the management controls a sufficiently high proportion of their own company shares, transaction costs of takeovers might easily become prohibitive. Of course, managerial entrenchment not only bars the inflow of outside expertise and finance into companies which are badly in need of restructuring. Likewise, it may perfectly 'protect' the management of a badly run company from the disciplining pressure of the market for corporate control. Therefore, it will slow down the pace of restructuring.

An example illustrating managerial entrenchment is the case of IPB presented in section 5.2.2. We remember, the management of the bank is effectively entrenched as it commands at least 40% of IPB's equity, either directly through holdings of the bank's group companies (like the big IPF family) or indirectly through holdings of 'friendly' firms. The case indicates the extent and danger of circular voting in the Czech economy. Self dealing and friendly relationships (old boys networks) are the keys to successful entrenchment. Once again, adequate laws and the inclusion of 'legal intent' into the deliberations of the courts would be the keys to break up the chains of mutual entrenchment in Czech enterprises.

NOTES

1. See Reflex, No. 46, 1995, p. 16.
2. See Hospodárské noviny, 27 July 1995, stock market supplement, p. IV.
3. Quotation from Ekonom, No. 40, 1995, p. 73. Indeed, there are few examples of successful minority shareholder resistance against unethical or unlawful actions of controlling owners. One example is the suit of the Swiss Discover Europe (DE) investment fund against the 'private' investment company PPF. On 27 March 1996, PPF had announced the convention of an extraordinary general meeting of the electrical engineering firm Elektromontázní závody (EZ) for the next day. The meeting took place on 28 March and decided a capital increase to strengthen PPF's equity interest in the company. The DE management, disposing of a minority stake in EZ, learned about PPF's action only after the meeting. It carried on a law suit, thereby convincing PPF to rescind the capital increase.
4. PIAS and Motoinvest clearly converted their funds to 'consolidate' the ownership structure of their financial groups and to entrench their fund managers. PIAS transformed only one fund, Bankovní IF. Today, the major part of Bankovní's portfolio consists of equity stakes in some other PIAS funds and in IPB. Motoinvest converted several funds legalizing thereby their sizeable stakes in other funds of the group as well as in Agrobanka. Other bank-sponsored funds so far have displayed a more conservative attitude towards the transformations, expressing typically that conversions would be inevitably connected with a loss of image and reputation.
5. An American lawyer reported in an interview carried out for this study that the conversions were mainly engineered by Czech law firms. Western law firms would have brought 'too much baggage', meaning that they would have asked whether this and that was 'fair and appropriate'. The quotation indicates that, at least in the view of Western law practitioners, 'Western' and Czech lawyers may have frequently a different understanding of ethical norms and fiduciary duties.
6. Tomas Jezek in an Interview with Ekonom, 31 January 1996, p. 41.
7. Some analysts estimate the amount of foreign portfolio investments withdrawn from the country in 1996 to as much as $ 500 million. Several large international funds like Flemings and Regent Kingpin are shifting their investment focus away from the Czech Republic. So did Swiss-based Discover Europe after the incurring of heavy losses when the market index declined dramatically between April and November 1996. Insiders trace the tumbling of the market back to the decision of many IPFs to escape market supervision and convert into more loosely regulated holdings. The fact is that Discover Europe has cut down the Czech portion of its $ 50 million fund from 60% in December 1995 to about 18% one year later, channelling most of the withdrawn funds to the Polish capital market. See Kaapor (1996/97, p. 55).
8. One major objective of the amendment was to relax the investment constraints of investment companies and investment funds so as to enable them to exert corporate governance more effectively. For changes in the regulation of the IPFs, see section 3.1.2.
9. See Hospodárské noviny, 21 March 1996, p. II.
10. Between July and December 1996, some 30 mandatory bids have been published on grounds of acquisitions of majority interests. Another five offers have been made after the abolition of public tradeability (Hospodárské noviny, 27 December 1996, capital market supplement, p. I). Besides, the amended Commercial Code requires a three-fourths majority of all voting stock participating in the general meeting to go private or to change the property rights linked to a certain class of shares. See also Dedic and Kopác (1996, p. 22 f.).
11. According to the head of the capital market supervisory department of the Ministry of Finance, Jan Veverka, the attribute 'public' refers only to the organized markets, that is at present the

PSE and the RMS. The minimum price is the weighted average price of an issue for the stipulated six-months trading period. The prices and trade volumes realized through direct trade at the Securities Centre are not included in the formula.

12. The mandatory bid after a conversion also concerns holdings which decided the conversion still before 1 July 1996, i.e. before the amendment took effect, but failed to register it before this date. According to the Ministry of Finance, several holdings missing the deadline convened extraordinary meetings to re-transform into investment funds as they couldn't pay off their shareholders. See Hospodárské noviny, 14 August 1996, capital market supplement, p. I.

13. As already mentioned, converted holdings are usually traded at high discounts. A compensation at market prices could give rise to perverse incentives of controlling owners or the fund managers themselves. The *ex ante* announcement of a voting on a transformation of the fund may be sufficient to send down the fund's market price considerably even before the general meeting. The actors in control of the fund's assets might try to use a transformation to decrease the price and hence cheaply enlarge their equity stake in the fund.

14. See Pokorný (1996), 'Novela obchodního zákoníku minoritním akcionárum prílis neslouzí', (The amendment of the commercial code doesn't help minority shareholders very much), Hospodárské Noviny, 23 August 1996, capital market supplement, p. VI.

15. Interview with Richard Sterling Surrey.

16. See Business Central Europe, June 1995, p. 21.

17. CCode §66b (b)

18. See Hospodárské noviny, 16 August 1996, capital market supplement, p. I.

19. See Hospodárské noviny, 19 August 1996, p. 1.

20. Spokesman Jan Rezek on the voting behaviour of the investment funds managed by IPB's investment Company: 'It's up to them how they vote'. Hospodárské noviny, 16 August 1996, capital market supplement, p. I.

21. In an interview carried out by the author in February 1996 (still before the amendment of the Commercial Code), a PIAS manager confirmed that the IPB group follows a common approach to the control of portfolio companies. The strategic decisions are made on a group level, including the bank itself. The fund managers then frequently only execute the common strategy and compose individual portfolios in accordance with given investment guidelines. With respect to the 'dozens of strategic enterprises' in the group portfolio, their investment decisions are undoubtedly not autonomous. This investment and governance approach is, however, typical for other financial groups, too (e.g. for Harvard, Motoinvest and the group of the Czech savings bank).

22. This is one important aspect of the 'self-enforcing model of corporate law' discussed by Black et al. (1994).

23. Expandia was originally the investment arm of the chemicals giant Chemapol. The company, running five funds, turned out one of the most successful collectors of voucher points in the second wave. In 1995, Expandia was taken over by the privately-held limited company Portum. The new Expandia managers were, at the same time, also the owners of the investment company.

24. A part of Expandia's stake comes from loans, promised to voucher holders during the second wave. Each individual who gave their voucher points to Expandia, was granted a cash loan backed by the voucher book. Many of the unit holders who received a loan decided to keep the money and let Expandia hold on to the units. As a consequence, the investment company already owned some 20% to 30% of both unit trusts prior to April 1996.

25. This is the US courts' interpretation of §10b of the 1934 Securities Exchange Act and the SEC's Rule 10b-5.

26. See Prague Business Journal, 28 October – 3 November, 1996, p. 1.

27. One member of the Ministry's supervisory department reports, for instance, that the control of the more than 400 funds is executed by only 14 employees. See Marie Jezková, member of the capital market supervision, in an interview in Ekonom, No. 6, 1997, p. 63.

28. See Hospodárské noviny, 22 July 1996, capital market supplement, p. I.

29. The *laissez-faire* attitude of the ministry is well reflected by a statement on minority shareholder rights made by former deputy minister Václav Rudlovcák: 'Our concern was not the capital market, but privatization. Talking about the robbing of minority shareholders, one

should realize that, if somebody gave his voucher points to a fund, this is a signal that he doesn't want to look after his investment. Robbing isn't a problem of the capital market, but of the courts and the police.' (Hospodárské noviny, 13 December 1996, stock market supplement, p. I). The statement well documents that, still months after the amendment has taken effect, a high-rank ministry official still rejects any responsibility of the supervisory department for the enforcement of minority shareholder rights.

30. Self-regulatory bodies with far-reaching sanctionary and supervisory competences are no peculiarities of the West. In this respect, other transitional countries like Poland, Hungary and also Bulgaria have already established independent SECs and thus outstripped the Czech Republic.

31. See Hospodárské noviny, 15 January 1997, capital market supplement, p. I.

32. Yet, the first intervention of this kind wasn't initiated by the ministry itself, but by the London-based Czech Value Fund (CVF) which had noticed unexplained losses in the balance sheets of the Czech Trend IF. CVF quickly and secretly lifted its holding from 2% up to some 40%, thereby wresting control of the fund. At an extraordinary general meeting, Trend's local managers were replaced by new ones. Finally, CVF requested the ministry for forced administration and an examination of the case.

33. AGB II bought the shares of Kreditní in end-1995. The supervisory department of the Ministry of Finance supposes the fund managers to have had detailed knowledge about the critical financial situation of the bank. According to the department, they should have known that the shares had virtually no value and thus consciously violated the interests of the fund's shareholders. Apparently the transaction was part of a deal between Motoinvest and the IPB group. In late 1995, both groups had been fighting for the control of Agrobanka. When IPB recognized that it wouldn't win the battle for control, it offered Motoinvest its complete holding in the bank, provided Motoinvest would buy, in addition, several other equity blocks IPB wanted to get rid of - among them the stake in Kreditní. Motoinvest agreed in order to ensure control of Agrobanka. The major proportion of the offered Kreditní stock was acquired by the funds AGB I and II. Meanwhile, AGB I is out of the Ministry's reach since it already transformed itself into a holding company in early 1996. Amazingly, Motoinvest spokesman J. Chudomel openly admitted that the Motoinvest management knew about the low quality of Kreditní's shares already at the time of the deal. His justification appears somewhat curious: 'From the point of view of the fund [AGB II], it is difficult to make an assessment of individual deals. Some cause losses, others are profitable.' (Quotation from Hospodárské noviny, 16 August 1996, p. 1).

34. Investment funds and unit trusts entering the main market must have a minimum of CZK 500 million registered capital.

35. Investment funds and unit trusts entering the side market must have a minimum of CZK 250 million registered capital.

36. In the end, firms tend to reveal information if they are dependent on or interested in doing so by themselves. Most American firms published their relevant financial data even before the emergence of a self-regulating body like the SEC as banks were too weak to provide them with enough capital (and the price of debt finance was relatively high respectively). Of course, the latter is due to regulation.

37. The PSE has formulated three basic exclusion criteria. Firstly, the trade volume of the given company for the past twelve months on the central market must be below CZK 200,000. This is equal to some $ 7,000. The rule hence targets issues which have been virtually ignored by investors. Secondly, the firm's market capitalization must not exceed CZK 5 million. Such companies can be reasonably assumed to be too small to really benefit from a listing at the stock exchange. Finally, the company mustn't have been traded on more than five days on the central market for the past twelve months. An issue will be de-listed if it meets either criteria one and two, or one and three. The 1996 overall transaction volume of the 400 stocks going to be excluded until June 1997 has been as little as CZK 29 million, i.e. CZK 72,500 per issue. This equals 0.1% of all deals made on the central market in the same year. See Hospodárské noviny, 28 January 1997, capital market supplement, p. I.

38. See Lubomír Sedlák: 'Czech accountancy practices still giving 'fuzzy' picture to investors', Prague Post, 24 January – 30 January 1996, p. 6.

39. There are, however, still wide differences in accounting principles even among Western economies like Germany and the US For instance, in contrast to the US principles, German accountancy rules make the inclusion of leased property in the balance sheet of the leaseholder dependent upon the design of the leasing contract. As a consequence of systemic differences, an American audit, carried out in 1995, certified German carmaker Mercedes Benz to be operating at a loss while, according to German accounting standards, it was profitable.

40. The proportion of deals made on the central market has reportedly been declining from the opening of the exchange. This indicates that the process of the 'third wave', the consolidation of companies' ownership structures, is far from being completed.

41. The agreement is modelled on the US National Association of Securities Dealers (NASD) rules, placing brokers under the obligation to report all traded shares, including their volumes and prices. See Borish and Noel (1996, p. 33).

42. In the run-up to the amendment of capital market regulation, several stock traders had even required legislatory changes to forbid all off-exchange trades. See e.g. Gary Bird in Prague Post, 5 July - 11 July 1995, p. 6: 'Low liquidity plagues even well-capitalized firms'.

43. Indeed, the belated reaction of the PSE is somewhat paradoxical. More than 95% of all off-exchange transactions are effected by dealers who are, for the major part, registered at the PSE. Since this is common knowledge, it is amazing that the exchange didn't enforce stricter trade disclosure much earlier.

44. Since the implementation of KOBOS, the PSE has been split up into three trading groups. The most liquid issues belong to the first group and are traded continuously in KOBOS. All other issues from the main and side markets and selected liquid issues from the free market are included in the second group which is traded daily at prices fixed once a day. The third group comprises the vast majority of companies and is traded only twice a week. Several weeks after the start of KOBOS, the three groups' shares of overall trading were fluctuating constantly at 26% (first group) to 72% (second group) to 2% (third group). See Hospodárské noviny, 29 April 1996, capital market supplement, p. I.

45. See also Václav Skolout, deputy general secretary of the PSE, in an interview in Ekonom, No. 11, 1996, pp. 11f.

46. Cook (1995a, p. 27) puts market illiquidity down to the funds' lacking buying power. The IPFs had spent heavily on advertising campaigns to attract voucher points in the mass privatization programme (some CZK 500 million according to CS First Boston in Prague). Quite logically, many of them didn't dispose of liquid funds to start portfolio trading immediately. However, the problem is linked more to the period until end-1995. Since then, several funds reportedly have put considerable pressure on portfolio companies to distribute dividends as soon as possible - no matter whether the financial and economic situation of the companies justifies such a policy or not. Meanwhile, most funds have rearranged their portfolios and added liquid stocks and bonds to it. Thereby, they have substantially increased their buying power.

47. Before 1994, interest income from bank deposits of both physical and legal persons had been subject to an identical tax rate of 15%.

48. Oldrich Neprac, director of EB Brokers, in Hospodárské noviny, 21 June 1996, capital market supplement, p. VI: 'Stát nechce mít tuzemské úspory na kapitalovém trhu' (The State Doesn't Want Domestic Savings on the Capital Market). In addition, double taxation considerably slows down the evolution of corporate groups and increases the costs of restructuring as it prevents enterprises from investing free cash flow with other companies (i.e. it lowers the marginal utility of such an investment as compared to other projects which might be relatively less profitable without double taxation of dividends).

49. According to an announcement of the Ministry of Finance, a withdrawal of the decree and thus of the discrimination of non-financial companies is not to be expected before 1998. While the withdrawal is far from certain, in the meantime it constitutes a serious barrier for the development of the young capital market.

50. §25 (3)(a) InvAct.

51. British regulation imposes on offerers an obligation to buy out the target's remaining stockholders after having obtained 30% of the target stock.

52. The price per share then is determined as at least the target stock's weighted average price on public markets in the six months prior to the day when the raider's stake went beyond 50%. Provided the raider offered a bid premium over the market price in the voluntary bid, the minimum price of the compulsory bid may then be below that of the voluntary bid.

53. An expression repeatedly encountered in interviews with fund managers. Flemings, managing a fund for the Czech and Slovak Republic, has radically restructured its portfolio. At the beginning of 1995 Flemings' portfolio consisted mainly of minority stakes. After the 'third wave' and the emergence of aggressive raiders such as Motoinvest or PPF, it decided to sell its stakes in companies where dubious funds and holding companies had stakes and built up considerably their stakes in the most promising firms. Considering the new amendment a 'farce', this was the only option to safeguard funds without having to rely on a law full of loopholes.

54. Black et al. (1994) also point to the practice of 'reverse triangular mergers, where a parent company acquires a target by merging a subsidiary into the target. The consideration for the acquisition is parent stock held by the subsidiary, which is exchanged for the stock of the target company. The advantage of the transaction is that it does not disturb the corporate identity or contractual relationships of the target'; p. 285, fn. 27.

55. Hospodárské noviny, 17 September 1996, p. 6.

56. The management of CZS had originally released an announcement that the subsidiaries would finance the transaction exclusively from their own funds. However, it turned out that they couldn't. The loans are secured by real estate assets and stocks of the subsidiaries.

57. Hospodárské noviny, 19 September 1996, fair supplement, p. 6.

Conclusion

From a technical and political viewpoint, the Czech voucher-based approach to privatization turned out most successful. The authorities effectively tied their hands to care for smooth ownership transfer by setting up a tight timetable and creating huge demand of an involved and therefore interested public for the 'good' privatization. Considering the combination of vouchers and other methods of ownership transfer in numerous enterprises, voucher privatization was the key accelerator of large-scale privatization. The Czech experience demonstrates that voucher privatization well fits a political environment with (as yet) weak interest groups and high public support of reforms. The authorities used this political window of opportunity to implement a privatization programme with a clear focus on speed, public commitment (in spite of low purchase power) and fairness.

The Czech approach to privatization is institutionally open, i.e. it creates a leeway for spontaneous developments. The voucher scheme didn't predetermine the ownership and governance structures of individual companies. It did, however, create a market for corporate control and trigger the process of spontaneous concentration of ownership, thereby helping companies to attract appropriate investors and, in the long-term, to get an efficient governance structure. It is thus part of the Czech overall approach to let the market forces spontaneously select the control system that best fits the economic and social setting of the country. The result of this evolutionary approach is a spontaneous mix of mechanisms of insider as well as outsider control. The latter is mirrored by the emergence of IPFs which are in part behaving like portfolio investors and largely contributing to the development of the nascent Czech capital market. However, a significant number of the funds are executing active corporate control.

Many of the most active funds are affiliated to bank-dominated financial groups. Two facts are decisive for the active involvement of the banks in corporate control. Firstly, the regulation of the bank's asset portfolios has been very loose. From the beginning, banks have been allowed to acquire direct equity stakes in the enterprise sector and to raise their voice in the boardrooms more indirectly through IPFs established and owned by the banks. Besides, law does not prevent directors and employees of the banks from getting involved in the management of the funds. Banks therefore can and largely do disregard firewalls between themselves and their investment companies. Of course, this allows banks and their funds to pool information to realize economies of scale and scope in the execution of corporate control. Moreover, personal ties considerably tighten the banks' grip of funds and portfolio companies. The regulatory framework hence supports universal banking and debt/equity finance.

Secondly, it turned out that banks are in fact interested in active corporate governance. In the course of voucher privatization, they set up managerial funds and started building up long-term equity ties with the enterprise sector. At the same time they pooled internal and external branch experts and top managers with the assignment to monitor and control the portfolio companies of the bank groups. With respect of both the regulatory environment and the 'governance preferences' of the banks, there are many parallels with the German financial system. Like Czech regulation, German law allows banks to establish strong equity links to the enterprise sector. Banks, in turn, have a strong interest in getting actively involved in the affairs of debtor firms and therefore accumulate substantial direct shareholdings and additionally increase their governance power by proxy voting. On the other hand, there are distinct differences between the Czech and the Anglo-Saxon banking systems. In the US, the 1933 Glass-Steagall Act (separation of commercial from investment banking) and the 1956 Bank Holding Company Act (restricting bank holding companies to no more than 5% of the voting stock of non-banks) have been effectively keeping banks from equity control. Historically, American banks had been deeply involved in the affairs of many corporations and had played an important role as active guardians of the enterprise sector. In the UK, portfolio regulation of banks is more liberal, but banks have shown no interest in becoming active guardians of the enterprise sector. At least in equity control, they are rather passive.

The Czech bank-centred groups have made substantial efforts to draw up and implement effective control structures in their portfolio companies. They are well-represented in the boardrooms and have sometimes even set up additional monitoring committees to strengthen equity control. Furthermore, they have participated in drafting restructuring plans, thereby contributing primarily financial and marketing expertise. In an economy suffering from a serious lack of managerial expertise and governance competence, they did an important job in bundling scarce expertise in their pools of internal and external governance experts. They ensured the allocation of that expertise to the boards of their portfolio companies. The banks frequently support the injection of external finance (loans, capital increases) to their enterprises. Superior and cheaper access to finance of companies controlled by bank-sponsored funds points to at least fairly efficient debt/equity finance. Banks are apparently drawing from economies of scope and scale in the execution of corporate control. Moreover, they let the enterprises participate in gains coming from reduced agency costs. Beyond financial restructuring, the bank-centred groups have also been carrying through deep restructuring, including the reengineering of production processes and a sometimes dramatic downsizing of the workforce. Of course, given the high number of portfolio companies, in most firms the bank funds rely heavily upon the loyalty and capability of the senior management. The latter is bearing the main responsibility for the turn-around of the firm. As a consequence, management exchanges have become an important means of IPF-control.

Given the portfolio restrictions of the funds as well as a natural preference to effectively diversify portfolio risks even in the case of strategic holdings, one may observe the emergence of implicit, yet obvious rules of cooperation between the IPFs. A common long-term interest in many portfolio firms has effectively promoted the mutual alignment of the interests of the bank-sponsored funds. Bank groups therefore show a high inclination for cooperation. Besides, the emergence of delegated monitoring arrangements between them has been increasingly adding to the efficacy of corporate control. Undoubtedly, along with direct foreign and domestic investors, the bank-sponsored funds are major executors of insider control in Czech enterprises.

Ownership allocation through mass privatization is a political rather than a purely market-based process. However, the ownership structures produced by the Czech voucher scheme were merely temporary. Indeed, voucher privatization was conditional for the quick emergence of a vivid market for corporate control. Considering the underdeveloped work ethic of many managers under conditions of transition, the market for corporate control has largely contributed to disciplining the management of companies with still quite unstable or dispersed ownership structures. Besides, the market for corporate control has somewhat mitigated the serious lack of both managerial and guardian competence, which is facing every transitional economy. The 'openness' of ownership structures has enhanced the chance to attract capable owners.

After voucher privatization and the distribution of shares to their new owners, heavy trading began among IPFs and banks. In the course of the 'third wave of privatization', the financial groups rearranged and consolidated their share portfolios. This led to an economy-wide concentration of ownership and a strengthening of the groups' governance power in strategic enterprises. During this period of ownership consolidation (which isn't yet finished) the Czech system of corporate control can be described appropriately as a hybrid of insider and outsider control. However, the significance of outsider control has been continuously declining. For the market of corporate control is eliminating itself: after lively takeover activities and considerable headway with the consolidation of ownership, the number of widely-held companies has been decreasing very quickly. More and more companies are in hands of strategic investors. The general tendency towards insider control is *inter alia* well documented by the increasing popularity of the dual board system in companies which have found long-term investors who gave them a clear strategic orientation. Nevertheless, there are and probably will be also in the future a number of corporations with dispersed ownership structures which are subject to outsider control.

While insider control is becoming the dominant mode of corporate control in Czech companies, the significance of the bank-centred financial groups as guardians of the enterprise sector is decreasing. This is for two reasons. Firstly, from an evolutionary view, the function of IPFs is *per se* a temporary one. With the entry of a growing number of managerially experienced and financially sound foreign direct investors in Czech companies and the ongoing accumulation of entrepreneurial know-how among domestic investors, the formerly basic function of the funds to bundle and allocate scarce resources like expertise and finance is becoming gradually redundant. As a result, the funds are leaving a considerable part of their portfolio companies and selling them to other classes of investors. This clearly is an evolutionary process. The second reason for the retreat of the financial groups from the boardrooms of many corporations is an active intervention of the government aiming to accelerate the evolutionary process outlined above. Recently, the authorities introduced a law restricting fund holdings in portfolio companies to no more than 11% of firm equity. The law's intention is to lower the governance power of the bank groups; corporate control should be executed rather by non-bank investors in the future. As a consequence, the large bank-sponsored funds have to sell a substantial part of their assets. This won't cause only a rise in agency and coordination costs due to reduced economies of scope and scale of the bank groups. It is highly questionable whether there are enough qualified investors to contribute the needed finance and expertise to the companies and thereby to replace the bank-sponsored IPFs. If not (and that seems rather probable), the new regulation will cause a lack of corporate control in many companies and serious delays in the restructuring process. It must be stressed, however, that the new law cannot push the bank groups completely out of corporate control. As most banks dispose of large funds families and other investment entities, they may frequently keep their strategic holdings by a mere redistribution of shareholdings between the portfolios of their subsidiaries.

While the evolutionary openness with respect to ownership and governance structures was a main strength of the voucher scheme, the Czech approach to privatization and corporate control was also fraught with at least four cardinal mistakes. One was the exclusion of a pool of 'strategic enterprises', containing many of the biggest and most powerful enterprises of the country. The state, as major owner, was proceeding in a very reactive way in those companies and was not able to actively contribute to the drafting of frequently badly needed restructuring plans, thereby effectively leaving the companies in a control vacuum. Moreover, in the aftermath of voucher privatization when the J-curve of transformation put the brakes on economic growth, political support of reform measures inevitably declined and the design of each single privatization project for a strategic enterprise became the object of public dispute. In the end, wafer-thin political majorities frequently undermined the government's ability to successfully carry through the privatization of large enterprises, especially if they were to be privatized into the hands of foreign strategic investors. As a result, the privatization of strategic enterprises has been largely stalled after the resignation of the *Klaus* government in November 1997. An important lesson to draw from the Czech experience is therefore to use a political window of opportunity even more than the Czechs. Only a speedy and comprehensive implementation of large-scale privatization permits the focusing of political energy and public debate on problems like the design and enforcement of regulation, supervisory bodies and the court system.

The second major mistake of large-scale privatization was the discrimination against foreign direct investors. Foreign investors with an interest in the acquisition of SOEs were obliged to charge a chartered accountant with the evaluation of company assets. The value guessed after an audit was then the basis for further negotiations with the authorities while domestic investors were allowed to draft privatization projects based upon book values. As the asset values estimated by independent accountants mostly exceeded the - in part quite arbitrary - book values which were frequently only taken from the old balance sheets, this represented a considerable edge for domestic investors. Later on, it turned out that many domestic investors couldn't provide companies with the finance, expertise and hard-nosed western management practices needed to carry out successful restructuring.

The third crucial deficiency was the postponement of banking privatization. In absence of capable and hard-nosed strategic investors, banks were not really given the incentive to implement an efficiency-oriented policy. Their payoff function was dominated by the political preferences of the government and personal goals of the senior management. The latter included the cultivation of 'old boys networks' and the allocation of loans according to personal likes and dislikes. In an environment allowing banks to play a central role in the execution of corporate control, delays in bank privatization effected inefficiencies in corporate control as well as misallocation of scarce capital. The Czech experience shows that the entry of foreign direct investors into the banking sector is inevitable to quickly channel both capital and expertise to the banks, to finally wipe out the bail-out expectations of bank managers and to accelerate the process of behavioural adaptation, including the adoption of certain ethical norms and the destruction of still existing personal networks. Only after the complete withering away of the state from equity control of banks, can one expect banks to pursue a profit-maximizing policy rather than adhere to political (and managerial) goals.

The fourth mistake involves inconsistencies between quick privatization and the sequencing of other institutional measures. In fact, the regulation and supervision of banks and capital markets has only been gradually approaching to western standards. There are still serious gaps in the legal framework, but even more in its enforcement. Too much reliance upon free market forces caused a lack of effective regulation and of political commitment to fight abuse of property rights. The regulation of banks and capital markets has been implemented incomplete and too late; the enforcement of rules was weak due to toothless instruments and insufficient training of the supervisory bodies. For a long time, political decisionmakers didn't realize the meaning of laws in guarding the economy against the consequences of unethical and unfair behaviour of managers and controlling shareholders. This largely reduced the efficacy of corporate control and enabled many investors to get rich at the expense of minority shareholders, lenders or – in the case of banks – small depositors. For instance, the delayed implementation of a bankruptcy law has seriously affected debtholders who could exert virtually no pressure on company managers and owners in order to harden the budget constraint of the debtor.

The Czech experience teaches us that ownership change and institutional change must be accomplished simultaneously to make private property efficient. Privatization must be accompanied not only by adequate changes of the laws, but likewise by their practical application. While the institutional environment should be sufficiently permissive to produce innovative institutional arrangements (like the spontaneous emergence of IPFs and their involvement in privatization and corporate control) and support a selection among them, the enforcement of existing regulation is a precondition to bar foreseeable inefficient and costly outcomes of economic activity. Therefore, it is of utmost importance to invest heavily, at a very early stage in transition, in core institutions with the task to enforce regulation. This concerns the courts as well as the supervisory bodies e.g. of the capital market and the banking industry. The quality of the system of corporate control largely depends upon the expertise (training), instruments and political independence of those institutions.

References

Aghion, Philippe and Patrick Bolton (1989), 'The Financial Structure of the Firm and the Problem of Control', *European Economic Review* 33, pp. 286-293.

Allen, Franklin (1993), 'Stock Markets and Resource Allocation', in: Colin Mayer and Xavier Vives (eds.), *Capital Markets and Financial Intermediation*, Cambridge, UK: Cambridge University Press, pp. 81-108.

Allen, Franklin and Douglas Gale (1995), 'A Welfare Comparison of Intermediaries and Financial Markets in Germany and the US', *European Economic Review* 39, pp. 179-209.

Aoki Masahiko (1995), 'Controlling Insider Control: Issues of Corporate Governance in Transition Economies', in: Masahiko Aoki and Hyung-Ki Kim (eds.), *Corporate Governance in Transitional Economies, Insider Control and the Role of Banks*, Washington: Economic Development Institute of the World Bank, pp. 3-30.

Arrow, Kenneth J. (1962), 'Economic Welfare and the Allocation of Resources for Invention', reprinted in: D.M. Lamberton (ed.) (1971), *Economics of Information and Knowledge*, Harmondsworth, pp. 141-160.

Arrow, Kenneth J. (1986), 'Agency and the Market', in: K.J. Arrow and M.D. Intriligator (eds.), *Handbook of Mathematical Economics*, Vol.3, North-Holland: Elsevier Science Publishers, pp. 1183-1195.

Baer, Herbert and Cheryl Gray (1995), *Debt as a Control Device in Transitional Economies: the Experiences of Hungary and Poland*, Policy Research Working Paper 1480, The World Bank, Washington DC.

Baumol, William J. (1959), *Business Behaviour, Value and Growth*, New York: Macmillan.

Baums, Theodor and Philipp von Randow (1995), Shareholder Voting and Corporate Governance: The German Experience and a New Approach, in: Masahiko Aoki and Hyung-Ki Kim (eds.), *Corporate Governance in Transitional Economies, Insider Control and the Role of Banks*, Washington: Economic Development Institute of the World Bank, pp. 435-458.

Bergström, Clas, Peter Högfeld, Jonathan Macey and Per Samuelson (1995), *The Regulation of Corporate Acquisitions: A Law and Economic Analysis of European Proposals for Reform*, International Center for Policy Research Working Paper no. 2/95, Torino.

Berle, Adolf A. and Gardiner C. Means (1932), *The modern corporation and private property*, new edition (1968), New York: Columbia University Press.

Bhide, Amar (1993), 'The Hidden Costs of Stock Market Liquidity', *Journal of Financial Economics* 34, pp. 31-51.

Bhide, Amar (1994), 'Efficient Markets, Deficient Governance', *Harvard Business Review*, November-December 1994, pp. 129-139.

Black, Bernard, Reinier Kraakman and Jonathan Hay (1994), *Corporate Law from Scratch*, Paper presented at the joint conference of the World Bank and the CEU Privatization Project on 'Corporate Governance in Central Europe and Russia', 15-16 December 1994, Washington DC.

Black, Fischer (1975), 'Bank Funds Management in an Efficient Market', *Journal of Economics* 2, pp. 323-339.

Borish, Michael S. and Michel Noel (1996), *Private Sector Development During Transition: The Visegrad Countries*, World Bank Discussion Paper no. 318, Washington, D.C.: The World Bank.

Bös, Dieter (1993), 'Privatization in Europe: A Comparison of Approaches', *Oxford Review of Economic Policy*, Vol. 9, no. 1, pp. 95-111.

Boycko, Maxim, Andrei Shleifer and Robert W. Vishny (1994), 'Voucher Privatization', in: *Journal of Financial Economics* 35, pp. 249-266.

Boycko, Maxim, Andrei Shleifer and Robert W. Vishny (1995), *Privatizing Russia*, Cambridge, US, and London, UK: The MIT Press.

Brom, Karla and Mitchell Orenstein (1994), 'The Privatized Sector in the Czech Republic: Government and Bank Control in a Transition Economy', *Europe-Asia Studies* 46, pp. 893-928.

Buch, Claudia (1996), 'Banken im Transformationsprozeß - eine Bestandsaufnahme für Polen, die Tschechische Republik und Ungarn', *Die Weltwirtschaft*, no. 1/1996, pp. 70-102.

Bulír, Ales (1992), 'Regional Aspects of Small-Scale Privatization', in: CERGE, *Privatization Newsletter of Czechoslovakia*, October 1992, no. 9, pp. 4-6.

Burzovní noviny (supplement to hospodárské noviny), various issues.

Cadbury, Sir Adrian (1995), *The Cadbury Report: How British Industry is Tackling the Governance Issue*, Lecture held at the conference 'Aufsicht und Rat', 15 February 1995, Frankfurt a.M.

Calbreath, Dean (1995), 'Checks and Balances', in: *Business Central Europe*, February 1995, pp. 47 f.

Capek, Ales (1995), *Privatization of Banks and their Credit Policy during the Transition in the Czech Republic*, Center for Social and Economic Research, Studies & Analyses no. 52, August 1995, Warsaw.

Capek, Ales and Pavel Mertlík (1996), *Organizational Change and Financial Restructuring in Czech Manufacturing Enterprises 1990-1995*, Czech National Bank Working Paper no. 55, Institute of Economics of the Czech National Bank, Prague.

Chudzik, Robert (1994), *Das polnische Bankenwesen*, unpublished manuscript, Europa-Universität Viadrina, Frankfurt (Oder).

Chudzik, Robert (1995), 'Comparative Analysis of the Bank Restructuring Programs in the Czech Republic, Hungary and Poland', in: Ewa Miklaszewska (ed.), *Competitive Banking in Central and Eastern Europe*, Kraków: Jagiellonian University, pp. 131-149.

Claessens, Stijn (1996), *Corporate Governance and Equity Prices; Evidence from the Czech and Slovak Republics*, mimeo, Washington, D.C.: The World Bank.

Coffee, John C., Jr. (1991), 'Liquidity versus Control: The Institutional Investors as Corporate Monitor', *Columbia Law Review* 91, pp. 1277-1368.

Coffee, John C. Jr. (1996), 'Institutional Investors in Transitional Economies: Lessons from the Czech Experience', in: Roman Frydman, Cheryl Gray and Andrzej Rapaczynski (eds.), *Corporate governance in Central Europe and Russia: Banks, funds and foreign investors*, Vol.1, Budapest: CEU.

Cook, Joe (1995a), 'Taking Stock of a Star', *Business Central Europe*, April 1995, pp. 27 f.

Cook, Joe (1995b), 'Picking Winners - Profile: Zdenek Bakala, Patria Finance', *Business Central Europe*, September 1995, p. 60.

Corbett, J. and C. Mayer (1992), 'Financial Reform in Eastern Europe: Progress with the Wrong Model', *Oxford Review of Economic Policy* 7, no. 4, pp. 57-76.

Czech Statistical Yearbook, various issues, Prague: Czech Statistical Office.

Davis, Lance E. and Douglas C. North (1971), *Institutional Change and American Economic Growth*, Cambridge, UK: Cambridge University Press.

Dedic, Jan and Ludvik Kopác (1996), 'Úvodní komentár' (Introductory Comment), in: Jan Dedic and Ludvik Kopác (eds.), *Obchodní Zákoník* (Commercial Code), Version of 1 July 1996, Prague: Prospektrum, pp. 1-32.

Deloitte & Touche (1995), *US AID Regional Bankruptcy Survey: Czech Republic*, unpublished manuscript, Prague: Deloitte Touche Tohmatsu International.

De Mott, Deborah (1988), 'Comparative Dimensions of Takeover Regulation', in: John C. Coffee Jr., Louis Lowenstein and Susan Rose-Ackerman (eds.), *The Impact of the Hostile Takeover*, Oxford: Oxford University Press, pp. 398-435.

Demsetz, Harold (1969), 'Information and Efficiency: Another Viewpoint', *Journal of Law and Economics* 12, pp. 1-22.

Dewatripont, Mathias and Jean Tirole (1993), 'Efficient Governance Structure: Implications for Banking Regulation', in: Colin Mayer and Xavier Vives (eds.), *Capital Markets and Financial Intermediation*, Cambridge, UK, Cambridge University Press, pp. 12-35.

Diamond, Douglas W. (1984), 'Financial Intermediation and Delegated Monitoring', *Review of Economic Studies* 51, pp. 393-414.

Dittus, Peter (1994), *Corporate Governance in Central Europe: The Role of Banks*, BIS Economic Papers, no. 42, August 1994, Basle: Bank for International Settlement.

Dittus, Peter and Stephen Prowse (1994), *Corporate Control in Central Europe and Russia: Should Banks Own Shares?*, Paper presented at the joint conference of the World Bank and the CEU Privatization Project on Corporate Governance in Central Europe and Russia, 15-16 December, Washington, DC.

Earle, John S., Roman Frydman and Anrzej Rapaczynski (1994*), Small Privatization: The Transformation of Retail Trade and Consumer Services in the Czech Republic, Hungary and Poland*, Budapest: CEU Press.

Easterbrook, Frank H. and Daniel R. Fischel (1981), 'The Proper Role of a Target's Management in Responding a Tender Offer', *Harvard Law Review* 94, pp. 1161-2003.

Economist, various issues.

Economist (1994), *A Survey of Corporate Governance*, 29 January.

Edwards, Jeremy and Klaus Fischer (1994a), *Banks, Finance and Investment in Germany*, Cambridge, UK: Cambridge University Press.

Edwards, Jeremy and Klaus Fischer (1994b), 'An Overview of the German Financial System', in: Nicolas Dimsdale and Martha Prevezer (eds.), *Capital Markets and Corporate Governance*, Oxford: Clarendon Press, pp. 257-283.

Egerer, Roland (1994), *Investment Funds and Corporate Governance in Emerging Markets: An Assessment of the Top Ten Voucher Funds in the Czech Republic*, mimeo, The World Bank, December 1994.

Ekonom (Economist, Czech weekly), various issues.

Ekonom (1995), 'Jak se (ne)zbavit drobných akcionáru' (How (Not) to Get Rid of Minority Shareholders), no. 40, pp. 73 f.

Ekonom (1996), 'Diagnóza neduhu' (Diagnosis of Disability), no. 45, pp. 83 f.

Elton, Edwin J. and Martin J. Gruber (1991), *Modern Portfolio Theory and Investment Analysis*, 4th edition, New York: John Wiley & Sons.

Engerer, Hella (1996), 'Privateigentum, Privatisierung und Transformation', in: *DIW*, Quarterly 1/1996, Schwerpunktheft Systemtransformation, pp. 14-30.

Fama, Eugene F. (1970), 'Efficient Capital Markets: A Review of Theory and Empirical Work', *Journal of Finance* 25, pp. 383-417.

Fama, Eugene F. (1976), *Foundations of Finance*, New York: Basic Books.

Fama, Eugene F. (1980), 'Agency Problems and the Theory of the Firm', *Journal of Political Economy* 88, pp. 288-307.

Fama, Eugene F. (1985), 'What's Different About Banks?', *Journal of Monetary Economics* 15, pp. 29-39.

Fama, Eugene F. (1991), 'Efficient Capital Markets II', *Journal of Finance* 46, pp. 1575-1617.

Fama, Eugene F. and Michael C. Jensen (1983), 'Separation of Ownership and Control', *Journal of Law and Economics* 26, pp. 301-325.

Fama, Eugene F., L. Fisher, M. Jensen and R. Roll (1969), 'The Adjustment of Stock Prices to New Information', *International Economic Review* 10, pp. 1-21.

Fama, Eugene F. and Merton H. Miller (1972), *The Theory of Finance*, Hinsdale, Illinois.

Flek, Vladislav (1993), *Efficiency Approach and Progress in Privatization in Ex-Czechoslovakia*, Working Paper 29/1993, Leuven: Leuven Institute for Central and East European Studies.

Fond národního majetku Ceské republiky (National Property Fund of the Czech Republic, 1995), *Kodex Fondu národního majetku Ceské republiky stanovující závazná pravidla pro zástupce FNM CR, vykonávající akcionárská práva u jeho majetkových úcastí v akciových spolecnostech* (Codex of the NPF of the Czech Republic determining binding rules for representatives of the NPF of the Czech Republic executing ownership rights for its equity interests in joint-stock companies), unpublished manuscript, Prague: Fond národního majetku Ceské republiky.

Frankel, A.B. and J.D. Montgomery (1991), 'Financial Structure - An International Perspective', *Brookings Papers of Economic Activity*, No. 1, pp. 257-310.

Franks, Julian and Colin Mayer (1990), *Capital Markets and Corporate Control: A Study of France, Germany and the UK*, Economic Policy 10, pp. 257-310.

Franks, Julian and Colin Mayer (1994), *Ownership and Control*, Paper written for the International Workshop at the Kiel Institute of World Economy on 'Trends in Business Organization: Competitiveness by Participation and Cooperation', 13-14 June 1994; Revised Version from 13 September 1994.

Friedman, Milton (1953), *Essays in Positive Economics*, Chicago: University of Chicago Press.

Friedrich, Alex (1996), 'Huge Share-Capital Reduction Aids Ekoagrobanka's Survival', *Prague Post*, 24-30 January 1996, p. 7.

Frydman, Roman and Andrzej Rapaczynski (1992), 'Privatization and Corporate Governance in Eastern Europe: Can a Market Economy Be Designed?', in: Georg Winckler (ed.), *Central and Eastern Europe Roads to Growth*, Washington, pp. 255-285.

Frydman, Roman; Andrzej Rapaczynski and John S. Earle (1993), *The Privatization Process in Central Europe*, Budapest et al.: Central European University Press.

Frydman, Roman and Andrzej Rapaczynski (1994), *Privatization in Eastern Europe: Is the State Withering away?*, Budapest: CEU Press.

Grosfeld, Irena (1995), *Financial Systems in Transition: Is there a Case for a Bank Based System?*, CEPR Discussion Paper no. 1062, London.

Grossman, Sanford J. and Oliver D. Hart (1980), 'Takeover Bids, the Free-rider Problem, and the Theory of the Corporation', *The Bell Journal of Economics* 11, 42-64.

Grossman, Sanford and Oliver Hart (1982), 'Corporate Financial Structure and Management Incentives', in: John McCall (ed.), *The Economy of Information and Uncertainty*, Chicago: Chicago University Press, pp. 107-137.

Grossman, Sanford and Joseph Stiglitz (1980), 'On the Impossibility of Informationally Efficient Markets', *American Economic Review* 70, pp. 393-408.

Hanousek, Jan (1996), *Asymmetry and the Voucher Scheme: Wait-and-See and Win. The Czech Voucher Privatization*, paper presented at the International CERGE-EI Workshop on 'Institutional Reform and Political Economy of European Integration', Prague, January 11-13, 1996.

Hanousek, Jan and Radek Lastovicka (1994), *Incorporation of Information into Models: A Methodology and Estimation Using Czech Voucher Privatization Data*, CERGE Working Paper no. 72.

Hart, Oliver (1991), 'Incomplete Contracts', *The New Palgrave*, Vol.2, pp. 752-759.

Hayek, Friedrich A. von (1967), 'The Corporation in a Democratic Society: In Whose Interest Ought It to and Will It Be Run?', in: Friedrich A. von

Hayek, *Studies in Philosophy, Politics and Economics*, London, pp. 300-317.

Hayri, Aydin and Gerald A. McDermott (1995), *Restructuring in the Czech Republic - Beyond Ownershp and Bankruptcy*, CERGE-EI, Working Paper no. 66, May 1995, Prague.

Hester, Donald D. (1994), 'On the Theory of Financial Intermediation', *De Economist* 142, pp. 133-149.

Holmström, Bengt R. (1987), 'Incentive Compensation: Practical Design from a Theory Point of View', in: Haig, G. Nalbantian (ed.), *Incentives, Cooperation, and Risk Sharing*, Totowa N.J., pp. 176-187.

Holmström, Bengt R. and Jean Tirole (1989). 'The Theory of the Firm', in: R. Schmalensee and R.D. Willig (eds.), *Handbook of Industrial Organization*, Vol.1, North-Holland: Elsevier Science Publishers, pp. 61-133.

Horcicová, Milena (1996a), 'Dan z nechteného dedictví (1)' (Tax on unwanted inheritance 1), *Ekonom* no. 33/1996, pp. 17 f.

Horcicová, Milena (1996b), 'Dan z nechteného dedictví (2)' (Tax on unwanted inheritance 2), *Ekonom* no. 34/1996, pp. 16 f.

Hospodárské noviny (Economic paper, Czech daily), various issues.

Hrncír, Miroslav (1993), *Financial Intermediation in the Czech Republic: Lessons and Progress Evaluation*, Discussion Paper on Economics of Transition no. DPET 9302, January 1993, Department of Applied Economics, Cambridge: University of Cambridge.

Hrncír, Miroslav (1994), 'Financial Intermediation in Former Czechoslovakia and in the Czech Republic: Lessons and Progress Evaluation', *Economic Systems* 17, pp. 301-32.

Hull, Robert M. and Richard Moellenberndt (1994), 'Bank Debt Reduction Announcements and Negative Signaling', *Financial Management* 23, no. 2, pp. 21-30.

James, Christopher (1987), 'Some Evidence on the Uniqueness of Bank Loans', *Journal of Financial Economics* 19, pp. 217-235.

Jenkinson, Tim and Colin Mayer (1994), *Hostile Takeovers: Defence, Attack and Corporate Governance*, London: McGraw-Hill.

Jensen, Michael C. (1986), 'Agency Costs of Free Cash Flow, Corporate Finance and Takeovers', *American Economic Review* 76, Papers and Proceedings, pp. 323-329.

Jensen, Michael C. (1988), 'Takeovers: Their Causes and Consequences', *Journal of Economic Perspectives* 2, pp. 21-48.

Jensen, Michael C. and William H. Meckling (1976), 'Theory of the Firm: Managerial Behaviour, Agency Costs and Ownership Structure', in: *Journal of Financial Economics* 3, pp. 305-360.

Jensen, Michael C. and Richard S. Ruback (1983), 'The Market for Corporate Control, The Scientific Evidence', *Journal of Financial Economics* 11, pp. 5-50.

Kaapor, Michael (1996/97), 'Self-destruction', *Business Central Europe*, December 1996/January 1997, pp. 55 f..

Keilhofer, Franz X. (1995), *Wirtschaftliche Transformation in der Tschechischen Republik und in der Slowakischen Republik: Das ORDO-liberale Konzept der Wettbewerbsordnung und seine Bedeutung für die wirtschaftspolitischen Herausforderungen in Mittel- und Osteuropa*, Schriften zum Vergleich von Wirtschaftsordnungen Bd. 51, Stuttgart et al.: Gustav Fischer Verlag.

Kenway, Peter and Eva Klvacová (1996), 'The Web of Cross-ownership among Czech Financial Intermediaries: An Assessment', *Europe-Asia Studies* 48, pp. 797-809.

Keren, Michael (1995), 'The Role of the Capital Market in the Transition from Socialism: Comment to C. Schütte and M. Groszek', in: Wolfgang Quaisser, Richard Woodward and Barbara Blaszczyk (eds.), *Privatization in Poland and East Germany: A Comparison*, Volume II, Working Papers no. 182/183, Osteuropa-Institut: München, pp. 503-510.

Kester, W. Carl (1992), Industrial Groups as Systems of Contractual Governance, Oxford Review of Economic Policy, vol. 8, no. 3, pp. 24-44.

Kikeri, Sunita; John Nellis and Mary Shirley (1994), 'Privatization: Lessons from Market Economies', *The World Bank Research Observer*, vol. 9, no. 2, pp. 241-272.

King, Neil Jr. (1995), 'The Great Czech Debate: Can Anything Tame The Fund Monsters?', *Central European Economic Review*, June 1995, pp. 24-26.

Klaus, Václav (1991), *Cesta k trzní ekonomice* (A Road to Market Economy), Prague: Top Agency.

Klaus, Václav (1996), *Mezi minulostí a budoucností* (Between Past and Future), Brno: Nadace Universitas Masarykiana.

Klvacová, Eva (1993), 'The Current Situation of Privatization in Czechoslovakia', *Prague Economic Papers* 1, 1993, pp. 19-28.

Kornai, János (1993), 'The Evolution of Financial Discipline under the Postsocialist System', *Kyklos*, vol.46, no. 3, pp. 315-336.

Kotrba, Josef (1995), Czech Privatization: Players and Winners, in: Jan Svejnar (ed.), *The Czech Republic and Economic Transition in Eastern Europe*, Academic Press: San Diego, CA, pp. 159-198.

Kotrba, Josef and Jan Svejnar (1994), 'Rapid and Multifaceted Privatization: Experience of the Czech and Slovak Republics', *Most* 4, pp. 147-185.

Lewandowski, Janusz and Jan Szomburg (1990), Strategia Prywatyzacji (Privatization Strategy), *Transformacja Gospodarski*, issue no. 7, Gdansk: The Gdansk Institute for Market Economies.

Lastovicka, Radek; Marcincin, Anton and Michal Mejstrík (1994), *Privatization and Opening the Capital Market in the Czech and Slovak Republics*, CERGE-EI, Working Paper no. 54, April 1994, Prague.

Lidové noviny (Czech daily), various issues.

Lummer, Scott L. and John McConnell (1989), 'Further Evidence on the Bank Lending Process and the Capital-Market Response to Bank Loan Agreements', *Journal of Financial Economics* 25, pp. 99-122.

Macey, Jonathan and Miller (1995), *Corporate Governance and Commercial Banking: A Comparative Economic Perspective with Emphasis on Germany, Japan and the United States*, International Centre for Economic Research Working Paper no. 1/1995, Torino.

Malkiel, Burton (1992), *A Random Walk Down Wallstreet*, New York: W.W.Norton.

Manne, Henry G. (1965), 'Mergers and the Market for Corporate Control', *Journal of Political Economy* 73, pp. 110-120.

Marris, R.L. (1964), *The Economic Theory of 'Managerial' Capitalism*, London: Macmillan.

Mayer, Colin (1988), 'New Issues in Corporate Finance', *European Economic Review* 32, pp. 1167-1188.

Mayer, Colin (1990a), 'Financial Systems, Corporate Finance, and Economic Development', in: R.G. Hubbard (ed.), *Asymmetric Information, Corporate Finance, and Investment*, Chicago, IL: University of Chicago Press, pp. 307-332.

Mayer, Colin (1990b), 'The Regulation of Financial Services: Lessons from the United Kingdom', in: Jean Dermine (ed.), *European Banking in the 1990s*, 2nd edition 1993, Oxford: Blackwell, pp. 43-63.

Meier, Russel and Joseph P. Saba (1995), *Improving State Enterprise Performance, The Role of Internal and External Incentives*, World Bank Technical Paper no. 306, October 1995, Washington D.C.: The World Bank.

Mejstrík, Michal (1994), *Czech Investment Funds as a Part of Financial Sector and Their Role in Privatization of the Economy*, Reform Round Table Working Paper no. 14, May 1994, Prague: Charles University.

Mejstrík, Michal (1995), 'The Banking and the Non-Banking Financial Sectors: Their Role in Privatization of the Economy', in: Ewa Miklaszewska (ed.), *Competitive Banking in Central and Eastern Europe*, Kraków: Jagiellonian University, pp. 113-130.

Mejstrík, Michal (ed.) (1997), The Privatization Process in East-Central Europe, Evolutionary Process of Czech Privatization, Dordrecht et al.: Kluwer Academic Publishers.

Mejstrík, Michael and James Burger (1994), 'Vouchers, Buy-Outs, Auctions: The Czech Battle for Privatization in the Czech and Slovak Republic', in: UNCTAD and Kopint-Datorg (eds.), *Privatization in the Transition Process, Recent Experiences in Eastern Europe*, New York and Geneva: United Nations, pp. 187-222.

Miklos, Ivan (1995), *Corruption Risks in the Privatisation Process, A Study of Privatization Developments in the Slovak Republic Focusing on the Causes and Implications of Corruption Risks*, mimeo, Bratislava, May 1995.

Milanovic, Branko (1991), 'Privatization in Post-Communist Economies', *Communist Economies and Economic Transformation* 3, pp. 5-39.

Ministry for the Administration of the National Property and Its Privatization of the Czech Republic (1993*), Report on the Privatization Process for the Years 1989 to 1992*, Prague.

Mladá fronta dnes (Czech daily), various issues.

Mládek and Mejstrík (1993), *The Privatization Newsletter of the Czech Republic and Slovakia*, p. 12 .

Modigliani, Franco and Merton Miller (1958), 'The Cost of Capital, Corporate Finance, and the Theory of Investment', *American Economic Review* 48, pp. 261-297.

Morck, Randall, Andrei Shleifer and Robert W. Vishny (1989), 'Alternative Mechanisms for Corporate Control', *American Economic Review* 79, pp. 842-852.

Müller, Holger (1993), *Finanzmärkte im Transformationsprozeß*, Stuttgart: Deutscher Sparkassenverlag.

Muth, John (1961), 'Rational Expectations and the Theory of Price Movements', *Econometrica* 29, 315-335.

Nesnídal, Jirí (1996a), 'Obchodní soudy ve stavu pretízení' (Business courts under strain), *Ekonom* no. 3/1996, pp. 26-30.

Nesnídal, Jirí (1996b), Úvod (Introduction) to: 'Zákon o konkurzu a vyrovnání' (Bankruptcy and Composition Act), supplement to *Ekonom* no. 16/1996, p. II.

Neumann, Manfred J.M. and Martin Klein (1982), 'Probleme der Theorie effizienter Märkte und ihrer empirischen Überprüfung', *Kredit und Kapital* 15, pp. 165-187.

Olson, Mancur (1968): *Die Logik des kollektiven Handelns - Kollektivgüter und die Theorie der Gruppen*, Tübingen: J.C.B. Mohr.

Pauly, Jan and Dusan Tríska (1994), 'Investment Funds in the Czech Republic', in: Marko Simoneti and Dusan Tríska (eds.), *Investment*

Funds as Intermediaries of Privatization, Ljubljana: Central and Eastern European Privatization Network, pp. 30-39.

Pistor, Katharina and Joel Turkewitz, 1994, 'Copying with Hydra-state ownership after Privatization', Paper presented at the joint conference of the World Bank and the CEU Privatization Project on 'Corporate Governance in Central Europe and Russia', 15-16 December 1994, Washington DC, p.44 published in: Roman Frydman, Cheryl Gray and Andrzej Rapaczynski (eds.), *Corporate governance in Central Europe and Russia: Banks, funds and foreign investors* (Volume 1)., Budapest: CEU.

Pohl, Gerhard, Robert E. Anderson, Stijn Claessens and Simeon Djankov (1996), *Privatization and Restructuring in Central and Eastern Europe*, Technical Paper no. 368, The World Bank, Washington, DC.

Pound, John (1992), 'Beyond Takeovers: Politics Comes to Corporate Control', *Harvard Business Review*, March-April 1992, pp. 83-93.

Pozen, Robert C. (1994), 'Institutional Investors: The Reluctant Activists', *Harvard Business Review*, January-February 1994, pp. 140-149.

Prague Business Journal (weekly newspaper), various issues.

Prague Post (weekly newspaper), various issues.

Pravda, Michal (1996), 'Proti neobezretným bankám' (Against Imprudent Banks), in: Ekonom no. 3/1996, pp. 61 f.

Právo (Czech daily), various issues.

Putterman, Louis (1993), 'Ownership and the Nature of the Firm', *Journal of Comparative Economics* 17, pp. 243-263.

Rock, Edward B. (1995), 'America's Fascination with German Corporate Governance', *Die Aktiengesellschaft*, July 1995, pp. 291-299 .

Roe, Mark J. (1990), 'Political and Legal Restraints on Ownership and Control of Public Companies', *Journal of Financial Economies* 27, pp. 7-41.

Roe, Mark J. (1991), 'A Political Theory of American Corporate Finance', *Columbia Law Review* 91, pp. 10-67.

Röhrich, Martina (1994), 'Die Wirksamkeit der Managementdisziplinierung über den externen Kontrollmechanismus des Marktes für Unternehmenskontrolle', *Zeitschrift für Wirtschafts- und Sozialwissenschaft* 114, 81-98.

Romano, Roberta (1992), 'A Guide to Takeovers: Theory, Evidence, and Regulation', *The Yale Journal of Regulation* 9, pp. 119-180.

Ross, Stephen A. (1973), 'The Economic Theory of Agency: The Principal's Problem', *American Economic Review* 63, pp. 134-193.

Ross, Stephen A. (1977), 'The Determination of Financial Structure: The Incentive Signaling Approach', *Bell Journal of Economics* 8, pp. 23-40.

Rudlovcák, Vladimír (1994), 'Investment Companies and Investment Funds as a Result of and a Remedy for Voucher Privatization', in: Marko Simoneti and Dusan Tríska (eds.), *Investment Funds as Intermediaries of Privatization*, Ljubljana: Central and Eastern European Privatization Network, pp. 21-24.

Sanda, Pavel (1995), *Pohled Fondu národního majetku* (View of the National Property Fond), Speech held at the Coopers & Lybrand Conference on 'Administration and Governance of Joint Stock Companies', Prague, June 27th, 1995.

Saunders, Anthony (1994), 'Banking and Commerce: An Overview of the Public Policy Issues', *Journal of Banking and Finance* 18, pp. 231-254.

Scherer, F.M. (1988), 'Corporate Takeovers: The Efficiency Argument', *Journal of Economic Perspectives* 2, pp. 69-82.

Schmidt, Reinhard H. (1990), 'Informationsökonomie und Preisentwicklung auf Finanzmärkten: Abschied von neoklassischen Optimierungsvor- stellungen?', in: Wolfgang Filc and Claus Köhler (eds.), *Kooperation, Autonomie und Devisenmarkt*, Berlin.

Schneider, Dieter (1987), *Allgemeine Betriebswirtschaftslehre*, 3rd edition, München and Wien: Vahlen.

Schütte, Clemens (1995), 'An Efficient-Governance Approach to Privatization and Financial Intermediation', in: Wolfgang Quaisser, Richard Woodward and Barbara Blaszczyk (eds*.): Privatization in Poland and Eastern Germany: A Comparison*, Vol.II, Osteuropa-Institut, Munich, pp. 471-502.

Schütte, Clemens (1998), *A theoretical analysis of information disclosure requirements in tender offers*, unpublished manuscript, Europe University Viadrina, Frankfurt/Oder.

Schütte, Clemens and Kevin Canty (1996), 'Takeovers, Shareholder Rights and Securities Regulation - The Legal Framework of Corporate Control in the Czech Republic', in: CERGE-EI (ed.): *The Economic, Political and Social Dimensions of Economic Transition and European Integration*, Discussion Paper no. 6/96, Special Issue, Prague, November 1996, pp. 282-302.

Sheard, Paul (1989), The Main Bank System and Corporate Monitoring and Control in Japan, Journal of Economic Behavior and Organization 11, pp. 399-422.

Sheard, Paul (1994), Main Banks and the Government of Financial Distress, in: Masahiko Aoki and Hugh Patrick (eds.): The Japanese Main Bank System, Its Relevance for Developing and Transforming Economies, Oxford University Press, Oxford, pp. 188-230.

Shleifer, Andrew and Lawrence Summers (1988), 'Breach of Trust in Hostile Takeovers', in: A. Auerbach (ed.), *Corporate Takeovers: Causes and Consequences*, Chicago, IL: University of Chicago Press, pp. 33-56.

Shleifer, Andrew and Robert W. Vishny (1990), 'Equilibrium Short Horizons of Investors and Firms', *American Economic Review* 80, Papers and Proceedings, pp. 148-153.

Simon, Herbert (1961), *Administrative Behavior*, New York: Macmillan.

Skalický, Jirí (1994), 'The Past and the Future of Investment Funds in the Czech Republic', in: Simoneti, Marko and Dusan Tríska (eds.), *Investment Funds as Intermediaries of Privatization*, Ljubljana: Central and Eastern European Privatization Network, pp. 17-20.

Smith, Adam (1776*), An Inquiry into the Nature and Causes of the Wealth of Nations*, reprinted in W.B. Todd (ed.)(1976), *Glasgow Edition of the Works and Correspondence of Adam Smith*, vol. II, Oxford: Oxford University Press.

Spiska, Jirí (1993), *Investicní Spolecnosti, Invesicní Fondy: Kolektivní investování a jeho právní úprava* (Investment Companies, Investment Funds: Collective Investment and its legal environment), Prague: Management Press.

Spremann, Klaus (1987), 'Zur Reduktion von Agency-Kosten', in: Schneider, Dieter (ed.), *Kapitalmarkt und Finanzierung, Schriften des Vereins für Socialpolitik*, Neue Folge 165, Berlin, pp. 341-350.

Stein, J. (1988), 'Takeover Threats and Manager Myopia', *Journal of Political Economy* 96, pp. 61-80.

Steinherr, Alfred and Ch. Huveneers (1994), 'On the Performance of Differently Regulated Financial Institutions: Some Empirical Evidence', *Journal of Banking and Finance* 18, pp. 271-306.

Stiglitz, Joseph E. (1974), 'Incentives and Risk Sharing in Sharecropping', *Review of Economic Studies* 41, pp. 219-257.

Stiglitz, Joseph E. (1985), 'Credit Market and the Control of Capital', *Journal of Money, Credit, and Banking* 17, pp. 133-152.

Sundarsanam, P. S. (1995), *The Essence of Mergers and Acquisitions*, London: Prentice Hall.

Svejnar, Jan (1989), 'A Framework for the Economic Transformation of Czechoslovakia', *PlanEcon Report*, vol. V, no. 52.

Svejnar, Jan and Miroslav Singer (1993), *Using Vouchers to Privatize an Economy: The Czech and Slovak Case*, CERGE Working Paper no. 9, second revision, April 1993.

Tichý, Lubos (1993), 'The Bankruptcy Code of the Czech Republic', in: OECD (ed.), *Corporate Bankruptcy and Reorganisation Procedures in OECD and Central and Eastern European Countries*, Paris, pp. 81-98.

Tirole, Jean (1994), 'On Banking and Intermediation', *European Economic Review* 38, pp. 469-487.

Tríska, Dusan (1994), 'Political, Legislative and Technical Aspects of Privatization in the Czech Republic', in: Marko Simoneti and Dusan Tríska (eds.), *Investment Funds as Intermediaries of Privatization*, Ljubljana: Central and Eastern European Privatization Network, pp. 25-29.

Tuma, Zdenek and Jeffrey E. Dotson (1994), 'The Privatization Process: The Problem of Bad Debts and Arrears', *The Privatization Newsletter of the Czech Republic and Slovakia*, no. 28, November 1994, pp. 1-4.

Tuma, Zdenek and Jeffrey E. Dotson (1995), 'Privatization Byproducts: Firms with Changed Property and Liquidations,' *The Privatization Newsletter of the Czech Republic and Slovakia*, no. 30, January 1995, pp. 1-3.

Ufer, Horst (1994), *Zum Transformationsprozeß in der Tschechischen und Slowakischen Republik: Versuch einer Bewertung*, Diskussionspapier Nr.96, Berlin: Deutsches Institut für Wirtschaftsforschung.

UNIDO (1992), *Czechoslovakia: Industrial Transformation and Regeneration*, Oxford, UK and Cambridge, US.: Blackwell Publishers.

Úspech (Success, weekly economic journal), various issues.

Vickers, John and George Yarrow (1988), *Privatization: An Economic Analysis*, reprinted 1989, Cambridge, Mass.: MIT Press.

Vláda Ceské a Slovenské federativní republiky (1990): 'Scénár ekonomické reformy' (Scenario of Economic Reform), published in: *Hospodárské noviny*, 4 September 1990, supplement.

Wagener, Hans-Jürgen (1994*), What type of capitalism is produced by privatization?*, mimeo, Frankfurt/Oder: Europe University.

Walter, Ingo (1993), *The Battle of the Sytems: Control of Enterprises and the Global Economy*, Kieler Vorträge, Neue Folge 122, Kiel: Institut für Weltwirtschaft an der Universität Kiel.

Wijnbergen, Sweder van and Anton Marcincin (1995), *Voucher Privatization, Corporate Control and the Cost of Capital: An Analysis of the Czech Privatization Programme*, CEPR Discussion Paper no. 1215, London Centre for Economic Policy Research.

Williamson, Oliver E. (1963), 'Managerial Discretion and Business Behavior', *American Economic Review* 53, pp. 1032-1057.

Williamson, Oliver E. (1985), *The Economic Institutions of Capitalism*, New York: The Free Press.

Williamson, Oliver E. (1988), 'Corporate Finance and Corporate Governance', *Journal of Finance* 18, pp. 567-591.

Williamson, Oliver E. (1992), 'Private Ownership and the Capital Market', in: Siebert, Horst (ed.), *Privatization*, Tübingen 1992, pp. 27-54.

Winiecki, Jan (1991), 'Transition and the Privatization Problem', in: *Cato Journal*, vol. 11, no. 2, pp. 299-309.

Winter, S.G. (1964), 'Economic 'Natural Selection' and the Theory of the Firm', *Yale Economic Essays* 4, pp. 225-272.

Winter, S.G. (1971), 'Satisficing, Selection and the Innovating Remnant', *Quarterly Journal of Economics* 85, pp. 237-261.

Wruck, Karen H. (1990), 'Financial Distress, Reorganization and Organizational Efficiency', *Journal of Financial Economics* 27, pp. 419-444.

Index

A-Invest 112
accountability, of directors 47
accountancy system 33, 275–6
adverse selection, small banks 213–15
Aero Vodochody 96
agency costs 6f
  asymmetric information 4
  debt 10–11
  secured creditors 231, 233
  standard-debt contracts 14–15
agency theory, corporate control 1–2, 3,
  4–5
Agrobanka 102, 112, 129, 235, 238, 248,
  270
allied brokerage, reselling of stock 255
Anglo-Saxon board model 45f, 46–7,
  156, 165, 187
arbitrageurs 22
arbitrators, debt 233
Armabeton Praha 192–7
asset stripping 255
asset structure, IPFs 103–4, 130–6
AssiDomän 125–6, 129
asymmetric information
  agency costs 4
  opportunism 2
audits, banks 238

bad debt 208–10, 248
bailiffs, shortage of 232
balance sheets
  big banks 219t, 220, 235
  clearing bad loans 209–10
  restructuring 211–12
  small banks 215
bank assets
  flow problem 213–20
  stock problem 208–12
Bank Holding Company Act (1956) 292

bank-based corporate control 5–19, 291–3
  versus market-based 34–48
bank-sponsored IPFs, cooperation
  between 160
banking system, outset of transition
  207–8
bankruptcy
  BCA amendment (1996) 227–30
  corporate control 9–11
  legislation 235
  position of creditors 230–1
  proceedings 226–7, 228f
  protection of debtors 223–5
Bankruptcy and Composition Act (BCA)
  223, 225, 226, 227–30, 236
banks
  competition between 246–8
  debt control 51, 207–37
  enterprise restructuring 42
  first wave performance 109–10
  governance structure, transitional
    countries 51
  informational efficiency 29
  privatization and ownership structure
    240–5, 248, 295–6
  prudential regulation and supervision
    237–40, 248
  regulation of 106–7, 296
  state intervention 96
  see also financial groups; financial
    intermediaries
beer industry, shareholders 140
bidding behaviour
  investment companies 111
  investors 86–7
bidding process
  tender regulation 281–2, 285
  transaction costs 31–3
  transitional countries 52–3

voucher privatization 80–1
see also hostile tenders; mandatory bids
Biocel Paskov 126
block transactions 276–7
board models
    control systems 44–8
    joint-stock corporations 152–68
    transitional countries 49–50
boards of directors 8
bonding costs 4, 11, 16
borrowers, bank information on 15–16

Cadbury Committee 47
capital base, debtholders 13
capital markets
    informational efficiency 23–9, 33
    pre-reform performance 255–9
    reform measures 259–62
    transition periods 41
capital stock, decreasing 256
capital structure
    efficient modern corporations 12–14
    universal banks 17–18
cash flow, managers' incentive to waste
    3, 39
centralized decentralization 62–3
Centres for Voucher Privatization 61–2,
    80–1
Ceská incasní 210
Ceská pojistovna (CP) 110, 122t, 133,
    177, 244
Ceská sporitelna (CS) 107–8, 117t, 133,
    134, 141, 142, 146, 177, 189, 210,
    212, 213, 217, 235, 238, 242, 245
Ceská Zbrojovka Strakonice 284
CEZ 132
Chemapol 102, 112, 126
chief executive officer (CEO), Anglo-
    Saxon board model 47, 161
circular voting 284
Cistá reka 102
City Code of Takeovers and Mergers 282
Civic Democratic Party 59
closed-end trusts 86, 267
co-determination 46, 154, 163
collateral 231–3
collective self-harming 5
Comecon 170, 209–10, 221
Commercial Code 92, 106, 169, 260,
    264, 266, 267, 280

commitment approach 34–7
common law system 271
company information 273–6
compensating balances 16
compensation price 261
competence, IPFs 85, 168–9
competition
    banking sector 246–7, 248
    imperfect 19–20
    perfect 20
    selection of control structures 41
concerted action 263–6
conditional bids 31, 282
consensus approach 37–9
consensus model 154
Consil 91
construction sector, IPF investment 134
Consus 161
contracts
    debt control 10
    equity control 5–7
    overdue debt 235–6
    profit transfers 266–7
    see also loan contracts; standard-debt
        contracts
control systems
    board models 44–8
    commitment approach 34–7
    consensus approach 37–9
    discretion approach 39–40
control transactions, regulation 260
controlled persons 263, 266
controlling persons 263, 264, 265, 266
controlling shareholders
    definition of 262–3
    protecting minority shareholders from
        30
    unethical actions by 255–7
cooperation
    bank groups 202–3, 293
    corporation owners 159–61
Coopers & Lybrand 162, 171
coordination costs 5, 6f
corporate control
    bank-based 5–19, 291–3
        versus market-based 34–48
    lessons, transitional countries 48–53
    market-based 19–33
    problem of modern 1–5
corporate finance, IPFs 170–1